T0330343

Digitalization and Sustainability

To my dad who taught me the power of possibility and the importance of persistence.
M. Kathryn Brohman

To my dad and mom who always believed in me.
Gregory S. Dawson

To my dad who always challenged me to a better version of myself everyday.
Kevin C. Desouza

Digitalization and Sustainability

Advancing Digital Value

Edited by

M. Kathryn Brohman

Associate Professor, Smith School of Business, Queen's University, Canada

Gregory S. Dawson

Clinical Professor, W. P. Carey School, Arizona State University, USA

Kevin C. Desouza

Professor, QUT Business School, Queensland University of Technology, Australia

Cheltenham, UK • Northampton, MA, USA

Published by
Edward Elgar Publishing Limited
The Lypiatts
15 Lansdown Road
Cheltenham
Glos GL50 2JA
UK

Edward Elgar Publishing, Inc.
William Pratt House
9 Dewey Court
Northampton
Massachusetts 01060
USA

A catalogue record for this book
is available from the British Library

Library of Congress Control Number: 2023941847

This book is available electronically in the **Elgar**online
Business subject collection
http://dx.doi.org/10.4337/9781800888807

ISBN 978 1 80088 879 1 (cased)
ISBN 978 1 80088 880 7 (eBook)

Printed and bound in Great Britain by TJ Books Limited, Padstow, Cornwall

Contents

Tables

Contributors

Behnam Abedin holds a PhD in Information Systems from Queensland University of Technology, with a multi-disciplinary background in data analytics, business, and entrepreneurship. His research is inspired by problems in practice and is rooted in information systems, business, and entrepreneurship theories. His research mainly focuses on the use of digital technologies to facilitate organisations' digital transformation, specifically small companies to use ICT to secure their survival, sustainability, and growth. In particular, he is interested in understanding both positive and negative aspects of using digital technologies by organisations.

Suchit Ahuja is an Assistant Professor, Supply Chain and Business Technology Management Department at the John Molson School of Business, Concordia University (Canada). He holds a PhD in Management Information Systems from the Stephen J.R. Smith School of Business at Queen's University and an MSc in IT from Purdue University. Since 2021, Suchit has also been serving as the Director of John Molson School's MSc Program in Business Analytics and Technology Management. Suchit's research focuses on digital strategy and innovation, digital platforms and ecosystems, frugal digital innovation, societal impacts of digital innovation, and community-based innovation. For his research, Suchit has worked with small- and medium-sized enterprises and startups in India, USA, and Canada. Suchit has obtained funding for his research from federal and provincial funding agencies including SSHRC, FRQSC, and Mitacs. He has published his research in international journals including *Information Systems Journal, Journal of Community Informatics*, and *Kindai Management Review*. His research has been presented at prestigious conferences including AoM, ICIS, AMCIS, PACIS, Conf-IRM, R&D Management, InnoFrugal, IEEE, ACM, and CCSBE. Suchit was awarded the Dean's Excellence in Teaching Award in 2021 and the President's Excellence in Teaching Award in 2022 at Concordia University. Suchit has served on prestigious committees such as the Standards Council of Canada and is a member of the board of advisors of BizSkills Academy, an EdTech startup in Ontario.

Sultana Lubna Alam is an Associate Professor of Information Systems at Deakin University, Australia. Lubna is the Director of Master of Information Systems and Coordinator for industry engagement at the Department of

Information Systems and Business Analytics. With nearly two decades working as an academic and an applied researcher, she is passionate about socio-technical and empowering impacts of emerging technologies and data analytics on individuals, government and not-for-profits. Her research has been published in journals such as *Information Systems Research*, *Information Technology and People*, and *Scandinavian Journal of Information Systems*. A recipient of Vice-Chancellor's Excellence Award for Outstanding Contribution to Student Learning, she has contributed on several industry panels and is regularly invited for social issue commentary on TV, radio and the print media. She has served on the judging panel for 'excellence in IT whole-of-government' award for Gov2.0 and digital transformation. She is the founder of Alo – Enlightened Women Incorporated, (https://www.alowomen .org.au/) as a voice for women, aims to uphold and promote gender equality, women's leadership and empowerment issues, specifically within the CALD communities.

Dorine Andrews - while consulting over 30 years assisting the US government, international companies and non-profits transform their businesses, Dorine Andrews co-authored two books on business and technology change management along with many industry articles. In 1998, she returned to school to become Dr. Dorine Andrews, earning a doctorate in digital communications design (DCD) at the University of Baltimore. She then joined academia teaching at Georgetown University in its Communications, Culture, and Technology graduate program and at the University of Baltimore in the Yale Gordon College of Arts and Sciences before returning to consulting work. She finally settled into her capstone job, a five-year tenure as the chief information officer for the Peace Corps, from 2010 to 2015.

Rainer Bernnat is a partner and senior vice president at PwC Strategy& Germany as well as an honorary professor of Information Systems and Management at the faculty of business and economics of the University of Augsburg, Germany. He leads the government practice of PwC in Germany and EMEA. His major consulting focus is on transforming strategic requirements of government clients into digital / IT strategies and architectures that meet their business needs and that increase efficiency and effectiveness by integrating digitization in their organizations and processes. Prof. Dr. Bernnat holds a Diploma and a PhD in business administration.

Reihaneh Bidar is a Lecturer in the Business Information Systems discipline at the UQ Business School, The University of Queensland, Australia. In 2018, Reihaneh received her PhD in Information Systems from the Queensland University of Technology. She conducts theoretical and systems research into the organizational and societal impact of digital collaboration and work digitalization. Her research interests contribute to interdisciplinary problems in IS and reside mainly at the intersection of individual practices, digital technologies, and managing collaborative work. A large share of Reihaneh's current research focuses on human-AI collaboration and how effective implementation of human-AI hybrid benefits organizations. Reihaneh employs both qualitative and quantitative methods to investigate emerging phenomena.

M. Kathryn Brohman is Associate Professor at Smith School of Business at Queen's University in Canada. She is a published author and thought leader in strategy execution and digital transformation and has pioneered academic programs on these subjects as well as worked with hundreds of organizations in North America to digitalize their business and translate strategy into action. Dr. Brohman is also an avid researcher and has published her work in top academic journals. On the global scale, she is the co-founder of the Digital Innovation, Transformation and Entrepreneurship special interest group, an academic community that helps to shape research and thought leadership in management practices that enable digitalization.

Dan Chenok is Executive Director of the IBM Center for The Business of Government. He oversees all of the Center's activities in connecting research to practice to benefit government, and has written and spoken extensively around government technology, cybersecurity, privacy, regulation, budget, acquisition, and Presidential transitions. Previously, Mr. Chenok served as Chief of Information Policy and Technology with the U.S. Office of Management and Budget, where he led activities for federal information and IT policy including electronic government, computer security, privacy and IT budgeting. Mr. Chenok has won numerous honors and awards, including a 2010 Federal 100 winner for his work on the presidential transition, the 2016 Eagle Award for Industry Executive of the Year, and the 2002 Federal CIO Council Azimuth Award for Government Executive of the Year. Mr. Chenok earned a BA from Columbia University and a Master of Public Policy degree from Harvard's Kennedy School of Government.

Jagdish Dalal - after over four decades of senior IT executive positions with Fortune 100 companies and a partnership with PwC, he is focused on working with non-profits and speaking at public and private events. As VP of Information Management at Xerox, he led the team outsourcing IT to EDS in 1994 in a $3.2 billion engagement. Harvard Business School has written a case study about the strategy, and it has been used as a teaching case study in many business schools. He was CIO and VP of E-business at Carrier Corp (a division of United Technologies at the time) before starting his consulting practice. He was one of the founding partners of the Business Process Outsourcing service line at PwC and was the leader of a then largest BPO contract by taking over

HR, Accounts Payable for a leading telecommunication company. In recognition of his contribution and pioneering work in the outsourcing field, he was inducted in the outsourcing Leadership Hall of Fame in 2014.

Gregory S. Dawson is Clinical Professor in the School of Accountancy in the W. P. Carey School of Business at Arizona State University and is also President of Dawson Consulting Services. He teaches accounting analytics in the graduate and undergraduate platforms and has won teaching awards in several different programs. His research explores the legal, social, technical and public policy ramifications of the adoption of artificial intelligence in the public and private sector. He recently completed a series of articles on national artificial intelligence strategy documents, which was published in Brookings. His PhD is from the University of Georgia and he has been at ASU since 2008. Prior to becoming an academic, he was a Partner in the Advisory Practice at PwC in Washington, D.C. and Sacramento, California.

Kevin C. Desouza is Professor of Business, Technology and Strategy in the School of Management at the QUT Business School at the Queensland University of Technology. He is a Nonresident Senior Fellow in the Governance Studies Program at the Brookings Institution. He formerly held tenured faculty posts at Arizona State University, Virginia Tech and the University of Washington and has held visiting appointments at the London School of Economics and Political Science, Università Bocconi, Shanghai Jiao Tong University, the University of the Witwatersrand, and the University of Ljubljana. Desouza has authored, co-authored, and/or edited nine books. He has published more than 150 articles in journals across a range of disciplines including information systems, information science, public administration, political science, technology management, and urban affairs. Several outlets have featured his work including: *Sloan Management Review*, *Stanford Social Innovation Research*, *Harvard Business Review*, *Forbes*, *Businessweek*, *Wired*, *Governing*, *Slate.com*, *Wall Street Journal*, BBC, *USA Today*, NPR, PBS, and *Computerworld*. Desouza has advised, briefed, and/or consulted for major international corporations, non-governmental organizations, and public agencies on strategic management issues ranging from management of information systems to knowledge management, innovation programs, crisis management, and leadership development. Desouza has received over $2.25 USD million in research funding from both private and government organizations. For more information, please visit: http://www.kevindesouza.net.

Christian Dremel is a recipient of the ERCIM 'Alain Bensoussan' Fellowship at the Norwegian University of Science and Technology (NTNU), guest lecturer at the Hasso Plattner Institute and the University of Bamberg, and senior research fellow at the University of St. Gallen. He holds a PhD from the University of St. Gallen which collaboratively was pursued with AUDI AG. His research interest focus on the required organizational and technological transformations and preconditions to realize business value and business models on digital technologies, such as artificial intelligence, Internet of Things, and big data technologies.

Robert D. Galliers is the University Distinguished Professor Emeritus and former Provost, Bentley University, and Professor Emeritus and former Dean, Warwick Business School. He received the AIS LEO Award for exceptional lifetime achievement in Information Systems in 2012 and was the founding editor-in-chief of *The Journal of Strategic Information Systems* until December 2018. His work on research methods, spanning three decades, is particularly well cited, alongside his ground-breaking contributions to unpacking the emergent nature of information systems strategizing.

Asif Qumer Gill is a result-oriented academic cum practitioner with extensive 20 plus years' experience in IT in various sectors including banking, consulting, education, finance, government, non-profit, software, and telecommunication. He is A/Professor and Leader of the DigiSAS Lab (P.K.A COTAR) and industry project delivery focused agile Software Development Studio (SDS) at the School of Computer Science, UTS. He is also director and founder of the start-up 'Infoagility' (Adapt Inn Pty Ltd). His earlier professional experience in agile software development, solution architecture, information architecture, information security, and program management provided a strong foundation for later work in digital strategy, architecture, and solutions. He is recognised as a leader and specialist in adaptive enterprise and information architecture for designing and implementing large scale digital data ecosystems and platforms. He received his PhD and MSc in computing sciences. He is also certified as a CISM, DVDM, DCAM, ITILv3, and TOGAF.

Thomas Haskamp is a researcher at the Chair for Design Thinking and Innovation Research at the Hasso Plattner Institute, Potsdam, Germany. As a member of the Hasso Plattner Design Thinking Research Program between Hasso Plattner Institute and Stanford University, Thomas is fascinated by topics around digital innovation and transformation, as well as design thinking. Specifically, he is interested in understanding the phenomenon of organizational inertia as part of incumbent's digital transformation activities.

Andreas Hein is a postdoctoral researcher and leader of the research group digital platforms and e-government at the Krcmar Lab, Technical University of Munich (TUM), Germany. He holds a PhD from TUM in Information Systems and has three years of experience as a Senior Strategy Consultant at IBM. His work has appeared in the *European Journal of Information Systems*, *Electronic Markets*, *Business & Information Systems Engineering*, and *Information Systems Frontiers* and refereed conference proceedings such as the International Conference on Information Systems or the European Conference on Information Systems.

Sebastian Hermes is a senior consultant for process mining at Deloitte Consulting. He holds a Doctoral degree in Information Systems from TUM, a master's degree in Entrepreneurship from the University of Liechtenstein and a Bachelor's degree from the Baden-Wuerttemberg Cooperative State University. Sebastian has worked for five years at Roche Pharma and co-founded Thinkfield. His work has appeared in *Electronic Markets and Business Research* as well as in refereed conference proceedings such as the International Conference on Information Systems or the European Conference on Information Systems.

Thomas Hess is Professor of Information Systems and Management at the Ludwig-Maximilians-Universität München (LMU), LMU Munich School of Management, Germany, where he also serves as director of the Institute for Digital Management and New Media. He is also director of the Bavarian Research Institute for Digital Transformation and is member of the board of the Internet Business Cluster Munich. Professor Hess holds a PhD from the University of St. Gallen, Switzerland, and a diploma in Business Informatics form the Technical University of Darmstadt, Germany. His research focuses on the potential of digital technologies for changes in value creation and management systems of companies. His work has appeared in international journals as the *Journal of Management Information Systems*, *European Journal of Information Systems*, *Information Systems Journal*, *Electronic Markets*, *Business and Information Systems Engineering* and *Long Range Planning*. Professor Hess has also been published in the proceedings of conferences such as International Conference on Information Systems (ICIS), European Conference on Information Systems (ECIS) and Americas Conference on Information Systems (AMCIS) and in journals for the management practice like *MIS Quarterly Executive*. His work has, according to Google Scholar, already been cited more than 17,000 times.

Philip Karnebogen is a research assistant at the Research Center Finance & Information Management (FIM) and the Branch Business & Information Systems Engineering of the Fraunhofer FIT where he is part of the digital value networks research group. His research focuses on digital transformation and emerging digital technologies such as artificial intelligence. Philip holds a Master of Science in Industrial Engineering from the University of Augsburg and has gained further experience in supporting digital transformation projects in large industrial companies.

Philipp Kernstock is a PhD student at the Chair of Information Systems at the Technical University of Munich (TUM), Germany. He holds a Master of Science in Information Systems from TUM. His research interests include digital platform ecosystems.

Helmut Krcmar is a Professor Emeritus of Information Systems with the Department of Informatics, TUM, with a joint appointment with the School of Management, where he is currently the Founding Dean and Delegate Officer of the President – TUM Campus Heilbronn. He has co-authored a plethora of research papers published in major IS journals including *Management Information Systems Quarterly*, *Journal of Management Information Systems*, *Journal of Information Technology*, *Information Systems Journal*, *Journal of Strategic Information Systems*, and the *European Journal of Information Systems*. Prof. Krcmar is a Fellow of the Association for Information Systems (AIS) and a Member of Acatech National Academy of Science and Engineering.

Kristina Kusanke is a research associate and PhD candidate at the Chair of Information Management at University of Hagen. Prior, she held various positions in the chemical and automotive industry. Her research interest lies in the fields of challenges and choices in organizational design resulting from business transformation endeavors.

Juuli Lumivalo is a postdoctoral researcher in the Faculty of Information Technology in University of Jyväskylä (Finland). Her current research interests include value co-creation & co-destruction, design of smart and cyber-physical services, and sustainable digital service innovation. Her doctoral dissertation (2020) focused on value co-creation and co-destruction from the perspective of users of digital services.

Carolin Marx is a researcher and PhD student at the Chair for Design Thinking and Innovation Research at the Hasso Plattner Institute in Potsdam, Germany who is passionate about interdisciplinary research at the intersection of psychology, management and information systems. In her research, Carolin applies a cognitive-affective lens on decision-making challenges in digital transformation and innovation initiatives with particular emphasis on understanding how 'escalation of commitment' – the failure to withdraw from losing courses of action – emerges and which mitigation strategies decision-makers can apply.

Anna Maria Oberländer is a postdoctoral researcher at the University of Bayreuth, the Research Center Finance & Information Management (FIM) and the Branch Business & Information Systems Engineering of the Fraunhofer FIT, where she co-heads a research group and manages the Digital Innovation Lab as a co-founder. Her research and teaching centre around digital innovation, digital transformation, and emerging digital technologies such as the (industrial) Internet of Things. Anna has a background in strategy consulting with McKinsey & Company, where she supported clients in large-scale digital transformations.

Tero Päivärinta is a Professor of Information systems at Luleå University of Technology, Sweden, and a Professor at M3S Research Group, University of Oulu, Finland. His current research focuses on digitalization of service ecosystems in e-government and in industry, information management, and benefits realization from IT investments.

Clay Pearson joined the City of Pearland, Texas as City Manager in March 2014. Pearson serves Pearland with nearly 25 years' experience in municipal government. Prior to Pearland, he served the City of Novi, Michigan including as the City Manager for eight years. He had 14 years total in Novi, including six as Assistant City Manager. Prior to Novi, Pearson served the City of Elgin, Illinois for a decade in various capacities, including Assistant City Manager, Budget Officer and Director Code Administration and Neighborhood Affairs. Pearson is active with the association of local government professionals, the International City/County Management Association (ICMA). Pearson has a Master of Public Administration degree from the University of Kansas and a Bachelor's degree from Gustavus Adolphus College (St. Peter, Minnesota). He serves currently on the Board of the Alliance for Innovation and the Swedish-American Chamber of Commerce of Houston.

Ulla Rinkes is an affiliate researcher at the Chair for Design Thinking and Innovation Research at the Hasso Plattner Institute, Potsdam, Germany. She holds a PhD from the Catholic University of Eichstaett-Ingolstadt, a DAS Corporate Learning of the Swiss Competence Center for Innovations in Learning and is a certified Scrum Master and Product Owner. Ulla has 15 years of practical experience in a Tier 1 consultancy as well as being a Managing Director at one of the world's leading financial service providers. She is passionate about driving large scale strategic change initiatives to a successful outcome with special emphasis on people development and innovation.

Patrick Rövekamp is a research assistant at the Research Center Finance & Information Management (FIM) and the Branch Business & Information Systems Engineering of the Fraunhofer FIT. His research focuses on incumbent's digital platform strategies and digital transformation. Patrick holds a Master of Science (with honors) in Finance and Information Management from the Technical University of Munich and gained further experience at Dr. Oetker, where he co-developed the incumbents' ecosystem strategy and now serves as managing director in the start-up crafts unfolded.

Arman Sadreddin is an Assistant Professor, Supply Chain and Business Technology Management Department at the John Molson School of Business, Concordia University (Canada). Arman's research focuses on digital entrepreneurship, digital innovation, technology-enabled organizational capabilities, entrepreneurial ecosystems, digital divide and community development. Arman has published his research in international journals including the *International Journal of Information Management*, the *International Journal of Technological Innovation, Entrepreneurship and Technology Management (Technovation)*, *Journal of Community Informatics*, and several international conference proceedings, such as International Conference on Information Systems (ICIS), Americas Conference on Information Systems (AMCIS), R&D Management Conference, and World Open Innovation Conference (WOIC). Arman received several research grants from different agencies including the Insight Development Grant from Social Sciences and Humanities Research Council (SSHRC) of Canada and Mitacs. Arman holds a PhD and an MSc in Management Information Systems from Smith School of Business at Queen's University in Canada, and an MSc in Quality Systems Engineering from Concordia University (Canada).

Christian Sciuk is a PhD student in Management Information Systems at the Institute for Digital Management and New Media at Ludwig-Maximilians-Universität München (LMU), LMU Munich School of Management, Germany. He holds an MSc in Business Administration from Ludwig-Maximilians-Universität München (LMU), Germany, and a BSc in Global Business Management from the University of Augsburg, Germany. His research focuses on the governance of digital transformation and the study of new management roles in this context, such as the Chief Digital Officer. Previously, Christian gained various professional experiences, such as in corporate strategy or as a consultant for digital transformation.

David Soto Setzke is a business analyst at Allianz and a PhD candidate at Technical University of Munich (TUM). His dissertation explores success and failure factors for digital transformation strategies in established organizations using a configurational research approach. He holds a Master of Science in Informatics from TUM. His research and practical interests include large-scale digital transformation projects and digital platform ecosystems. His research has been published in journals such as *Information Systems Frontiers*, *Electronic Markets*, and the *Journal of Competences, Strategy and Management* as well as all major IS conference proceedings.

Tuure Tuunanen is Chair Professor of Information Systems at the Department of Informatics and Media at the Uppsala University and Professor of Information Systems and Vice Dean of Research in the Faculty of Information Technology at the University of Jyväskylä. He leads the Value Creation for Cyber-Physical Systems and Services Research Group and Finnish Hub for Digitalization. He is also a global faculty fellow at the Center for Service Leadership at Arizona State University. He holds M.Sc. and D.Sc. (Econ.) from the Aalto University School of Business.

Falk Uebernickel is a professor at the Hasso Plattner Institute, one of Europe's leading institutes for IT. He received his PhD in Business Administration from the University of St. Gallen. Since then, he has pursued research in digital innovation, transformation, and design thinking, of which he has a particular focus on automotive companies (BMW Group, Porsche, Audi, VW, Hyundai). Falk is also the spokesman of the SUGAR network – a global movement and initiative of over 20 universities and more than 100 companies to apply Design Thinking to real-world problems.

Daniel J. Veit is a full professor and chair of Information Systems and Management at the faculty of business and economics of the University of Augsburg, Germany. His research focuses on transformational effects of information systems and digitalization in society with a specific focus on sustainability. His publications have appeared in outlets such as the *MIS Quarterly*, *Journal of Management Information Systems*, *Information Systems Journal, European Journal of Information Systems,* and others. He serves as a Senior Editor for the *Journal of the Association for Information Systems* and as a Senior Editor for the *Information Systems Journal*.

Verena Kessler Verzar is a research assistant at the Chair of Information Systems and Management at the faculty of business and economics of the University of Augsburg, Germany. She gained practical experience in customer relationship management at Cultural Care Germany GmbH and in system development and project management at Ludo Fact GmbH. Her research interests lie mainly in the areas of digital usage behavior, privacy, and electronic government.

Christina Wagner is a senior doctoral student in Information Systems and Management at the faculty of business and economics of the University of Augsburg, Germany. She completed her master's degree in business and economics at the University of Augsburg. Her research interests lie in general on the impact of technologies on individuals' perceptions and behaviors, and more specifically on individuals' privacy in the face of digitalization. She has presented her works at European and international conferences on information systems and served as reviewer for several information systems journals and conferences.

Gongtai Wang is an Assistant Professor in Digital Technology at Smith

School of Business, Queen's University, Canada. He teaches and researches topics related to digital innovation, specifically focusing on how to fundamentally rethink and strategically redesign traditional products/services and business models with emerging digital technologies such as the Internet of Everything, mixed reality, artificial intelligence, and blockchain. His research has been published in *MIS Quarterly* and the *Journal of Product Innovation Management* and honored with awards at flagship information systems conferences. Prior to his academic career, he worked as a system engineer in the information technology industry.

Jörg Weking is visiting PostDoc at the Queensland University of Technology (QUT) and a research group leader at the Krcmar Lab at the Technical University of Munich (TUM). He studied Information Systems at the University of Münster, at the Turku School of Economics, and the QUT, and holds a doctoral degree in Information Systems from TUM. His research focuses on digital business models and digital platform ecosystems. His work has been published in the *European Journal of Information Systems*, *Electronic Markets*, *International Journal of Production Economics*, *Communications of the AIS*, and in refereed conference proceedings such as the International Conference on Information Systems or the European Conference on Information Systems.

Foreword

Robert D. Galliers

I was pleased and honoured to have been asked to write a brief Foreword to this welcome addition to the literature on digital value – especially so because, while much has been written on what has been called the 'age of digitalization', many treatments of the topic reflect a somewhat simplistic assumption that digital advances are with us, will continue, and will – more or less automatically – add value. While we may accept the first two aspects of this assumption, it is the third that requires more thought and critical reflection … and this is where this book is itself *of value*.

There is no doubting that digital technologies are pervasive and have impacted many facets of individual, organisational and societal activity in the twenty-first century. But what value ensues? This is a central question that this book considers … and does so in the balanced and reflective style that is required. Reflections by practitioners – alongside academic contributions – add more value. Opportunity and innovation can of course arise from the astute adoption and utilisation of digital technologies, but it is important to understand the complicated nature of the world we live in and the opposing forces at play in many of the contexts in which digital technologies are being applied.

Recognition of these – at times opposing – forces, the different worldviews, aims and objectives, and the possibility – or rather, the likelihood – of there being cross purposes, misunderstandings and misconceptions at play, is crucial to the gaining of value. Harvesting the 'good', without falling victim to the 'bad' requires this recognition: an open-minded approach amongst the actors involved, an understanding of the different *weltanschauungen*, which require surfacing in order for actors to work together – collectively and with common purpose – and at times, necessarily leaving their own requirements and objectives behind.

Adding value – to society – on the part of for-profit organisations and, conversely, adding value – by governments and public sector organisations – to private sector operations is a consideration that requires the kind of holistic treatment that is required, and that this book provides, for mutual benefit. Thus, a holistic treatment of digital value is the focus of this collection and a range of functional, organisational and societal considerations are dealt with. The structures, processes and eco systems necessary for actors to work together with common purpose are brought to the fore, as are the contradictions and issues arising.

The editors have sought contributions from a wide variety of sources and bring coherence to the subject matter by combining academic material with practical examples. I commend the work to students, academics and practitioners who seek to understand better the complexities of the digital world in which we live, with a view to avoiding the pitfalls associated with the unthinking application of the technology and to gaining real value from their endeavours.

Acknowledgements

This book project has persevered through the COVID-19 pandemic. We began this project early September 2020. During this time, the three of us, spread across Canada, the US, and Australia were experiencing different realities due to variances in lockdowns, mask mandates, vaccination rates, and border controls. One thing that became immediately clear as we witnessed various responses from governments and the private sector is that digital technologies have a significant role to play in creating public value. The use of Zoom for organising work and staying in touch with colleagues and friends, delivering lectures, and even to help families connect with their elderly loved ones became standard. We would first like to thank all the first responders who worked tirelessly through the pandemic to ensure that we would make it out of it.

Second, this book would not have been possible without the contributions from our authors. We thank each of them for taking the time to work with us on this project. We hope you enjoy the overall product and look forward to collaborating with you in the future.

Third, Samar Fatima provided much needed research and editorial assistance to prepare the final submission while still managing to complete her doctoral studies on time. Thank you, Samar!

Fourth, our appreciation goes to the entire team at Edward Elgar. Ellen Pearce believed in this project and encouraged us to pursue the book project. Francine O'Sullivan and team ensured that the production process was smooth and efficient.

Last, but definitely, not the least, each of us would like to thank a few individuals personally.

Kathryn - I started this project just over a year after I lost my Dad. It was through his prolonged battle with chronic disease that I experienced the challenges of navigating our healthcare system in Canada. This project provided me the opportunity to reflect on why those challenges exist and how my work as an academic researcher might influence positive change. Thank you Dad – you were always ahead of your time, I hope I can continue your legacy.

Greg – I owe a deep thank you to my mother who proudly showed me the bookshelf where she had the books that were written by friends and family and pointed out the spot where this book would go. The desire to fill that spot was motivating. Although my much loved Dad is no longer with us, his presence and support was felt through the entire process. Additionally, I owe deep thanks to my family and my friends – especially Dana -- who listened to me talk incessantly about this book and how it was going.

Kevin – 2021 was a year I will never forget. I would not have been able to make it through it if not for my family, friends, and colleagues. There are too many to name here, but you know who you are. I thank you for the support, kindness, and tolerance shown to me. I dedicate this book to my dad who passed away on March 7th 2021.

Kathryn, Kingston, Ontario, Canada
Greg, Phoenix, Arizona, USA
Kevin, Brisbane, Queensland, Australia

1. Digital value systems and sustainability

M. Kathryn Brohman, Gregory S. Dawson and Kevin C. Desouza

INTRODUCTION

Over the last decade, organizations have invested significant resources in digital transformation efforts with the intent to change the way their business generates value. However, despite major advances in digital technologies, the complexity of implementing those technologies in ways that create and disseminate value has proven to be no easy feat (Dabrowska et al. 2022). In fact, research has found that about 70 percent of digital transformation initiatives fail to achieve their goals (Bellantuono et al. 2021).

Although it is plausible to blame high failure rates on neglect of well-known organizational change management factors (e.g., lack of management support, lack of clearly defined objectives, poor communication) it would be unfair to ignore other key factors at play. One such factor is the fundamental change in business environment, commonly known as the Fourth Industrial Revolution. This new digital age is breaking precedent by increasing the speed of business, expanding the breadth and depth of change beyond traditional organizational boundaries, and unleashing new technological powers to organizations that control digital infrastructures such as social platforms and pervasive surveillance systems. Amongst other things, this fundamental change in environment has uncovered a great deal of uncertainty. Today, organizations need to consider how their business fits into a broader network of organizations involved in value producing activities related to an offering. In this book, we conceptualize the broader network of organizations as a 'value system'. The accelerated use of technology through the pandemic allowed organizations to leapfrog generations with regard to digital transformation (Hovestadt et al. 2021). Although there is some trepidation about the negative impacts, transformational efforts have increased the impact of digital in value creation.

Hence, we converge our focus on a specific type of value system we define as a 'digital value system'.

> Digital value system is *value generated when value creation for organizational systems is complemented by increases in value from other systems using digital technologies.*

As the socioeconomic impact of a digital value system is evident, we adopt Dabrowska et al.'s (2022) extended definition of digital transformation as 'a socioeconomic change across individuals, organizations, ecosystems, and societies that are shaped by the adoption and utilization of digital technologies'. This book organizes academic thought leadership and gains practitioner insights to define this next generation of value creation inherent in the digital age. Prior to moving on, let us consider a simple example of a 'digital value system' to identify the key components examined and outline the overall structure of the book. The simple example is a family vacation that includes cooperation between a network of organizations involved in providing the family with travel (flights, car rental) and a seven-night stay at a resort.

The highest level value system is defined by a collection of organizations that establish rules and regulations that are closely linked to the protection of the consumer, or in this example, protection of the family. We call this the '*societal value system*' and it is related to the need to establish sustainable business practices. In travel, the societal value system includes the cooperation of a wide array of organizations involved in enabling sustainable travel services and keeping people safe. For example, border control mitigates the risk of a family attempting to travel with banned goods, the Department of Transportation ensures appropriate accommodation is arranged if the family's flight is cancelled, and a regional bureau (e.g., consular affairs) may need to assist if the family wants to depart early due to hurricane warnings. At the core of this value system is a range of publicly-inspired interests including human rights, environmental sustainability, and anti-corruption.

The '*organizational value system*' is any given company or institution involved in the travel experience. In the digital age, organizations can take many forms. Using the travel example, a family can choose to book activities through an independent company webpage (e.g., Delta, Marriott, Budget) or use a booking platform such as Expedia, TripAdvisor, and Booking.com. A common platform is an example of a more complex organizational value system, or what many call a platform, that often delivers greater potential value (e.g., additional savings for booking more than one product, access to payment plans and last-minute deals). One of the challenges with today's travel platforms is that they are helpful in booking, but are less effective in providing the family with a seamless experience enabled by the network of organizations sharing information and working together. As such, when navigating the organizational value system, a customer is often left to resolve issues that arise between companies. Some may naturally consider the role of inter-organizational systems here; however, an alliance between organizations is still considered to be an organizational value system. It is the disconnects between alliances or even departments within a single organization that are a common cause of value degradation in the digital age.

The '*functional value system*' leverages digital technology to enable the integration and coordination of technology-related activity in complementary and impactful ways. Before investigating this value sub-system in more detail, it is important to note that the use of digital technology to manage this component is what makes this book most unique. Although scholars and practitioners have been using terms such as corporate social responsibility and environmental sustainability for over a decade, yielded results are primarily symbolic rather than substantial (Bowen, 2014). New blueprints (e.g., millennium development goals to sustainable development goals) and actionable mechanisms (e.g., ESG principles) have only recently started to emerge and require private and public sector organizations to become more interdependent (Lim, 2021). It is this third sub-system that introduces the potential for digital technology to serve as an actionable mechanism for integrating components of the digital value system.

Now some may question the novelty of this sub-system approach as enterprise systems such as Customer Relationship Management (CRM) came into vogue in the mid-1990s and academic scholars have highlighted the potential benefit of using this technology to create better customer relationships and personalized services based on a better understanding of customer needs and behaviors (Coltman, 2007). This is true; however, almost 30 years later, one would expect that investment in this technology would mean that customers should feel more personally connected to companies and trust that companies have their best interest in mind. Yet customer challenges continue to this day, with a recent study pointing to CRM as an example of the 70 percent of digitalization initiatives that fail to achieve their expected outcomes (Farhan et al., 2018).

We contend that although gaps may exist within these value sub-systems, digital value emerges when digital technology enables complementarities and resolves tensions between them. Returning to our simple example of a family vacation, there are many examples of technology enabling complementarity in travel. For example, social media companies create opportunities for families to create social value (e.g., staying in touch with loved ones, monitoring animals through home access to home cameras) and platforms can respond quickly in times of crisis (e.g., offering new flights, altering supply chains). It is also important to note that when complementarity is lacking, technology can create harm. Take, for example, social media sharing images and videos of the war in Ukraine that resulted in negative impacts to mental health (Riad et al. 2022).

It was indeed these gaps and negative consequences that inspired us to explore the relationship between digital technology and sustainability and develop the concept of digital value systems. The remainder of this chapter will set the stage for digital value systems by providing a brief history of Internet technology, outlining the evolution from decentralized to centralized, through Web 2.0 technologies and then finally to Web3 that promises a return to decentralized models. This discussion leads to an overview of paradoxical tensions and their role across value system components. The next section introduces our framework and describes the three value systems in more detail.

A BRIEF HISTORY OF INTERNET TECHNOLOGY

In the early 1990s, the first generation of the Internet commercialized network technologies and introduced new potential for value creation by changing the way people, organizations and society connected and shared information. The rise of near instant communication by email, instant message, telephone (Voice over Internet Protocol (VoIP)), two-way interactive video calls, and the World Wide Web influenced the mean annual growth in number of Internet users to average between 20 and 50 percent per year (Coffman and Odlyzko, 1998) and enabled organizations to establish a corporate presence in the new world of 'online'. Interestingly, it was around the same time that John Elkington changed the narrative on business value. In 1994, he coined the term 'triple bottom line' or 3BL to highlight the need for organizations to move beyond profitability by adding people and planet to their formula for success. We are not suggesting a direct correlation here, but one must admit – the overlap in timing between Web 1.0 and 3BL is indeed interesting.

In and around 2005, the next era of the Internet emerged (Web 2.0). High speed Internet and wider adoption rates were complemented by improvements to the worldwide web that changed static content to dynamic, or user-generated content. Rich web applications, web-oriented architecture and social web fundamentally changed the way people shared information, collaborated with others, and expressed themselves online. In the computer industry, the growth and influence of companies like Google, Facebook, Amazon, and Netflix connected people and organizations across the globe and made real-time communication and user-generated content a day-to-day reality. What emerged was a change in the way companies created value from traditional linear, value-chain models to platforms. Linear business models continued to create value by leveraging resources to create products and services, but a new type of value emerged from companies that created and facilitating the means of connection. A platform is a business model that helps to facilitate interactions of participants where interactions can take the form of short-term exchanges like connecting buyers to sellers (e.g., Amazon) or longer-term collaboration to achieve a shared outcome or sustained effort (e.g., Wikipedia).

As organizations worked to understand how business models were changing from linear production to connected platform, society began to make demands related to work-life balance, fairer salaries for workers, sustainability, and diversity, equity and inclusion as the exposure of unethical human and labour practices became more prominent. The fair treatment of people was not new, effective human resource management had always been deemed important for good business practice. However, when people were given a platform to get their voice heard, it became apparent that some of the most respected and admired companies and industries were plagued by unethical behavior, internal conflict, anxiety and unhappy employees (Conway et al., 2019; Ravazzani & Mazzai, 2018). For example, Mini-Microsoft[1]was a blog maintained by an anonymous Microsoft employee for a decade (2004–14), on which that employee as well as other Microsoft employees discussed and, on many occasions, criticized the firm's policies. Around the same time, other social media tools emerged that allowed employees to rate their employers on various categories, or allowed women to rate their employers on how they treated female employees (Donkin, 2007). Gradually, leaders came to realize the direct influence of social capital on performance and placed higher priority on managing the well-being of their people (Carmelli et al., 2009; Norrish et al., 2013). Firm and industry initiatives as well as academic research projects addressing questions of employee well-being, inclusion, and diversity in the technology sector have been ongoing for about two decades now (Trauth, 2017), partly driven by genuine beliefs and partly as a result of legal and regulatory pressures (Dobbin and Kalev, 2016). Yet questions of digital divide and digital inclusion remain as relevant today (Sieck et al., 2021; Trauth, 2017).

Although it can be argued that many social advances were made during the Web 2.0 era, areas of concern also arose. Several governmental entities, NGOs and industry sources reported that greenhouse (GHG) emissions from the use of IT in 2007 amounted to two per cent of the global GHG emissions, in addition to generating vast amount of electronic waste, yet at the same time acknowledged the potential for IT to help other industries reduce their environmental footprints significantly (Elliot, 2011). This gave rise to the emergence of two complementary streams of research and practice in IS: Green IT which was concerned with reducing the environmental footprint of IT, and Green IS, which was focused on using IT-enabled innovative solutions to help other industries reduce their environmental footprints (Loeser et al. 2017).

Today, enterprises and corporations are pursuing environmental and social sustainability goals under the umbrella acronym ESG, which stands for environmental, social and governance (Ketter et al., 2020; Kotsantonis & Serafeim, 2019). ESG practices emerged from a realization between the private and public sector that a movement toward low-carbon economy, net-zero emissions, fair treatment of people, and competent governance will require substantial investment beyond the public sector, more specifically private sector capital and expertise will be needed to meet our climate and societal objectives. In Canada, for example, the federal government launched the Sustainable Finance Action Council in May 2021 to help lead the Canadian financial sector toward developing integrated financial activities that take into account environmental, social, and governance (ESG) factors to encourage companies to finally put action to their environmental sustainability and social impact agendas.

Concurrent with the rise of ESG, Web3 is emerging as a group of technologies that has been rapidly developed over the last several years (Cao, 2022). At the core of Web3 are blockchains, open and interconnected community-owned databases and computing platforms that place strong emphasis on security and return control of data and identity back to users (Sheridan et al., 2022). Although Web3 is still nascent and potentiality overhyped, core Web3 applications are emerging such as DeFi (decentralized finance), DeSci (decentralized science), open digital wallets, tokens, decentralized autonomous organizations (DAOs) and open metaverses (Cao, 2022). In addition, companies like JPMorgan, Nike, Alphabet, and Disney have begun to strategize how Web3 can generate value for their business.

Like any new group of emerging technologies, both academics and practitioners will need to consider how these technologies may impact the way organizations approach strategy, structure, and business model innovation (Lumineau et al., 2021). A core promise of Web3 is decentralizing coordination and governance (Davidson et al., 2018). Some argue that this decentralizing logic goes against the centralizing logic of Web 2.0 that resulted in early social networks evolving into giant centralized platform ecosystems that collect and retain data on users and control many aspects of our daily lives, from our social interactions to our political attitudes to our shopping habits and financial data (Edelman, 2021). In fact, experts argue that this decentralizing logic is more in line with the open protocols of web 1.0 and predict a return of control to individual firms (Edelman, 2021). Therefore, if the promises of Web3 are realized beyond hype and in the right way, the benefit of leveraging technology to integrate profitability with ESG the payoffs could be significant (Baker, 2021).

Despite great potential inherent in Web3, early adopters will need to find ways to ensure that emerging Web3 decentralized solutions can co-exist with the dominant Web 2.0 grounded in centralized principles. This brings up the question of how firms can manage the opposing forces of centralizing and decentralizing at the same time, which sets the stage for the second theme in the book, paradoxical tensions.

DIGITAL VALUE AND PARADOXICAL TENSIONS

By combining an emerging set of advanced technologies with the rise of ESG, we came to the realization that corporate executives will soon (if they have not already) be looking to IT and other digital business functions to identify and define 'what they can do' to support ESG performance. After a careful review of literature, we identified research areas within the information systems field that have addressed ESG enthusiastically, but done so in a somewhat disconnected manner.

- In the area of environmental sustainability, the aforementioned Green IT and Green IS research streams are flourishing, generating insights on a range of topics from encouraging energy-efficient behaviors in households (Loock et al., 2013) to sustainable business practices (Seidel et al., 2013) and strategies (Loeser et al., 2017), to achieving the United Nations Sustainable Development Group (UNSDG) goals through smart cities (Corbett & Mellouli, 2017).
- With regard to generating social value, IS scholars have also studied a range of interesting topics, from addressing rural-urban healthcare divides through online health communities (Goh et al., 2016) to responsible innovation (Ahuja et al., 2022), to socioeconomic development (Bonina et al., 2021), to emancipatory machine learning (Kane et al., 2021), to engaging with indigenous peoples (Myers et al., 2020) and to postcolonial perspectives on IT offshoring (Ravishankar et al., 2013).
- IS has a long history of studying governance, from early studies of hierarchical, market, outsourced, and hybrid governance structures (Loh & Venkatraman, 1992; Sambamurthy & Zmud, 1999), to the implications of cloud computing (Choudhary & Vithayathil, 2013; Vithayathil, 2018) and platform ecosystems (Huber et al., 2017; Song et al., 2018) for governance.

Our literature review also demonstrated that as a field, we are far from a unified ESG perspective (Evans et al., 2017). One can hardly find studies that examine the interrelations and interactions of environmental sustainability, social value, and governance, as well as the relation between these ESG components and the business value of IT (BVIT) – the expected business payoffs from IT investments (Kohli & Devaraj, 2003; Sabherwal & Jeyaraj, 2015). Adding to these missing parts is the disconnect between academic research and industry practices and needs. As such, we anticipate the journey toward leveraging technology to improve ESG principles will be long and uncertain.

In this book, we take the first steps on this journey. However, even with a unified view, we expect the paradoxical tension between business viability (e.g., profitability, fiscal responsibility) and ESG principles will remain 'contradictory yet interrelated elements that exist simultaneously and persist over time' (Smith and Lewis 2011, p. 382). Framing this as a paradoxical tension (Agarwal et al., 2022; Gregory et al., 2015; Schultze & Bhappu, 2022; Wimelius et al., 2021) as opposed to trade-off provides a new perspective that may help uncover ways to pursue competing objectives (i.e., profitability and ESG) at the same time. Exploring paradoxes, we also identified mechanisms to address paradoxical tensions. The best-known mechanism is ambidexterity defined as 'an organization's ability to pursue two disparate things at the same time' (Gibson and Birkinshaw 2004, p. 210); however, others are beginning to emerge, such as collaborative governance (Agarwal et al., 2022).

To ensure the chapters in the book explored our two themes (digitalization and paradoxical tension), we approached known scholars who were exploring topics such as resolving competing objectives, paradoxical tensions and/or exploring mechanisms related to ambidexterity and collaborative business and governance practices.

DIGITAL VALUE SYSTEMS

It is sufficed to say that the transformation toward digital value systems that enable ESG practices will be most difficult on large incumbent organizations. The larger and more established the business is, the greater the impact of corporate inertia to sustain 'business as usual' and resist change induced by environmental and social demands as well as technological innovation. As such, this book positions the large incumbent organization at the core of our overarching Digital Value System framework and chapters and practitioner viewpoints are written with the intent to help guide senior leadership along their digital transformation journey.

To reiterate, the definition of a digital value system is value generated when value creation for organizations is complemented by increases in value for people and planet using digital technologies. In addition to this chapter, two other chapters bring to light the importance for our field to explore digital value systems. Chapter 2 draws on institutional theory to investigate how digital technology enabled public and private organizations to come together to deliver smart, regional services. Chapter 3 takes a critical look at value co-creation in social enterprises to discuss how digital technology can create value; however, it also introduces co-destruction activities that emerge when digital technology is not used and applied in appropriate ways.

The remaining chapters are structured into three sections that describe each value system (societal, organizational, functional). Each section starts with a practitioner overview that provides some key insights and practical ways to apply some of the academic findings. The first chapter in each section is a review of academic literature followed by two academic research studies that examine the value system. When all chapters come together, they inform the Digital Value System framework illustrated below.

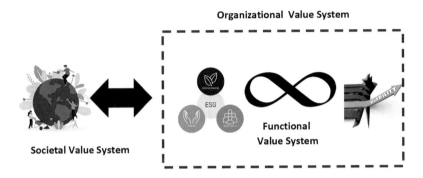

Figure 1.1   Components of a digital value system

The *societal value system* draws attention to the rise of the fourth industrial revolution characterized as a rapid epochal shift from traditional industrial industry to an economy built upon information technology. The two-sided arrow into the organizational value system illustrates the interaction between these systems. It is the societal value system that encapsulates the technological revolution that is fundamentally altering the way people live, work and relate to one another. On the other hand, existing organizational practices emerged from assumptions inherent in the industrial revolution. As such, the paradoxical tension most dominant in this value system is between the traditional business and new economic models and organizing frameworks to effectively do business in the digital age making this value system most relevant to senior executives. The term 'ecosystem' is a good example of a new organization of interacting actors (e.g., supplier, distributors, customers, competitors, government agencies etc.) involved in the delivery of a specific product or service through both competitive and cooperative practices (Jacobides et al., 2018). Actors in an ecosystem are drawn together by a shared fate of a community as a whole (Iansiti & Levien, 2004) where intimate and continual interactions may be permanent and direct or merely ad-hoc or temporal. When it comes to business, the critical differentiator of ecosystems compared to traditional business is that no entity can exist in isolation – survival of every actor is co-dependent on the survival of others (Purao & Desouza, 2010).

The practitioner perspective on this first set of chapters offers many interesting insights that are reminiscent of the age-old saying, 'where there's a will there's a way'. The author explains that for societal value to emerge, 'desire' amongst organizational leaders is necessary to first come to terms with the fact that changes in the environment are important. He follows up with the need to conduct a critical evaluation to determine if the organization has the tools it needs to find its way. Looking ahead, the author paints a positive outlook stating that more and more local governments are leveraging value from technology to create improved and more equitable services. Chapter 4 offers a review of digital transformation literature from both the societal and organizational level of analysis and draws out the tension between 'me and we' giving examples such as the UN Glasgow Financial Alliance for Net Zero raising monetary commitments from banks and other investors for green finance which in the end could mean less profitability for them. Chapters 5 and 6 are both case studies that adopt a digital platform approach to examine digital value. Chapter 5 demonstrates how digital entrepreneurs can leverage technology to be profitable and frugal at the same time. Chapter 6 describes different ways government is using social media to resolve competing objectives with businesses and citizens and provides examples of both value creation and value deterioration as a result of social media use.

The *organizational value system* is confined within the dotted lines to represent the argument that digital technology is fundamentally changing the organization's scope of responsibility. Value creation in the digital age will move away from organizations (for-profit business, government) being fully vertically integrated, which is in stark contrast to traditional business models where value is created by the actions and investments of either a single organization or a container of partner organizations in a strategic alliance that have carefully negotiated how value will be distributed. This increasing scope of responsibility also incorporates the need to embrace ESG principles. As such, chapters in this section coalesce around an emerging tension between competition, profitability (inside-out) and cooperation, ESG (outside-in). This tension demonstrates how digital technology and ecosystem-driven business models can help organizations cooperate and compete at the same time. As such, this value system is most relevant to middle managers responsible for changing business models and transforming the nature of work. Examples include online services that create opportunities for firms to co-create value with customers (Malar et al. 2019) and digital platforms that aim to resolve the tension between commodity and value-generating business processes (Markus and Loebbecke, 2013). Increased use of communication and social media technologies in organizations inspired the rise of the Icarus paradox

(Pinsonneault and Rivard, 1998) and the connectivity paradox (Leonardi et al. 2010). More recently, artificial intelligence and automation are highlighting tensions between digital/human work configurations (Baptista et al., 2020) that are fundamentally changing business models and extending the role of digital technology in managing organizational change (Sund et al., 2016).

What we learn from our practitioner in this section is that organizations need to get better at keeping customer-defined value at the forefront of their day-to-day operations. Whether it be data, social media, or the emerging metaverse, environmental scanning has become a daily, if not a real-time organizational capability. Chapter 7 sets up the challenges in organizational digital transformation by conducting a literature review on organizational inertia and presenting a framework for practice. Chapter 8 describes the evolution of the technology-enabled organizational value from traditional value-in-exchange and value-in-use perspectives to a new value-in-configuration that assembles a target set of digital technologies in a way that the intended value can be realized. Finally, Chapter 9 describes how the organizations evolve through different levels of digital maturity and presents recommendations for practice.

The *functional value system* is represented by the infinity sign that aims to help organizations resolve tensions between competition and cooperation. Embedded in the notion of infinity is that resolving organizational-level tensions is an ongoing, continuous effort, but it is also important to note that the symbol illustrates paradoxical tensions that live within the functional value system (e.g., IT, digital lab) itself. As such, this value system is most relevant to leaders of technology-related functions. We anticipate these leaders may be somewhat ahead of middle managers and senior leaders as they have been resolving tensions since the 2001 release of the agile manifesto that offered an alternative to traditional waterfall software development practices. In the early days, agile implementations played out more like a hostile takeover than a resolve of paradoxical tension. It was not until development teams were empowered with tools like Slack and JIRA that they started to orchestrate value by using both traditional and agile practices (Haffke et al., 2017). Other tensions in the functional view include IT and business governance practices (Huber et al., 2017) and a range of topics in human-computer interaction such as rational versus privacy in context (Badillo-Urquiola et al., 2018).

In this section, the practitioner overview walks readers through a history of leadership within the IT function and explains how a movement toward platforms and ecosystems are blurring boundaries between other functions (e.g., data analytics, security). Chapter 10 is a literature review on bimodal IT and uncovers a long list of functional tensions that emerge from previous research on structural ambidexterity and IT ambidexterity. Chapter 11 introduces new terms such as generativity and affordances and describes four configurations of functional platform types based on a comprehensive analysis. Chapter 12 wraps up the book by describing the evolution of IT leadership from its beginnings to the present day to shed light on how value generation has changed across different leadership approaches. Authors conclude with an outlook on the further evolution of IT leadership.

THE PURSUIT OF DIGITAL VALUE

Despite the fact that we anticipate paradoxical tensions to emerge from three distinct digital value systems, we contend that for systems-level change to occur, the boundaries between these value systems need to dissolve to some degree. In the digital age, increased economic volatility, environmental concerns, customer-focus, and continued erosion of societal trust in traditional capitalist and government systems are just a few examples of the many conditions that are expanding the scope of responsibility for value creation. As such, we reiterate the idea that value creation in the digital age will move away from any society, organization or function being fully vertically integrated and encourage organizational leaders to realize that the protection of boundaries can have serious consequences.

That being said, full cooperation is also not the answer as keeping boundaries intact to some degree remains essential – hence the dotted line. An expanded scope of responsibility does not negate the fact that rivalry between private sector companies and the fight for resources across government sectors remains intense. As such, we posit that competitive versus cooperative behavior may be the most challenging paradoxical tension to address in the digital age.

This book does not contribute to the macro-level debate on the topic of ecosystems versus industry; however it does recognize that when faced with competing objectives, expanding the scope of responsibility is helpful for value creation. Related to the societal value system, we anticipate connections between economic actors and political actors in the form of digitally-enabled, public-private partnerships and inter-organizational collaboration will become vital. In the organizational value system, silos will need to remain intact but digital technology will enable effective data transfer, cooperation, and communication across silos. Finally, in the functional view, departments will become more dependent on the IT function for operational support but the development of digitally-enabled products and services will expand across all departments.

To illustrate the opportunity for digital value creation across all systems, we end this chapter with a real-life story about digital transformation in government. We set the stage by recognizing that although government leaders are expected to prioritize people and planet, citizens across all countries are growing impatient with poor practices related to fiscal responsibility. Next, government at federal, states, and municipal levels have leveraged digital technology to resolve tensions between automation and human work by stream-lining mundane, repeatable tasks so personnel can focus on more value-added work. In 2015, the Australian government estimated that 40 percent of the 800 million transactions at the federal and state government each year were completed by phone, mail or in person. They created an AU$6.1 billion plan to reduce to 20 percent over a 10-year period estimating benefit to both citizens and government valued at AU$26.6 billion. This would equate to a net benefit of around AU$2,000 per Australian household.

Resolving tensions to automate mundane work is definitely a good starting point and the good news is that additional success stories stemming from digital technology use in government continue to emerge. Take for example the US government decision to halt a plan to build a $14 million Army Museum when people on social media raised awareness about the 47 Army Museums that already exist across the country. The bad news is that efforts to address paradoxical tensions have not really changed the fact that bureaucrats across every nation have little incentive to spend taxpayer dollars responsibly. So, despite good intentions, evidence of outrageous public sector waste continues. As such, chapters in this book provide several examples of how government initiatives that expand the scope of responsibility across government ministries are enabling system-level changes in government. It is the possibility for this level of change that became most evident during response to the COVID-19 pandemic. Initiatives such as Operation Warp Speed is an example of how private and public sector organizations worked together to accelerate the development, manufacturing, and distribution of COVID-19 vaccines (Winch, 2021). Stakeholders involved recognized the need to extend beyond traditional industry boundaries to collaborate with partners and even competitors to unleash the resources, talent and skills needed to achieve a seemingly impossible outcome.

NOTE

1.   http://minimsft.blogspot.com/ (accessed October 18, 2022).

REFERENCES

Agarwal, N., Soh, C., & Yeow, A. (2022). Managing paradoxical tensions in the development of a telemedicine system. *Information and Organization, 32*(1), 100393.

Ahuja, S., Chan, Y. E., & Krishnamurthy, R. (2022). Responsible innovation with digital platforms: Cases in India and Canada. *Information Systems Journal*, n/a(n/a), 1–54.

Badillo-Urquiola, K., Yao, Y., Ayalon, O., Knijnenurg, B., Page, X., Toch, E., ... & Wisniewski, P. J. (2018, October). Privacy in context: Critically engaging with theory to guide privacy research and design. In Companion of the 2018 ACM Conference on Computer Supported Cooperative Work and Social Computing (pp. 425–31).

Baker, J. (2021). Blockchain and sustainability: Oxymoron or panacea? *Forbes*. https://www.forbes.com/sites/jessibaker/2021/05/25/blockchain-and-sustainability -oxymoron-or-panacea/

Baptista, J., Stein, M. K., Klein, S., Watson-Manheim, M. B., & Lee, J. (2020). Digital work and organisational transformation: Emergent Digital/Human work configurations in modern organisations. *The Journal of Strategic Information Systems*, *29*(2), 101618.

Bellantuono, N., Nuzzi, A., Pontrandolfo, P., & Scozzi, B. (2021). Digital transformation models for the I4. 0 transition: Lessons from the change management literature. *Sustainability*, *13*(23), 12941.

Bonina, C., Koskinen, K., Eaton, B., & Gawer, A. (2021). Digital platforms for development: Foundations and research agenda. *Information Systems Journal*, *31*(6), 869–902.

Bowen, F. (2014). After greenwashing: Symbolic corporate environmentalism and society. Cambridge University Press.

Cao, L. (2022). Decentralized AI: Edge intelligence and smart blockchain, Metaverse, Web3, and DeSci. *IEEE Intelligent Systems*, *37*(3), 6–19.

Carmeli, A., Ben-Hador, B., Waldman, D. A., & Rupp, D. E. (2009). How leaders cultivate social capital and nurture employee vigor: Implications for job performance. *Journal of Applied Psychology*, *94*, 1553–61.

Choudhary, V., & Vithayathil, J. (2013). The impact of cloud computing: Should the IT department be organized as a cost center or a profit center? *Journal of Management Information Systems*, *30*(2), 67–100.

Coffman, K., & Odlyzko, A. (1998). The size and growth rate of the Internet. *First Monday*.

Coltman, T. (2007). Why build a customer relationship management capability? *The Journal of Strategic Information Systems*, *16*(3), 301–20.

Conway, E., Rosati, P., Monks, K., & Lynn, T. (2019). Voicing job satisfaction and dissatisfaction through Twitter: Employees' use of cyberspace. *New Technology, Work and Employment*, *34*(2), 139–56.

Corbett, J., & Mellouli, S. (2017). Winning the SDG battle in cities: How an integrated information ecosystem can contribute to the achievement of the 2030 Sustainable Development Goals. *Information Systems Journal*, *27*(4), 427–61.

Dąbrowska, J., Almpanopoulou, A., Brem, A., Chesbrough, H., Cucino, V., Di Minin, A., ... & Ritala, P. (2022). Digital transformation, for better or worse: a critical multi-level research agenda. *R&D Management*.

Davidson, S., Filippi, P. D., & Potts, J. (2018). Blockchains and the economic institutions of capitalism. *Journal of Institutional Economics*, *14*(4), 639–58.

Dobbin, F., & Kalev, A. (2016). Why Diversity Programs Fail. Harvard Business Review. https://hbr.org/2016/07/why-diversity-programs-fail

Donkin, R. (2007). Blogging cuts both ways. FT.Com, 1. https://www.proquest.com/ trade-journals/blogging-cuts-both-ways/docview/229027257/se-2

Edelman, G. (2021). The father of Web3 wants you to trust less. Wired. https://www .wired.com/story/web3-gavin-wood-interview/

Elliot, S. (2011). Transdisciplinary perspectives on environmental sustainability: a resource base and framework for IT-enabled business transformation. *MIS Quarterly*, 197–236.

Farhan, M. S., Abed, A. H., & Ellatif, M. A. (2018). A systematic review for the determination and classification of the CRM critical success factors supporting with their metrics. *Future Computing and Informatics Journal*, *3*(2), 398–416.

Gibson, C. B., & Birkinshaw, J. (2004). The antecedents, consequences, and mediating role of organizational ambidexterity. *Academy of Management Journal*, *47*(2), 209–26.

Goh, J. M., Gao, G. (Gordon), & Agarwal, R. (2016). The creation of social value: Can an online health community reduce rural-urban health disparities? *MIS Quarterly*, *40*(1), 247–63.

Gregory, R. W., Keil, M., Muntermann, J., & Mähring, M. (2015). Paradoxes and the nature of ambidexterity in IT transformation programs. *Information Systems Research*, *26*(1), 57–80.

Haffke, I., Kalgovas, B., & Benlian, A. (2017). Options for Transforming the IT Function Using Bimodal IT. *MIS Quarterly Executive*, *16*(2).

Hovestadt, C., Recker, J., Richter, J., Werder, K. (2021). Digital Responses to Covid-19: Digital Innovation, Transformation and Entrepreneurship During Pandemic Outbreaks. SpringerBriefs in Information Systems.

Huber, T. L., Kude, T., & Dibbern, J. (2017). Governance practices in platform ecosystems: Navigating tensions between cocreated value and governance costs. *Information Systems Research*, *28*(3), 563–84.

Iansiti, M., & Levien, R. (2004). The keystone advantage: what the new dynamics of business ecosystems mean for strategy, innovation, and sustainability. Harvard Business Press.

Jacobides, M. G., Cennamo, C., & Gawer, A. (2018). Towards a theory of ecosystems. *Strategic Management Journal*, *39*(8), 2255–76.

Kane, K., Young, A., Majchrzak, A., & Ransbotham, S. (2021). Avoiding an oppressive future of machine learning: A design theory for emancipatory assistants. *MIS Quarterly*, *45(1)*, 371–96.

Ketter, W., Padmanabhan, B., Pant, G., & Raghu, T. S. (2020). Special issue editorial: Addressing societal challenges through analytics: An ESG ICE framework and research agenda. *Journal of the Association for Information Systems*, *21(5)*, 1115–27. https://doi.org/10.17705/1jais.00631

Kohli, R., & Devaraj, S. (2003). Measuring information technology payoff: A meta-analysis of structural variables in firm-level empirical research. *Information Systems Research*, *14(2)*, 127–45.

Kotsantonis, S., & Serafeim, G. (2019). Four things no one will tell you about ESG data. *Journal of Applied Corporate Finance*, *31*(2), 50–58. https://doi.org/10.1111/jacf.12346

Leonardi, P. M., Treem, J. W., & Jackson, M. H. (2010). The connectivity paradox: Using technology to both decrease and increase perceptions of distance in distributed work arrangements. *Journal of Applied Communication Research*, *38*(1), 85–105.

Lim, W. M., & Weissmann, M. A. (2021). Toward a theory of behavioral control. *Journal of Strategic Marketing*, 1–27.

Loeser, F., Recker, J., Brocke, J. vom, Molla, A., & Zarnekow, R. (2017). How IT executives create organizational benefits by translating environmental strategies into Green IS initiatives: Organizational benefits of Green IS strategies and practices. *Information Systems Journal*, *27*(4), 503–53.

Loh, L., & Venkatraman, N. (1992). Diffusion of information technology outsourcing: Influence sources and the Kodak effect. *Information Systems Research*, *3*(4), 334–58.

Loock, C.-M., Staake, T., & Thiesse, F. (2013). Motivating energy-efficient behavior with Green IS: An investigation of goal setting and the role of defaults. *MIS Quarterly*, *37*(4), 1313–32.

Lumineau, F., Wang, W., & Schilke, O. (2021). Blockchain governance—A new way of organizing collaborations? *Organization Science*, *32*(2), 500–21.

Malar, D. A., Arvidsson, V., & Holmstrom, J. (2019). Digital transformation in banking: Exploring value co-creation in online banking services in India. *Journal of Global Information Technology Management*, *22*(1), 7–24.

Markus, M. L., & Loebbecke, C. (2013). Commoditized digital processes and business community platforms: New opportunities and challenges for digital business strategies. *MIS Quarterly*, *37*(2), 649–53.

Myers, M. D., Chughtai, H., Davidson, E., Tsibolane, P., & Young, A. (2020). Studying the other or becoming the other: Engaging with indigenous peoples in is research. *Communications of the Association for Information Systems*, *47*(1).

Norrish, A., Biller-Andorno, N., Ryan, P., & Lee, T. H. (2013, November 20). Social capital is as important as financial capital in health care. *Harvard Business Review*. https://hbr.org/2013/11/social-capital-is-as-important-as-financial-capital-in-health-care

Pinsonneault, A., & Rivard, S. (1998). Information technology and the nature of managerial work: From the productivity paradox to the Icarus paradox? *MIS Quarterly*, 287–311.

Purao, S., & Desouza, K. (2010, October). Large IT projects as interventions in digital ecosystems. In Proceedings of the International Conference on Management of Emergent Digital EcoSystems (pp. 9–16).

Ravazzani, S., & Mazzei, A. (2018). Employee anonymous online dissent: Dynamics and ethical challenges for employees, targeted organisations, online outlets, and audiences. *Business Ethics Quarterly*, *28*(2), 175–201.

Ravishankar, M. N., Pan, S. L., & Myers, M. D. (2013). Information technology offshoring in India: A postcolonial perspective. *European Journal of Information Systems*, *22*(4), 387–402.

Riad, A., Drobov, A., Krobot, M., Antalová, N., Alkasaby, M. A., Peřina, A., & Koščík, M. (2022). Mental Health Burden of the Russian–Ukrainian War 2022 (RUW-22): Anxiety and Depression Levels among Young Adults in Central Europe. *International Journal of Environmental Research and Public Health*, *19*(14), 8418.

Sabherwal, R., & Jeyaraj, A. (2015). Information technology impacts on firm performance: An extension of Kohli and Devaraj (2003). *MIS Quarterly*, *39*(4), 809–36.

Sambamurthy, V., & Zmud, R. W. (1999). Arrangements for information technology governance: A theory of multiple contingencies. *MIS Quarterly*, *23*(2), 261–90.

Schultze, U., & Bhappu, A. D. (2022). Examining the viability of organization-sponsored sharing platforms. *Journal of the Association for Information Systems*, *23*(4), 889–912.

Seidel, S., Recker, J., & vom Brocke, J. (2013). Sensemaking and sustainable practicing: Functional affordances of information systems in green transformations. *MIS Quarterly*, *37*(4), 1275–99.

Sheridan, D., Harris, J., Wear, F., Cowell Jr, J., Wong, E., & Yazdinejad, A. (2022). Web3 challenges and opportunities for the market (arXiv:2209.02446). arXiv. https://doi.org/10.48550/arXiv.2209.02446.

Sieck, C. J., Sheon, A., Ancker, J. S., Castek, J., Callahan, B., & Siefer, A. (2021). Digital inclusion as a social determinant of health. *NPJ Digital Medicine*, 4, 52.

Smith, W. K., & Lewis, M. W. (2011). Toward a theory of paradox: A dynamic equilibrium model of organizing. *Academy of Management Review*, *36*(2), 381–403.

Sund, K. J., Bogers, M., Villarroel, J. A., & Foss, N. (2016). Managing tensions between new and existing business models. *MIT Sloan Management Review*, *57*(4), 8.

Trauth, E. (2017). A Research Agenda for Social Inclusion in Information Systems. ACM SIGMIS Database: *The DATABASE for Advances in Information Systems*, *48*(2), 9–20.

Vithayathil, J. (2018). Will cloud computing make the Information Technology (IT) department obsolete? *Information Systems Journal*, *28(4)*, 634–49.

Wimelius, H., Mathiassen, L., Holmström, J., & Keil, M. (2021). A paradoxical perspective on technology renewal in digital transformation. Information Systems Journal, *31(1)*, 198–225.

Winch, G. M., Cao, D., Maytorena-Sanchez, E., Pinto, J., Sergeeva, N., & Zhang, S. (2021). Operation Warp Speed: Projects responding to the COVID-19 pandemic. *Project Leadership and Society*, 2, 100019.

2. Value co-creation for smart villages: the institutionalization of regional service ecosystems

Juuli Lumivalo, Tero Päivärinta and Tuure Tuunanen

INTRODUCTION

Norrbotten, the largest region in Sweden, covers 25 percent of the country area, while its population represents only 2.56 percent of the Swedes (Regionfakta, 2022). Suboptimal availability of local services affects livability in such rural regions in developed countries. Livability refers to the degree to which the physical and social features of a living environment fit an inhabitant's requirements and desires. High livability improves individual and community well-being (Newman, 1999). Vast distances to public and private service hubs pose challenges to inhabitants. Fortunately, the Internet and fast broadband connections have become widely available allowing integration of local and digital service resources (McKinsey & Co., 2014; Regionfakta, 2022). Thus, opportunities for innovating smart services for inhabitants' needs have increased. For instance, on-demand delivery of goods and health services can be provided in rural regions as service constellations combining public and private services, such as a mobile service booth for distributing health and convenience services as well as appointments for unemployment services and leisure activities.

However, designing, developing, and providing services for sparse village populations is challenging due to the scarcity of municipal resources. Given these villages' low population densities and distance from larger cities and towns, traditional market mechanisms may not sustainably secure the availability of public or private services on site. Further, each inhabitant has their personal needs, values, and goals, and therefore, one service model may not fit all, which may create tension between the actors involved. For instance, while some of the inhabitants seek to maintain face-to-face social connections with service providers, such as health care professionals, some may perceive the transition to a digitalized or hybrid service model most beneficial. Structures and processes at the regional, national, and global scales significantly influence the development of small towns and municipalities (Leetmaa et al., 2015, p. 148). However, public and private service providers across sectors may also have conflicting priorities, potentially preventing the establishment of collaboration structures. Thus, smart services are needed in rural areas to develop and facilitate synergies, connecting individual inhabitants with government and businesses at the micro-level, as well as networks of rural actors at the meso level (inhabitants, businesses, and municipalities) and municipalities at the macro level.

Such value co-creation with smart services may be crucial in maintaining rural, sparsely populated regions in developed countries livable by facilitating both individual and community well-being (Newman, 1999). Connections are also needed between emerging smart city initiatives and the initiatives of surrounding rural regions, with a focus on higher-scale innovation and sustainability (Kar et al., 2019). However, extant literature on smart city and regional initiatives tends to focus on large cities or densely populated regions, overlooking rural regions in developed countries, e.g., (Markkula & Kune, 2015). Typically, the larger the population of the area, the more urgently the need for smart services is considered (Dwivedi et al., 2012).

Thus, an improved understanding of how to create value in regional service ecosystems is needed. We address this need by answering the following research question: how can value be derived for actors in regional service ecosystems through smart services? To attain an understanding of what is of value for inhabitants and the municipality, we employ the Service-Dominant Logic (SDL) framework (Vargo & Lusch, 2004, 2016) and investigate value as an outcome of a co-creation process in which actors integrate available resources into a joint venture. Due to sparse customer bases in rural areas, transformation of the prevailing ways and means of providing and consuming services may be required for enabling such co-creation. Thus, we draw from institutional theory (Barley & Tolbert, 1997) in innovating smart, sustainable services for regional service ecosystems (Vargo et al., 2015).

To understand how to create value using smart services in regional service ecosystems, we conducted qualitative interviews (n = 53) in Norrbotten County, Sweden. Utilizing the laddering interview method (Ken Peffers et al., 2003; Reynolds & Gutman, 1988), we establish an understanding of the regional service ecosystem's value structures to inhabitants by constructing thematic maps of the laddering chains. We employ the concept of scripts, i.e., the 'observable, recurrent activities and patterns of interaction characteristic of a particular setting' (Barley & Tolbert, 1997, p. 98) in understanding value co-creation in a regional service ecosystem. Depicting links between institutionalization and actors' practices we observe institutional work (Wieland et al., 2016) that may be employed in developing sustainable public and private services in smart villages for the purpose of attaining a regional service ecosystem.

The findings contribute to the e-government literature with a novel investigation of the development of smart villages in rural areas capturing the interplay between higher-order scales and individual actors. We also contribute to the SDL discourse with empirical evidence of institutionalization for potential value co-creation in a regional service ecosystem. Our findings showcase that also disruptive innovations are required for co-creating value with novel combinations of digital-enabled services to maintain rural regions' livability.

THEORETICAL BACKGROUND

The Service-Dominant Logic Perspective and Service Ecosystems

One of the main interests of service providers when designing, developing, and providing services is to determine how value can be derived from the service. Over the past two decades, research has begun to emphasize the role of customers in the creation and determination of value e.g., (Prahalad & Ramaswamy, 2004). Interactivity and relationship-focused perspectives have emerged, suggesting that companies ought to consider customers as active co-creators of experience and value, e.g., (Ballantyne, 2004; Prahalad & Ramaswamy, 2000). According to SDL (Vargo & Lusch, 2004) service providers may merely propose value propositions to their customers, which customers may choose to accept by integrating their resources into a value co-creation process. Here, products and services have no embedded value. Instead, value is co-created through the process of resource integration between the involved providers and customers (ibid.). In other words, SDL underscores operant resources (e.g., knowledge and skills) as primary subjects of economic and social exchange. Furthermore, institutions – the rules, norms, and beliefs set by people (Scott, 2008) – coordinate the actions and experiences of individual actors, thus constraining or enabling the co-creation of value (Vargo & Lusch, 2016). Accordingly, each benefiting actor determines derived value contextually and phenomenologically.

As actors integrate possessed resources, they fundamentally become connected to other actors by those resources, and vice versa. For instance, actors can build on one another's knowledge through the collective innovation of services. Such processes occur not only in dyads between two actors but also in triads and networks of multiple connected actors (Vargo & Lusch, 2016). These networks form service ecosystems, which are fundamental to understanding value co-creation (Chandler & Vargo, 2011) and are defined as 'relatively self-contained, self-adjusting system[s] of resource-integrating actors connected by shared institutional arrangements and mutual value creation through service exchange' (Vargo & Lusch, 2016, pp. 10–11). Service ecosystems involve 'large-scale social structures and institutions' that evolve with actors' unique service efforts in dyads, triads, and complex networks (Chandler & Vargo, 2011, p. 44). Thus, to understand how value is derived by individual actors (at the micro level), it is essential to understand meso- and macro-level influences. This understanding may include institutionalized meanings of practices and public procedures. To make sense of such discrepancies in deriving value, understanding the context and acknowledging value as a contextually contingent concept are essential (Vargo et al., 2008).

Institutional Change in Re-forming Service Ecosystems

We adopt the SDL lens and view that institutional arrangements guide actors' sensemaking of service situations and the emerging value for beneficiaries in nested and overlapping service ecosystems (Vargo & Lusch, 2016). The institutionalized view draws from the social systems perspective, which claims that actors draw meaning from social systems and societal beliefs and norms (Edvardsson et al., 2011). Barley and Tolbert (1997, p. 6) discuss institutions as having 'shared rules and typifications that identify categories of social actors and their appropriate activities or relationships'. Vargo and Lusch (2016, p. 6) offer a more simplified definition in which institutions consist of 'rules, norms, meanings, symbols, practices, and similar aides to collaboration'. Wieland et al. (2016) state that institutions are the glue in service ecosystems enabling and constraining value co-creation within these social systems.

Barley and Tolbert (1997) modelled how institutions are created, altered, and reproduced. They posit that 'scripts' may be viewed as bridges that gauge how institutions affect actions and, at the same time, how actions iteratively maintain, modify, and create new institutions. The authors structure a methodology, stating that scripts may first be used to encode institutional principles in specific settings and then enacted on to maintain or enforce such principles (Barley & Tolbert, 1997). In a similar vein, Wieland et al. (2016) argue that value co-creation practices, which are enacted by actors, simultaneously shape those very same practices by creating, maintaining, or disrupting the institutions that are guiding their (re)enactment. Wieland et al. (2016, p. 5) define such value co-creation practices as 'sets of overlapping and interlinked bundles of integrative, normalizing, and representational practices through which actors make sense of and integrate public, private, and market-facing resources'. Furthermore, Barley and Tolbert (1997) suggest that a setting that involves disturbances (e.g., new technological developments or regulations) can be particularly fruitful for observing institutional change through scripts.

Value Co-creation in Regional Service Ecosystems: Need for Institutional Work

While localizing public services in sparsely populated (but highly connected) areas may be ineffective with the traditional market mechanisms (McKinsey & Co., 2014), government-driven reformation of service ecosystems is needed to support inhabitants' well-being. Accordingly, e-government research has acknowledged that future challenges require a shift in conducting and organizing innovation, and embracing technological advancements, such as artificial intelligence and big data (Liu & Zhenghong, 2014; Mulder, 2014). Drawing from the SDL lens, collaboration between individuals as well as governmental, commercial and other stakeholders may be key for co-creating such service innovations and public value in the era of digitalization. Previous research has attempted to obtain an understanding of technology-enabled public value co-creation (Cronemberger & Gil-Garcia, 2019) and citizen value co-creation in smart cities, e.g., (Owais et al., 2017). While value co-creation with smart services may be particularly crucial in maintaining rural, sparsely populated regions as livable, the literature tends to focus on large cities or densely populated regions, overlooking rural regions in developed countries (e.g., Markkula & Kune, 2015). More research is needed also for linking smart city initiatives with surrounding rural regions, focusing on sustainable higher-scale innovation (Kar et al., 2019).

Further, while acknowledging the network of multiple stakeholders is considered essential to the e-government domain (e.g., Axelsson et al., 2013; Balta et al., 2015), previous research has provided little knowledge of public sector value co-creation in rural villages on the service ecosystem level, which involves networks of villages, municipalities, citizens, businesses, and citizen organizations. Co-creation of value by utilizing new technologies in smart cities also remains understudied (Cronemberger & Gil-Garcia, 2019). At the same time, it is well-understood that the most significant challenge in developing smart city services is not technological, but rather attitudinal (Mulder, 2014). Thus, to understand how to facilitate ecosystem-level value co-creation in smart villages, it is essential to understand interconnectedness between actors' (i.e., inhabitants', public/private service providers' and other stakeholders') practices and institutions to identify the government-driven institutional work required for the transformation (Wieland et al., 2016). For instance, institutions such as the norm of having a face-to-face doctor's appointment in a hospital, may need to be disrupted in order to successfully provide public digital health care services for rural regions – and this may be established by creating new norms through governmental institutional work, which includes practices such as providing and using digital services in the public sphere and inviting/facilitating new era collaborations.

METHODOLOGY

Our objective was to investigate rural residents' preferred practices for value co-creation building on Barley and Tolbert's (1997) guidelines for observing scripts. Scripts illustrate how individual actors construct and commit to new rules and interpretations of appropriate behavior in particular settings. The authors suggest that a setting that involves disturbances (e.g., new technological developments or regulations) can be particularly fruitful for observing institutional change through scripts (ibid). Thus, by employing the uncovered scripts, we were able to depict institutional work required for value co-creation in the interplay between particular smart service offerings (the micro-level) and the regional service ecosystem of Norrbotten County (the macro-level). We conducted laddering interviews with citizens of nine rural villages and towns in Sweden's Norrbotten County, one of the EU's most sparsely populated regions (Regionfakta, 2022). Employing the laddering interview technique (Peffers et al., 2003; Reynolds & Gutman, 1988; Tuunanen & Peffers, 2018), the goal of the interviews was to map the villagers' views regarding what kinds of public or private digital-enabled services would provide opportunities for value co-creation in the region and why.

Norrbotten inhabitants of different occupations and age groups (ranging between 24–78 years) were interviewed in 53 individual interviews. In accordance with the laddering technique, informants were first introduced to a stimuli collection of six written scenarios (Peffers et al., 2003). The informant then selected two most appealing scenarios, and the researcher asked the informant to describe a particular desired use experience with regard to the first-selected scenario; this was briefly recorded as attribute ladders. Thereon, the researcher continued asking 'Why would this be important for you?' (Reynolds & Gutman, 1988). The informant continued providing their reasoning to a series of 'why' questions; these were recorded as consequence ladders. When no further reasoning could be provided, the ultimate personal goal of the informant was identified as value ladders. Then, the researcher moved on to asking questions related to the second stimulus, continuing until both stimuli were thoroughly covered.

In total, 688 chains (laddering structures) were collected showcasing potential future institutional innovations required for the sustainability of villages in Norrbotten, with a particular focus on service portfolios for citizens and livability. Moreover, another level of analysis emerged with respect to the service ecosystem. For instance, a localized digital-enabled service point would require rethinking of service models, and collaboration between the public domain as well as private sector actors, e.g., transportation. Following Peffers et al. (2003), the coded dataset totaled 873 laddering structures, derived from the original chains. A clustering analysis was conducted on these coded chains, graphing thematic maps for each emerging digital service theme by connecting 'pathways' between attribute-, consequence-, and value-level constructs (Ken Peffers et al., 2003; Tuunanen & Kuo, 2015).[1] The following eight unique thematic maps emerged: (1) digital health services; (2) service points; (3) digital services for tourism; (4) service buses; (5) accelerating social life; (6) logistics of goods; (7) service portals, and (8) facilitating citizen transportation. Investigating the pathways (i.e., connections between the constructs) in the thematic maps, we found diversity across attribute-level constructs, but also overlap of the consequence and value constructs across the thematic maps.

Labelling each unique pathway on the formed thematic maps, we derived institutional scripts (Barley & Tolbert, 1997), illustrating informants' descriptions of the perceived structures behind co-creation practices enabled by digital service innovations. Each emerging script comprehended structures showcasing how particular service features (attribute constructs) may benefit the focal actor (consequence constructs) and co-create value establishing an ultimate goal of service use (value constructs). The emerging value constructs were, subsequently, clustered according to their contents and their appearance in the laddering chains. For instance, the value constructs comfort and easiness in life, right to choose, coping with daily life, independence, ease of use, and prosperity were all clustered under the title 'Comfort and easiness in life.'

As an example, altogether 10 scripts emerged in the thematic map of 'Digital health services' (cf. Figure 1.1). For instance, in the first script, the attribute constructs access to public health services, and access to related educational resources therein, were found important, as they allowed for improved interaction with health services. Thus, the first script indicates that the creation of new institutions would lessen the related frustration, stress, and workload. Consequently, informants claimed that it would aid in enhancing competence, thus leading to the ultimate values of public resource and service efficiency, accessibility, saved time, comfort and ease of life, health benefits, and social inclusion. The second script was constructed with similar consequence- and value-level constructs; the difference was in the focus on creating new institutions in the digital booking of health services. The third script had an identical value-level structure as script 2; however, at the consequence level, it delved into the informative aspects of the access and booking of health services, reasoning that these are important for seeking advice directly from health care personnel and thus have more services available and are better able to work from rural villages. The script showcased that creation of new institutions by remotely consulting health care personnel may trigger a new challenge in which urgent care needs may be recognized too slowly in remote mode. Thus, we identified the need to maintain current institutions, i.e., the option of physical appointments. The scripts 7 and 8 suggested the creation of new institutions that would allow more efficient use of public health care resources due to less expensive consultation and faster access to such services, thus saving time and lowering infection risks. In turn, script 6 suggested disrupting prevalent institutions as by accessing and booking digital services, on-demand services could be provided on site. This would reduce the need for current types of face-to-face services, as the new practices would be formalized. Moreover, the institution of driving a car to a city to receive health services would also be disrupted in script six.

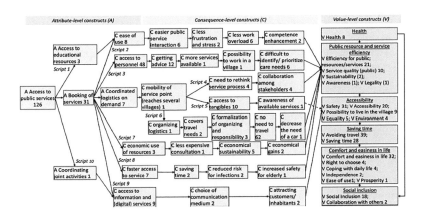

Figure 2.1　　*Thematic map, 'access to public health services' scripts 1–10: constructs and their frequency (hits)*

In the analysis, cross-thematic script overlaps were considered particularly fruitful in terms of defining smart, sustainable joint service offerings relevant across seemingly distinct service themes. Thus, we set out to employ the overlapping value co-creation scripts across divergent themes for developing *encoding scripts*, that may be utilized for formulating bundles of digital services and creating institutional change in the form of a rural service ecosystem (Barley & Tolbert, 1997; Wieland et al., 2014). For theory building purposes, we focused on connections that were relatively frequent across the divergent digital service themes. Through several threshold tests, ≥3 was selected as an appropriate threshold for ensuring that the emerging scripts were not overly cluttered, while a suitable level of detail remained. Thereafter, we assessed all the connections between linked attribute, consequence, and value constructs appearing with the threshold of ≥3 (i.e., scripts overlapping in at least three distinct service themes), which derived altogether six encoding scripts (Barley & Tolbert, 1997). As manifestations of institutional work, the value co-creation practices that underlined the emerging encoding scripts simultaneously shaped those very same practices by creating, maintaining, or disrupting the institutions that are guiding their (re)enactment. Accordingly, the shared encoding scripts between distinct themes were considered to have high potential to build institutional change through value co-creation practices suggested by the informants not only at the level of a single service idea but also at the level of bundled service exchange at the level of the rural service ecosystem (Wieland et al., 2016).

ENCODING SCRIPTS FOR INNOVATING BUNDLES OF DIGITAL-ENABLED SERVICES

In our analysis, we derived six encoding scripts, each overlapping across at least three divergent digital service themes. The scripts were distributed across the digital service themes with six hits in the theme of local service point; four hits in the themes of health services, and service bus; two hits in the theme of online service portal; and single hits in the themes of tourism and recreation, logistics of goods, and social life. Each encoding script, comprehending connected attribute (service feature), consequence (reasoning), and value constructs (ultimate goals and outcomes) (Peffers et al., 2003; Reynolds & Gutman, 1988). As institutional arrangements guide actors' sensemaking of the emerging value for beneficiaries of service exchange (Vargo & Lusch, 2016), each of the emerging encoding scripts showcase the value co-creation potential of the script in question across the linked digital service themes. Such value co-creation synergies manifesting across divergent digital service themes as the emerging encoding scripts showcase institutional principles for innovating bundles of digital-enabled services for a regional service ecosystem. Table 1 presents the six emerging encoding scripts overlapping across the divergent digital service themes. In the following, we depict each emerging encoding script one by one.

In the first encoding script, the service offering is based on providing access to information and services, meaning the construction of infrastructures that allow fast broadband connections and digitalized services that can be accessed through devices the inhabitants possess. The requisite institutional work involves creating a shift from the need to travel long distances for public and private services toward enjoying such services from the convenience of one's home or another local access point. Thus, the encoding script is connected with the digital service themes of local service point, online service portal, and service bus, which indicate a roadmap for developing the offering of internet connections not only through personal hotspots and broadband connections, which would allow at-home access to a versatile online service portal, but also through publicly constructed physical sites, such as a local booth where village

Table 2.1   Encoding scripts overlapping in divergent digital service themes (threshold ≥3)

Encoding scripts (connected attribute, consequence, and value constructs)			**Overlapping digital service themes** (threshold ≥3)						
Attribute constructs	Consequence constructs (number of connections)	Value constructs (number of connections)	Health services	Local service-point	Online service-portal	Service-bus	Tourism	Logistics of goods	Social Life
1. Access to Internet & services	No need to travel (5)	Avoiding travel (5)		X	X	X			
2. Access to public services	Access to personnel (34) No need to travel (32) Access to information and (digital) services (5) Access to tangibles (3)	Accessibility (14) Avoiding travel (21)	X	X		X			
3. Coordinated logistics on demand	Access to tangibles (14) No need to travel (13)	Accessibility (8) Comfort and easiness in life (13) Avoiding travel (14)	X	X		X		X	

Encoding scripts (connected attribute, consequence, and value constructs)		Overlapping digital service themes (threshold ≥3)			
4. Digital service portal and website	Access to information and (digital) services (3)	Accessibility (5)	X	X	X
5. F2F/hybrid public services	End-user support needed (5) Access to personnel (14) No need to travel (26) Preserving human interaction (8)	Self-efficacy (3)	X		
		Accessibility (7)	X	X	
		Avoiding travel (7)			
		Comfort and easiness in life (10)			
		Safety (8)			
		Social inclusion (3)			
6. Social informing and meeting	Preserving human interaction (8)	Social inclusion (8)	X	X	

inhabitants may visit and have access to digital public and private services. Furthermore, a service bus circulating between villages was also elevated as a focal corner stone for providing access to the internet and services. The service bus may offer access to physical services, such as personalized advice and municipal services, as well as digital services through provision of internet access and devices required for accessing public and private services. A commonly shared value and goal was the avoidance of travel, meaning having requisite services available locally and online. Thus, the synergies in bundling public and private services in accessible physical and digital outlets was found particularly important due to its negative impact on the traveling needs in the investigated rural communities.

The second encoding script focuses on institutional work on creating and improving access to public service offerings, such as employment, health, and social services. Due to sparse populations, such services are often located distances away from rural areas, which means that services may not be equally accessible to rural inhabitants. While access to digital services (provision of digital public service offerings and access to an internet connection) may partially address the dilemma, some public services are required to be provided face-to-face. For instance, the informants were keen to consume some health services (such as doctors' appointments for diagnoses) more likely at a local service point or a service bus. Our findings indicate that institutional work is required to create a shift in the appropriate manner of using and consuming public services, and particularly the conduct of information intensive tasks such as managing one's job seeking profile and booking of appointments, which do not necessarily require face-to-face service. Bringing public service and infrastructures close to the rural inhabitants was seen important as it improved inhabitants' access to information and (digital) services, and tangibles, such as in-person service, and equipment. Overall, these were seen to meet the values and goals of accessibility and avoiding traveling long distances.

The third encoding script revolves around physical goods relating to both public and private services, from clinical health equipment to convenience shopping. The interviewed inhabitants agreed that a systemic solution to coordinated logistics is needed. As a result, our findings point toward a need for institutional work toward creating a shift in the application of logistics systems that simultaneously serve the needs of public services as well as firms operating locally and globally. For instance, it would be beneficial to distribute heart rate monitoring equipment to rural homes ad-hoc, while the villagers' private online purchases and convenience goods could be shipped to rural households using the same logistics mechanisms. Our findings suggest that a circulating service bus could be one solution in coordinating such logistics, and a local service point offering access to digital services may be beneficial also in providing a local collection outlet for the shipped tangibles. Such mechanisms open for any market actors would be highly needed due to rural inhabitants' limited access to goods and products without traveling. Our findings illustrate that a coordinated logistics system operating on demand without restrictions between ecosystem actors would increase the rural inhabitants' comfort and easiness in life as well as accessibility, also serving the purpose of avoiding travel.

The fourth encoding script is based on the development of an accessible digital service portal open for divergent ecosystem actors such as tourism operators and other local companies, as well as public services. The umbrella of an open online service portal and website holding together all available services would improve the accessibility to not only existing service providers, but also the entrance of new market actors. Implementing such a service would require institutional work with respect to creating new practices for gaining access to information, and divergent public and private services. Thus, the traditional means of providing physical services could be digitalized to an appropriate extent, and new digitalized features may also be used for complementing the extant physical (yet less accessible) ones. For instance, citizen consultation could be provided via chats or built-in conference calls, and simultaneously, local private service providers could display and distribute their services digitally. Further, our findings indicate that an open digital service portal and website may allow for facilitating the growth of a local sharing economy by improving the visibility of closely available resources, such as accommodation units and produce. Here, a local service point was considered an important structure not only making the service portal physically visible for locals and visitors, but also by providing access to the online services.

In the fifth encoding script, a requirements-based combination of face-to-face and hybrid service offerings emerges as a focal requisite institutional work for both creating new and maintaining extant practices. The complexity of the need and potential of hybrid service offerings is highlighted with respect to health services, such as doctors' appointments and physical checkups. While some of the offerings requiring traditionally physical appointments may be dealt with by online tools, the use of digital services is not equally possible for all inhabitants, especially with respect to the need of support and guidance. Such facilitation is needed particularly to increase accessibility and inhabitants' skills, improving their self-efficacy. Thus, a local service point is needed, wherein hybrid services may be provided with technical and other support at hand. With attentive service at a local service point or a circulating service bus, some of the otherwise physically facilitated appointments could be organized in a hybrid mode. For instance, blood pressure could be measured by a physical person at the service point whereas a doctor's control consultations could be organized virtually when appropriate. At the same time, face-to-face service offerings were found crucial in a variety of service offerings. For instance, public services ought not only to be available through online channels, rather, physical face-to-face interactions ought to be preserved to some extent. Our findings underscore that such locally available physical appointments and assistance would not only improve safety and accessibility, but they would also increase social interactions and improve rural inhabitants' comfort and easiness in life.

Finally, the sixth encoding script focused on mitigating the potential adverse effects of digitalization on personal interactions. Especially in rural areas, public and private services may make up a great proportion of the social interactions an inhabitant has outside the family. Thus, institutional work is required for maintaining human-to-human interactions, which was found particularly integral with respect to facilitating social inclusion. Accordingly, the local service point was depicted as a focal physical structure at the village, providing face-to-face interactions on site not only between service providers (such as the municipality), but also among the inhabitants. It was found particularly important that public services, such as employment advice, or social and health consultation were alternatively provided also in person to ensure social inclusion. The service point was also viewed as a local meeting point, where resources could be integrated and exchanged.

DISCUSSION

The goal of the study was to investigate synergies between script structures emerging from divergent digital service themes, indicating constellations of smart services promoting overreaching value for a regional service ecosystem. Having conducted a detailed analysis of all the scripts emerging across the eight divergent thematic maps, we dissect six encoding scripts overlapping across the digital service themes of health services: local service point, online service portal, service bus, tourism and recreation, logistics of goods, and social life. The emerging encoding scripts bring forth evidence of practices for digital value co-creation (as structures of linked attributes, consequences and ultimate values/goals) suggested by rural village inhabitants in Norrbotten, Sweden. Accordingly, our findings illustrate how several attribute constructs within the encoding scripts lead to overlapping consequence and value constructs, showcasing potential synergies in bundling smart services. Here, resultant values are contributed by small streams of several attributes and consequences, concretizing the village-level value as a whole. Drawing from institutional theory (Barley & Tolbert, 1997), we argue that the depicted encoding scripts may be viewed as bridges for understanding and planning actions that may maintain, modify, and create new institutions manifesting as new appropriate practices for sustainable bundling of public and private services. Investigating synergies between the encoding scripts is particularly important as their underlying institutions may act as glue enabling value co-creation in the developed regional service ecosystem (Wieland et al., 2016).

For practitioners, the depicted encoding scripts and their implications illustrate concrete recommendations concerning interrelated stakeholder ensembles for ecosystem-level institutionalization practices. Table 2.2 illustrates how digital value co-creation may be facilitated through the emerging scripts, and respective actions needed from the (public) facilitator of the regional service ecosystem. In the era of digitalization, accessibility is one of the most recurring values focal to inhabitants. The value of accessibility touches on the topic of digital connectivity, but also the tacit and tangible resource exchange taking place between and among human actors and technology. We can see that fostering digital accessibility may link to the values of self-efficacy, safety and comfort and easiness, and even social inclusion, for rural inhabitants. While our findings highlight the manyfold value co-creation potential of the regional service ecosystem, continuous strategic actions, such as construction of infrastructures, development of digital and hybrid offerings, fostering of human interactions and coordination of logistics are needed from the facilitator role. The local service point emerged as the single most recurring digital service theme within the six encoding scripts, indicating strong value co-creation potential and synergies with other digital service themes. As implications, we find that the values of accessibility, self-efficacy, avoiding travel, comfort and easiness in life, safety, and social inclusion may evidently be co-created for village inhabitants through local availability of physical service points.

With a close connection with the local service point theme, our findings indicate that the rural service ecosystem would benefit from developing hybrid and face-to-face health services, which could be distributed through the physical service points locally available. Thus, our findings suggest the local service point as the most prominent steppingstone for practitioners toward innovating bundles of digital-enabled services, particularly with respect to public and private health services. In the related encoding scripts, access to information, services, and tangibles, as well as mitigating the need to travel emerged among the most focal consequence constructs in such health services provided through the physical service point. Further, also social inclusion and the need for end-user support were elevated as focal consequence constructs for co-creating value through health services at a physical service point. Thus, we see that the practices related to organizing physical service points for health services ought to be harnessed not only for providing access, but also for fostering social inclusion, connectedness, and support.

However, such initiatives may not be effectively facilitated with the means of traditional market mechanisms in sparsely populated rural areas, such as Norrbotten, Sweden. For example, a village-based service point providing health services may not attract a critical mass of users unless it offered

Table 2.2   *Digital value co-creation potential of encoding scripts and implications to practice*

Encoding script	*(Attribute construct)*	> *Consequence construct*	> *Value construct*	***Digital value co-creation potential***
1. Access to Internet & services	> No need to travel	> Avoiding travel		An emerging need to facilitate digital value creation through construction of infrastructures for fast broadband connections and digitalized services that can be ubiquitously accessed employing the devices possessed by the inhabitants.
2. Access to public services	> Access to personnel > No need to travel > Access to information and (digital) services > Access to tangibles	> Accessibility > Avoiding travel	Progressive digital value propositions and fast broadband infrastructures at the smart village support digital resource integration between public/private service providers and inhabitants, allowing inhabitants to avoid travel and engage in digital value co-creation from the place and time of their choosing.	An emerging need to develop and provide locally accessible digital and hybrid value propositions, such as a service point or a service bus for facilitating synergies and bundling public and private services.

Encoding script	*(Attribute construct)*	*> Consequence construct*	*> Value construct*	*Digital value co-creation potential*
3. Coordinated logistics on demand	> Access to tangible > No need to travel	> Accessibility > Comfort and easiness in life > Avoiding travel	Fully or partially digitalized service offerings locally available at the smart village supports digital resource integration between public/ private service providers and inhabitants, allowing for digital and physical resource integration and inhabitants engaging in digital/hybrid service exchange from home or in the local neighborhood.	An emerging need to coordinate smart and systemic logistics of necessities and conveniences to and from villages through a local smart service hub or a mobile service point (such as a service bus).
4. Digital service portal and website	> Access to information and (digital) services	> Accessibility	A ubiquitous and accessible digital platform for enabling and facilitating digital and physical resource integration between and among public and private service providers and inhabitants.	An emerging need to develop an open digital service portal for facilitating engagement, interaction, and delivery between and among public and private stakeholders of the regional service ecosystem.

Encoding script	(Attribute construct)	> Consequence construct	> Value construct	Digital value co-creation potential
5. F2F/hybrid public services	> End-user support needed > Access to personnel > No need to travel > Preserving human interaction	> Self-efficacy > Accessibility > Avoiding travel > Comfort and easiness in life > Safety > Social inclusion	A locally situated or mobile physical service point proposes on-demand value in face-to-face and hybrid resource integration between the inhabitants and public/private service providers improving patient safety and accessibility, and increasing social interactions, comfort and easiness in life for rural inhabitants.	An emerging need to facilitate the omni-channel model in public services through implementation of physical on-demand service points complementing a variety of services offered via a digital platform.
6. Social informing and meeting	> Preserving human interaction	> Social inclusion	In the era of digital services, a locally situated or mobile service point proposes social and inclusive value through face-to-face interactions between the service provider (such as the municipality) and inhabitants and also among inhabitants.	An emerging need to allocate physical structures for fostering social face-to-face interactions between and among service providers and inhabitants.

a diverse bundle of other service features. Informants' ideas emerging for service-bundling include involvement of social meeting places (e.g., a café or shared office space), commercial services (e.g., a village shop or self-service kiosk) or tourism/recreation services, combining deliveries of goods and even transportation hubs, etc. However, a new ecosystem value facilitator role is required for active development and bundling of adjacent service offerings. Thus, to enhance well-being for the individual inhabitants as well as the public and private service providers and other stakeholders, we recognize a need for adopting institutionalized value co-creation practices for involving multiple stakeholders in smart service portfolios (Wieland et al., 2016). To facilitate such synergies, smart services ought to connect individual inhabitants with private and public stakeholders at the micro-level, as well as networks of stakeholders at the meso level and municipalities at the macro level. For instance, the digital service theme of tourism and recreation surfaced with respect to the encoding script of digital service portal and website, manifesting the need to bundle private services with the local digital service portal and website as well as the physical service point. While the economic sustainability of local actors was one of the key drivers indicating the need to bundle both public and private services in a physical service point, interestingly, the variety of services in one physical place was also seen as a focal institutional work for maintaining human-to-human interactions and fostering social inclusion in rural areas.

Further, our findings indicate that while digital service provision deserves great attention in the design of a rural service ecosystem, also tangibles, such as goods and physical services offered by public and private actors ought to be integrated in the service portfolio. Accordingly, the service bus emerged as another focal digital service theme for organizing logistics of goods and tangibles. In practice, the service bus ought to be closely connected with the physical local service point, which could be adopted as a platform for the bus. Furthermore, the service bus was found to relate to the digital service theme of logistics of goods, indicating a strong connection also to the open market actors and the shipping of goods, such as convenience products and produce to the rural areas operated by the service bus.

According to our analysis and the emerging six encoding scripts and the underlying ecosystem-level institutional work practices, we argue for considering the development of smart villages as regional service ecosystems (Vargo & Lusch, 2016) for several, initially even seemingly unconnected, stakeholders. Overall, to establish a shift toward regional service ecosystems, our findings indicate that a smart village would require institutional work (maintaining, creating new and simultaneously disrupting prevalent institutions) and institutionalized practices at the ecosystem level. For example, when bringing health services to the village service point, ecosystem-level actions are required for a mutual understanding of appropriate levels of availability of physical or online health services at the service point. This would cover the creation and maintenance of (new) adequate norms and practices of service behavior for both the customers and service providers. For example, individual customers, and healthcare and service point providers would be included, further connecting with logistics providers for shipping medicines to customers. Thus, as implications we see that institutionalized service inno-vation at the ecosystem level would likely require new institutionalized actor roles to orchestrate heterogeneous service portfolios. This may disrupt prev-alent institutionalized practices, traditional producer-initiated service models, and assumptions held by service providers and citizens alike. Thus, a 'positive disruptor' role may be needed – beyond the roles suggested by Wieland et al. (2016), let alone stakeholder roles in typical e-government projects (e.g., Balta et al. 2015) – to operationalize ecosystem-level service portfolio institutionali-zation. Establishing and maintaining such an ecosystem-level stakeholder role would require wide acceptance in co-operation of policymakers, public and private service providers, and active citizens, among other actors.

With our analysis, we contribute to the e-government literature by bring-ing forth novel insights into the development of smart villages as regional service ecosystems viewing institutionalization at the level of particular digital service themes and their interconnections. To understand how to facilitate ecosystem-level value co-creation in smart villages, it is essential to under-stand interconnectedness between actors' practices and institutions as a means to identify the institutional work required for the transformation (Wieland et al., 2016). Considering the employed analytical framework (Wieland et al., 2016), smart villages require institutional work and institutionalized practices at the ecosystem level, including integrative, normalizing, and representa-tional practices to guide the integration of public, private and market-facing resources in the smart villages. For example, to bring health services to the local service point (partially on-line, partially face-to-face), ecosystem-level actions are required to reach a joint understanding of appropriate levels of availability of physical or on-line health-services at the service point, estab-lishing and maintaining adequate (new) behavioral norms and practices of the customer, service provider and facilitator in the new service contexts, and altogether ecosystem-level work on continuous development of both a particu-lar service domain and the whole regional service ecosystem. We propose that such institutional work and related actors' practices may drive institutional change for co-creation of digital-enabled value such as inhabitants improved safety, accessibility, self-efficacy, and social inclusion.

Further, we contribute to the SDL (Vargo & Lusch, 2004, 2016) discourse with an empirical study that analyzes institutional work and practices for value co-creation in smart villages through the derived encoding scripts. As research implications, we see our findings provide opportunities for future action design research initiatives on practices. While institutionalization is a well-established area of investigation, harnessing the understandings of prevailing institutions for new service design remains understudied. As our study reveals that institutionalization may be the underlying key for developing bundled service ensembles for rural service ecosystems, more research is needed in particular toward building reflexivity, i.e., 'an awareness of existing social structures' in this context (Vink & Koskela-Huotari, 2021, p. 1). While a contextualized study brings forth important contextual insights, it may also pose a limitation for development of theoretical knowledge. As such, our study may not be generalizable to all rural areas in developed countries. Accordingly, we see that we have only scratched the surface investigating institutional work required in transforming rural areas into smart villages. Thus, we call for more studies to investigate value co-creation for regional service ecosystems.

CONCLUSION

Our study concretized the essence of considering smart villages from the viewpoint of regional service ecosystems. Due to tensions between different stakeholders' priorities and scarce public resources, we propose that smart services for rural villages cannot be developed on the prevailing basis of single-service offerings and their market mechanisms. An ecosystem facilitator role ought to be established by a public stakeholder to create an open agora for building a sustainable, many-sided, service portfolio of mutually dependent, smart service offerings. As one model does not fit all, research is needed for obtaining insights on potential tensions between rural inhabitants' as well as divergent public and private service providers' preferences. Once obtained, the new insights may be harnessed for establishing and managing a rural service ecosystem for co-creation of digital-enabled value. However, we find that the design of such a rural service ecosystem requires institutional work and openness to potentially disrupting prevalent public and private-sector institutions. Further, smart services are needed for connecting rural villages and larger cities, meaning that smart city initiatives ought to increasingly stretch toward the peripheries. It follows that new roles and co-creation practices are required between actors at the ecosystem level, and such practices ought to be commonly acknowledged among several actors. Currently, such ecosystem-level institutionalization practices seem to be missing in establishing public and private services in the context of rural villages in developed countries. This may partially explain the prevailing challenges in developing smart villages, despite the availability of necessary technological solutions and infrastructures. Our study and analysis presented one way of scrutinizing such latent synergies across divergent digital service themes and derived six encoding scripts for developing value co-creation practices that complement a smart service portfolio for a regional service ecosystem. The study depicts in a novel manner institutional work and actors' practices required for institutional change and for co-creation of digital-enabled value. Pinpointing overlap between encoding scripts across the digital service themes for developing the Swedish Norrbotten area, our findings indicate that the suggested institutional work may facilitate co-creation of digital-enabled public value when implemented at not only the level of particular services but also at the level of the regional service ecosystem.

KEY TAKEAWAYS

- Sustainable digital-enabled value co-creation in rural yet digitally connected areas require development of smart service bundles and adoption of new institutionalized value co-creation practices.
- As a means to facilitate regional service ecosystem-level value co-creation in smart villages and identify the institutional work required therein, it is essential to understand interconnectedness between actors' practices and institutions.
- A new ecosystem value facilitator role is required for active development and successful bundling of adjacent service offerings.
- Laddering interviews were found a helpful technique for deriving institutional scripts required for institutional change and for understanding actors' practices required for digital-enabled value co-creation.

NOTE

1. Additional details on the conduct of the study can be retrieved by contacting the authors and from (Lintula et al., 2020).

REFERENCES

Axelsson, K., Melin, U., & Lindgren, I. (2013). Public e-services for agency efficiency and citizen benefit—Findings from a stakeholder centered analysis. *Government Information Quarterly*, *30*(1), 10–22. https://doi.org/10.1016/j.giq.2012.08.002

Ballantyne, D. (2004). Dialogue and its role in the development of relationship specific knowledge. *Journal of Business & Industrial Marketing*, *19*(2), 114–123. https://doi.org/10.1108/08858620410523990

Balta, D., Greger, V., Wolf, P., & Krcmar, H. (2015). E-government Stakeholder Analysis and Management Based on Stakeholder Interactions and Resource Dependencies. *2015 48th Hawaii International Conference on System Sciences*, 2456–65. https://doi.org/10.1109/HICSS.2015.294

Barley, S. R., & Tolbert, P. S. (1997). Institutionalization and Structuration: Studying the Links between Action and Institution. *Organization Studies*, *18*(1), 93–117. https://doi.org/10.1177/017084069701800106

Chandler, J. D., & Vargo, S. L. (2011). Contextualization and value-in-context: How context frames exchange. *Marketing Theory, 11*(1), 35–49. https://doi.org/10.1177/1470593110393713

Cronemberger, F., & Gil-Garcia, J. R. (2019). Big Data and Analytics as Strategies to Generate Public Value in Smart Cities: Proposing an Integrative Framework. In M. P. Rodriguez Bolivar (Ed.), *Setting Foundations for the Creation of Public Value in Smart Cities* (pp. 247–67). Springer International Publishing. https://doi.org/10.1007/978-3-319-98953-2_10

Dwivedi, Y. K., Weerakkody, V., & Janssen, M. (2012). Moving towards maturity: Challenges to successful e-government implementation and diffusion. *ACM SIGMIS Database: The DATABASE for Advances in Information Systems, 42*(4), 11–22. https://doi.org/10.1145/2096140.2096142

Edvardsson, B., Tronvoll, B., & Gruber, T. (2011). Expanding understanding of service exchange and value co-creation: A social construction approach. *Journal of the Academy of Marketing Science, 39*(2), 327–39. https://doi.org/10.1007/s11747-010-0200-y

Kar, A. K., Ilavarasan, V., Gupta, M. P., Janssen, M., & Kothari, R. (2019). Moving beyond Smart Cities: Digital Nations for Social Innovation & Sustainability. *Information Systems Frontiers, 21*(3), 495–501. https://doi.org/10.1007/s10796-019-09930-0

Ken Peffers, Charles E. Gengler, & Tuure Tuunanen. (2003). Extending Critical Success Factors Methodology to Facilitate Broadly Participative Information Systems Planning. *Journal of Management Information Systems, 20*(1), 51–85. https://doi.org/10.1080/07421222.2003.11045757

Leetmaa, K., Kriszan, A., Nuga, M., & Burdack, J. (2015). Strategies to Cope with Shrinkage in the Lower End of the Urban Hierarchy in Estonia and Central Germany. *European Planning Studies, 23*(1), 147–65. https://doi.org/10.1080/09654313.2013.820100

Lintula, J. M. K., Päivärinta, T., & Tuunanen, T. (2020). *Value Co-creation for Smart Villages: The Institutionalization of Regional Service Ecosystems.* International Conference on Information Systems (ICIS 2020), Online, December 13-16, 2020. http://urn.kb.se/resolve?urn=urn:nbn:se:ltu:diva-83076

Liu, P., & Zhenghong, P. (2014). China's Smart City Pilots: A Progress Report. *Computer, 47,* 72–81. https://doi.org/10.1109/MC.2013.149

Markkula, M., & Kune, H. (2015). Making Smart Regions Smarter: Smart Specialization and the Role of Universities in Regional Innovation Ecosystems. *Technology Innovation Management Review, 5*(10), 7–15.

McKinsey & Co. (2014). *Offline and Falling Behind: Barriers To Internet Adoption | PDF | Internet | Online And Offline.* McKinsey & Co. https://www.scribd.com/document/241605895/Offline-and-falling-behind-Barriers-to-Internet-adoption

Mulder, I. (2014). Sociable smart cities: Rethinking our future through co-creative partnerships: Second international conference, DAPI 2014, HCI Interational 2014, Heraklion, Crete, Greece. *Proceedings of Distributed, Ambient, and Pervasive Interactions 2014 (DAPI 2014) Second International Conference, DAPI 2014,* 566–574. https://doi.org/10.1007/978-3-319-07788-8_52

Newman, P. W. G. (1999). Sustainability and cities: Extending the metabolism model. *Landscape and Urban Planning, 44*(4), 219–26. https://doi.org/10.1016/S0169-2046(99)00009-2

Owais, S. T., Khanna, S., & Mani, R. S. (2017). Building Multi-Channel e-Service Delivery Platform: Opportunities and Challenges. *Proceedings of the Special*

Collection on EGovernment Innovations in India, 58–63. https://doi.org/10.1145/3055219.3055233

Prahalad, C. K., & Ramaswamy, V. (2000, January 1). Co-opting Customer Competence. *Harvard Business Review*. https://hbr.org/2000/01/co-opting-customer-competence

Prahalad, C. K., & Ramaswamy, V. (2004). Co-creation experiences: The next practice in value creation. *Journal of Interactive Marketing, 18*(3), 5–14. https://doi.org/10.1002/dir.20015

Regionfakta. (2022). *Norrbottens län—Regionfakta.* Regionfakta. http://www.regionfakta.com/Norrbottens-lan/

Reynolds, T. J., & Gutman, J. (1988). Laddering theory, method, analysis, and interpretation. *Journal of Advertising Research, 28*(1), 11–31.

Scott, W. (2008). Institutions and Organizations: Ideas and Interests. *Institutions and Organizations: Ideas and Interests.* https://digitalcommons.usu.edu/unf_research/55

Tuunanen, T., & Kuo, I.-T. (2015). The effect of culture on requirements: A value-based view of prioritization. *European Journal of Information Systems, 24*(3), 295–313. https://doi.org/10.1057/ejis.2014.29

Tuunanen, T., & Peffers, K. (2018). Population targeted requirements acquisition. *European Journal of Information Systems, 27*(6), 686–711. https://doi.org/10.1080/0960085X.2018.1476015

Vargo, S. L., & Lusch, R. F. (2004). Evolving to a New Dominant Logic for Marketing. *Journal of Marketing, 68*(1), 1–17. https://doi.org/10.1509/jmkg.68.1.1.24036

Vargo, S. L., & Lusch, R. F. (2016). Institutions and axioms: An extension and update of service-dominant logic. *Journal of the Academy of Marketing Science, 44*(1), 5–23. https://doi.org/10.1007/s11747-015-0456-3

Vargo, S. L., Maglio, P. P., & Akaka, M. A. (2008). On value and value co-creation: A service systems and service logic perspective. *European Management Journal, 26*(3), 145–52. https://doi.org/10.1016/j.emj.2008.04.003

Vargo, S. L., Wieland, H., & Akaka, M. A. (2015). Innovation through institutionalization: A service ecosystems perspective. *Industrial Marketing Management, 44*, 63–72. https://doi.org/10.1016/j.indmarman.2014.10.008

Vink, J., & Koskela-Huotari, K. (2021). Building Reflexivity Using Service Design Methods. *Journal of Service Research*, 10946705211035004. https://doi.org/10.1177/10946705211035004

Wieland, H., Koskela-Huotari, K., & Vargo, S. L. (2016). Extending actor participation in value creation: An institutional view. *Journal of Strategic Marketing, 24*(3–4), 210–26. https://doi.org/10.1080/0965254X.2015.1095225

Wieland, H., Polese, F., Vargo, S., & Lusch, R. (2014). Toward a Service (Eco) Systems. Perspective on Value Creation. *International Journal of Service Science, Management, Engineering, and Technology, 3.* https://doi.org/10.4018/jssmet.2012070102

3. Co-creation and co-destruction paradoxes for social enterprises

Reihaneh Bidar and Behnam Abedin

INTRODUCTION

Social Enterprises (SEs), as organizations with hybrid and innovative business models (Battilana & Lee, 2014; Luisa & Magdalena, 2017), have gained considerable attention during the last decade in the entrepreneurship sector. SEs play a significant role in modern societies as they address the rise for ethical consciousness of citizens and the need for businesses to be socially responsible (Agostinelli, 2010), and benefit society in different ways, such as providing employment and training opportunities for marginalized people. There are many examples of how social enterprises may create benefits for society. Consider Food Connect, for example, they provide farm and farmer support programs and eater for South-East Queensland and promote fair access to healthy, fresh, ecologically grown food. Its mission is to promote sustainable development in zero hunger, climate action, good health and well-being, and work and economic growth for Australians. Gray New is another example of how SEs that aim to connect communities across Australia through training and community-building activities to boost well-being and mental health, reduce inequalities, and promote justice and gender equality.

SEs play a pivotal role in the future of communities because they fill the gaps in providing community services for the public by governments or private companies and support groups of marginalized people due to their disadvantages (Gray et al., 2003; Mason et al., 2007). Although the focus of SEs is on solving social problems and making a difference in society, they need to generate their own revenue to become self-sustainable and cover costs, and they need to overcome their resource barriers. Online collaborative platforms can improve such barriers by facilitating co-creation activities for SEs and consequently help to maximize social impacts and value creation. Small SEs, specifically, are vulnerable organizations and operate in resource-scarce environments that could benefit from collaborative value creation to address their challenges in relationship with resources and grant funding and consequently secure their survival and sustainability.

Co-creation is a collaborative creation of value through the participation of a network of actors (i.e., within the ecosystem[1] of stakeholders) (Grönroos & Voima, 2013). Participation of multiple stakeholders in value co-creation can create valuable knowledge and resources for the ecosystem since each stakeholder has their own set of unique capabilities, experiences, and resources (Kazadi et al., 2016) and can have a contribution of financial or altruism to fulfill stakeholders' needs (Bidar et al., 2017). Online platforms have extended co-creation activities to digitally mediated collaborations with distributed resources to solve problems through open communities (Bidar et al., 2021). Social and sustainability problems and inequalities can be reduced if harnessed through open platforms, which can create possible collective solutions to the world's problems (Halmos et al., 2019) and crises. An example of this can be seen through #WirVsVirus ('We Versus Virus'), an open call to action via Twitter initiated in Germany during COVID-19 by seven organizations and social enterprises supported by the German government. The mission was to pool creative potential civil society and co-create solutions on challenges related to COVID-19, such as to help citizens during the lockdown, respond to an increase in domestic violence, and fast-track digital healthcare services.[2] #WirVsVirus created a new way to think about value creation in a digital environment, co-created by various actors – industry, civil society, and public authorities.

The use of co-creation practices can have adverse impacts, which means that not all interactions between stakeholders lead to positive outcomes (Järvi et al., 2018). Previous research has shown that where value is co-created through interactions, value co-destruction can also emerge as an opposing phenomenon (Echeverri & Skålén, 2011; Plé & Chumpitaz Cáceres, 2010). Online collaboration is paradoxical in nature and needs to be managed in order to maximize online value creation. Information Systems (IS) research should consider value co-destruction as an emerging topic when they study the value co-creation concept (Vartiainen & Tuunanen, 2016) since technological advancements may add complexity to organizations and lead to loss of control and value destruction (Zhang et al., 2020). Considering the #WirVsVirus example and the importance of value co-creation through the online platforms, it would be equally important to explore if any adverse outcomes and/or co-destruction activities emerged through the engagement of civil society, SEs, and public authorities.

This chapter draws on the importance of the co-creation and co-destruction paradox and new ways of thinking about value creation in the digital age for SEs. While co-creation and co-destruction research has attracted attention in the delivery of public services and the social innovation process (Engen et al., 2021), it is yet to be unpacked in the SE domain as well as how they can manage co-creation and co-destruction in an integrated manner. Considering that little is known about online value co-creation and co-destruction and their potential impact on the challenges for SEs, and the rise of interest in online co-creation because of pervasive changes in the world (Bidar et al., 2021), we aim to understand co-creation and co-destruction concerning SEs collaboration. We aim to address: (i) What are the co-creation and co-destruction factors emerged through online communities in the ecosystem of SEs?; (ii) What are the outcomes resulting from online value co-creation and co-destruction interactions of stakeholders?; and (iii) What challenges do SEs face in their ecosystem that can be addressed through online value co-creation? Firstly, we conducted a systematic literature review to investigate existing literature on SEs' co-creation and co-destruction in online collaboration. A framework was developed as the result of analyzing the literature. Secondly, we conducted a semi-structured interview to refine the model and evaluate the identified factors in the framework.

Adopting the paradox lens enables SEs to develop better response and management strategies in a paradoxical situation. Paradoxical situations emerge between environmental, social, and economic challenges (Hahn et al., 2018). Given that SEs' collaboration in online communities helps them promote their social and financial missions and sometimes compete with other SEs for financial and non-financial resources, co-creation and co-destruction paradoxes can emerge through their interaction. A paradoxical view of organizational relationships, motivated by divergent goals and perceptions of what constitutes value, can lead to tensions in resource management in value co-creation (Niesten & Stefan, 2019). Such dynamics are outlined in the paradox theory and are referred to as 'contradictory yet interrelated elements that exist simultaneously and persist over time' (Smith & Lewis, 2011, p. 387). The paradox here refers to a persistent contradiction (tradeoffs) between different alternatives (Smith & Lewis, 2011) in the online collaboration process- co-creation and co-destruction interactions.

This chapter provides insight on how online co-creation among stakeholders provides more financial and non-financial opportunities related to philanthropy, government funding, and value generation. But we acknowledge that value destruction can occur due to SE's negative online interactions, especially in regard to SE's resource development. This chapter brings an interesting perspective on how stakeholders' online co-creation helps social enterprises to meet their dual objectives (social missions and financial objectives) and address their challenges, and how the negative dynamics in their interaction can be balanced through adopting a paradoxical thinking approach.

The remainder of this chapter flows as follows. First, a literature review will be provided on the definition, challenges of SEs, and the potential of online value co-creation and co-destruction. Next, we will discuss the theoretical background of this research, followed by presenting a conceptual framework for online value co-creation and co-destruction in the ecosystem of SEs (published in the European Conference of Information Systems 2019). Then, we present the findings of the interview, the discussion, and the contributions of this research.

THEORETICAL BACKGROUND

Previous research has studied the effect and role of face-to-face co-creation in SEs context (e.g., Ge et al., 2019; Luisa & Magdalena, 2017) but have not investigated the role of online communities to support value co-creation in the SE context. Online value co-creation through online communities has been explored in different disciplines (Barrett et al., 2016; Yan et al., 2016), however, little is known about the role of online communities as the facilitator of SE's value co-creation to address their challenges. Furthermore, during the last years, SEs have used Information and Communication Technologies (online communities and digital platforms) for different purposes such as marketing (Mitchell et al., 2015), scaling up (Braund & Schwittay, 2016), and communication amongst social enterprise employees (Keane et al., 2017). However, the main focus of these cases has not been on value co-creation. Therefore, we aim to fill this gap in the literature by investigating the role of online communities as the facilitator of value co-creation in the SE context. We follow the definition of value co-creation as a process where actors are involved in resource integration and service exchange (Vargo & Lusch, 2016) rather than a dyadic interaction process between two entities (Pera et al., 2016). According to this definition of value co-creation, two essential elements of value co-creation are the existence of multiple actors and resource integration and the exchange of services or resources.

Social Enterprises

The social enterprise (SE) field has become increasingly important with a growing presence in IS literature as SEs play an essential role in social and economic development. However, there exists a lack of agreement on how SEs can be distinguished from other types of organizations (Powell, 2015). Although different researchers have provided various definitions for 'social enterprise', there is no consistent definition for SE in the literature (Wry & York, 2017). Despite the inconsistency in the definition of SE in the literature, most scholars agree that SEs have a dominant mission to create social value while also generate revenue to ensure financial sustainability and commercial business operations requirements (Bradford et al., 2020; García-Jurado et al., 2021). SEs attempt to deal with social and/or environmental missions in society and achieve financial performance by applying innovative business models and commercial strategies to create social value within their ecosystem (Battilana & Lee, 2014). SEs do business differently in comparison with traditional for-profit enterprises, charities, and not-for-profit organizations by offering innovative products/services to benefit the social economy and their stakeholders and have social and environmental impacts (Kay et al., 2016). SEs have been identified as an essential element of modern economy and societies because they benefit members of the ecosystem by providing different employment and training opportunities for marginalized people and offering different services to the public (Mason et al., 2007).

SEs, like any other organizations, have a network of multiple stakeholders including communities, groups, other enterprises, and individuals and interact with them in their ecosystem (Smith et al., 2013). SEs have a diverse ecosystem with multiple stakeholders, including founders and/or managers, employees, and volunteers as internal stakeholders and other SEs, non-profit organizations, government agencies, donors, private and public investors, beneficiaries, customers, academics, trade unions, political parties, commercial banks, media and the community as external stakeholders (Barraket et al., 2017). In the process of scaling up, the interaction boundaries become blurred as different stakeholders are geographically dispersed from each other. Therefore, increasingly, SEs are adopting digital technologies to keep the growing business efficient and the social impact effective (Pankaj & Seetharaman, 2021).

Challenges of SEs

SEs are the foundation of national economies, yet they face many challenges to survive and become viable organizations. Seeking to achieve their objectives, SEs need to address social and economic challenges. SEs tend to serve a combination of social and financial returns at the same time (Dual Objectives) (Doherty et al., 2009), therefore, challenges in addressing a social or environmental problem as part of social missions can result in failure in financial return, and contrariwise (Jay, 2013). SEs should implement suitable mechanisms in governance, finance, marketing, human resourcing, and performance measurement to achieve financial and societal goals (Liu et al., 2014; Staessens et al., 2019) and scale up their impact (Lyon & Fernandez, 2012). The liability of smallness affects opportunities for SEs to acquire and manage financial capital and limited finance reduces their access to all resources, including human and information recourses (Lefebvre, 2020). Due to limited financial resources, SEs rely on volunteers, especially when they have an environmental or social mission, such as reducing poverty or social disadvantage (Kelly et al., 2019).

The process of leveraging resources is often complicated for SEs, especially during the start-up phase. SEs require intangible resources and capabilities to operate effectively (Doherty et al., 2014). Networks then become a pathway to engage resource bricolage and build collaborative partnerships (Tasavori et al., 2018). As such, a capacity for SEs to locate and engage outsiders with a stewardship culture is a valuable internal resource (Bacq & Eddleston, 2018). Online communities have become a valuable source of facilitating relationships and collaboration among actors for value co-creation (Barrett et al., 2016; Füller et al., 2009). For example, sharing information and knowledge among stakeholders can address the challenge of SEs related to the lack of information in this sector (Barraket & Collyer, 2010), or an effective marketing strategy for introducing SEs' innovative products/services through online communities can address market development challenges (Barraket et al., 2016). Therefore, online value co-creation activities can be an innovative way for SEs to find resources and secure their survivability.

Online Value Co-Creation in SEs

Actors within an ecosystem need to collaborate with each other not only to build competitive advantages (Romero & Molina, 2011) but also to create networks and partnerships which allow them to access new resources, revenue streams, and knowledge as well as reduce their risk (Hynes, 2009; Romero & Molina, 2011). The interactions between actors in the ecosystem and partnerships can lead to value co-creation in different aspects, including: 'co-produced, co-manufactured, co-developed, co-designed, co-serviced and/ or co-processed' (Romero & Molina, 2011, p. 448). For SEs, it is highly crucial to be a member of such partnerships to develop their market, access customers' information, identify opportunities, apply for funding sources and gain local support (Shaw & Carter, 2007). In addition, the availability of low-cost technologies, such as online communities and digital platforms, facilitates the accessibility of resources and collaboration with stakeholders for SEs.

Online communities enable actors to interact and collaborate with other like-minded peers with shared interests to achieve different goals (Barrett et al., 2016) such as co-creation and innovation (Füller et al., 2009) and knowledge sharing. The value perception toward co-creation is identified as informational, personal-psychological (e.g., Hedonic, Utilitarian, Financial, Social), and service-related values (e.g., Quality, Support) (Bidar et al., 2021). Online communities offer numerous cost-effective and multi-stakeholder interaction opportunities, and can result in value co-creation (Füller et al., 2009). The use of such technologies could help organizations co-create new value through knowledge sharing, increasing transparency, identifying and integrating resources or capabilities, as well as reducing transaction costs that the organization is not able to do so on its own (Grover & Kohli, 2012). The use of online technologies (e.g., online communities) transforms entrepreneurship (Autio et al., 2018), by not only opening opportunities for innovation but also expanding their social relationships (Nambisan et al., 2019). This value co-creation for SEs usually happens on resource-based networks that can be facilitated by online communities (Luisa & Magdalena, 2017).

Value co-creation can provide extensive benefits to SEs who operate in resource-scarce environments with limited financial, physical, and human resources making it difficult for them to achieve their goals on their own (Barraket et al., 2016; Desa & Basu, 2013; Di Domenico et al., 2010; Doherty et al., 2009). Scholars referred to the importance of value co-creation among SEs' stakeholders to generate both social and economic opportunities simultaneously (De Silva et al., 2019), and increase the sustainability of their business (Bandyopadhyay & Ray, 2019; Sun & Im, 2015). However, very few studies looked at the role of online value co-creation for SEs. Tung and Jordann (2017) found that SEs use online communities as powerful tools for crowdsourcing to find the required human resources or volunteers that they need for their projects. Luisa and Magdalena (2017) found that SEs are willing to use online communities and networks to access best practices, available opportunities, marketing, and the latest news relating to the sector and other SEs. Also, they proposed that implementing a new online platform for SEs is needed, but it still requires more investigation on how the new online platform can facilitate social entrepreneurs' value co-creation.

Online Value Co-Destruction in SEs

While previous research has emphasized value co-creation through interactions among actors, it is essential to consider the fact that value might be co-destroyed through online interactions (Plé & Chumpitaz Cáceres, 2010). Value co-destruction has been defined as an interactional process between different parties that causes a decline in at least one of the actors' well-being (tangible or intangible) (Järvi et al., 2018; Plé & Chumpitaz Cáceres, 2010). According to Vafeas et al. (2016), value co-destruction can be rooted in resource deficiencies and resource intentional or unintentional misuse by involved actors, separately or jointly. While information and knowledge exchange in online communities can lead to value co-creation, value co-destruction can emerge when the integration of resources such as information (Vafeas et al., 2016), knowledge and skills (Zhang et al., 2018) are not achieved in online communities. Unsuccessful integration of resources in online interactions can be caused by different factors such as the absence of trust (Järvi et al., 2018; Vafeas et al., 2016), poor communication (Bidar et al., 2021; Vafeas et al.,

2016), lack of transparency (Frau et al., 2018), low-quality information (Frau et al., 2018) and insufficient competencies (Bidar et al., 2021) to name a few.

In line with calls for further research on value co-destruction in different industries and business models (Echeverri & Skålén, 2011; Prior & Marcos-Cuevas, 2016) as well as in different online platforms (Frau et al., 2018), we aim to study value co-destruction in the context of SEs through using online communities. The importance of this investigation is that co-destruction interactions may happen more frequently in less structured collaboration settings (i.e., open community co-creation) (Bidar et al., 2021) and can impact costs, customer loss, and negative word of mouth (Smith, 2013). Also, such destructive interactions may be considered a 'dark side' of interactions (Plé & Chumpitaz Cáceres, 2010), and value may not always be positive for SEs. Specifically, because of the resource constraint situation for small SEs, examining value co-destruction efforts for SEs emerged through their online interaction, and its impact on their financial and non-financial resources is important.

Conceptualizing Online Value Co-Creation and Co-Destruction in the Social Enterprise Context

In the entrepreneurship literature, SEs and their ecosystem have been theorized as complex and unique (Wry & York, 2017), resulting in a need to generate/extend theories (Dacin et al., 2010; Haugh, 2012) to apply to the SE context. To contribute to this need, we developed a framework (Figure 3.1) based on literature-informed insights drawn from IS and management disciplines. We use the Service-Dominant (S-D) Logic paradigm in the social enterprise context to demonstrate that value is co-created through the integration of resources and interaction among multiple actors (Vargo & Lusch, 2004) and that value might be co-destroyed through lack of resource integration in relationships among actors (Plé & Chumpitaz Cáceres, 2010). As these phenomena are driven by positive and negative SE interactions in the online environment, we aim to explore co-creation and co-destruction factors in SE's ecosystem and how it affects the outcome and SE's challenges.

The most important resources for the co-creation of value through interactions between actors are knowledge, information, and skills (Lusch et al., 2007; Vargo & Lusch, 2004), which can also be co-destructed during interactions (Echeverri & Skålén, 2011). Figure 3.1 illustrates SEs interaction with stakeholders in online communities and exchange resource to achieve values in return. We found two different types of benefits and costs for stakeholders: (1) the positive impacts of value co-creation on the challenges that SEs face and the adverse impacts of value co-destruction on the challenges are considered benefits and costs of participating in online interactions; (2) the outcomes

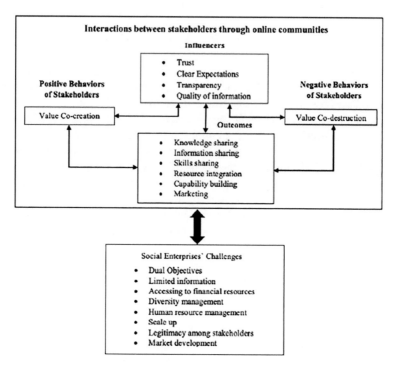

Figure 3.1   *Framework for online value co-creation and co-destruction*
              in small social enterprises

of online value co-creation and value co-destruction can be considered benefits
(positive outcome) and costs (negative outcome). We demonstrate that there
are some factors (influencers) that influence the behavior of stakeholders
in online communities' ecosystems that can lead to value co-creation or
co-destruction, including trust, clear expectations, transparency, and quality
of information (Frau et al., 2018; Järvi et al., 2018; Vafeas et al., 2016). These
environmental factors influence the formation of value or destruction of value
(Bidar et al., 2016) and will lead to the outcome of the SEs' participation in
online communities.

METHODOLOGY

Since social entrepreneurs' online value co-creation is a new area of research,
and the concepts of value co-creation and co-destruction are not well defined
in the SE context, exploratory qualitative research with an in-depth inves-

tigation of the phenomenon is appropriate (Yin, 2013). We interviewed 24 Australian social entrepreneurs. Interviewing social entrepreneurs provided us with in-depth knowledge regarding co-creation and co-destruction activities and outcomes resulting from participating in online communities since they are key informants of their respective organizations (Ince & Hahn, 2020).

We transcribed all interviews, which enabled rigorous coding and analysis (Rubin & Rubin, 2011). Coding was completed following a series of cross-checking exercises or coding bias. Saturation is achieved in terms of richness in data collection, and interviews were continued until no new insights were apparent in the responses (Fusch & Ness, 2015). A deductive-inductive thematic analysis was used as a strategy for data analysis (Fereday & Muir-Cochrane, 2006) to explore our initial framework. Considering the factors in the initial model, we categorized the findings based on the themes of challenges as drivers for SEs to interact with others online, co-creation and co-destruction efforts of stockholders, influencers, and positive and negative outcomes of SEs' interactions.

FINDINGS

This section discusses the results and emerging themes addressing the role of online communities and value co-creation and co-destruction paradoxes in the social enterprise context. Depending on what challenges SEs aim to address using the online communities, they can go through a paradoxical tension. Figure 3.2 represents three paradoxical layers situated on trust or mistrust, driven by resource intensively, headwinds and tailwinds, and actor's intention.

Social Enterprises Challenges Addressed Through Online Collaboration

In order to survive, SEs are required to address their challenges related to limited financial and non-financial resources (including human and information resources) and balance their dual objectives. Digital technologies, such as online platforms, affect the ability of SEs to address such challenges and achieve and sustain a competitive advantage over time (Markides & Sosa, 2013).

SEs' co-creation facilitated by online platforms often helps SEs build, maintain and grow their financial resources. Almost all interview participants identified that financial challenges affected their enterprises. They believed that 'the financial sustainability is always going to be a risk and something that we need to manage' (e.g., SE9, SE17). Even if they try to be 'self-sufficient economically' and attract financial support in different ways, such as attracting funds but building 'sustainable revenue sources will continue to be a challenge' (e.g., SE1, SE8). Even if they receive some donations, this is not sufficient for

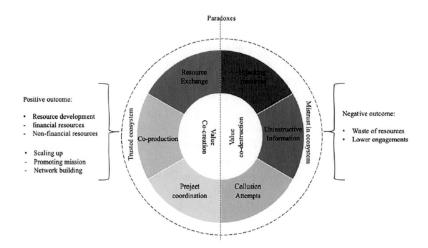

Figure 3.2   Online co-creation and co-destruction paradoxes for SEs

the middle term of long-term financial sustainability. Lots of the work that SEs do 'requires a lot of partnerships, management of partnerships, management of those relationships to make the most of funding, [service opportunities] to be able to continue building sustainability within our organization' (SE13), which can be facilitated better by the use of online platforms. Online platforms facilitate SEs' co-creation where SEs can build relationships with other like-minded social enterprises, engage in financial opportunities, collaborate in fundraising activities, and attract 'external grant funding' (SE5), and coordinate their collaborations.

Accessing human resources and skilled staff was a challenge for some of the social enterprises. Resourcing personnel was challenging for the owners or founders of small social enterprises, especially when 'working with a disengaged or disadvantaged cohort' (SE2). Because they 'employ disadvantaged people, and [and this is] not a commercially viable method [...] but it is a need, and it is what we should be doing because of the impact that generates' (SE6). Many SEs employ their target beneficiaries as paid staff, which creates additional costs in providing support for the disadvantaged employees. Insufficient human resources were also related to the lack of financial stability. SE22 explained, 'I would love to add two or three staff [...] and a few volunteers, but then there are funding issues.' This is where online communities are helpful and enable SEs 'to find other volunteers or people that want to come on board and help in any shape or form' (SE7). Although most of the small- to medium-sized SEs use online communities to source information and volunteers and address their non-financial challenges to some extent, the use of a co-creation-based digital platform can be a step change for SE's resourcing and scaling up. Ushahidi[3] is an example of a digital-based SE that sources information and volunteers for crisis mapping. Ushahidi is built based on co-creation and crowd-based strategies to create a human rights observatory and helpline. Juliana Rotich, co-founder and former Executive Director of Ushahidi, refers to the use of technology as 'one of the most important factors of success.'

Participants explained that scaling up their enterprise was a challenge for them. Participants associated this challenge with networking and financial issues. For example, SE22 has planned to expand to Queensland and then Australia, but 'we do not have enough funding to support this'. Another participant stated that to strengthen their business model, they struggle with 'how [to] expand our vision of the new economy beyond Brisbane […] and become economically self-sufficient' (SE23). SE10 explained that they focus on 'how to maintain our structure but also be able to grow our business past Queensland and New South Wales'. They believed that in order to grow their enterprise, they needed to grow their 'network'. Participants believed that collaboration via online communities helps them strengthen their network and provide opportunities such as funding opportunities, which can drive scaling their enterprise vision.

The mission of SEs is to maximize the social value, but also the need to gain financial value for their sustainability. As SEs are hybrid organizations with dual objectives, it is a complex task for SEs to achieve their social purpose while also become sustainable and financially viable organizations (Battilana & Lee, 2014; Smith et al., 2013). The use of IS supports SEs in balancing their dual goals and paradoxes. For example, the use of IS (social media platforms and mobile apps) helped Jaipur Rugs to be more efficient and profitable while also accommodating the social missions such as rural women empowerment, thus helping Jaipur Rugs balance the dual objectives as it provided access to real-time information, activity monitoring, and richer communication (Pankaj & Seetharaman, 2021).

Trust Paradox

The trust-mistrust threshold in online collaboration is low because of the openness of online interactions and weak relationships between actors. Depending on the sensitivity of resources being exchanged, at times SEs benefit from trusting the co-creation process, but at other times trusting others does not meet their expectations; therefore, mistrust can spread through their interactions. Trust and mistrust tensions then influence the collaboration process.

For a co-creation ecosystem to function properly and for successful resource exchange, *trust between social enterprisers* must be nurtured. Participants reported that they do not participate in initiatives if they do not trust other participants in those initiatives because there are 'a lot of fake users, you have got a lot of hidden agendas. [...] I've seen people who've created businesses and called it a social enterprise, but the main goal is far from the public good' (SE5). They believed that it is important to 'get to work with people that are very much like-minded and [...] you do business with people you know you trust' (SE6). Others stated that they 'trust the shared information in the ecosystem only if there is credibility in [the provided] information, and multiple sources for any information' (SE2). In our study of service co-creation in collaborative systems (Bidar et al., 2021), we found that an actor's level of trust about the quality of a provided information depended on an evaluation of the quality of the offered information through a collective agreement among the ecosystem members supported by platform features which helps decision-making. Establishing trust is an absolute requirement for efficient resource exchange and shared understanding development within the ecosystem. For SEs, trusting collaborative relationships are essential to establishing clarity in the co-creation of dual objectives (Jenner & Oprescu, 2016). Co-creation does not occur without integrity and trust amongst stakeholders (Abela & Murphy, 2008). However, actors need to decide when is best to trust others when it comes to sensitive information and resource-sharing requirements.

Co-Creation and Co-Destruction Paradox

In this chapter, co-creation refers to situations in which a network of social entrepreneurs collaborate in online activities to create value and address their challenges, such as resource development and scaling up. While social entrepreneurs could achieve positive outcomes through co-creation with their stakeholders and other SEs, not all collaborations were positive. The co-creation and co-destruction[4] paradox represents a tension between actors' interaction influenced by trust and mistrust, which are driven by three underpinning interaction drivers: resource-intensiveness, headwinds and tailwinds, and actors' intentions. Analysis of the interview identified three dimensions of this paradoxical tension: (1) resource exchange versus hijacking resources, driven by resource intensively nature of interactions; (2) co-production versus uninstructive information, driven by collaboration headwinds and tailwinds; and (3) project coordination versus collusion attempts, driven by SE's intention in the collaboration process.

Resource exchange versus hijacking resources

The first interaction paradox is related to the trade-off between resource exchange and hijacking of resources by others in the ecosystem concerning resource insensitivity. Resource exchange refers to the entrepreneur's collaboration on exchanging information about different resources and opportunities, clients, and volunteers. Most participants stated that they exchange information about news related to the sector to inform other members about new policies, grants, and other opportunities to create collective knowledge and support other SEs in their sector. For example, they exchange information 'if there is a new policy' (SE24), or 'new information coming out about social enterprise, and various programs, and articles' (SE4) in order to 'grow collective knowledge, […] and increase awareness about social enterprise outside of the network' (SE4). They also exchange recourses about grants and co-create through 'sharing grants' (SE9), since there are very few governments or philanthropic grants available in Australia, getting a grant is a highly competitive process. Online co-creation can lead SEs to a more dynamic exchange of resources (e.g., skills, experience, knowledge), and scaling up their impact through 'the interconnected and distributed activity of various stakeholders acting independently' and is in line with the Australian national strategy for social enterprises objectives.[5] As multi-stakeholder co-creation is influential in the sustainability of SEs and unpacks new opportunities (Bandyopadhyay and Ray (2019), the centrality of multi-actor resource exchange within the co-creation concept needs to be theoretically and practically reflected in SE.

Contrasted with resource exchange, the openness of online collaboration increases the risk of hijacking resources by others. The identified activities associated with hijacking resources were referred to by participants as misuse of ideas and resources for their own profit without the permission of other SEs. SEs believed that some social entrepreneurs pirated and hijacked other ideas, plans, and events for self-promotion during some of the collaborations. Participants stated that sometimes hijacking is limited to ideas and information. For example, SE21 stated that 'people may have taken an idea away from a collaboration and then used it for their own means, and they are not being, let's say collegiate'. However, SE1 stated that sometimes 'the collective campaign and project that we're running amongst a number of people and organization, got hijacked by one of the partners for their own, [for] self-promotion'. However, sometimes the gained value is higher for SEs than the cost of the hijacked resource.

Co-production versus uninstructive information

The tension between co-production and uninstructive information represents the tailwind and headwind situation where the integration of resources exchanged can be seen as being valuable on the one hand and problematic on the other hand.

On one hand, the engagement with partners helped SEs to build new relationships and resources through collective mindset. Online co-production helped them to find partners who 'have similar ideas and values and engage further and collaborate in projects' (SE4). For example, SEs collaborate in creating a 'financial planning for sale' (SE15). To further expand their partnership, they co-create by facilitating 'collective events with partners and promote that out to [their] network'(SE1). Online co-production eventually has positive value for SEs and the sector. 'The power of what [they] do together is obviously more than what [they] could do individually' (SE13) and advantage longer term benefits. Online co-production 'provides credibility to the sector more broadly' (SE2). New digital technologies, such as online platforms, support new ways of collaborating, managing resources, and creating new solutions (Markus & Loebbecke, 2013), which can promote entrepreneurial activity and expand their partnership. Through online co-creation, SEs that are interested in working collaboratively can co-develop future work based on mutual interest and co-invest with some of the better-resourced SEs in the sector.

By contrast, producing uninstructive information was found to be destructive when the actual value does not fit the SE's expectation and can lead to a waste of resources. Participants believed that the created content by SEs is not 'necessarily [based on] informed opinions' (SE1) and are sometimes 'useless noise' (SE2). They explained they 'spend a lot of time filtering and deleting content, [which] can be quite resource-intensive' (SE1). Sometimes, it is not possible 'to control the content and the trolls' (SE5), and the 'false information' (SE3) provided by other SEs. Considering that social enterprises are more likely to face a shortage of human resources and capital than commercial enterprises, uninstructive information and insufficient resource provided may reduce value (Ge et al., 2019). The misalignment between actors' value perceptions and exchanging value propositions creates a headwind and prevents an effective progression of a collaboration.

Project coordination versus collusion attempts
This paradox refers to the tension between actors' intention to support and lubricate relationships through online communities versus impeding the collaboration efforts.

SEs coordinated 'different events and campaigns, project development and management programs with their partners and other organization' (SE1). Participants stated that online collaboration enabled them to effectively 'coordinate their partnership [...] and monitor groups' (SE17) and to 'galvanize people around a specific issue' (SE1), which resulted in effectively promoting their work and build relationships and get others' supports on issues (SE1,

SE17). In our recent study on co-creation (Bidar, et al., 2021), we found that project maintenance, moderating, and altering activities are the main activities showing actor administrative behavior through online co-creation. While coordination was traditionally done within the boundary of a social enterprise, now digital platforms facilitate required coordination through collaboration and co-creation. Australia's social enterprise sector is fragmented and underserved, and it needs 'critical coordination support to and facilitate ongoing engagement between core sector groups, networks and bodies' (Social Enterprise National report[6]). Establishing effective online co-creation strategies to support coordination and collaboration can improve the performance of SEs and increase visibility through the distribution of activities with other stakeholders and the community.

We found collusion activities as an act of co-destruction in which social entrepreneurs attempt to promote themselves and their enterprises by perusing others to act in their favor, sometimes, in exchange for intrinsic or extrinsic incentives. SE22 experienced situations where they have been asked 'to promote [someone's] business to [their] network'. Participants believed that some SEs intend to manipulate others and use collaborations for self-promotion. For example, SE5 explained that 'many communities where the founder, the people who own the discussions, especially forums, are run by people for profit, for business, and they are directing all the answers in that direction [...] that will always be manipulated by someone else for profit'. Such self-promotion intentions could cause the targeting of other SEs negatively. SE3 stated that an incident occurred in their business 'where we did have a disgruntled individual making false accusations about our business, and there was some defamation involved. They were going to jump online and release all this false Information about our business'. In our previous study (Bidar et al., 2020) we found collusion as a co-destruction pattern that emerges through actors' negative interaction in online collaborative systems. The openness of online communities allows destructive patterns such as collusion to form through actors' dynamics (Bidar et al., 2020). We believe that for SEs, collusion diminishes the trust of other SEs participating in online co-creation and can negatively affect their future collaboration. Collusion efforts can hinder SEs resource development and scale up.

Paradoxical Outcomes

The analysis of interviews indicated that participants perceived positive and negative outcomes from their participation and engagement in Online communities. The participants' perception of value outcome was 'anything that brings benefit on a range of levels'. They believed that 'value does not necessarily have to be financial, [value] can be reputation, it can be value to a network, it can be value around awareness and building brand awareness' (SE1). We categorize the positive outcome as promoting mission, accessing financial and non-financial resources, and network building. The adverse outcomes included a waste of resources and lower engagement. Such negative contribution towards others' collaboration could prevent further engagement and 'cause people to withdraw' (SE21). It can cause 'damage [...], distrust and unwillingness to engage' (SE1). Although the identified co-destruction activities for SEs could occur in any collaborative environment, the outcome of such co-destruction activities could be a significant loss for a small social enterprise, especially hijacking their resources. However, the experience in value co-creation/co-destruction is not necessarily the same for all actors. Because of SE's diverse value perception in the online environment, when one can experience value co-destruction from an interaction, the other actor may experience value co-creation. In other words, participation in co-creation does not always lead to value creation but may lead to value loss, and contrariwise co-destruction activities may lead to value generation.

Positive outcome

Promoting mission and marketing. Since most small enterprises do not have a dedicated marketing budget to promote their work, social entrepreneurs use online communities as a cost-effective option to promote their services and activities. SE3 explained that 'online communities allowed us to promote [our] business and continue pushing out both our brand'. Participants believed that contributing to online communities helped them inform others about their activities, ultimately leading to their marketing support. 'I think support in getting my business in what I do in my services out there would be great marketing-wise' (SE17). One participant believed that collaborations in online communities do not only benefit SEs to promote their work but also 'advocate for the sector [...] and provide credibility to the sector' (SE2). This outcome is valuable to SEs located in regional areas with limited access to SE hubs in capital cities.

Easy access to Information, knowledge and skill. Engaging in online communities helped SEs to access information so as 'to quickly identify the funding opportunities' (SE2); find 'current programs and events' (SE17); to enable 'access to business planning resources' (SE1, SE2); and access 'case studies' (SE24, SE1). Also, online co-creation provided SEs with news about their industry and social enterprises in general. For example, 'if there have been any legal changes, and financial changes' (SE15). Previous studies conducted on online value co-creation activities have mainly focused on sharing activities, particularly knowledge sharing, information sharing, and skills sharing (Savolainen, 2017; Yan et al., 2016). Access to information, knowledge, and skills (e.g. product materials, processes) for SEs means accessibility to a variety of resources at various points of the value chain that are mutually beneficial (Jenner & Fleischman, 2017). Openness, collaboration, and democratization of information and knowledge access are key principles for online community initiatives. Using online communities, SEs reach outside their organizational boundaries to share information with their stakeholders, facilitating future co-creation and engagement.

Access to financial resources. Financial issues were typically the first challenge that these participants discussed. Insufficient finance and cash flow problems influenced all stages of their business development. It is mainly because some social enterprises offer their services and/or products to their beneficiaries for free. Moreover, there are very few governments or philanthropic grants available in Australia, so getting a grant is a highly competitive process. In addition to the lack of financial resources for social enterprises, they also reported challenges in acquiring more physical space to expand their business and access human resources. The majority of social entrepreneurs explained that one positive outcome from their engagement in online communities was to receive financial resources for their social enterprise through fundraising. They try to 'drive income' (SE15), which occurs through accessing 'fundraising and crowds founding' (SE12, SE15, SE22) activities in online communities. Engagements in online communities ultimately 'can translate to [the] financial benefit, when it comes to other growing client opportunities, or crowdfunding opportunities, or other partner and investment opportunities' (SE1). Financial resources are essential for SEs to secure their survival and sustainability (Doherty et al., 2014; Haugh, 2009; Ince & Hahn, 2020), however, they are often not able to access these resources. SEs entirely generate income from commercial activities, including selling services and products, and also, they are not dependent on donations or governmental funds (Choi et al., 2020; Weaver, 2020). Value co-creation can enable SEs to access the resources that they need to create competitive advantages and improve their sustainability and development (Ge et al., 2019; Jenner & Fleischman, 2017). Online communities can also help with their crowdfunding and financial sourcing strategies and develop innovative financial approaches to improve their performance (Braund & Schwittay, 2016).

Network building. Participants emphasized the importance of engaging in online communities on building new relationships and growing their domestic and international network with other social entrepreneurs. They believed that their engagement improved the 'way social entrepreneurs connect to each other regardless of their geographic locations' (SE15). Participants evidenced that the result of their co-creation through online communities enabled them to find and 'recruit staff and volunteers' (SE12, SE13, SE14), and 'find new clients' (SE15) they needed for their social enterprises' operations. For example, (SE4) stated that: 'I've been able to connect with people all across

Australia who work in this space because of online communities. I think without [online connections] it would have been a very long journey, and a lot harder than it was without having the ability to reach out to other people who were doing something similar' (SE4). Participants' comments reflected that the use of online communities is crucial for SEs in order to build and maintain relationships with other social entrepreneurs across Australia's vast landscape. Building relationships and expanding personal networks are fundamental pillars of online social networks and online communities. Online communities support building internal and external networks, with larger SEs and government bodies to create awareness and visibility and attract financial/ non-financial resources.

Negative outcome

The findings showed that SE's interactions are not only linked to positive outcomes, their interactional lead to collective destruction of value (e.g., Makkonen & Olkkonen, 2017). We found that SE's collaboration can discourage others, result in lower engagement, and waste resources. Self-promotion and negatively contributing towards other SEs lower the 'likelihood that we would work in that capacity again and a number of those partners would work in that capacity again... I think there's a bit of damage that was done. So, there's a bit more distrust and unwillingness to engage on that level' (SE1).

Another negative outcome from the participants' perspective was that sometimes it is a 'waste of time and energy' (SE1, SE23) to engage with others in online communities. For example, sometimes you need to 'spend a lot of time filtering and deleting content' because either the collaborators tried to 'hijack the conversation' or produced unconstructive feedback. Co-destruction has not been thoroughly discussed in the social enterprise collaboration context and can have a profound effect on the SEs. Thus, it is important to examine the impacts of value co-destruction such as cost reduction, customer loss, and negative word of mouth (Smith, 2013) and its consequences for SEs.

DISCUSSION

This research is one of the first studies that contributes to theoretical knowledge by extending value co-creation and co-destruction concepts to the SE context and provides a paradox model of SEs' online collaboration. Considering the need for exploring co-destruction in different contexts and environments (Plé, 2017; Plé & Chumpitaz Cáceres, 2010; Vartiainen & Tuunanen, 2016) and co-existence of co-creation and co-destruction we take a paradox perspective to explore SE's online collaboration. First, we presented an initial conceptual model representing the key constructs involved in the interactions between SEs and their stakeholders through online communities in the ecosystem of

Ses (adapted from Abedin & Bidar 2019). Then, we evaluated the initial conceptual model by exploring the Australian SE's perspective of how they collaborated in online communities and the value created or diminished through their collaboration.

Unlike medium and large SEs, small SEs struggled with networking and communicating their challenges associated with financial and non-financial resources and scaling up their mission. SEs are particularly vulnerable to financial challenges due to their propensity to prioritize their social motive over commercial necessities (Ince & Hahn, 2020). Due to limited financial resources, small SEs rely on volunteers, especially when they have an environmental or social mission, such as reducing poverty or social disadvantage (Kelly et al., 2019). We found that co-creation through online communities facilitated collaboration amongst social enterprises within or across specific industries to mitigate those challenges. Financial sustainability was found to be a challenge for SEs that influences their growth and social impact (Bacq & Eddleston, 2018) and that SEs rely on external grants to secure their long-term financial sustainability (Abedin et al., 2021). We argued that SEs can potentially practice and mitigate financial sustainability through opportunities provided through resource exchange and co-production activities online (e.g., fundraising activities). Online co-creation enables SEs to strategically manage their human resources through community engagement and network building. For those SEs looking to scale their impacts by growing their enterprises, building and maintaining collaboration at the national and international levels was viewed as an opportunity facilitated by online communities. The development of co-creation and crowd-based paradigm mediated with an online platform can support SEs in seeking investors and other financial/non-financial resources. Initiatives that emerged from COVID-19 and recovery, such as #WirVsVirus and 'All of Us: Combat Coronavirus'",[7] are great examples of the successful role of digitalization and use of online communities by SEs. Such initiatives advance SEs by fostering engagement in co-creation activities, which is critical to strengthen their capability to help solve social and economic issues caused by COVID-19.

We did not find any support in the interviews for challenges related to limited information (Barraket & Collyer, 2010), diversity management (Smith et al., 2013), legitimacy among stakeholders (Doherty et al., 2014), and market development (Barraket et al., 2016). We believe that challenges associated with diversity management, legitimacy among stakeholders, and market development, can be of more concern for middle to large social enterprises. We found that financial sustainability, access to human resources, and scaling up mainly impacted small SEs. Limited information was not a concern for SEs, since online communities enabled access to diverse resources such as learning materials, start-up resources, business planning, case studies, and information related to different opportunities and events.

SEs, as organizations with limited resources (Bridgstock et al., 2010), need to interact with their stakeholders to co-create value (Romero & Molina, 2011). The use of online communities helps SEs access new knowledge and new resources, as well as new markets (Hynes, 2009). Online communities as a tool for supporting value co-creation (Füller, 2010) can facilitate the interactions between SEs and their stakeholders. It is crucial for SEs to build a network and interact with their stakeholders because each stakeholder brings their own unique knowledge, skills, capabilities, and resources in the value co-creation process (Kazadi et al., 2016). We found that the importance of online co-creation for small SEs is to facilitate coordination across different internal and external stakeholders and strengthen their financial/non-financial collaboration, which is fundamental for the survival of small SEs. Small SEs are apt to prioritize scaling and promoting their social mission over financial performance. Scalability and financial growth for small SEs was associated with how better they can meet their social missions and objectives. Therefore, online co-creation facilitates their objective of promoting their mission and strengthening their network. However, the type of co-creation activities may change over the enterprise's life course.

We found that SEs' online interactions might cause a co-destruction of value (i.e., reduce or destroy potential value) by hijacking resources, unin-structive information exchange, and collusion efforts. We found that such co-destruction activities can create distrust and unwillingness to engage and lead to negative outcomes such as waste of resources. SEs often have limited access to resources. Almost 73 percent of SEs in Australia are small and operate in resource-scarce environments (Di Domenico et al., 2010; Doherty et al., 2009; Islam, 2020), making them vulnerable organizations. Although SEs can grow through online interactions and have access to resources, loss of resources through negative interactions can negatively affect their surviva-bility and performance. For example, the negative side of engaging in funding for SEs would be hijacking resources such as human resources and volunteers and funding opportunities. Environment dynamics negatively affect the rela-tionship between offline value creation and social enterprise growth (Ge et al., 2019). Similarly, in the online context, negative dynamics among actors generate co-destruction patterns (Bidar et al., 2020), and for SEs, such negative contribute to their expected value outcome.

CONCLUSION

The findings presented here are helpful for SEs that seek to create or maintain their collaboration through online communities. We suggest that SEs generate value for their business and coordinate the challenges related to financial problems, human resources and scaling up through online co-creation activities. The chapter distinguished between different co-destruction activities that may occur through SE's online interaction and might negatively affect SEs and lead to cost rather than benefits. Although mitigation strategies can be determined for detecting co-destruction efforts when designing online communities, SEs need to be trained to identify and avoid co-destruction efforts that can lead to waste of resources. The findings of this chapter can be used as a foundation for developing a digital platform that can serve as a social enterprise tool to facilitate SE collaborations. The development of such dedicated online platforms can benefit small SEs and their beneficiaries by providing open access information, fostering co-creation, and generating value from their investments in digital collaboration efforts. Furthermore, the development of crowd-based online initiatives enables a distributed model for SEs where the crowd has the opportunity to work with any SEs that share a common interest, and SEs can collect resources and solve social issues.

The list of key lessons learned is that co-creation and co-destruction paradoxes are intertwined with each other. The online environment benefits SEs with increasing visibility, scaling up, and resource accessibility. Nevertheless, in online collaboration, adverse effects on SEs can also occur. We should take into account that actors perceive the value received as positive (value co-created) or negative (value co-destroyed). However, one's value perception may be different from another and one's value perception can change over time. Also, sometimes the gained value through SE's online collaboration outweighs the cost (e.g., hijacked resource). SEs need to be aware of such paradoxes in the online ecosystem and find ways to manage these contradictory pressures.

Value co-creation and co-destruction are determined as dynamic processes that co-exist (Chowdhury et al., 2016). By acknowledging the coexistence of such contradictory elements, 'paradoxical thinking creates a cognitive frame that enables to develop more creative solutions for responding to complex problems and contributes to sustainable development' (Brix-Asala et al., 2021, p. 2). Given the complexity of co-creation and co-destruction and the dynamic nature of SEs' interactions, managing such paradox requires different cycles of thinking and strategies. Brix-Asala et al. (2021) suggested either the acceptance strategy can be applied to live with the current form of the paradox or resolution strategies that will further transform the situation. In response to the paradox, SEs can choose to either separate two opposite poles (separation strategy) or accept both extremes (acceptance strategy) (Vafeas & Hughes, 2020). In this chapter, we set the foundation for co-creation, co-destruction, and social enterprisers research that adopts paradox view using acceptance and resolution strategies.

In some situations, SEs need to accept that because of the openness of online communities, co-creation and co-destruction interactions co-exist. The acceptance strategy helps SEs in the short term to acknowledge and confront both contradicting elements (co-creation and co-destruction) incompatibility instead of resolving the contradict (Lewis, 2000). This involves appreciation of the differences (Smith & Lewis, 2011) but coordinating contradictory elements in a mutually beneficial way. For example, we found that whereas some SEs were suggesting uninstructive information being created by others, they are more likely to embrace the co-creation of new knowledge and resources and accessibility to constructive information and opportunities. Acceptance in this example is that an SE is aware but avoids negative elements such as uninstructive information provided by other SEs. Considering Ushahidi's example, although co-destruction efforts can exist in the form of trolling and incorrect incidents, the value gain outweigh the value reduction in terms of crisis management. In other instances, SEs contradictory aims can lead to paradoxical situation, one may view a situation as value creation and others as value reduction. Therefore, resolving strategy is not suitable because both opposing forces are necessary and entwined (Lüscher & Lewis, 2008). Acceptation or adoption mindset sets the stage for integration and novel solution in a longer term (Vafeas & Hughes, 2020).

Resolution strategies can be beneficial for the longer-term paradoxes' impacts, e.g., when co-destruction leads to a persistent negative outcome. These paradoxes can be addressed by separation (spatial and temporal) strategies (Smith & Lewis, 2011). Separation strategies facilitate the management of tensions by keeping the paradox elements separated (Hahn 2015). While temporal separation deals with contradictory elements at different points of time, spatial separation situates them at different social and physical locations (individual, organizational, systemic). We believe that the separation strategy can be determined at the individual and systemic levels. For example, at the individual level, to prevent co-destruction efforts such as hijacking resources, SEs can reinforce co-creation activities with trusted parties rather than share key information about their social and economic development with the open community. This can follow a self-regulatory approach for resource management and relational governance and requires identifying reliable parties rather than those with competing demands and goals. At the systemic level, paradoxes provide good opportunities to better govern and design the platform. For example, there should be a mechanism for online communities to detect and separate destructive efforts from creative efforts (e.g., group members' suspiciousness and group plagiarism detection mechanisms for detecting collusion (Chen et al., 2018), or line up strategies to reinforce co-creation engagement among SEs. In another example, the ability to post anonymously increases the chance of destructive efforts and acts of vandalism. This can be improved through the design and identity management of collaborators. In terms of temporal separation, maintaining longer-term relationships with different parties to gradually strengthen their trust and financial/ social engagement rather than negative relationships.

It is the scope of this research that can guide future work. For example, the data was collected from small enterprises. Future research could analyze co-creation and co-destruction in medium and large enterprises to generalize the findings. A comparison of different size SEs can provide insights into which challenges SEs are seeking to address when collaborating in online communities. In the future, it would be interesting to gain additional insights into SE's co-creation and co-destruction by observing their collaboration in online communities over time. This chapter serves to encourage other researchers to extend our view of SEs interactions in online communities by exploring how this model can be applied in a specific industry. We propose potential future research avenues in co-creation and co-destruction areas. Future research can focus on multiple paradoxes and their interactions and issues of more importance to the digital ecosystem. Future research can also investigate how our proposed co-creation and co-destruction paradox framework can be applied to different online platforms facilitating SE's collaboration. How does the nature of paradoxes change in online versus offline contexts? One can also investigate how the emerging co-creation and co-destruction paradoxes can be balanced to facilitate effective collaboration?

KEY TAKEAWAYS

- Paradoxical tensions of resource exchange versus hijacking resources, co-production and uninstructive information, and project coordination versus collusion attempts are the most important paradoxical tensions representing SE's online co-creation and co-destruction.
- Viewed as a paradox, co-creation and co-destruction are no longer separate but are reinforcing one another.
- The online collaboration benefits SEs with increasing visibility, scaling up, and resource building. However, in online collaboration, adverse effects on SEs can also occur. SEs need to find ways to balance and manage these contradictory pressures.

NOTES

1. 'A network of various stakeholders in the social enterprise domain (e.g., government, intermediary organizations, social enterprises, and consumers), their interaction and resource and experiences that form ecosystem' (Hazenberg et al., 2016).

2.   https://innovationinpolitics.eu/showroom/project/wirvsvirus-hackathon-support
        -programme/; https://ssir.org/articles/entry/open_social_innovation.
3.   A non-profit digital social enterprise: https://www.ushahidi.com/.
4.   We analyze the insights collected from interviews and our previous publications
        in the co-destruction context. In our previous studies in the co-destruction
        context, we looked at the negative impact of co-destruction in online collabo-
        rative systems as we believed that the destructive behavior might happen more
        frequently in open community co-creation (Bidar et. al., 2021; Bidar et. al.,
        2020). We found that paradoxical nature of online interactions might cause
        a co-destruction of value (i.e., reduce or destroy potential value) by providing
        low-quality service, having insufficient competencies, and/or through destruc-
        tive communication.
5.   https://www.griffith.edu.au/__data/assets/pdf_file/0014/1360400/SENS
        -Directions-Report_Part-Two.pdf.
6.   https://www.griffith.edu.au/__data/assets/pdf_file/0014/1360400/SENS
        -Directions-Report_Part-Two.pdf.
7.   https://www.give4cdcf.org/.

REFERENCES

Abedin, B., Douglas, H., Watson, J., & Bidar, R. (2021). Mitigating challenges of small
    social enterprises to improve performance. *International Journal of Productivity and
    Performance Management, ahead-of-print* (ahead-of-print).
Abela, A. V., & Murphy, P. E. (2008). Marketing with integrity: ethics and the
    service-dominant logic for marketing. *Journal of the academy of marketing science,
    36*(1), 39–53.
Agostinelli, J. (2010). The proof is in the pudding: social enterprise in Australia. *Fine
    print, 33*(2), 19–23.
Autio, E., Nambisan, S., Thomas, L. D., & Wright, M. (2018). Digital affor-
    dances, spatial affordances, and the genesis of entrepreneurial ecosystems. *Strategic
    Entrepreneurship Journal, 12*(1), 72–95.
Bacq, S., & Eddleston, K. A. (2018). A resource-based view of social entrepreneurship:
    how stewardship culture benefits scale of social impact. *Journal of Business Ethics,
    152*(3), 589–611.
Bandyopadhyay, C., & Ray, S. (2019). Marketing in social enterprises: The role of
    value creation through relationship marketing. In *Strategic marketing for social
    enterprises in developing nations* (pp. 32–52). IGI Global.
Barraket, J., & Collyer, N. (2010). Mapping social enterprise in Australia: Conceptual
    debates and their operational implications. *Third Sector Review, 16*(2), 11–28.
Barraket, J., Douglas, H., Eversole, R., Mason, C., McNeill, J., & Morgan, B. (2017).
    Classifying social enterprise models in Australia. *Social Enterprise Journal, 13*(4),
    345–61.
Barraket, J., Mason, C., & Blain, B. (2016). Finding Australia's social enterprise sector
    2016: Final report. *Social Traders and Centre for Social Impact Swinburne.*
Barrett, M., Oborn, E., & Orlikowski, W. (2016). Creating value in online communi-
    ties: The sociomaterial configuring of strategy, platform, and stakeholder engage-
    ment. *Information Systems Research, 27*(4), 704–23.

Battilana, J., & Lee, M. (2014). Advancing research on hybrid organizing–Insights from the study of social enterprises. *The Academy of Management Annals, 8*(1), 397–441.

Bidar, R., Barros, A., & Watson, J. (2021). Co-creation of services: an online network perspective. *Internet Research,* (ahead-of-print).

Bidar, R., ter Hofstede, A. H., & Sindhgatta, R. (2020). Co-destruction Patterns in Crowdsourcing. International Conference on Advanced Information Systems Engineering.

Bidar, R., Watson, J., & Barros, A. (2016). Literature review to determine environmental and cognitive factors underlying user value cocreation behaviour. Proceedings of the 20th Pacific Asia Conference on Information Systems (PACIS) 2016.

Bidar, R., Watson, J., & Barros, A. (2017). Classification of service co-creation systems: An integrative approach.

Bradford, A., Luke, B., & Furneaux, C. (2020). Exploring Accountability in Social Enterprise: Priorities, Practicalities, and Legitimacy. *Voluntas: International Journal of Voluntary & Nonprofit Organizations, 31*(3).

Braund, P., & Schwittay, A. (2016). Scaling inclusive digital innovation successfully: the case of crowdfunding social enterprises. *Innovation and Development, 6*(1), 15–29.

Bridgstock, R., Lettice, F., Özbilgin, M. F., & Tatli, A. (2010). Diversity management for innovation in social enterprises in the UK. *Entrepreneurship and Regional Development, 22*(6), 557–74.

Brix-Asala, C., Seuring, S., Sauer, P. C., Zehendner, A., & Schilling, L. (2021). Resolving the base of the pyramid inclusion paradox through supplier development. *Business Strategy and the Environment.*

Chen, P.-P., Sun, H.-L., Fang, Y.-L., & Huai, J.-P. (2018). Collusion-proof result inference in crowdsourcing. *Journal of Computer Science and Technology, 33*(2), 351–365.

Choi, D., Berry, F. S., & Ghadimi, A. (2020). Policy design and achieving social outcomes: A comparative analysis of social enterprise policy. *Public Administration Review, 80*(3), 494–505.

Chowdhury, I. N., Gruber, T., & Zolkiewski, J. (2016). Every cloud has a silver lining—Exploring the dark side of value co-creation in B2B service networks. *Industrial Marketing Management, 55*, 97–109.

Dacin, P. A., Dacin, M. T., & Matear, M. (2010). Social entrepreneurship: Why we don't need a new theory and how we move forward from here. *Academy of Management Perspectives, 24*(3), 37–57.

De Silva, M., Khan, Z., Vorley, T., & Zeng, J. (2019). Transcending the pyramid: opportunity co-creation for social innovation. *Industrial Marketing Management.*

Desa, G., & Basu, S. (2013). Optimization or bricolage? Overcoming resource constraints in global social entrepreneurship. *Strategic Entrepreneurship Journal, 7*(1), 26–49.

Di Domenico, M., Haugh, H., & Tracey, P. (2010). Social bricolage: Theorizing social value creation in social enterprises. *Entrepreneurship Theory and Practice, 34*(4), 681–703.

Doherty, B., Foster, G., Meehan, J., & Mason, C. (2009). *Management for social enterprise*. Sage Publications.

Doherty, B., Haugh, H., & Lyon, F. (2014). Social enterprises as hybrid organizations: A review and research agenda. *International Journal of Management Reviews, 16*(4), 417–36.

Echeverri, P., & Skålén, P. (2011). Co-creation and co-destruction: A practice-theory based study of interactive value formation. *Marketing theory, 11*(3), 351–73.

Engen, M., Fransson, M., Quist, J., & Skålén, P. (2021). Continuing the development of the public service logic: a study of value co-destruction in public services. *Public Management Review, 23*(6), 886–905.

Fereday, J., & Muir-Cochrane, E. (2006). Demonstrating rigor using thematic analysis: A hybrid approach of inductive and deductive coding and theme development. *International journal of qualitative methods, 5*(1), 80–92.

Frau, M., Cabiddu, F., & Muscas, F. (2018). When Multiple Actors' Online Interactions Lead to Value Co-Destruction: An Explorative Case Study. In *Diverse Methods in Customer Relationship Marketing and Management* (pp. 163–180). IGI Global.

Füller, J. (2010). Refining virtual co-creation from a consumer perspective. *California Management Review, 52*(2), 98–122.

Füller, J., MüHlbacher, H., Matzler, K., & Jawecki, G. (2009). Consumer empowerment through internet-based co-creation. *Journal of Management Information Systems, 26*(3), 71–102.

Fusch, P. I., & Ness, L. R. (2015). Are we there yet? Data saturation in qualitative research. *The Qualitative Report, 20*(9), 1408.

García-Jurado, A., Pérez-Barea, J. J., & Nova, R. (2021). A new approach to social entrepreneurship: A systematic review and meta-analysis. *Sustainability, 13*(5), 2754.

Ge, J., Xu, H., & Pellegrini, M. M. (2019). The effect of value co-creation on social enterprise growth: Moderating mechanism of environment dynamics. *Sustainability, 11*(1), 250.

Gray, M., Healy, K., & Crofts, P. (2003). Social enterprise: is it the business of social work? *Australian Social Work, 56*(2), 141–54.

Grönroos, C., & Voima, P. (2013). Critical service logic: making sense of value creation and co-creation. *Journal of the Academy of Marketing Science, 41*(2), 133–50.

Grover, V., & Kohli, R. (2012). Cocreating IT value: New capabilities and metrics for multifirm environments. *MIS Quarterly, 36*(1), 225–32.

Hahn, T., Figge, F., Pinkse, J., & Preuss, L. (2018). A paradox perspective on corporate sustainability: Descriptive, instrumental, and normative aspects. *Journal of Business Ethics, 148*(2), 235–48.

Halmos, A., Misuraca, G., & Viscusi, G. (2019). From public value to social value of digital government: Co-creation and social innovation in European Union initiatives. ProProceedings of the 52nd Hawaii International Conference on System Sciences| 2019.

Haugh, H. (2009). A resource-based perspective of social entrepreneurship. *International Perspectives on Social Entrepreneurship, 2009*, 99–116.

Haugh, H. (2012). The importance of theory in social enterprise research. *Social Enterprise Journal, 8*(1), 7–15.

Hynes, B. (2009). Growing the social enterprise–issues and challenges. *Social Enterprise Journal, 5*(2), 114–25.

Ince, I., & Hahn, R. (2020). How dynamic capabilities facilitate the survivability of social enterprises: A qualitative analysis of sensing and seizing capacities. *Journal of Small Business Management*, 1–35.

Islam, S. M. (2020). Unintended consequences of scaling social impact through ecosystem growth strategy in social enterprise and social entrepreneurship. *Journal of Business Venturing Insights, 13*, e00159.

Järvi, H., Kähkönen, A.-K., & Torvinen, H. (2018). When value co-creation fails: Reasons that lead to value co-destruction. *Scandinavian Journal of Management, 34*(1), 63–77.

Jay, J. (2013). Navigating paradox as a mechanism of change and innovation in hybrid organizations. *Academy of Management Journal, 56*(1), 137–59.

Jenner, P., & Fleischman, D. (2017). Enhancing social enterprise sustainability: A value co-creation pathway. *e-Journal of Social & Behavioural Research in Business, 8*(1), 57.

Jenner, P., & Oprescu, F. (2016). The sectorial trust of social enterprise: friend or foe? *Journal of Social Entrepreneurship, 7*(2), 236–61.

Kay, A., Roy, M. J., & Donaldson, C. (2016). Re-imagining social enterprise. *Social Enterprise Journal, 12*(2), 217–34.

Kazadi, K., Lievens, A., & Mahr, D. (2016). Stakeholder co-creation during the innovation process: Identifying capabilities for knowledge creation among multiple stakeholders. *Journal of Business Research, 69*(2), 525–40.

Keane, O., Hall, P. V., Schuurman, N., & Kingsbury, P. (2017). Linking online social proximity and workplace location: social enterprise employees in British Columbia. *Area, 49*(4), 468–76.

Kelly, D., Steiner, A., Mazzei, M., & Baker, R. (2019). Filling a void? The role of social enterprise in addressing social isolation and loneliness in rural communities. *Journal of Rural Studies, 70*(2019), 225–36.

Lefebvre, V. (2020). Performance, working capital management, and the liability of smallness: A question of opportunity costs? *Journal of Small Business Management.*

Lewis, M. W. (2000). Exploring paradox: Toward a more comprehensive guide. *Academy of Management Review, 25*(4), 760–76.

Liu, G., Takeda, S., & Ko, W.-W. (2014). Strategic orientation and social enterprise performance. *Nonprofit and Voluntary Sector Quarterly, 43*(3), 480–501.

Luisa, G. M., & Magdalena, R. A. (2017). Assessing the value dimensions of social enterprise networks. *International Journal of Entrepreneurial Behavior & Research, 24*(3).

Lusch, R. F., Vargo, S. L., & O'brien, M. (2007). Competing through service: Insights from service-dominant logic. *Journal of Retailing, 83*(1), 5–18.

Lüscher, L. S., & Lewis, M. W. (2008). Organizational change and managerial sensemaking: Working through paradox. *Academy of Management Journal, 51*(2), 221–40.

Lyon, F., & Fernandez, H. (2012). Strategies for scaling up social enterprise: lessons from early years providers. *Social Enterprise Journal, 8*(1), 63–77.

Makkonen, H., & Olkkonen, R. (2017). Interactive value formation in interorganizational relationships: Dynamic interchange between value co-creation, no-creation, and co-destruction. *Marketing theory.*

Markides, C., & Sosa, L. (2013). Pioneering and first mover advantages: the importance of business models. *Long Range Planning, 46*(4-5), 325–34.

Markus, M. L., & Loebbecke, C. (2013). Commoditized digital processes and business community platforms: New opportunities and challenges for digital business strategies. *MIS Quarterly, 37*(2), 649–53.

Mason, C., Kirkbride, J., & Bryde, D. (2007). From stakeholders to institutions: the changing face of social enterprise governance theory. *Management Decision.*

Mitchell, A., Madill, J., & Chreim, S. (2015). Marketing and social enterprises: implications for social marketing. *Journal of Social Marketing.*

Nambisan, S., Wright, M., & Feldman, M. (2019). The digital transformation of innovation and entrepreneurship: Progress, challenges and key themes. *Research Policy, 48*(8), 103773.

Niesten, E., & Stefan, I. (2019). Embracing the paradox of interorganizational value co-creation–value capture: A literature review towards paradox resolution. *International Journal of Management Reviews, 21*(2), 231–55.

Pankaj, L., & Seetharaman, P. (2021). The balancing act of social enterprise: An IT emergence perspective. *International Journal of Information Management, 57,* 102302.

Pera, R., Occhiocupo, N., & Clarke, J. (2016). Motives and resources for value co-creation in a multi-stakeholder ecosystem: A managerial perspective. *Journal of Business Research, 69*(10), 4033–41.

Plé, L. (2017). Why do we need research on value co-destruction? *Journal of Creating Value, 3*(2), 162–69.

Plé, L., & Chumpitaz Cáceres, R. (2010). Not always co-creation: introducing interactional co-destruction of value in service-dominant logic. *Journal of Services Marketing, 24*(6), 430–37.

Powell, M. (2015). *Social Enterprise in Adult Day Care: Marketing and Sustainability.* University of York.

Prior, D. D., & Marcos-Cuevas, J. (2016). Value co-destruction in interfirm relationships: The impact of actor engagement styles. *Marketing Theory, 16*(4), 533–52.

Romero, D., & Molina, A. (2011). Collaborative networked organisations and customer communities: value co-creation and co-innovation in the networking era. *Production Planning & Control, 22*(5-6), 447–72.

Rubin, H. J., & Rubin, I. S. (2011). *Qualitative interviewing: The art of hearing data.* Sage.

Savolainen, R. (2017). Information sharing and knowledge sharing as communicative activities. *Information Research: an International Electronic Journal, 22*(3), n3.

Shaw, E., & Carter, S. (2007). Social entrepreneurship: Theoretical antecedents and empirical analysis of entrepreneurial processes and outcomes. *Journal of Small Business and Enterprise Development, 14*(3), 418–34.

Smith, A. M. (2013). The value co-destruction process: a customer resource perspective. *European Journal of Marketing, 47*(11/12), 1889–1909.

Smith, W. K., Gonin, M., & Besharov, M. L. (2013). Managing social-business tensions: A review and research agenda for social enterprise. *Business Ethics Quarterly, 23*(3), 407–42.

Smith, W. K., & Lewis, M. W. (2011). Toward a theory of paradox: A dynamic equilibrium model of organizing. *Academy of Management Review, 36*(2), 381–403.

Staessens, M., Kerstens, P. J., Bruneel, J., & Cherchye, L. (2019). Data envelopment analysis and social enterprises: analysing performance, strategic orientation and mission drift. *Journal of Business Ethics, 159*(2), 325–41.

Sun, S. L., & Im, J. (2015). Cutting microfinance interest rates: An opportunity co–creation perspective. *Entrepreneurship Theory and Practice, 39*(1), 101–28.

Tasavori, M., Kwong, C., & Pruthi, S. (2018). Resource bricolage and growth of product and market scope in social enterprises. *Entrepreneurship & Regional Development, 30*(3-4), 336–61.

Tung, W. F., & Jordann, G. (2017). Crowdsourcing social network service for social enterprise innovation. *Information Systems Frontiers, 19*(6), 1311–27.

Vafeas, M., & Hughes, T. (2020). Resource integration: Adopting a paradox perspective to inform the management of tensions in customer resource allocation. *Industrial Marketing Management, 91*, 596–609.

Vafeas, M., Hughes, T., & Hilton, T. (2016). Antecedents to value diminution: A dyadic perspective. *Marketing Theory, 16*(4), 469–91.

Vargo, S. L., & Lusch, R. F. (2004). Evolving to a new dominant logic for marketing. *Journal of Marketing, 68*(1), 1–17.

Vargo, S. L., & Lusch, R. F. (2016). Institutions and axioms: an extension and update of service-dominant logic. *Journal of the Academy of Marketing Science, 44*(1), 5–23.

Vartiainen, T., & Tuunanen, T. (2016). Value co-creation and co-destruction in an is artifact: Contradictions of geocaching. System Sciences (HICSS), 2016 49th Hawaii International Conference.

Weaver, R. L. (2020). Social enterprise and the capability approach: Exploring how social enterprises are humanizing business. *Journal of Nonprofit & Public Sector Marketing, 32*(5), 427–52.

Wry, T., & York, J. G. (2017). An identity-based approach to social enterprise. *Academy of Management Review, 42*(3), 437–60.

Yan, Z., Wang, T., Chen, Y., & Zhang, H. (2016). Knowledge sharing in online health communities: A social exchange theory perspective. *Information & Management, 53*(5), 643–53.

Yin, R. (2013). *Case study research: Design and methods.* Sage Publications.

Zhang, T., Lu, C., Torres, E., & Cobanoglu, C. (2020). Value co-creation and technological progression: a critical review. *European Business Review.*

Practice 1. Paradoxes and progress: perspectives on collaboration for digital value

Dan Chenok

Over the last several decades, new technologies have transformed how organizations can be structured and operated for success – specifically, digital change has enabled horizontal and collaborative organizations to increase their value, relative to that typically offered by traditional vertical hierarchies. This paradigm is reshaping public and private sector enterprises in both multinational and very local settings, including government agencies using automation to improve service delivery to veterans, expand loan assistance to small business, and service families in need.

The elements of digital change that mature organizations bring involve multiple factors, especially for government organizations, including:

- the move to cloud computing networks that allows organizations to access, assess, and share information and deliver service at faster speed and lower costs (see more discussion below);
- the development of artificial intelligence and machine learning applications that accelerates the analysis of massive amounts of data to support more accurate and more personalized decision making – value here relies on AI that builds in ethical protocols to reduce risk of bias from the data against particular groups;
- strong cybersecurity that is built into digital technologies, not added after the fact – securing the data and ensuring legitimate access while also leveraging more traditional firewalls and sensors, assuming that digital networks are always vulnerable and require 'zero trust' approaches that focus on protection across multiple threat vectors;
- a skilled workforce that has the tools to operate in a twenty-first century economy – this will require hiring, training, and partnering to ensure that that teams working on digital enablement can drive user-centered design, open source development, and customer experience in their work.

In Chapter 1 of this volume, the authors provide powerful evidence of the shift to horizontal and collaborative organizations, and also explore its differential impact based on organizational and technological maturity – maturity to harness digital technologies like those identified above in delivering value. Brohman et al. describe how twenty-first century companies and governments are expanding the definition of 'value' to fuse private and public sector objectives. Rather than only assessing value through a lens of either commercial profit or government serving the people, the authors note the importance of both and add a third lens that crosses sectors: that of a sustainable planet. Together, the three elements comprise a sort of balanced scorecard for a new age, referred to as the 'triple bottom line' or '3BL'. Sustainability represents a critically important – some would say existential – domain to measure value; the IBM Center for the Business of Government recently published two reports that address how digital technologies can promote sustainable outcomes across the public and private sectors.[1]

Technological advances now allow organizations to meet these multiple objectives not through a Weberian evolution of the singular organization, but rather through an array of formal and informal networks in which people interrelate in unconventional ways to develop and apply technology innovation and analytics in achieving mission objectives. Through a networked approach, organizations can bring the power of 'collective action' – which occurs when technology enhances the ability to cross boundaries in order for people to interact – that drives greater value than any one enterprise could bring.

As the former US Government leader for technology policy at the Office of Management and Budget, and now as the director of the IBM Center,[2] I have experienced and advanced successful and problematic applications of technology. These divergent paths tend to co-exist as the power of new horizontal applications does not align well with the structure of vertical organizations. They create a paradox to be managed, one where successful outcomes emerge after co-creation in the development and implementation of policy and strategy. I have witnessed this firsthand in the development of regulations to deliver student financial aid more efficiently by developing regulations jointly with student and financial institution representatives; moreover, our Center has published research on the value of co-creation for governments as well,[3] providing a research frame that supports further exploration.

Chapters in this section explore this paradox in different contexts. Authors Reihaneh Bidar and Behnam Abedin write in Chapter 2 that 'co-creation' among multiple interests can provide mutual benefit for 3BL, while those same interests can also engage in 'co-destruction' by suboptimizing operations as part of a network. This point reflects the benefits and risks of collective action – a recent Center report on network-service delivery[4] demonstrates the proposition that I have witnessed in working with government – specifically, bringing organizations together upfront to co-create a delivery process that can benefit those receiving services, and reduce risk of destruction from one part of the network taking an outsized role in the production of those services.

Evidence of the importance of leverage among organizations even appears when assessing value created across rural communities. In Chapter 3, , authors Juuli Lintula, Tero Päivärinta, and Tuure Tuunanen study a rural area of Sweden to write about the greater value derived from 'smart villages' that act collectively to co-deliver services, as opposed to the traditional case where each community seeks to provide a complete set of services that are redundant with those of their neighbors. Using 'service dominant logic' can help smart villages find common delivery methods through 'regional services ecosystems' – and digital technologies exist today that bring geographically dispersed areas together in new ways. Service-dominant logic approaches service design from the perspective of the outcome being received in a way that meets a user's expectations and capacity to access services; our Center published a report describing how this principle informed service design across a range of localities through integrating ethnographic research to support villages, including a case from West Africa.[5]

So how do digital technologies foster collective organizational action? Brohman et al identify several that resonate with my work in and out of government. These include:

- Cloud computing platforms, which allow multiple enterprises to share common technology infrastructure rather than recreate redundant IT stores. The US Government has moved toward greater cloud adoption through 15 years of policy, starting with the development of the 'Cloud First' Strategy by President Obama's Transition Team in 2008 (I Chaired the Technology and Government subgroup, and the group architect of that policy, Vivek Kundra, went on to serve as the first Federal CIO of the Obama Administration) and now enshrined as 'Cloudsmart'[6] that can be implemented as a 'hybrid' of existing and new cloud systems.
- Open standards and APIs ('application programming interfaces'), which provide a common lexicon and integrate application development so that enterprises no longer have to own or contract for homegrown software. The IBM Center report *Aligning Open Data, Open Source and Hybrid Cloud Adoption in Government*[7] describes the value of linking open source software and hybrid cloud environments to allow collaborative action and collective data management across organizations.
- Online service delivery, which can enable producers and consumers – as well as governments and the public – to co-develop the value chain for access services. This has been a public sector goal ever since early e-government strategies were introduced in the US while I was still at

OMB in 2001. Of course, as Bidar and Abedin note, organizations that do not adapt or incentivize around collaboration can follow this path only to experience collusion, inaccurate information, and increased cost and waste – elements of 'co-destruction'.

- Agile IT governance, where capacity is built in iterative fashion by cross-organizational teams that assess customer feedback; in the last few decades, agile has increasingly replaced older 'waterfall' systems where large components are built and released after significant development and cost timeframes. The success of the agile software movement has led a number of organizations to adapt agile tenets to other functions of governance, including policy development and program implementation – evidenced by recent initiatives from the World Economic Forum, the Organization for Economic Cooperation and Development, and the IBM Center's collaboration with the National Academy of Public Administration on the 'Agile Government Center'.[8]

Each of these technologies can help modern companies and governments work in multi-sector partnerships to realize greater digital value – serving people more effectively, doing so more sustainably by reducing the amount of redundant technology infrastructures that expend energy in a physical location, and driving greater cost efficiency and profit. Indeed, these technologies enable co-creation: cloud computing creates value by customizing ready-made software and hardware, APIs allow capabilities across organizations to be integrated, online services can allow customers to reach across silos and develop recommendations that inform future service improvements, and agile approaches rely on user feedback to iterate new solutions.

But, as each of the authors note, the paradox of risk and value, co-creation and co-destruction, can manifest if organizations are not well-managed – where business processes are set up to support vertical and hierarchical structures that do not match the need to collective action, and do not leverage the collective power of digital technologies like cloud computing and APIs. Based on my experience, this paradox becomes both more likely to occur and with greater impact in organizations that fail to adapt how they manage people and processes to a new era. Organizations that remain siloed will limit value and can even lead destructive outcomes; as the authors note, collaboration as a standard procedure and cultural norm can conversely expand digital value for profit, people, and planet.

NOTES

1.   https://www.businessofgovernment.org/report/digital-technology-and
      -environment and https://www.businessofgovernment.org/report/rise-sustainable
      -enterprise.
2.   https://www.businessofgovernment.org.
3.   https://www.businessofgovernment.org/report/engaging-citizens-co-creation
      -public-services.
4.   https://www.businessofgovernment.org/report/collaborative-networks-next
      -frontier-data-driven-management.
5.   https://www.businessofgovernment.org/report/integrating-big-data-and-thick
      -data-transform-public-services-delivery.
6.   https://cloud.cio.gov/strategy.
7.   https://www.businessofgovernment.org/report/aligning-open-data-open-source
      -and-hybrid-cloud-adoption-government.
8.   https://napawash.org/the-agile-government-center/overview.

4. Unlocking digital value at the intersection of organizational digital transformation and digital business ecosystems

Philip Karnebogen, Anna Maria Oberländer and Patrick Rövekamp

INTRODUCTION

Organizations recognize that to survive and thrive in the digital age, investment in digitalization is needed to challenge traditional economies and enable new business models for value creation and capture Lansiti & Lakhani, 2020). One inherent challenge is that 'value' from an organizational perspective does not always align with what is considered 'valuable' by a broader ecosystem of stakeholders. Take for example, the high priority placed on profitability from a publicly-traded company perspective. To keep their stock price competitive, profitability needs to take precedence over people and planet. To survive, most for-profit organizations cannot lose sight of 'what's in it for me' as the need to be profitable remains essential. However, for-profit organizations increasingly recognize the need to place value and importance on 'what's in it for we'. In the digital age, contributing to an industry-level mandate to reduce harm to people and planet is also essential for survival. For example, the UN Glasgow Financial Alliance for Net Zero raised commitment from the world's banks and investors from US$5 trillion in 2020 to US$130 trillion in 2022 to deliver the financing needed to get the world on the pathway to reducing carbon emissions. This commitment will definitely cut into the profitability of financial institutions, however, for-profit firms also recognize that a collective agreement to contribute will level the playing field in terms of competition. For government institutions, this tension between me and we looks slightly different but it is equally important. In many countries, taxpayers are putting more and more pressure on the government to embrace the spirit of 'profitability' to ensure ministries and sectors are fiscally responsible. People recognize that the cost of reducing harm to people and planet ultimately falls on the taxpayer. With some countries such as Japan, Denmark, and Austria operating with personal income tax rates over 55 percent, tax rates in the world's wealthiest countries are rising. Of course, taxing higher incomes is never welcomed by the rich, but it also reduces burgeoning inequality that economists say will benefit markets long term.

So, despite the complexity that emerges when one considers the creation and capture of value from different perspectives, the simple takeaway is that all organizations need to orchestrate business models that consider both 'me' and 'we'. Pioneers in this space have learned that adopting digital technologies such as social media, analytics, and artificial intelligence (AI) is critical in orchestrating value across perspectives. In some cases, the results are positive, but others are raising some concerns. Let us look at a few examples. In 2019, Chipotle's launched its use of TikTok and ran campaigns such as #ChipotleLidFlip and #GuacDance to create a fun and social experience to complement its fast food offerings. In just the first six days, 111,000 videos were submitted to the challenge, resulting in 104 million video views. Through continued use of the TikTok platform, digital sales growth increased by 88 percent in 2020. Salesforce packaged their own lessons learned on achieving NetZero emissions into an analytics-based product called Sustainability Cloud that they now offer to other organizations to manage their climate initiatives in economically viable ways. Finally, Google and DeepMind collaborated in developing an advanced AI approach to orchestrating the intense cooling mechanisms necessary to operate Google's server infrastructure. Through the help of this new AI approach, they achieved a reduction of energy costs by 40 percent and, at the same time, lowered associated emissions. Similar applications of AI to raise operational efficiency are being experimented with by companies such as Siemens and Amazon, but potential benefits are matched by raising concerns. In fact, for example, Amazon's AI system that would automatically identify low-productive workers and initiate serious consequences such as dismissals has caused an outcry.

Unlocking value using digital technology requires today's leaders to transform their internal organization while navigating the broader ecosystem simultaneously. Similarly, they need to use digital technologies in ways that enable the creation of value but also recognize the potential for harm that can destroy value if risks are not appropriately mitigated. The good news is that academia has studied value creation and capture in organizational digital transformation (ODT) and digital business ecosystems (DBE) in great depth. The bad news is that to date, academia has provided limited insight into how organizations might manage the intersection between ODT and DBE to orchestrate business models that consider both 'me' and 'we'. That is the purpose of this chapter. By joining the forces of both research streams, our work aims to assess what empirical evidence and theoretical perspectives exist at their intersection and draw implications of our insights to guide practitioners in managing through this complexity.

Organizations, Ecosystems and What's in Between

ODT builds on the transformative impact of digital technologies on incumbent organizations (Vial, 2019) to refine the nature of business strategy (Bharadwaj, El Sawy, Pavlou, & Venkatraman, 2013) and highlight the importance of self-understanding of organizations (Wessel, Baiyere, Ologeanu-Taddei, Cha, & Jensen, 2020). From a strategy perspective, ODT pushes beyond traditional processes to business models to unlock digital value (Soluk & Kammerlander, 2021) and offers new digital technologies that open up pathways for digital value creation (Vial, 2019).

The literature on DBEs originated in the strategic management domain (Moore, 1993) and benefited from connecting the theory of biological eco-systems to research on networked value chains (Iansiti & Levien, 2004). Here attention is primarily divided between digital platforms (Tiwana, 2014) and (digital) innovation ecosystems (Dattée, Alexy, & Autio, 2018) that can unlock digital value. Offering theoretical statements for the understanding of various ecosystems, researchers emphasized structures of interdependent organiza-tions (Adner, 2017), the balance of collaboration and competition (Hannah & Eisenhardt, 2018), and specific types of complements (Jacobides, Cennamo, & Gawer, 2018). Scholars then further illuminated the role of digital technol-ogies for spreading innovations across DBEs (Wang, 2021), while empirical evidence suggests that non-digital business ecosystems develop through ODT into DBEs (Tan, Ondrus, Tan, & Oh, 2020).

The ODT and DBEs research streams has evolved with only loose interac-tions (Nischak & Hanelt, 2019; Nischak, Hanelt, & Kolbe, 2017; Tan et al., 2020). We know digital technologies empower organizational networks in which organizations depend on each other's to unlock digital value, as outlined by various case studies (e.g., Hansen and Kien (2015), El Sawy, Amsinck, Kraemmergaard, and Lerbech Vinther (2016), Alfaro et al. (2019), or Du, Pan, Xie, and Xiao (2020)). We have also developed some preliminary frameworks that emphasize how one research stream refers to the other (e.g., Biedebach and Hanelt (2020) or Tanriverdi and Lim (2017)). However, even though initial work has shed some light on the intersection between ODT and DBEs, the research community has yet to find 'common ground'. In other words, a deeper understanding of the intersection of ODT and DBEs is required for future theory building to guide managerial practice. With this purpose in mind, we pose the following research question: What are shared theoretical founda-tions and practical implications on ODT's and DBEs' intersection?

Following the theoretical development methodology introduced by Leidner (2018), our research approach was also inspired by similar work done by Mendling, Pentland, and Recker (2020) that explores the intersection of business process management and digital innovation. As such, the subsequent section outlines our research method. Briefly, we first synthesize the existing knowledge at the intersection of both research streams to extract underlying assumptions in isolation and then derive convergent assumptions for both research streams and provide real-world examples for each assumption. We then assess where ODT and DBEs are in isolation, describe their intersection, derive four convergent assumptions, and present overarching propositions and managerial implications to orchestrate value creation and capture.

METHODOLOGY

Our research consisted of two phases (see Table 4.1). In Phase A, we conducted a structured literature review to ascertain that the identified research gap does indeed exist (vom Brocke et al., 2015) and is not, instead, a false assumption rooted in the limited perception of the authors. Following Leidner (2018) and Rivard (2014), the purpose of this assessing review was not to comprehensively summarize the literature on ODT and DBEs. Instead, the purpose was to capture and describe the research gap at their intersection and form a sound basis for our convergent assumptions. We reviewed the literature on what has already been done and discovered, based on guidelines by Templier and Paré (2018). We managed to identify "patterns in the research streams and uncover what is missing" (Leidner 2018, p. 554).

Leidner's (2018) proposition inspired phase B that a literature review may not always be sufficient to develop novel insights supporting theory development. The latter may occur if insights are offered beyond what the current literature has to say. As such, in this phase we performed a specific theorizing review to identify critical assumptions that converge ODT and DBEs, present real-world examples for each convergent assumption, and draw implications for practitioners. This involved uncovering the assumptions made in prior research, which 'is as much about understanding the importance of what is left unsaid as it is about interpreting what is said' (Leidner 2018, p. 562).

The assessing review (Phase A) followed a six-step process inspired by several literature review methodologies used in information systems research (Templier & Paré, 2018; vom Brocke et al., 2015; Webster & Watson, 2002). During this phase, a search of literature identified 336 articles and after screening the abstract for each, 50 were deemed to be directly related to the subject under consideration. An additional nine articles were added through forward and backward search of relevant papers. Our team refined the quality of our assessment through a full-text screening of all 59 articles. At this stage, we

Table 4.1   *Research methodology*

Phase	Methodological Approach	Steps per Phase	Methodological Guidance
Phase A	Assessing review (synthesize and describe)	a.1 Problem definition a.2 Literature search a.3 Screening for inclusion a.4 Quality assessment a.5 Data extraction a.6 Data interpretation	Webster and Watson (2002); vom Brocke et al. (2015); Templier and Paré (2018).
Phase B	Specific theorizing review (theorize and identify research gaps)	b.1 Iterative assumption extraction b.2 Discussion of extracted assumptions b.3 Proposal of convergent assumptions b.4 Derivation of managerial implications	Dubin (1978); Whetten (1989); Bacharach (1989); Leidner (2018); Rivard (2014).

excluded another 12 articles which did not fall within the scope of the study, e.g., due to a lack of relevance for the intersection of both research streams or an inappropriate study context (vom Brocke et al., 2015). Knowledge was extracted from the remaining 47 papers to clarify our understanding of ODT, DBEs, and their intersection and meaning, considering both research streams have a relevant but theoretically unsubstantiated intersection.

In Phase B, a four-step approach ensured we alternated between abstractions and specific instances as Rivard (2014) recommended to guide theory construction. Throughout this creative and analytical process, the authors aimed to use existing literature as a springboard toward a foundation for theory at the intersection of ODT and DBEs. A particular benefit of this work is its attention to the interrelationships of these two research streams, which have hardly been investigated to date. This phase began by two authors screening all 47 articles to identify assumptions, whereby one author focused on the intersection from the perspective of ODT and the other on the intersection from the perspective of DBEs. The authors discussed their respective lists of assumptions until they reached a consensus on a final assumption list. The third author was invited to participate in the next step, which included three rounds of discussions on the preliminary list of assumptions. The focus of these discussions was not to converge but rather to validate and identify additional unstated assumptions. A final list of convergent assumptions was formulated by identifying missing links between individual assumptions from ODT and the DBEs research streams. This list was presented and discussed with 11 IS scholars who validated our assumptions and provided feedback to refine our results. In the final step, the authors identified managerial implications by discussing each assumption as it related to organizational action using real-world examples.

FINDINGS

Results of the Assessing Review (Phase A)

Before discussing our observations of ODT and DBE literature in isolation, it is important to provide insights about the fuel that inspires both phenomena – specifically, emergent digital technologies. There was no widely accepted definition of digital technologies, instead digital technology was commonly used as an umbrella term for a combination of information, computing, communication, and connectivity technologies (Bharadwaj et al., 2013; Denner, Püschel, & Röglinger, 2018; El Sawy et al., 2016). Complicating any attempt at a single definition, digital technologies are still evolving rapidly, as technological progress and the recombination of existing digital technologies lead to ever new manifestations (Yoo, Boland, Lyytinen, & Majchrzak, 2012). Nevertheless, our review concluded that digital technologies share common characteristics including re-programmability, homogenization of data, self-referential nature (Yoo, Henfridsson, & Lyytinen, 2010), convergence, and generativity (Ciriello, Richter, & Schwabe, 2018; Yoo, 2013). We also found evidence that digital technologies that are not merely representations of the physical world but are able to create their own artifacts to which there is no physical counterpart shaping reality (Baskerville, Myers, & Yoo, 2020). This is consistent with the notion of ontologic reversal that embodies the creation and capture of digital value opportunities (Baskerville et al., 2020). With examples such as streaming music, movies, or series, digitally reading books, getting tickets, or receiving other documents, the opportunity is for digital artifact to be generated before or instead of a physical representation.

As it relates to the intersection of ODT and DBE, these characteristics of digital technologies increasingly blur traditional organizational and industry boundaries (Yoo et al., 2010) and support the growing consensus that digital technologies contribute to profound changes in society at large and in a wide variety of industries, asking and enabling incumbent organizations to transform (Vial, 2019). Scholars also explain the significant changes in value creation and capture as facilitated by the emergence of digital platforms (Tan et al., 2020; Vial, 2019). With the rise of ODT, scholars have labelled digital platforms as a vital sub-form of DBEs (Rietveld & Schilling, 2020) and used different theory angles (e.g., transaction costs or strategic management) to conceptualize their impact (Evans & Schmalensee, 2016; Parker, van Alstyne, & Choudary, 2016; Tiwana, 2014).

In the following, we present our synthesis of reviewed articles for both ODT and DBE in isolation as well as at their interaction. A list of analyzed articles is available in our supplemental materialsupplemental material.[1]

Organizational Digital Transformation (ODT) in Isolation

ODT literature explains the transformation of organizations driven by the adoption of digital technologies (Vial, 2019). Bharadwaj et al. (2013) propose the relevance of digital technologies beyond IT/IS strategy for the entire strategy of an organization. What is more, they can profoundly impact value creation and capture (Iansiti & Lakhani, 2020) as well as resolve the trade-offs that hinder unlocking digital value. Accordingly, digital innovation can have 'transformative effects' on incumbent organizations to achieve digital value (Fichman, Dos Santos, & Zheng, 2014; Nambisan, K. Lyytinen, A. Majchrzak, & M. Song, 2017; Oberländer, Röglinger, & Rosemann, 2021). Adopting digital technologies makes it possible to improve existing processes, products, and services and facilitates even more radical innovations (O'Reilly & Tushman M., 2013). This explains why digital technologies trigger wave upon wave of changes in the business world, such as transforming processes, customer offers, business models (Baiyere, Salmela, & Tapanainen, 2020; Soluk & Kammerlander, 2021), and organizational identities (Wessel et al., 2020). Ultimately, contributions propose ODT might be a 'highly dynamic process involving iterating between learning and doing' (Chanias et al. 2019, p. 17) while asking organizations for continuous change (Hinsen, Jöhnk, & Urbach, 2019).

Scholars have developed a multitude of definitions of ODT (Vial (2019), Chanias, Myers, and Hess (2019), Soluk and Kammerlander (2021), and Wessel et al. (2020)). At the end of Phase A, we developed a common understanding of ODT as 'an ongoing process to improve an organization through adopting digital technologies, enabling it to (re)define its value proposition. ODT involves dealing with dynamic strategy making, significant structural changes, and an emergent organizational identity'.

Research on ODT focuses on constructs of *individual organizations* that transform through their *adoption of digital technologies* to create new *value propositions*. Adopting digital technologies may enable new value propositions for existing customers and new customers (Hinings, Gegenhuber, & Greenwood, 2018). To date, ODT literature has tended to focus merely on individual aspects of digitally enhanced networks, such as the increased networking of value chains (Bilgeri, Wortmann, & Fleisch, 2017; Fuerstenau et al., 2019; Pelletier & Cloutier, 2019) or innovation cycles (Steiber, Alange, Ghosh, & Goncalves, 2020; Wang, 2021), while hardly accounting for aspects unique to ecosystems and their interaction with ODT. Though the profound impacts of DBEs tend to be neglected when considering ODT literature in isolation. Our review of literature supported the notion that digital technologies facilitate far-reaching business changes beyond established organizational parameters (Yoo et al., 2010; Yoo et al., 2012) and identified the following observations:

1. Organizations can extend their reach to new environments, while others beyond traditional industry boundaries can move into theirs. If these new arrivals are not approached as partners, they may quickly become competitors and a source of disruption (Blume, Oberländer, Roeglinger, Rosemann, & Wyrtki, 2020; Nadkarni & Prügl, 2021).
2. The need to explore beyond established business practices grows as customer expectations change through the adoption of digital technologies (Gregory, Kaganer, Henfridsson, & Ruch, 2018; B. Li, Li, & Liu, 2018). Thus, the relations between digital technologies and individual organizations fuel disruption, trigger strategic responses, and enable new paths of value creation (Vial, 2019).
3. ODT involves organizational complexity expressed in structural changes and organizational barriers beyond missing assets and capabilities (Mocker & Ross, 2018; Vial, 2019). Thus, the challenges of ODT often cannot be tackled with the resources of individual organizations, which is why they draw on their ecosystem. Therefore, organizations may need to adopt digital technologies to enable modularity, i.e., a standardized exchange of complements (Jacobides et al. 2018; Nadkarni and Prügl 2021).

Digital Business Ecosystems (DBE) in Isolation

DBE literature explains organizational networks that extend to business ecosystems where the definition of an ecosystem has matured by extending or rejecting existing theories from biological ecosystems (Bogers, Sims, & West, 2019; Moore, 1993). Business ecosystems literature contributes to the definition of spatial boundaries that separate it from other inter-organizational networks and relationships.

*   Organizations depend on other organizations' co-existence, e.g., through co-specialization and exchange of specific complements (Jacobides et al., 2018).
*   Organizations pursue a self-sustaining set of relationships within the ecosystem, e.g., through an ongoing balance of collaboration and competition in value creation and capture (Hannah & Eisenhardt, 2018).
*   The ecosystem is in ongoing co-evolution, e.g., through a continuing search for the alignment of organizations (Adner, 2017).
*   There is no single ecosystem in which an organization can interact. Instead, many overlap or comprise each other, corresponding to a holarchy of ecosystems (Wang, 2021).

The 'digital' component of DBEs emerged with the evolution of digital technologies (Nischak et al., 2017; Tan et al., 2020). DBEs represent a specific type of ecosystems that are supported by the construct of digital technologies (Tan et al., 2020) and can unlock digital value. While they are not exclusive to DBEs, three main propositions are noteworthy:

1. Modularity enables a standardized exchange of complements, which helps to explain the dependence on co-existence (Baldwin & Clark, 2000; Kallinikos, Aaltonen, & Marton, 2013). Organizations are thus bound together by the non-redeployability of their collective investments (Jacobides et al., 2018).
2. Generativity allows non-generic complements to facilitate new value propositions across different contexts (Adner, 2017; Yoo, 2013) – either unique or supermodular complements where the whole is more than the sum of its parts (Jacobides et al., 2018).
3. Reductions in transaction costs and the creation of network effects enabled by digital technologies are important factors to explain DBEs' economies of scale and scope (Iansiti & Lakhani, 2020; Rolland, Mathiassen, & Rai, 2018; Shapiro & Varian, 1999).

Scholars have also developed a multitude of definitions of DBE. We build on the work of (Adner, 2017), (Jacobides et al., 2018), and (Tan et al., 2020) to define a DBE as 'a set of organizations that interact in a standardized exchange of non-generic complements in both the production and consumption of a focal value proposition. Digital technologies may facilitate both the exchange of and the complements themselves. Moreover, there is a notion of value co-creation (including consumers), whereby organizations balance cooperation to create and competition to capture value in a nascent environment.'

Research on DBE focuses on constructs that define groups of organizations (e.g., industries) and are transforming through their *adoption of digital technologies, the goals of individual organizations within DBEs, the complex dependencies within DBEs*, and the *interdependencies of the goals of different organizations* (Bogers et al., 2019; Zhu, Li, Valavi, & Iansiti, 2018). Adopting digital technologies enable how DBEs evolve through the creation of digital innovation (c.f. Dattée et al. (2018) or Nambisan et al. (2017)). To date, DBE literature has tended to focus on how this innovation diffuses through ecosystems (Wang, 2021) but focusing on understanding these networks of organizations, literature currently lacks an explanation for how DBEs influence ODT of individual organizations as well as DBEs that emerge or transform through the ODT of individual organizations. Like ODT, DBE literature offers empirical support that ODT and DBEs have a valuable intersection (Nischak et al., 2017;

Tan et al., 2020; Vial, 2019). This intersection with ODT may hold answers to improve our understanding of DBEs.

The Intersection of ODT and DBE

The intersection of ODT and DBEs has historical roots in advancing IT-based networking of value chains (Fredriksson & Vilgon, 1996) that has been used to shed light directly on the interplay between ODT and DBEs. IS scholars tend to focus on how organizational adoption of digital technologies enables DBEs to emerge (Aragon, Alonso-Zarate, & Laya, 2018; Nischak et al., 2017). Another phenomenon frequently observed is how partnerships and platforms enable organizations to join forces to meet the challenges of ODT (El Sawy et al., 2016; Hansen & Kien, 2015; Stamas, Kaarst-Brown, & Bernard, 2014) and transform line value chains and markets (L. Li, Su, Zhang, & Mao, 2018). Research has also provided insights on how digital innovation changes the relationships of individual organizations within existing ecosystems, referring to the example of Sony Ericsson (Selander, Henfridsson, & Svahn, 2010). Below is a list of insights that emerged from our assessing review of the inter-section of ODT and DBE.

- Characteristics of digital technologies (e.g., modularity, generativity) foster the ongoing reconfiguration and recombination of complements in changing environments (Karim & Capron, 2016).
- Organizations build IS-enabled capabilities to survive within ecosystem competition (Tanriverdi & Lim, 2017). Such capabilities allow organizations to create specific complements (Jacobides et al., 2018; Yoo, 2013).
- Partnerships play a vital role in generating IT-enabled value propositions (Ye & Agarwal, 2003) to sustain competitive advantage (Dong, Xu, & Zhu, 2009). Organizations partner up to exchange specialized resources and, in doing so, compensate for the lack of specific assets and capabilities (Berghaus & Back, 2017).
- Digital platforms provide an infrastructure for exchanging complements, serve as a marketplace, and foster recombination (Benlian, Kettinger, Sunyaev, & Winkler, 2018; Fuerstenau et al., 2019; Hein et al., 2019; Hein et al., 2020). Platforms challenge linear supply chains (Parker et al., 2016) and extend the managerial practice to include collaborators and comple-mentors in addition to competitors, suppliers, and customers (Shapiro & Varian, 1999).
- Digital platforms require different governance and orchestration mech-anisms (Mukhopadhyay & Bouwman, 2019). Empirical platform litera-ture frequently focuses on an actor within a DBE (e.g., Google, Apple, Facebook, Amazon, Alibaba, Tencent) who occupies a central position

as sponsor or owner of a digital platform (Fink, Shao, Lichtenstein, & Haefliger, 2020).

• The Identification of the roles that organizations may play in their eco-systems (Biedebach & Hanelt, 2020), including coordination and control mechanisms (Adner, 2017) and a balance of value creation and capture (Teece, 2018).

• DBEs are innovation accelerators (Henfridsson & Yoo, 2014; Wang, 2021) where multiple organizations collaborate on recombining resources (W. Li, Liu, Belitski, Ghobadian, & O'Regan, 2016) and implement business changes in digital products, services, or processes. Multiple studies tested the hypothesis on the advantages of value co-creation (Kim, 2018; Taylor, Hunter, Zadeh, Delpechitre, & Lim, 2020) for ODT in an evolving envi-ronment (Thomson, Kamalaldin, Sjodin, & Parida, 2021). Examples are buyer-supplier collaborations that lead to new customer offerings (Ayala et al., 2020; Kathuria, Karhade, & Konsynski, 2020), the LEGO group lever-aging digital platforms for co-creating products with consumers (El Sawy et al., 2016), or the paper company Mohawk using cloud computing to share resources with multiple other organizations to provide new offerings (Stamas et al., 2014).

In summary, the intersection of ODT and DBEs is rich in literature, but con-tributions exploring it theoretically and providing practical implications and recommendations are still few and far between. Our review concluded that few publications shed light on the need for theory development to explain the intersection, and empirical statements are 'rich in detail but strictly bounded in space or time' (Bacharach 1989, p. 500). Examples include Tan et al. (2020), who analyzed the Korean pop industry and studied how an existing business ecosystem relies on ODT to advance into a DBE, and Biedebach and Hanelt (2020) who identified archetypes of organizations within DBEs but do not explain how those archetypes came to be or why they are essential. With regard to theory development, there has been some progress to date, for example, Vial (2019) proposes that the challenges of ODT may be resolved by moving to ecosystems for the creation of joint value propositions. In response, (Wang, 2021) presented a theory on how innovation impacts DBEs in part-whole relationships that represent a holarchy – an ecosystem (whole) which in turn consists of several levels of sub-ecosystems (parts), e.g., individ-ual organizations.

Results of the Theorizing Review (Phase B)

Following the four steps outlined in Phase B of our methodology, our analy-sis coalesced around four convergent assumptions (Table 4.2) related to the intersection between ODT and DBE. This section of the chapter elaborates on the convergence of these respective assumptions and explains why they represent a 'missing link' between existing research streams in ODT and DBEs, following the example of Mendling et al. (2020). It is worth noting that these assumptions do not represent an exhaustive set of assumptions within both research streams, and we do not mean to suggest that something is 'misunderstood'. Instead, we derive these convergent assumptions (CAs) along with real-world examples to take the first step towards explaining why, where, and how research on ODT and DBEs intersect (Bacharach, 1989) and what implications arise for practitioners.

CA1: ODT requires and enables resource-sharing in DBEs

ODT literature tends to view the challenge of organizations' digitally-enabled value creation by tackling requirements for additional resources (i.e., assets and capabilities) (Nadkarni & Prügl, 2021; Vial, 2019). However, the adoption of digital technologies is non-trivial (Yoo et al., 2012). Where an individual organization cannot answer a demand for value creation by itself, it may need to leverage resources from DBEs and depend on others (Berghaus & Back, 2017; Nischak et al., 2017). Vice versa, if the organization in question develops valuable resources for digitally-enabled value creation, it can share these resources with others (Ayala et al., 2020). Due to the characteristics of digital technologies, combining resources can result in what has been defined as 'supermodular complements' (Jacobides et al., 2018). Supermodular complements refer to combinations of different resources that achieve higher benefits when their utilization is jointly coordinated rather than utilizing them in isolation. For example, two coordinated investments may achieve higher returns than the same two uncoordinated investments. This characteristic is often described through the phrase 'the whole being more than the sum of its parts' and explains why previously separate organizations may agree to join forces (Jacobides et al., 2018; Thomson et al., 2021). Either way, driven by the emergence of digital technologies, organizations increasingly depend on others for co-specialization and a modular, standardized exchange of resources (Jacobides et al., 2018). However, before sharing resources (as complements) for digitally-enabled value creation, organizations must build the (modular) digital infrastructure for that exchange as part of their ODT (Baldwin & Clark, 2000). As a result, organizations are bound together by the non-redeployability of their collective investments that form DBEs (Jacobides et al., 2018). Ultimately, DBEs are higher-level networks of organizations that depend on co-existence and share their resources for superior, digitally enabled value (co-)creation (Adner, 2017).

As an example, Du et al. (2020) have shown how *GSE*, a Chinese garment company, adopted advanced analytics technology in the context of their ODT.

Table 4.2   Derived convergent assumptions of ODT and DBEs

Nr.	Topic of Assumption	Assumption in ODT Literature	Assumption in DBEs Literature	The Missing Link in Assumptions	Convergent Assumption
1	**Resource** *interdependence*	Organizations require external resources for digitally-enabled value creation.	Organizations mutually share resources for digitally-enabled value (co-)creation.	Organizations can leverage resources from DBEs for ODT. Vice versa, DBEs require organizations to contribute resources for mutual, digitally-enabled value (co-)creation.	*ODT requires and enables resource-sharing in DBEs.*
2	**Coopetition** *dynamics*	Organizations must act due to digitally-driven competition and disruption.	Organizations balance collaboration and competition (coopetition).	Organizations engage in ODT to protect against disruption. In DBEs, organizations shield each other from digital disruption through coopetition.	*ODT seeks protection that can be provided by the coopetition dynamics of DBEs.*
3	*Structural* **evolution**	Organizations transform in an ongoing process fueled by digital technologies.	Organizations realign in an ongoing process required for digitally-enabled value (co-)creation.	Organizations need to continuously evolve in ODT and DBEs driven by digital technologies. Evolution is triggered if an organization facilitates new value propositions or (re-)aligns with others who have done so.	*DBEs require organizations to co-evolve, fueling their ongoing ODT.*

Nr.	Topic of Assumption	Assumption in ODT Literature	Assumption in DBEs Literature	The Missing Link in Assumptions	Convergent Assumption
4	*Locus of **control***	Organizations need to overcome hierarchy-based value creation and static control paradigms.	Organizations are engaged in ecosystem-based value (co-) creation and dynamic holarchies.	Organizations need to develop dynamic control for activities across DBEs. That offers a way forward for hierarchy-based control mechanisms, which ODT aims to overcome.	*DBEs facilitate dynamic control structures that organizations need to develop within ODT.*

Then, *GSE* shared these analytics resources to orchestrate a network of organizations in which they seized their partners' production facilities to create novel value propositions. *GSE* and its partners cooperated to unlock supermodular complements. Thus, ODT and DBEs intersect when sharing resources to solve the challenges of digitally enabled value (co-)creation. Asadullah, Faik, and Kankanhalli (2020) provide a further example of Singaporean e-commerce platforms illustrating how digital platforms create the basis for the mutual exchange of resources in a DBE (Asadullah et al., 2020). The authors show how multiple small and medium-sized e-commerce companies in Singapore leveraged digital platforms for the mutual exchange of infrastructural, informational, and reputational resources to develop new products and services. Thus, these e-commerce companies used digital platforms (as one form of DBEs) to access necessary resources for their ODT.

CA 2: ODT seeks protection that can be provided by the coopetition dynamics of DBEs

ODT literature outlines the urgency to act due to increased digitally-driven competition. The unfathomability of digital disruption may 'hit' organizations' systems of value creation as exogenous shocks (Blume et al., 2020; Schoemaker, Heaton, & Teece, 2018). Particularly, linear value chains are perceived as being under 'attack' by digital competitors or entire DBEs (Iansiti & Lakhani, 2020). Against this backdrop, ODT emboldens organizations to act and seek protection against digitally-driven competition and disruption, e.g., by creating new digital value streams (Stelzl, Röglinger, & Wyrtki, 2020). Joining organizations to balance collaboration and competition leads to a dynamic environment of *coopetition* that can offer a shield to disruptions in a nascent ecosystem (Hannah & Eisenhardt, 2018; Jacobides et al., 2018). If another organization is disrupted or withdraws resources that complement a DBE, the respective DBE's overall value (co-)creation is hampered. To some extent, the ecosystem shares a fate in that it has to replace the complements for the benefit of all parties, even in cases where some organizations are competitors for certain value propositions or complements (Iansiti & Levien, 2004). Therefore, organizations within a DBE have the incentive to protect each other, even if they are partly in competition. In other words, the ecosystem is only as strong as its weakest link.

For example, (Stamas et al., 2014) have examined how Mohawk, a paper company, used DBEs to transform its business model when it was threatened with disruption through digital media. Mohawk adopted cloud technologies during their ODT to facilitate new forms of value co-creation with partners, some of which were previously competitors. In doing so, they protected their business models against disruption due to their diversity and shared interest in co-creation with others. Hence, ODT and DBEs intersect where organizations shield each other against disruption and enable digital value streams through coopetition. Cozzolino, Corbo, and Aversa (2021) further exemplify how different advertising companies reacted to new market entrants. Viewing these digital advertising companies from 2005 to 2019, the authors show how incumbents overcame the inherent risk of being disrupted and the challenges of ODT. Here incumbents engaged new platform-based market entrants by carefully balancing collaboration and competition. Using the example of advertising companies, the authors show how the challenges of ODT can be countered by thoughtfully balancing both in a DBE.

CA 3: DBEs require organizations to co-evolve, fuelling their ongoing ODT

ODT literature considers an organization's evolution by adopting digital technologies and altering positions within their environment (Riasanow, Jaentgen, Hermes, Boehm, & Krcmar, 2020). Fueled by the development of digital technologies, ODT is an ongoing (and potentially never-ending) process (Chanias et al., 2019; Hinsen et al., 2019). Furthermore, by offering new resources as complements, an organization changes its alignment to others within DBEs (Biedebach & Hanelt, 2020; Jacobides et al., 2018). Thus, re-alignment across organizations and, thereby, the ODT of other organizations within these DBEs is triggered. Consequently, DBEs require organizations to co-evolve and follow an ongoing process of ODT (Selander et al., 2010; Tan et al., 2020). In other words, organizations are driven by digital technologies and continuously (re-)align themselves to changing digital value streams and their altered complements. Thus, individual organizations transform with changing DBEs, and vice versa.

To give an example, we refer to Tan et al. (2020): The ODT of companies of the Korean pop industry began with individual organizations in the same industry adopting digital technologies to democratize content delivery within an ecosystem. The subsequent adoption of digital technologies by content providers, content creators, and content users led to their integration on digital platforms. Ultimately, all existing organizations had to realign themselves and co-evolve in a DBE. Hence, ODT and DBEs intersect where digital technologies drive evolution by facilitating new value propositions. Hansen and Kien (2015) provide a further example of how Hummel, a European sports fashion company, utilized an ecosystem of partners to meet the challenges of ODT and provide a holistic omnichannel experience for its customers. Thereby, Hummel leveraged its broad network of partners for a globally aligned online branding. In this process, Hummel created a platform on which licensors, retailers, and other partners could integrate to provide a unified user experience for customers. This example shows how Hummel's ODT and the development of a digital platform led to the co-evolution of partners within Hummel's DBE, that adopted Hummel's platform solution and changed how they create value.

CA 4: DBEs facilitate dynamic control structures that organizations need to develop within ODT

ODT is predicated on the proposition that existing hierarchy-based value creation structures must be overcome (Kapoor, 2018). Organizations within ODT thus need to transform static control paradigms and break silos of functional units to enable new value propositions (Vial, 2019; Wessel et al., 2020). However, overcoming existing control paradigms does not relieve an organization from the general need to control its activities. In this course, ecosystem-based value creation features holarchies – where every ecosystem forms a part of the whole of other higher-level ecosystems (Henfridsson & Yoo, 2014; Wang, 2021). In consequence, activities in DBEs influence each other throughout the DBEs holarchy. Thus, DBEs facilitate organizations to build dynamic control structures for their activities and ensure a coherent outcome for themselves and other organizations. For example, another organization might be a partner in one and a competitor in another DBE (Karhu, Gustafsson, Eaton, Henfridsson, & Sørensen, 2020; Karhu & Ritala, 2020). The dynamic control paradigms of holarchies offer a way forward to advance the static control paradigms which ODT aims to overcome during the transformation from hierarchical- to ecosystem-based value (co-)creation (Jacobides et al., 2018).

Wang (2021) illustrated DBEs' part-whole relations in the tech landscape. Where so-called category DBEs of cloud computing or e-commerce form a holarchy's top-level, business DBEs of Amazon, eBay or Alibaba form a lower level. Throughout ODT, an organization may face the question of how to engage with partners for which value propositions in which DBE. For example, an organization can build a marketplace DBE competing with the

Amazon marketplace and simultaneously partner with the latter for different value propositions. However, the organization still must control its activities for a coherent collective outcome for value propositions to consumers and the other organizations within the overall e-commerce category ecosystem. Hence, ODT and DBEs intersect where organizations develop new control structures within their ODT to manage their activities across DBEs. Rövekamp, Ollig, Buhl, and Keller (2022) explain how an organization learns to switch control structures dynamically for engaging in different DBEs at a time. Viewing Dr. Oetker's (a globally active consumer good industry company) ODT journey from 2017 to 2021, they synthesize that Dr. Oetker started with a strong focus on competing to build digital platforms and hence control valuable resources for value co-creation. However, the ODT journey of Dr. Oetker made relatively slow progress until the organization changed its approach to dynamic control structures and started to differentiate between individual DBEs. Thus, they differentiated their control structures depending on different goals per DBE. For example, Dr. Oetker decided to aim for a role in developing control structures that shape the DBE in an ecosystem forming around the value proposition of adaptable recipes by using AI-based forecasting of alternative ingredients. In another example, the distribution of recipes, they adopted existing control structures from social media platforms to complement these ecosystems in value co-creation rather than pushing for their own digital platforms as at the beginning of their ODT journey.

DISCUSSION

At the intersection of ODT and DBEs and inspired by the four derived convergent assumptions, we suggest an overarching proposition: *ODT and DBEs are a means to an end of the other, which is to say that there is a cyclical and iterative interrelationship between the two*, as shown in Figure 4.1. On the one hand, explaining organizational networks that form an ecosystem requires looking at *why*, *how*, and *when* individual ODTs (inside-out perspective) transform to and with DBEs (Bacharach, 1989). Thus, contributing organizations and individual digital transformations significantly influence a DBE (Tan et al., 2020). On the other hand, digital technologies significantly influence the constellation of existing DBEs (outside-in perspective) and trigger the digital transformation of the involved individual organizations (Jacobides et al., 2018; Tan et al., 2020).

The fundamental practitioner implication that arises from this overarching proposition is that *organizations may not be able to master the challenges of digital transformation without DBEs*. For researchers, this implication requires scholars to move beyond conceptualizing DBEs as merely 'some kind of interconnectivity that comes with digital' and recognize the need for deeper reflection on its theoretical embedding and statements. ODT and DBEs are not separate means, they are a collective mean to an end required to survive and thrive in the digital age. As illustrated in Figure 4.1, ODT is a business practice that leverages digital technologies as a way to embrace an inside-out perspective. At the end of the day, every organization is composed of processes, systems, tools, and products that determine how the organization thinks and acts. So, the design and use of digital technologies must consider what already exists, embrace what still works, and thoughtfully change what is obsolete. DBE is a business practice that leverages digital technologies to counteract the

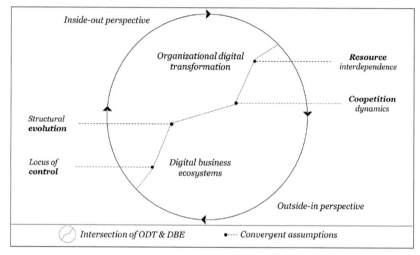

Figure 4.1   The shared foundation at the intersection of ODT and DBE

bias inherent to inward focus by deliberately challenging organizational-level assumptions to change the value proposition based on what is going on in the outside world. We relate this difference back to the chapter's introduction when we discuss the importance of balancing 'what's in it for me' with 'what's in it for we'.

The other key component of this illustration is the cyclical nature of the relationship between ODT and DBEs. Depicted by the arrows, we argue that organizations go through phases where they change their mode of thinking to identify new opportunities through imagination and creativity and incorporate discipline to execute the new opportunities most efficiently and effectively. When operating in a phase of DBE, organizations are encouraged to adopt a divergent thinking approach to generate creative ideas and explore possible solutions. After the process of divergent thinking from an outside-in perspective, organizations then organize and structure ideas and information around the existing set of processes, systems, tools, and products that define the way the organization thinks and acts. This thinking approach is synonymous with convergent thinking. This cyclical relationship allows ODT and DBE to be managed as a single 'mean to an end of the other' and effectively exploit digitally induced opportunities while addressing digitally induced challenges.

The crucial relationships between ODT and DBEs have not yet been fully explored. To pave the way to such an understanding, we argue that ODT and DBEs converge on four assumptions regarding *resources, coopetition dynamics, evolution*, and *control* that can be used to guide future research.

- *Interdependence* in leveraging and sharing *resources* requires adopting digital technologies and expediting digitally enabled value creation.
- Dynamics of *coopetition* where organizations balance their necessities to shield each other from disruption and enable new value streams by adopting digital technologies.
- Structural *evolution* driven by DBEs requires organizations to co-evolve in an ongoing ODT by adopting digital technologies and (new) value propositions.
- A new locus on dynamic *control* that manages activities across DBEs, especially as ODT is seeking new paradigms of control that transform existent and static paradigms of their 'value chain past'.

As illustrated by the line in Figure 4.1, ODT and DBE neither oppose each other nor run side by side. It is the intersection that lies between where new opportunities emerge. Our results support Chanias et al. (2019) in that managing this intersection is an ongoing process that continuously realigns ODT with other actors in DBEs (Adner, 2017). Chipotle's continuous use of TikTok to run campaigns such as #ChipotleLidFlip and #GuacDance and Google's track record for leveraging AI to raise its operational efficiency are an example of this. Our results also support and extend work by Soluk and Kammerlander (2021) as we found DBEs can facilitate and extend the transformation of organizational processes, products, and business models where the intersection allows DBEs to resolve some of ODT's severe challenges. The UN Glasgow Financial Alliance for Net Zero is a good example of how a DBE can influence legacy businesses by providing an outside-in perspective.

Taking the two perspectives one step further, we posit that incumbent organizations may start their ODT without a deliberate focus on DBEs, yet in doing so, learn that digitalization is 'a game played by partners'. Thus, organizations that embark on an ODT journey end up in collaborating in DBEs. Resistance to engage in DBEs, especially the willingness to share resources to open up new pathways of value creation (Vial, 2019), may result in ODT failure. Nevertheless, although examples of this can be found in empirical research

(Du et al., 2020; El Sawy et al., 2016; Stamas et al., 2014), so far there is no theoretical development to support this discussion. As such, future research is needed to explain why the intersection is important, what defines its effectiveness, and how organizations need to adapt (Bacharach, 1989; Whetten, 1989). Since ODT and DBEs will change organizations in the long term (Teubner & Stockhinger, 2020), continuing to study the advances in digital technologies will be fundamental to interlocking disparate research streams (Riasanow et al., 2020).

Finally, we conclude that our set of convergent assumptions are subject to several boundary conditions. First, they assume that a DBE exists from the outset of ODT, and we do not focus on new DBEs that may develop throughout ODT. Second, the first three assumptions do not account for the fact that an organization may engage in multiple DBEs simultaneously. Our four assumptions establish a foundation, further theorizing on ODT and DBEs is essential to understanding phenomena related to organizations, ecosystems, and digital technologies. Future research may either confirm or reject our proposed assumptions by way of building and testing theory.

IMPLICATIONS

Organizations must define what 'value' means at the intersection of their organization's digital transformation and related digital business ecosystems. Incumbent organizations will most likely have a 'dominant logic' that drives the way they have traditionally thought about the products, markets, business models, and performance – at the core of this logic is an assumption about how value is generated from the organizational perspective. This common way of thinking about business strategy and value generation acts like a cultural glue and anchoring point that is often misaligned to what is considered 'valuable' by a broader ecosystem of stakeholders. As such, it is imperative organizations recognize this dominant logic may need to be challenged. Returning to the example of the UN Glasgow Financial Alliance for Net Zero that raised US$130 trillion in 2022, the profitability implications of this commitment explain why internal resistance to joining the alliance might be expected but pushing beyond the organization, a redefinition of value will be important to encourage organizations to pursue it.

From a managerial point of view, we also draw implications related to each of the four assumptions.

1. Related to resource interdependence, practitioners may need to develop new budget practices to deliberately contribute resources to a DBE initiative as well as practices that determine when it is appropriate to access resources from a DBE and how those resources will be managed. Further,

it is recommended that practitioners embrace sharing existing or newly developed resources with a DBE from the outset of an ODT development. In other words, organizations are encouraged to think strategically about resource sharing and interdependence from the beginning of a digital innovation lifecycle.

2. Coopetition will be enhanced by organizations that seize strategic partnerships with partners and/or competitors to accelerate their ODT activities and success. Practitioners need to develop guidelines for how and when they want to focus on cooperation or competition throughout their ODT when engaging with other organizations within DBEs.

3. Organizations need to develop ODT as an ongoing business process, not treat it as a single strategic project with a defined end. DBEs are constantly evolving, and so developing ODT as a continuous business process is essential for organizations to remain viable in the long term. A critical component of the ongoing business process is to learn how to discover, design, and implement the right digital technologies that allow them to sense and seize new opportunities, reconfigure organizational routines, and scale business processes for growth and survival. Incumbent organizations are encouraged to explore practices inspired by innovation pioneers such as Google, Amazon, and Facebook, including design thinking, prototyping, and experimentation. To investigate further, these business practices are becoming commonly known as 'digital' product management.

4. Lastly, established organizational policies and procedures need to be made more flexible to ensure they balance the needs and wants of the ecosystem (e.g., coopetition, social and environmental value) with the needs and wants of the business (e.g., competition, profitability). This includes flexible controls for managing the provision of and access to resources.

CONCLUSION

By synthesizing academic thought leadership in ODT and DBE research streams, we reveal assumptions and managerial implications to guide organizations at their intersection. In many ways, doing this well requires organizations to fundamentally rethink their strategy and execute on value propositions by reengineering the way they do business. We provide seven practical questions that managers can use as a checklist to anchor your business as you attempt to dissolve the cultural glue that currently holds your business together.

1. Are you challenging orthodoxies as a way to abandon the old rules of success and find new ways to deliver value in co-creation with other organizations?

2. Do you know what resources to share and what resources to protect?
3. What resources do you require from others for your own ODT?
4. Are you collaborating with the right set of strategic partners?
5. Who is responsible for managing the business processes that enable digital transformation?
6. Is your organization investing in developing business practices related to 'digital' product management?
7. What organizational policies and procedures are preventing the business from embracing ecosystem opportunities?

In closing, it is essential to state that navigating this checklist is not for the faint of heart. Leading the intersection between digital transformation and business ecosystems requires courage as this work is not only difficult, but can also be dangerous. Dissolving cultural glue takes more than good strategy, day-to-day execution of a digital transformation agenda brings with it fundamental changes in mindset and business practices. Like the old fable of the tortoise and the rabbit, senior leaders and legacy business practices need time to adapt – so, slow and steady is key to winning this race.

NOTE

1.   https://figshare.com/s/7d3ba25d807c11df0672.

REFERENCES

Adner, R. (2017). Ecosystem as Structure. *Journal of Management*, *43*(1), 39–58. https://doi.org/10.1177/0149206316678451
Alfaro, E., Bressan, M., Girardin, F., Murillo, J., Someh, I., & Wixom, B. H. (2019). BBVA's Data Monetization Journey. *MIS Quarterly Executive*, *18*(2). Retrieved from https://aisel.aisnet.org/misqe/vol18/iss2/4
Aragon, B. M. de, Alonso-Zarate, J., & Laya, A. (2018). How connectivity is transforming the automotive ecosystem. *Internet Technology Letters*, *1*(1). https://doi .org/10.1002/itl2.14
Asadullah, A., Faik, I., & Kankanhalli, A. (2020). *Can Digital Platforms help SMEs Develop Organizational Capabilities? A Qualitative Field Study*. Retrieved from https://aisel.aisnet.org/icis2020/sharing_economy/sharing_economy/12
Ayala, N. F., Le Dain, M. A., Merminod, V., Gzara, L., Valle, E. D., & Germán, F. A. (2020). The contribution of IT-leveraging capability for collaborative product development with suppliers. *The Journal of Strategic Information Systems*, *29*(3), 101633. https://doi.org/10.1016/j.jsis.2020.101633
Bacharach, S. B. (1989). Organizational Theories: Some Criteria for Evaluation. *The Academy of Management Review*, *14*(4), 496. https://doi.org/10.2307/258555
Baiyere, A., Salmela, H., & Tapanainen, T. (2020). Digital transformation and the new logics of business process management. *European Journal of Information Systems*, *29*(3), 238–59. https://doi.org/10.1080/0960085X.2020.1718007

Baldwin, C. Y., & Clark, K. B. (2000). The Power of Modularity. *The Academy of Management Review*, *26*(1), 130. https://doi.org/10.2307/259400

Baskerville, R. L., Myers, M. D., & Yoo, Y. (2020). Digital First: The Ontological Reversal and New Challenges for Information Systems Research. *MIS Quarterly*, *44*(2), 509–23. https://doi.org/10.25300/MISQ/2020/14418

Benlian, A., Kettinger, W. J., Sunyaev, A., & Winkler, T. J. (2018). Special Section: The Transformative Value of Cloud Computing: A Decoupling, Platformization, and Recombination Theoretical Framework. *Journal of Management Information Systems*, *35*(3), 719–39. https://doi.org/10.1080/07421222.2018.1481634

Berghaus, S., & Back, A. (2017). *Disentangling the Fuzzy Front End of Digital Transformation: Activities and Approaches*. Retrieved from https://aisel.aisnet.org/icis2017/PracticeOriented/Presentations/4

Bharadwaj, A., El Sawy, O. A., Pavlou, P. A., & Venkatraman, N. (2013). Digital Business Strategy: Toward a Next Generation of Insights. *MIS Quarterly*, *37*(2), 471–82. https://doi.org/10.25300/MISQ/2013/37:2.3

Biedebach, M., & Hanelt, A. (2020). *Towards a Typology of Ecosystem Roles in the Era of Digital Innovation – An Inductive Empirical Analysis*. Retrieved from https://aisel.aisnet.org/icis2020/general_topics/general_topics/7

Bilgeri, D., Wortmann, F., & Fleisch, E. (2017). *How Digital Transformation Affects Large Manufacturing Companies' Organization*. Retrieved from https://aisel.aisnet.org/icis2017/PracticeOriented/Presentations/3

Blume, M., Oberländer, A. M., Roeglinger, M., Rosemann, M., & Wyrtki, K. (2020). Ex ante assessment of disruptive threats: Identifying relevant threats before one is disrupted. *Technological Forecasting and Social Change*, *158*, 120103. https://doi.org/10.1016/j.techfore.2020.120103

Bogers, M., Sims, J., & West, J. (2019). What Is an Ecosystem? Incorporating 25 Years of Ecosystem Research. *Academy of Management Proceedings*, *2019*(1), 11080. https://doi.org/10.5465/AMBPP.2019.11080abstract

Chanias, S., Myers, M. D., & Hess, T. (2019). Digital transformation strategy making in pre-digital organizations: The case of a financial services provider. *The Journal of Strategic Information Systems*, *28*(1), 17–33. https://doi.org/10.1016/j.jsis.2018.11.003

Ciriello, R. F., Richter, A., & Schwabe, G. (2018). Digital Innovation. *Business & Information Systems Engineering*, *60*(6), 563–69. https://doi.org/10.1007/s12599-018-0559-8

Cozzolino, A., Corbo, L., & Aversa, P. (2021). Digital platform-based ecosystems: The evolution of collaboration and competition between incumbent producers and entrant platforms. *Journal of Business Research*, *126*, 385–400. https://doi.org/10.1016/j.jbusres.2020.12.058

Dattée, B., Alexy, O., & Autio, E. (2018). Maneuvering in Poor Visibility: How Firms Play the Ecosystem Game when Uncertainty is High. *Academy of Management Journal*, *61*(2), 466–98. https://doi.org/10.5465/amj.2015.0869

Denner, M.-S., Püschel, L. C., & Röglinger, M. (2018). How to Exploit the Digitalization Potential of Business Processes. *Business & Information Systems Engineering*, *60*(4), 331–49. https://doi.org/10.1007/s12599-017-0509-x

Dong, S., Xu, S. X., & Zhu, K. X. (2009). Research Note —Information Technology in Supply Chains: The Value of IT-Enabled Resources Under Competition. *Information Systems Research*, *20*(1), 18–32. https://doi.org/10.1287/isre.1080.0195

Du, W., Pan, S. L., Xie, K., & Xiao, J. (2020). Data Analytics Contributes to Better Decision-Making Beyond Organizational Boundaries. *MIS Quarterly Executive*, *19*(2). Retrieved from https://aisel.aisnet.org/misqe/vol19/iss2/5

Dubin, R. (1978). *Theory building* (Rev. ed.). New York: Free Pr.

El Sawy, O., Amsinck, H., Kraemmergaard, P., & Lerbech Vinther, A. (2016). How LEGO Built the Foundations and Enterprise Capabilities for Digital Leadership. *MIS Quarterly Executive*, *15*(2). Retrieved from https://aisel.aisnet.org/misqe/vol15/iss2/5

Evans, D. S., & Schmalensee, R. (2016). *Matchmakers: The new economics of multisided platforms*. Boston, Massachusetts: Harvard Business Review Press.

Fichman, R. G., Dos Santos, B. L., & Zheng, Z. (2014). Digital Innovation as a Fundamental and Powerful Concept in the Information Systems Curriculum. *MIS Quarterly*, *38*(2), 329–43. https://doi.org/10.25300/MISQ/2014/38.2.01

Fink, L., Shao, J., Lichtenstein, Y., & Haefliger, S. (2020). The ownership of digital infrastructure: Exploring the deployment of software libraries in a digital innovation cluster. *Journal of Information Technology*, *35*(3), 251–69. https://doi.org/10.1177/0268396220936705

Fredriksson, O., & Vilgon, M. (1996). Evolution of inter-organizational information systems in industrial distribution: the cases of Luna and Pappersgruppen. *European Journal of Information Systems*, *5*(1), 47–61. https://doi.org/10.1057/ejis.1996.11

Fuerstenau, D., Rothe, H., Baiyere, A., Schulte-Althoff, M., Masak, D., Schewina, K., & Anisimova, D. (2019). *Growth, Complexity, and Generativity of Digital Platforms: The Case of Otto.de*. Retrieved from https://aisel.aisnet.org/icis2019/is_heart_of_innovation_ecosystems/innovation_ecosystems/12

Gregory, R., Kaganer, E., Henfridsson, O., & Ruch, T. J. (2018). IT Consumerization and the Transformation of IT Governance. *MIS Quarterly*. (42), 1225–53.

Hannah, D. P., & Eisenhardt, K. M. (2018). How firms navigate cooperation and competition in nascent ecosystems. *Strategic Management Journal*, *39*(12), 3163–92. https://doi.org/10.1002/smj.2750

Hansen, R., & Kien, S. S. (2015). Hummel's Digital Transformation Toward Omnichannel Retailing: Key Lessons Learned. *MIS Quarterly Executive*, *14*(2). Retrieved from https://aisel.aisnet.org/misqe/vol14/iss2/3

Hein, A., Schreieck, M., Riasanow, T., Setzke, D. S., Wiesche, M., Böhm, M., & Krcmar, H. (2020). Digital platform ecosystems. *Electronic Markets*, *30*(1), 87–98. https://doi.org/10.1007/s12525-019-00377-4

Hein, A., Weking, J., Schreieck, M., Wiesche, M., Böhm, M., & Krcmar, H. (2019). Value co-creation practices in business-to-business platform ecosystems. *Electronic Markets*, *29*(3), 503–518. https://doi.org/10.1007/s12525-019-00337-y

Henfridsson, O., & Yoo, Y. (2014). The Liminality of Trajectory Shifts in Institutional Entrepreneurship. *Organization Science*, *25*(3), 932–50. https://doi.org/10.1287/orsc.2013.0883

Hinings, B., Gegenhuber, T., & Greenwood, R. (2018). Digital innovation and transformation: An institutional perspective. *Information and Organization*, *28*(1), 52–61. https://doi.org/10.1016/j.infoandorg.2018.02.004

Hinsen, S., Jöhnk, J., & Urbach, N. (2019). Disentangling the Concept and Role of Continuous Change for IS Research – A Systematic Literature Review. *International Conference on Information Systems, Munich*. Retrieved from https://aisel.aisnet.org/icis2019/business_models/business_models/12/

Iansiti, M., & Lakhani, K. R. (2020). *Competing in the age of AI: Strategy and leadership when algorithms and networks run the world*. Boston MA: Harvard Business Review Press.

Iansiti, M., & Levien, R. (2004). Strategy as ecology. *Harvard Business Review*, *82*(3), 68–78.

Jacobides, M. G., Cennamo, C., & Gawer, A. (2018). Towards a theory of ecosystems. *Strategic Management Journal*, *39*(8), 2255–76. https://doi.org/10.1002/smj.2904

Kallinikos, J., Aaltonen, A., & Marton, A. (2013). The Ambivalent Ontology of Digital Artifacts. *MIS Quarterly*, *37*(2), 357–70. https://doi.org/10.25300/MISQ/2013/37.2.02

Kapoor, R. (2018). Ecosystems: broadening the locus of value creation. *Journal of Organization Design*, *7*(1), 39. https://doi.org/10.1186/S41469-018-0035-4

Karhu, K., Gustafsson, R., Eaton, B., Henfridsson, O., & Sørensen, C. (2020). Four Tactics for Implementing a Balanced Digital Platform Strategy. *MIS Quarterly Executive*, *19*(2). Retrieved from https://aisel.aisnet.org/misqe/vol19/iss2/4

Karhu, K., & Ritala, P. (2020). Slicing the cake without baking it: Opportunistic platform entry strategies in digital markets. *Long Range Planning*, 101988. https://doi.org/10.1016/J.LRP.2020.101988

Karim, S., & Capron, L. (2016). Reconfiguration: Adding, redeploying, recombining and divesting resources and business units. *Strategic Management Journal*, *37*(13), E54-E62. https://doi.org/10.1002/smj.2537

Kathuria, A., Karhade, P. P., & Konsynski, B. R. (2020). In the Realm of Hungry Ghosts: Multi-Level Theory for Supplier Participation on Digital Platforms. *Journal of Management Information Systems*, *37*(2), 396–430. https://doi.org/10.1080/07421222.2020.1759349

Kim, A. (2018). Doubly-Bound Relationship Between Publisher and Retailer: The Curious Mix of Wholesale and Agency Models. *Journal of Management Information Systems*, *35*(3), 840–65. https://doi.org/10.1080/07421222.2018.1481651

Leidner, D. (2018). Review and Theory Symbiosis: An Introspective Retrospective. *Journal of the Association for Information Systems*, *19*(06), 552–67. https://doi.org/10.17705/1jais.00501

Li, B., Li, X., & Liu, H. (2018). Consumer Preferences, Cannibalization, and Competition: Evidence from the Personal Computer Industry. *MIS Quarterly*, *42*(2), 661–78. https://doi.org/10.25300/MISQ/2018/13803

Li, L., Su, F., Zhang, W., & Mao, J.-Y. (2018). Digital transformation by SME entrepreneurs: A capability perspective. *Information Systems Journal*, *28*(6), 1129–57. https://doi.org/10.1111/isj.12153

Li, W., Liu, K., Belitski, M., Ghobadian, A., & O'Regan, N. (2016). E-Leadership through Strategic Alignment: An Empirical Study of Small- and Medium-sized Enterprises in the Digital Age. *Journal of Information Technology*, *31*(2), 185–206. https://doi.org/10.1057/jit.2016.10

Mendling, J., Pentland, B. T., & Recker, J. (2020). Building a complementary agenda for business process management and digital innovation. *European Journal of Information Systems*, *29*(3), 208–219. https://doi.org/10.1080/0960085X.2020.1755207

Mocker, M., & Ross, J. (2018). *Digital Transformation at Royal Philips*. Retrieved from https://aisel.aisnet.org/icis2018/education/Presentations/4

Moore, J. F. (1993). Predators and prey: a new ecology of competition. *Harvard Business Review*, *71*(3), 75–86.

Mukhopadhyay, S., & Bouwman, H. (2019). Orchestration and governance in digital platform ecosystems: a literature review and trends. *Digital Policy Regulation and Governance, 21*(4), 329–351. https://doi.org/10.1108/DPRG-11-2018-0067

Nadkarni, S., & Prügl, R. (2021). Digital transformation: a review, synthesis and opportunities for future research. *Management Review Quarterly, 71*(2), 233–341. https://doi.org/10.1007/s11301-020-00185-7

Nambisan, S., K. Lyytinen, A. Majchrzak, & M. Song (2017). Digital innovation management: reinventing innovation management research in a digital world. *Management Information Systems Quarterly, 41,* 223–38.

Nischak, F., & Hanelt, A. (2019). *Ecosystem Change in the Era of Digital Innovation – A Longitudinal Analysis and Visualization of the Automotive Ecosystem.* Retrieved from https://aisel.aisnet.org/icis2019/is_heart_of_innovation_ecosystems/innovation_ecosystems/5

Nischak, F., Hanelt, A., & Kolbe, L. M. (2017). *Unraveling the Interaction of Information Systems and Ecosystems - A Comprehensive Classification of Literature.* Retrieved from https://aisel.aisnet.org/icis2017/General/Presentations/20

O'Reilly, C., & Tushman M. (2013). Organizational Ambidexterity: Past, Present, and Future. *Academy of Management Perspectives, 27,* 324–38.

Oberländer, A. M., Röglinger, M., & Rosemann, M. (2021). Digital Opportunities for Incumbents – A Resource-centric Perspective. *The Journal of Strategic Information Systems, 30*(3), 101670. https://doi.org/10.1016/j.jsis.2021.101670

Parker, G., van Alstyne, M., & Choudary, S. P. (2016). *Platform revolution: How networked markets are transforming the economy - and how to make them work for you* (First edition). New York, London: W.W. Norton & Company.

Pelletier, C., & Cloutier, L. M. (2019). Conceptualising digital transformation in SMEs: an ecosystemic perspective. *Journal of Small Business and Enterprise Development, 26*(6/7), 855–76. https://doi.org/10.1108/JSBED-05-2019-0144

Riasanow, T., Jaentgen, L., Hermes, S., Boehm, M., & Krcmar, H. (2020). Core, intertwined, and ecosystem-specific clusters in platform ecosystems: analyzing similarities in the digital transformation of the automotive, blockchain, financial, insurance and IIoT industry. *Electronic Markets.* Advance online publication. https://doi.org/10.1007/s12525-020-00407-6

Rietveld, J., & Schilling, M. A. (2020). Platform Competition: A Systematic and Interdisciplinary Review of the Literature. *Journal of Management,* 0149206320969791. https://doi.org/10.1177/0149206320969791

Rivard, S. (2014). Editor's comments: The ions of theory construction. *MIS Quarterly, 38,* iii–xiii.

Rolland, K. H., Mathiassen, L., & Rai, A. (2018). Managing Digital Platforms in User Organizations: The Interactions Between Digital Options and Digital Debt. *Information Systems Research, 29*(2), 419–43. https://doi.org/10.1287/isre.2018.0788

Rövekamp, P., Ollig, P., Buhl, H. U., & Keller, R. (2022). How Dr. Oetker's Digital Platform Strategy Evolved to Include Cross-Platform Orchestration. *MIS Quarterly Executive, 21*(1) Article 5).

Schoemaker, P. J. H., Heaton, S., & Teece, D. (2018). Innovation, Dynamic Capabilities, and Leadership. *California Management Review, 61*(1), 15–42. https://doi.org/10.1177/0008125618790246

Selander, L., Henfridsson, O., & Svahn, F. (2010). TRANSFORMING ECOSYSTEM RELATIONSHIPS IN DIGITAL INNOVATION. *ICIS 2010 Proceedings.* Retrieved from https://aisel.aisnet.org/icis2010_submissions/138

Shapiro, C., & Varian, H. R. (1999). *Information rules: A strategic guide to the network economy*. Boston, Mass.: Harvard Business School Press.

Soluk, J., & Kammerlander, N. (2021). Digital transformation in family-owned Mittelstand firms: A dynamic capabilities perspective. *European Journal of Information Systems*, 1–36. https://doi.org/10.1080/0960085X.2020.1857666

Stamas, P. J., Kaarst-Brown, M. L., & Bernard, S. A. (2014). The Business Transformation Payoffs of Cloud Services at Mohawk. *MIS Quarterly Executive*, *13*(4). Retrieved from https://aisel.aisnet.org/misqe/vol13/iss4/3

Steiber, A., Alange, S., Ghosh, S., & Goncalves, D. (2020). Digital transformation of industrial firms: an innovation diffusion perspective. *European Journal of Innovation Management.* Advance online publication. https://doi.org/10.1108/EJIM-01-2020-0018

Stelzl, K., Röglinger, M., & Wyrtki, K. (2020). Building an ambidextrous organization: a maturity model for organizational ambidexterity. *Business Research.* Advance online publication. https://doi.org/10.1007/s40685-020-00117-x

Tan, F. T. C., Ondrus, J., Tan, B., & Oh, J. (2020). Digital transformation of business ecosystems: Evidence from the Korean pop industry. *Information Systems Journal*, *30*(5), 866–898. https://doi.org/10.1111/isj.12285

Tanriverdi, H., & Lim, S.-Y. (2017). *How to Survive and Thrive in Complex, Hypercompetitive, and Disruptive ecosystems? The Roles of IS-enabled Capabilities.* Retrieved from https://aisel.aisnet.org/icis2017/ResearchMethods/Presentations/9

Taylor, S. A., Hunter, G. L., Zadeh, A. H., Delpechitre, D., & Lim, J. H. (2020). Value propositions in a digitally transformed world. *Industrial Marketing Management, 87*, 256–63. https://doi.org/10.1016/j.indmarman.2019.10.004

Teece, D. J. (2018). Business models and dynamic capabilities. *Long Range Planning*, *51*(1), 40–49. https://doi.org/10.1016/j.lrp.2017.06.007

Templier, M., & Paré, G. (2018). Transparency in literature reviews: an assessment of reporting practices across review types and genres in top IS journals. *European Journal of Information Systems*, *27*(5), 503–50. https://doi.org/10.1080/0960085X.2017.1398880

Teubner, A., & Stockhinger, J. (2020). Literature review: Understanding information systems strategy in the digital age. *The Journal of Strategic Information Systems*, *29*(4), 101642. https://doi.org/10.1016/j.jsis.2020.101642

Thomson, L., Kamalaldin, A., Sjodin, D., & Parida, V. (2021). A maturity framework for autonomous solutions in manufacturing firms: The interplay of technology, ecosystem, and business model. *International Entrepreneurship and Management Journal.* Advance online publication. https://doi.org/10.1007/s11365-020-00717-3

Tiwana, A. (2014). *Platform Ecosystems*. Elsevier. https://doi.org/10.1016/C2012-0-06625-2

Vial, G. (2019). Understanding digital transformation: A review and a research agenda. *The Journal of Strategic Information Systems*, *28*(2), 118–44. https://doi.org/10.1016/j.jsis.2019.01.003

Vom Brocke, J., Simons, A., Riemer, K., Niehaves, B., Plattfaut, R., & Cleven, A. (2015). Standing on the Shoulders of Giants: Challenges and Recommendations of Literature Search in Information Systems Research. *Communications of the Association for Information Systems, 37.* https://doi.org/10.17705/1CAIS.03709

Wang, P. (2021). Connecting the parts with the whole: Toward an information ecology theory of digital innovation ecosystems. *MIS Quarterly*. Retrieved from https://socialdatascience.umd.edu/wp-content/uploads/2021/01/Ecosystems-2021-01-13-TitleAbstract.docx.pdf

Webster, J., & Watson, R. T. (2002). Analyzing the Past to Prepare for the Future: Writing a Literature Review. *MIS Q, 26.*

Wessel, L., Baiyere, A., Ologeanu-Taddei, R., Cha, J., & Jensen, T. (2020). Unpacking the difference between digital transformation and IT-enabled organizational transformation. *Journal of Association of Information Systems.* Advance online publication. https://doi.org/10.17705/1jais.00655

Wessel, L., Baiyere, A., Ologeanu-Taddei, R., Cha, J., & Jensen, T. (2020). Unpacking the difference between digital transformation and IT-enabled organizational transformation. *Journal of Association of Information Systems.* Advance online publication. https://doi.org/10.17705/1jais.00655

Whetten, D. A. (1989). What Constitutes a Theoretical Contribution? *The Academy of Management Review, 14*(4), 490. https://doi.org/10.2307/258554

Ye, F., & Agarwal, R. (2003). Strategic Information Technology Partnerships in Outsourcing as a Distinctive Source of Information Technology Value: A Social Capital Perspective. *ICIS 2003 Proceedings.* Retrieved from https://aisel.aisnet.org/icis2003/26

Yoo, Y. (2013). The Tables Have Turned: How Can the Information Systems Field Contribute to Technology and Innovation Management Research? *Journal of the Association for Information Systems, 14*(5), 227–36. https://doi.org/10.17705/1JAIS.00334

Yoo, Y., Boland, R. J., Lyytinen, K., & Majchrzak, A. (2012). Organizing for Innovation in the Digitized World. *Organization Science, 23*(5), 1398–1408. https://doi.org/10.1287/orsc.1120.0771

Yoo, Y., Henfridsson, O., & Lyytinen, K. (2010). Research Commentary —The New Organizing Logic of Digital Innovation: An Agenda for Information Systems Research. *Information Systems Research, 21*(4), 724–35. https://doi.org/10.1287/isre.1100.0322

Zhu, F., Li, X., Valavi, E., & Iansiti, M. (2018). Network Structures and Entry into Platform Markets. *SSRN Electronic Journal.* Advance online publication. https://doi.org/10.2139/ssrn.3310477

5. Frugal digital innovation: delivering healthcare services in rural India

Suchit Ahuja and Arman Sadreddin

INTRODUCTION

Digital innovation is the process of creation of new combinations of digital and physical components to produce novel products, services, and businesses (Yoo et al., 2010). Research on digital innovation has gained significant prominence recently in several academic disciplines as well as with practitioners and policymakers looking to exploit novel digital technologies, tools, and platforms to generate, diffuse, and appropriate value (Nambisan et al., 2017). Digital innovation is seen both as a process and as an outcome. As long as there are underlying digital technologies and digitized processes, the outcomes themselves do not need to be digital (Autio et al., 2018; Nambisan et al., 2017). Digital innovation has been criticized for being resource-intensive, exclusionary, and consumption-driven, often locking out marginalized populations and low-income consumers from the benefits (Chan et al., 2020; Heeks et al., 2014). Outcomes of digital innovation not only consider profit, but also technological, societal, governmental, environmental, sustainability, and social impact factors. Digital technologies interact with other aspects of the socio-technical environment to create economic, social, and environmental impacts. To achieve profitability, competitive advantage, and societal impact simultaneously, firms fuse digital technologies, platforms, and business models with physical resources and capabilities within ecosystems. The digital platform may remain proprietary, but the resources and capabilities that revolve around it are ordinary in value, scarcity, and distinctiveness (Fréry et al., 2015). It is the orchestration and fusion of these physical, social, and digital entities that leads to competitive advantage and broader impacts within and beyond the ecosystem (Ahuja & Chan, 2017).

Although research exists on how to address the needs of customers at the bottom of the pyramid, it is mainly focused on customers in low-income countries (Hall et al., 2012; Prahalad & Mashelkar, 2010). The COVID-19 pandemic has imposed resource constraints and shortages on high-income countries as well, forcing them to focus on more sustainable and inclusive ways of innovating (Harris et al., 2020). Frugal innovation thus provides a paradigm of innovation for working within resource constraints rather than an environment of accumulating resources.

From Frugal Innovation to Frugal Digital Innovation

Frugal innovation has mainly been practiced in emerging economies such as India, China, Brazil, and Kenya (Radjou et al., 2012) that face severe infrastructure, financial, social, and technological constraints. This paradigm redefines business models, reconfigures value chains, redesigns products to use available resources, and create more inclusive markets for users with affordability constraints, often in a scalable and sustainable manner (Bhatti & Ventresca, 2012). Frugal innovation is gaining widespread global acceptance in research, practice, and society. Frugal solutions are centered on the development of products, services, technologies, and business models that target affordability, minimize use of resources, and create simultaneous business, social, and/or environmental impact through innovation networks and ecosystems. Recent frugal innovation practices are also enabled by the digitalization of processes, products, and services, that leverage existing asset-light SMACIT (Social Media, Mobile, Analytics, Cloud, and IoT) technologies as well as new technologies such as AI, 3D printing, blockchain, etc. For example, Raspberry Pi is a computing device which consists of a single board and costs around US$35. It is the epitome of 'frugal' and 'miniature' product mindset required for frugal innovation and has seen applications ranging from teaching programming to high school students to deployment of robotics and scalable cloud networking equipment.

A reasonable amount of research has been conducted on the conceptualization of frugal innovation. Frugal innovation was initially defined as 'innovation with fewer resources to generate greater value for more consumers' (Radjou et al., 2012). This definition has evolved. Weyrauch and Herstatt (2016) showed that substantial cost reduction, concentration on core functionalities, and optimized performance level were three core components of product-based frugal innovation. Subsequent research showed that several other dimensions of frugal innovation emerged from the challenging socio-economic contexts within which frugal solutions were embedded (Sarkar & Mateus, 2022). These included socio-economic considerations around product-feature fit, product-price fit, and product-market fit as well as broader impacts related to societal and ecological outcomes. More recent discussion of frugal innovation has been taking a multidisciplinary perspective, exploring intersections among frugal and digital concepts (Ahuja, 2021), frugal innovation and strategic thinking (Santos et al., 2020), frugal innovation and sustainability (Albert, 2019), and frugal innovation during the pandemic (Corsini et al., 2021). In essence, frugal innovation has moved beyond its initial conceptualization as a purely cost-cutting concept, to a more comprehensive multidimensional concept. The core value proposition remains focused on affordability, accessibility, and simplicity within resource-constrained contexts and relative to other solutions that might be available. As these principles gain mainstream attention, frugal innovation is being adopted even in advanced economies where organizations and governments are now looking to leverage frugal innovation principles to achieve UN sustainable development goals (SDGs), drive sustainability, and transform into circular economic models. Thus, frugal innovation is moving from applications at the bottom-of-the-pyramid to applications that are relevant to customers in the middle-of-the-pyramid. Frugal innovation has the potential to strike a balance between cost, features, and value while creating a much broader impact than existing paradigms of innovation. Overall, frugal innovation is an evolving phenomenon in practice and a maturing concept in theory. Frugal innovation can be studied as an outcome (Brem et al., 2020), process (Knizkov & Arlinghaus, 2021), business model (Winterhalter et al., 2017), strategy (Santos et al., 2020), or accounting mechanism (Anderson & Lillis, 2011).

Given the increasing use of digital technologies for development of frugal solutions, frugal digital innovation can be seen as an extension of frugal innovation where digital technologies play a crucial, enabling role. Thus, frugal digital innovation is a combination of business innovation, information technology/systems innovation, and social innovation to deliver higher value products and services by redesigning processes, business models, ecosystems, and value chains to drive affordability and sustainability (Ahuja, 2021). The use of digital technologies coupled with frugal innovation practices provides firms with frugal capabilities along with opportunities for competitive advantage and strategic differentiation (Ahuja & Chan, 2019). The technologies alone do not lead to frugal solutions in environments with limited resources; it is rather the unit economics-based, 'frugalized' business models centered on affordability that drive those frugal solutions (Ahuja & Chan, 2019; McMurray & Waal, 2019). EzeRx, a startup in India is a great example of frugal digital innovation, as it has developed a device that can non-invasively detect anemia and other liver and lung diseases and has designed an affordable business model that provides this service at 35 Rupees (approx. US$0.50) per test to patients (https://ezerx.in/products/).

Frugal digital innovations seek to replace the multitude of inefficient, complex and pervasive digital innovations (e.g., digital tools, technologies, platforms, value chains, and business models) (Howell et al., 2018) grounded in previous traditional mindsets, instead serving previously underserved parts of the population. Like other digitized solutions, frugal digital products and services take advantage of underlying affordances of digital technologies, platforms, and infrastructures (Nambisan et al., 2019) to innovate in resource-constrained contexts enabling value co-creation and distribution. Frugal digital innovation often develops in ecosystems with physical, digital, and social actors and transactions (Agarwal & Brem 2021; Ahuja, 2021). Frugal digital innovation ecosystems consist of firms, entrepreneurs, government, non-government agencies (NGOs), citizen volunteers, and other entities that develop and promote 'frugal solutions' rooted in constraints (Ahuja, 2021). For example, the affordable solution 'M-Pesa' in Kenya has enjoyed unprecedented success with adoption by more than 70 percent of the population (Van Hove & Dubus, 2019), especially those who do not have access to a bank account. M-Pesa is a simple mobile payment platform that works via SMS and does not require expensive 4G/5G mobile data or apps.

Exploring New Avenues

There is much remaining to be analyzed regarding the evolution of a frugal platform ecosystem, building upon previous studies (Ahuja, 2021; Ahuja & Chan, 2019). The development of such ecosystems is full of challenges, both positive and negative, that force them to find peculiar, locally grounded solutions to problems that are rarely seen elsewhere (George et al., 2016). This chapter addresses this gap in the literature and derives insights from a case study of a healthcare platform ecosystem in India that is working towards delivery of last-mile healthcare services to remote and rural populations. It aims to broaden the discussion on how platform ecosystems can drive both profitability as well as societal value while being committed to innovating responsibly in challenging contexts (Ahuja et al., 2023; Knizkov & Arlinghaus, 2020).

RURALHEALTH CASE

RuralHealth was founded to address the healthcare services delivery gap in rural areas. Although healthcare is relatively accessible in urban areas in India, rural areas suffer higher costs of service delivery. RuralHealth strategically addresses this issue with its digital platform ecosystem for simple, affordable, and community-driven solutions. Before RuralHealth, with no universal healthcare coverage, there was an extreme shortage in the supply of health services to poor, rural, and remote communities. It was impossible to provide services in these areas that suffered from illiteracy and a lack of access to technology. Government did not have data regarding neo- and post-natal care, nor did it know how to manage contagious diseases. There was a growing threat of chronic diseases. On the demand side, cost and difficulty of access were major factors that prevented these populations from seeking healthcare services. Government programs for health were unable to deliver last-mile care. Despite having a huge number of community workers (ASHAs), ASHAs found it difficult to deliver care and collect data in an efficient and timely manner. They still relied on field notes and memory. The high cost of travel to city hospitals was also creating barriers. Compounding the problem, private doctors and hospitals saw rural communities as less lucrative and were therefore less likely to invest in these areas.

'The whole premise of starting RuralHealth was to provide affordable and accessible healthcare to the last mile using technology intervention. There is a huge demand and supply gap in the rural space, especially when it comes to healthcare. And the only way we would be able to solve that problem is to use technology effectively, in an optimized way so that whatever the resources in terms of the doctors, paramedics, and others, they are used effectively in delivering healthcare.' (Founder)

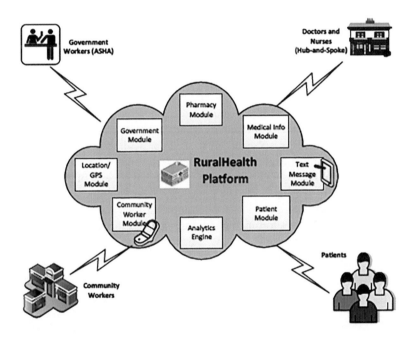

Figure 5.1   RuralHealth platform and ecosystem participants

RuralHealth encountered a multi-pronged dilemma. The cost of healthcare on the supply side kept rising due to the difficulty of delivering care at the last mile in remote areas. The cost on the demand side must be kept at affordable levels due to the low income levels of the patient communities. It was difficult to find well-educated, trained nurses and doctors in these areas and communities. Some ASHA workers had been trained as tertiary-care nurses by government, but this was not enough. Tools and technologies from city-based contexts could not be applied in rural areas. The government started to shift to cellphone-based data collection, but due to poor cellular coverage and non-existent Wifi coverage, it was difficult to work with them. Also, not all ASHA workers could afford to buy a phone or interact with it in an English language interface.

RuralHealth decided to address these issues with a platform solution that was able to connect various stakeholders physically, digitally, and socially. RuralHealth did not have any funds to roll out healthcare services directly to the public. It had to spend significant time and effort building a grassroots-driven ecosystem and then adding capabilities to its platform that addressed the needs of the participants of the ecosystem.

Establish Affordable Business Model, Resolve Existing Tensions (Market Creation)

RuralHealth defined itself as a for-profit social enterprise with a mission to enable access to healthcare services. It received funding from a social impact incubator and ran weekly pilot Rural Healthcare Clinics (around 2014) where it physically brought resident doctors from the city to rural areas where they interacted with patients, screening them using basic diagnostic tests. For rural villagers, this model represented an affordable and accessible option that ensures they do not lose a day's wages plus the travel costs of accompanying family members.

However, there were pressures to ensure that their focus on affordability does not create barriers to funding and long-term sustainability. The pressure of being cost-effective and proving that their solution was sustainable for investors was a major challenge.

> 'We are a for-profit entity and we got the initial funding...but the proving of the business model was difficult initially...proving of the business model was really tough...because how do you identify the revenue model? How do you ensure that the patients are willing to pay for the services and they can afford those services as well? So, that really took time. There are hardly any for-profit sustainable business models in India in terms of healthcare. So, we have learnt through the hard way.' (CEO)

When RuralHealth was founded, India did not have universal healthcare insurance. The system was fragmented, including various pay-for care provider services with little to no quality assurance. In that context, RuralHealth's

Figure 5.2   Rural health clinic

Figure 5.3   Van to transport doctors and nurses

initial business model would provide healthcare services to rural populations at affordable costs, but would also direct revenue away from doctors and care providers in nearby cities. The state government-run healthcare centers and services would also suffer from loss of paying patients. RuralHealth needed to resolve these demand-side and supply-side issues simultaneously. The CEO of RuralHealth illustrates these challenges.

> 'In India, it is difficult to prove your revenue model. Our investors were cautious about this. This is the most difficult thing to achieve, you have to bring people affected by your services to the same table. It is not easy to convince government officers that we can be successful. The doctors and hospitals in the adjacent areas will suffer losses if these rural patients stop going to them. We had to work with them to give them assurance of our business model. Government clinics would also need to be integrated in the future. It was tough to start.' (CEO)

Leverage Digital Technology to Meet Immediate Needs

The weekly rural clinics were successful, but there was still a data gap issue to solve. The doctors, nurses, and pharmacists could not keep track of the patients from one week to the next on paper files. Thus, a local firm was hired to help develop a SaaS-based platform to handle workflows and processes with appropriate modules and security settings. The platform was digitally linked to various biomedical equipment to seamlessly transfer data for plug-and-play functionality. It stored reports of image-based data and made them available at the point of care. It allowed for centralized monitoring of key metrics such as doctors' attendances and treatments prescribed. The RuralHealth platform enabled effective communication and data transfer between rural clinics and city-based hospitals. A business analyst described the platform and its modules.

> 'We built a cloud hosted platform, which captures the entire flow of the patient right from the last mile, from remote locations like villages, etc. The data is captured on smartphones by community health workers who are actually members picked up from the rural community, mostly women in the age range of 22 to 50 years of age, who are trained on technology and healthcare ...We did this because turnaround time in case of ASHAs and the pregnant mothers is pretty high because from the information captured by ASHAs on a hand written note, by the time it reaches the doctor, in many cases they are not able to quickly react to any high risk pregnancies and issues whereas in our case, since everything is digitized, the reaction time is pretty quick. So, we are able to quickly identify any high-risk pregnancies or any issues and take precautionary measures, so, thereby reduction of MMR and IMR.' (Business Analyst)

Embrace Constraints, Repurpose Resources

RuralHealth faced many technological constraints, especially around rugged, remote locations. RuralHealth had to design its hardware, software, data protocols, and other equipment in a customized manner and then train the end-users. Furthermore, due to financial constraints, it was impossible to provide all ASHA workers with technology devices and training. RuralHealth hired additional community health workers from within target communities. They picked women who were more educated than average and also had a strong understanding of local cultural norms and beliefs.

'These health workers are our own employees; they are not ASHA workers … they work with the ASHA workers of the government for various information gathering and optimization. The doctors are also on our payroll in a combination like full time, part time, consultants … depending on the type of need which we have. So, that's the arrangement we have with these people.' (CEO)

'Just to give an example, when we introduced smartphones to be given to these health workers, in their life they had never seen a phone … let alone a smartphone. So, when we did a project on mother and childcare, they were supposed to enter roughly around 50 sets of data … and we did some research on how much time it takes to enter the data on a paper versus a tablet versus a smart phone. And around one and half years back, the time taken to enter the data on smartphone was double the time taken on a manual paper. Within a year and a half, it has totally reversed, meaning that the time taken on smart phone is almost one third the time that they need to enter the data on paper. So, because of the training which we have given to these people, these health workers, initially there was lot of inhibition, they were thinking that they can't use and handle phones - like even a small swipe on a smart phone was very difficult for them because we had to consider the case like their hands are sweaty or having dust and other issues. So, we had some issues on the smartphone behaviour as well in the rural areas, in heat, dust, sweat … we managed all of that.' (Business Analyst)

Digitalize Services Inclusively, Co-Create Affordable Value

RuralHealth's platform was designed to capture end-to-end workflow of patients and their interactions with doctors. This was done to capitalize on the opportunity to generate historic patient data that could be tracked over time to provide timely health interventions.

'The platform comprises of a web-based version that has the entire gamut of right-from-patient registration, billing, admin section, inventory, pharmacy admin that captures all the data, data analytics like what is the patient footfall, what kind of diseases, what is the age profile of that, what is the terrain in that area, how many clinics are there, all of that. So, that's the admin side. Then on the clinical side it captures the various vitals of the patients, how many times this patient has visited, what kind of prescriptions, medicines and all of that.' (Business Analyst)

Figure 5.4   Telemedicine

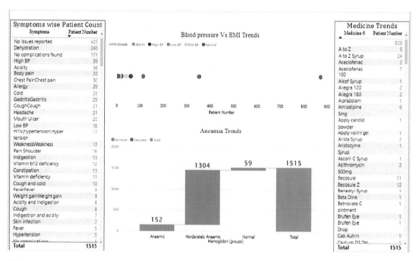

Figure 5.5   Patient chart

RuralHealth designed its platform to be modularized. This meant that the underlying infrastructure code would remain the same, and the interfacing modules built on top could be developed in a plug-and-play manner. This reduced code duplication and provided flexibility in creation of new modules. Furthermore, integration with affordable IoT devices for biometrics and QR codes made it easy for health workers and patients to interact with the apps in the low-literacy context. A business analyst at RuralHealth described the process of patient health data capture by health workers.

'And in the app we have several modules right from the health worker module. So, the health workers can capture all the vitals of the patients ... we have a QR code-enabled system ... that really ensures that the moment the health worker goes to a home, we are capturing the biometric thumb impression or a finger impression of the patient. GPS location of the patient is captured just to ensure that the health worker has gone to the ground and captured the data. And then that is pushed across the platform, and we have a centralized dashboard which keeps all this information ... whenever let's say a health worker is on the ground and they have this app, then they can scan the QR code and the entire patient information is pulled from the cloud. And the health worker will be able to enter all the vitals of the patient into the system which is being pushed back to the cloud. And then the doctors should be able to see the follow up immediately.' (Business Analyst)

RuralHealth designed specialized devices that attached to their workers' smartphones so that all patient health data could be collected at the patient's doorstep. These devices, designed to be affordable, used IoT and Bluetooth technologies and were compatible with low-cost android smartphones and tablets.

'So, all the data is captured at the patient end with the smartphone loaded with our app and a health worker that has various point of care devices like BP, ECG, blood glucose testing equipment, hemoglobin testing device and off late we are introducing a charm-like device for pneumonia detection, fetal doppler and several others.' (Business Analyst)

RuralHealth knew that it could not afford certain high-cost medical devices for all its health workers and was beginning to investigate the use of drones to share devices. For example, a portable ECG machine could be shared by health workers within a particular region as drone delivery of the machines would be much faster than via unpaved roads. The CEO explained the value of this strategy.

'Well, we are now working on some of the internet of things type solutions in an early stage. For example, we are considering using drones to enable equipment sharing among health workers ... let's say there is a device which cost Rs. 50,000 (US$750) and we know that if we assign this one device to one health worker that will not be affordable for us. So, it has to be shared ... for example a portable ECG machine...through drones maybe the health worker can request for the ECG for a particular patient and then the drone can come to that health worker, and they would be able to test the patient and again go off to another health worker.' (CEO)

Expand the Ecosystem Without Sacrificing Affordability Value Proposition

Once its regular rural health initiatives stabilized, RuralHealth established effective and strategic partnership with key stakeholders, creating a wider ecosystem to provide accessible and affordable health care and preventive services. At the ground level it connected with local NGOs, which helped to build trust with the local communities and assess service demand. Through hospital partnerships, patients could avail discounts during a hospital visit. Such collaboration improved patient access to high quality care. RuralHealth also worked with CSR partners to organize health camps and mega camps. Research partners in collaboration with RuralHealth were able to access rural markets which helped them understand the spread of chronic diseases and epidemics as well as efficacious treatments. RuralHealth worked with the global research partners to find the cause of these illnesses and provided specific health solutions to treat them. They also expanded their service offerings through a hub-and-spoke system to manage the limited resources it had at its disposal. A business analyst and the CEO explained how the hub and spoke model worked.

'We have community-based health workers that collect data at the patient's homes. Then the patient can come to a clinic which we call as a "Spoke". At the Spoke there are physical doctors who are available few days a week and on the other days these health workers act as the interface between patients and the doctors. The health worker can go to the patient's home, capture all the vitals and then upload that into the system which will help the doctor to decide the treatment ... and then we have something called as a "Hub" which could be at a maximum distance of 20 km from the last mile. That's the radius of the Hub. And at the Hub there are some advanced services which are available like the doctors, pathology, diagnostics, telemedicine services, eye related services and several others. So, through these step-by-step approaches, in case the patient needs access to secondary or tertiary care, they can be referred to various hospitals for that. So, this is the combination of technology and effective Hub and Spoke model. We are able to provide these services at a very nominal cost.' (Business Analyst)

'We partnered with an NGO and this is how we have been able to create a Hub and Spoke model. We set up meetings with their federations, self-help groups, designed the pricing and the features...we took care of the entire ground mobilization and community engagement because they enjoyed the trust factor of these people, while we purely focused on the healthcare, the entire healthcare delivery process, choosing doctors, identification of community health workers, and training them ... and working with them on technology adoption...on the government side, we met with a lot of people ... from the Chief Medical Officer of Health who is in charge of the district, to the Block Medical Officer of Health who in charge of a block. We explained to them our mission ... so it's more of a collaborative effort with the government instead of conflicting with them.' (CEO)

Capture Value within Ecosystem with Simple and Sustainable Digital Services

RuralHealth quickly realized that it needed to sustain its business by taking advantage of the expanded ecosystem. Since patients were provided with valuable services at affordable costs, they were ready to pay for services that they needed as long as the price remained affordable. RuralHealth launched its Digital Health Cards (DHC) for an annual fee of Rs. 600 (US$10) per family per year. Families could use this card to pre-pay for services, then leverage the benefits of RuralHealth's platform to tap into the government's 'direct benefits transfer and savings account scheme for the unbanked' (Pradhan Mantri Jan Dhan Yojana or PMJDY). DHCs are a transformative approach in rural public healthcare delivery and ensure additional revenue for RuralHealth through pre-purchase and patient loyalty.

> 'We have introduced something called health cards. So, it's a health card which is just a QR code-enabled card which has a unique number which is assigned and given to the patients. So, these health cards cost Rs. 600 ($10) per family per year which is only like Rs. 10 per member per month. And this health card entitles them for like five free consultations in a year, 10% discount on medicines, 10% discount on pathology, subsidized treatment given in case of malaria like in Jharkhand (Indian State) wherein we are serving 95% of the population that has been affected by malaria in the last five years. So, we have really kept that simple and affordable and even if we are selling just 50% of the cards in a territory, we are operationally breaking even. So, the model has been designed in that way. On a volume game the price point for the people is much lower whereas we are able to make money.' (CEO)

Economic, Social, Technology, and Environmental Impacts

Ruralhealth accomplished three primary innovations. First, RuralHealth successfully delivered healthcare services in geographical areas that were ignored by public health services. This created enormous social value for communities in those areas as health outcomes started to improve. Second, many people who belonged to those communities achieved employment as health workers, providing them with the opportunity to earn their livelihoods. Local workers simultaneously provided RuralHealth with social credibility within their communities, interfacing between the communities and RuralHealth. Third, although RuralHealth was continuously innovating with its technologies, it kept services on those platforms relatively simple and affordable.

> 'Yeah, we have served an area covering 3.5 million people in the last two years ... in the next 2-3 years it will be 10 million. High demand in India, so, yes we are growing at a steady rate ... there aren't any competitors in India...there are some

very few small players like either you will find NGOs who are doing pure healthcare or you'll find tech companies who are just limiting themselves to apps without any ground presence. At RuralHealth it is a combination of technology as well as the last mile healthcare delivery. So, these two things make us very unique. And here we have created a platform and ecosystem wherein we integrate the world's best solutions, simply and affordably ... in our case the entire model design has been on a bottom-up approach, meaning that we try to understand the limitations of the people, the limitations of the infrastructure, no high-speed internet available in the rural areas, etc. So, keeping all these constraints in mind we have designed the technology solutions.' (Founder)

From a social and environmental perspective, RuralHealth was able to address some adjacent problems and combat societal stigma attached to those problems. For example, pregnant mothers refused to take folic acid tablets, citing fear that the child would be born with dark skin. Through its community workers, RuralHealth educated these communities about nutritional requirements for pregnant mothers.

'We work also on a lot of messaging and dissemination because there are a lot of behavioral, cultural, social issues ... like even if the doctor prescribes iron and folic acid the mother won't take it thinking that the baby would be dark in color. So, we had to work on three-dimensional messaging one at the patient level, one at the family, one at the community level to try and tell that yes, these are good for your health and all of that.' (CSR Lead)

RuralHealth was also able to address malnutrition, which is an important health issue closely related to primary health. RuralHelath established partnerships among communities and NGOs to ensure that its patients had access to a healthy diet with high nutritional value. As a result, NGOs focused on locally-sourced millets and pulses instead of high-priced food grains with lower nutrition.

'We don't focus only on healthcare, because rural area health is linked to water, sanitation, and nutrition. So, we do converge in innovation also. For example, if there are like 90% of the people suffering from anemia, definitely we can't treat with medicines alone. So, we try to do agricultural intervention through our NGO partners, they grow pulses, broccoli, millets and we try and see that how these things can become a natural diet and supplement. In case of water, for example, we try and see whether water treatment solutions are able to help people, removal of arsenic and other issues. So, with technology and data mappings we are able to do social good.' (CSR Lead)

Patients who have benefitted from RuralHealth's services have provided video testimonials comparing RuralHealth favorably over the basic government-run public health services. The two main issues raised were affordability and accessibility. They also mention trust. Because they worked with health workers from within their own communities, they were able to trust RuralHealth's services more easily. Finally, they touched on the positive socio-economic impact of RuralHealth that has enabled them to live a more peaceful and dignified life, knowing that they have access to the best possible medical care within hours if needed. Their village has experienced improved survival rates of newborns and postpartum care for mothers among other positive changes.

'My village is far away from the city. I had problems traveling to the doctors in the city. I would lose my daily wages and pay for transportation. Now, we have nurses and doctors at our doorstep. We have our community care worker. She helps whenever we need anything. I have bought the health card for my family. It is cheaper than going to the city. I am very happy to support RuralHealth and encouraged others in the village to sign up with them.' (Patient 1)
'Earlier, whenever a pregnant woman would give birth, we used to be worried about the survival of the child and mother. Now, the mother and child receive care throughout the pregnancy and a lot of support after delivery. RuralHealth's people are very nice! They give the right medicines and take care of the health problems of the village. We have to pay, but it is much less than before. I have seen them running so many clinics for blood tests, eye care, diabetes, and even cancer and TB. We never had this type of care before.' (Patient 2)

DISCUSSION

Frugal Digital Innovation is a socio-digital phenomenon that enables innovation within resource-constrained environments by leveraging the capabilities of digital technologies, platforms, value chains, and ecosystems. To innovate frugally, it is necessary to understand the inter-twined nature of digital-social innovation (Qureshi et al., 2021). To understand the nuances of frugal digital innovation, we need to open the black-box of digital-social innovation and contextualize it within environments of resource constraints and concerns of affordability. There are several distinct phases of the development of frugal digital solutions. Planning and consideration of the context is necessary, for example, before any digital artifacts are designed. As in the case of RuralHealth, each phase includes consideration of positive and negative pressures that help shape frugal digital solutions.

Stage 1: Building the Foundations of a Platform Business

This stage begins with an assessment of the constraints and challenges of the environment. These constraints and challenges force the platform firm to embed itself within the context and devise solutions that work within those constraints. Traditional innovation studies focus on acquisition of resources and development of capabilities. When resources and capabilities are scarce, however, the platform firm needs to consider available resources and leverage local, contextual knowledge. RuralHealth understood the last-mile healthcare delivery problem and the affordability constraints of its target low-income population, so it developed a business model with affordability as its core value proposition. There may be no digital solution at this stage and the platform firm may need to work only with social and physical entities. At this stage, pushing for a digital solution may lead to poor long-term sustainability.

Stage 2: Framing A Resource-Constrained Digital Platform

At this stage a viable business model has been established. The next step is to create the necessary digital interfaces for the platform to be widely adopted. There may be pressure to scale quickly to reach paying customers, but a cautious approach must be adopted. The platform is usually built on asset-light, flexible technologies that are modular and offer lower cost of operations. This includes cloud-based technologies with minimal infrastructure costs and use of free/open-source technologies such as social media and social media aggregators for standard business operations such as customer relationship management. The platform firm focuses on the necessary technologies instead of offering high-end capabilities. The goal is to embed 'just enough' technology to build a frugal framework of technologies that can be operated at a low cost and can provide customers with the appropriate features. Digital elements emerge as important factors in addition to social and physical elements that interact with the platform.

Stage 3: Repurposing Resources to Build Plug-and-Play Capabilities

Once the technology framework is in place, the platform must identify the physical and social resources at its disposal. In adapting to the constraints of the context further, the platform may need to re-calibrate its resources to be able to accomplish its reach and network effects. In resource-constrained environments with populations that are inaccessible, the platform services may need to go in search of customers instead of depending on customers searching for services. RuralHealth adapted by re-organizing its physical workforce, by working with ASHAs, and hiring/training health workers from the communities. The platform must be able to take advantage of social capital embedded within its customer communities and zoom in on their needs. It will need to re-design or re-configure its digital resources and tools to match the capabilities of its customers and employees. The health workers needed to be trained in operating medical devices and smart phones to run the RuralHealth app. It helped that the devices could plug directly into the platform to send and receive patient data. The physical form factor of the devices also needed to be adapted to match environmental factors. Once again, we see an amalgamation of social, physical, and digital elements.

Stage 4: Creating Social Value via Digital Platform Capabilities

At this stage, the biggest gap a platform can fill is the creation of records and data where none existed previously. Data generation allows for future value capture and for establishment of downstream revenue within the ecosystem and communities. Leveraging various digital mechanisms, the focus is on making the ecosystem as inclusive as possible to generate maximum participation and network effects. The platform offers potential for economic inclusion, social inclusion, and digital inclusion for otherwise marginalized populations. By focusing on simplicity of design and right product-feature fit at the right price, the platform can pursue 'miniaturization' of its digital services and thereby 'frugalize' their offering. Using IoT devices, drones, and 3D printers, digital platforms can achieve the right product-market-feature-price fit. In the RuralHealth case, low-cost devices could plug data directly into the platform, and interfaces were kept simple to drive inclusion. The platform was able to harness the affordances of the technology and drive adoption with consideration of user expertise levels within the constraints of the spatial contexts.

Stage 5: Scaling the Platform Sustainably

At this stage, both the physical and the digital frameworks of the platform have been established. There is a viable revenue model, and the ecosystem has been set up. To grow further, the platform leverages partnerships within and outside of the ecosystem. This allows it to take advantage of growth opportunities as well as economies of scale. The platform can revisit its business model and re-calibrate its physical, digital, and social elements to meet simultaneous needs of multiple stakeholders (i.e., generativity). It can also build on the previous stage and expand the variety of physical-digital products/services for its existing and new customers. It can allow its existing customers to take advantage of economies of scale by partnering with government services and NGOs to offer complimentary services. RuralHealth partnered with NGOs to expand its workforce, collaborated with the government to allow direct money transfers to rural patients, offered its digital health card to take advantage of economies of scale and to setup an additional revenue stream, and strategized for long term sustainability of its business model.

Stage 6: Measuring Impacts

This stage is perhaps the most important part of frugal digital innovation utilizing digital platforms. Impact measurement of frugal digital innovations is complex. Frugal digital platform ecosystems focus on key metrics that span economic, social, and environmental domains. Furthermore, impact is highly contextual. Therefore, it is important for the platform business to track the right metrics on affordability, accessibility, and scale of impact. Through its various dashboards and in its partnership with government and NGOs, RuralHealth was able to keep track of its impact metrics as it was engaged both within and outside its ecosystem. By filling the data gap on rural health, it was able to provide a wealth of data on population health improvements as well as design technology and health interventions that governments and NGOs alone were struggling to achieve. Overall, its focus on affordable last-mile healthcare services brought economic, social, and environmental impacts.

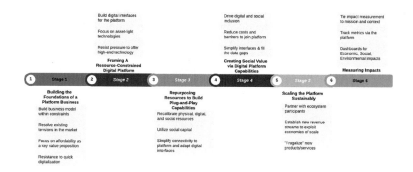

Figure 5.6   Frugal digital platform evolution

CONCLUSION

We have demonstrated how a healthcare platform innovates within constraints to deliver frugal digital solutions to patients within its ecosystem. Frugal innovation is an evolving phenomenon that emphasizes affordability, accessibility, and simplicity. In a digitalized world, these principles need to be achieved via digital mechanisms. We highlight how contextual conditions of scarcity and poor affordability enforce 'frugal innovation' by a digital platform in the healthcare sector. We describe the process of strategizing a business model centered on affordability and how characteristics of accessibility, inclusion, and simplicity are embedded in various physical, digital, and social aspects of the platform ecosystem. The tight fusion of the contextual conditions, platform capabilities, and the digital services offered by the platform provide theoretical as well as practitioner insights. From a theoretical point of view, we explore both antecedents and outcomes of frugal digital solutions considering the various contextual challenges to the development of a platform business model. For practitioners, we provide rich insights into the development of a healthcare platform that is used to provide last-mile services to a rural population. For policymakers, we provide an example of the role of government services and NGOs in providing digital health services to remote rural populations. The chapter shows how a platform ecosystem can drive a sustainable and affordable business while achieving economic and social impacts simultaneously.

KEY TAKEAWAYS

- Frugal digital innovation can be used in resource-constrained contexts where economic, social, and environmental value need to be created simultaneously.
- In combination with contextually-suited digital tools and technologies, frugal innovation can lead to rapid scaling and creation of value across the ecosystem.
- To successfully create economic and social value, frugal digital innovation solutions need to balance physical, social, and digital needs of multiple stakeholders.
- A digital platform operating in a resource-constrained setting must be able to define and track the right metrics to be able to prove its impact.
- The success of a digital platform in resource-constrained settings is dependent on the inclusion of stakeholders through provision of affordable services.
- To create long term value and impact, a strong ecosystem with an affordable business model are as important as digital technologies.

REFERENCES

Ahuja, S. (2021). Frugal Digital Innovation: Leveraging the Scale and Capabilities of Platform Ecosystems. In N. Agarwal & A. Brem (eds.), *Frugal Innovation and Its Implementation: Leveraging Constraints to Drive Innovations on a Global Scale* (pp. 279–300). Springer International Publishing. https://doi.org/10.1007/978-3-030-67119-8_13

Ahuja, S., & Chan, Y. (2017). *Resource Orchestration for IT-enabled Innovation.*

Ahuja, S., & Chan, Y. (2019). Frugal innovation and digitalisation: A platform ecosystem perspective. In *Frugal Innovation* (pp. 89–107). Routledge. https://doi.org/10.4324/9780429025679-5

Ahuja, S., Chan, Y. E., & Krishnamurthy, R. (2022). Responsible innovation with digital platforms: Cases in India and Canada. *Information Systems Journal, na.* https://doi.org/10.1111/isj.12378

Albert, M. (2019). Sustainable frugal innovation—The connection between frugal innovation and sustainability. *Journal of Cleaner Production, 237,* 117747. https://doi.org/10.1016/j.jclepro.2019.117747

Anderson, S. W., & Lillis, A. M. (2011). Corporate Frugality: Theory, Measurement and Practice*. *Contemporary Accounting Research, 28*(4), 1349–87. https://doi.org/10.1111/j.1911-3846.2011.01107.x

Autio, E., Nambisan, S., Thomas, L. D. W., & Wright, M. (2018). Digital affordances, spatial affordances, and the genesis of entrepreneurial ecosystems. *Strategic Entrepreneurship Journal, 12*(1), 72–95. https://doi.org/10.1002/sej.1266

Bhatti, Y. A., & Ventresca, M. (2012). *The Emerging Market for Frugal Innovation: Fad, Fashion, or Fit?* (SSRN Scholarly Paper No. 2005983). https://doi.org/10.2139/ssrn.2005983

Brem, A., Wimschneider, C., de Aguiar Dutra, A. R., Vieira Cubas, A. L., & Ribeiro, R. D. (2020). How to design and construct an innovative frugal product? An empirical examination of a frugal new product development process. *Journal of Cleaner Production, 275,* 122232. https://doi.org/10.1016/j.jclepro.2020.122232

Chan, Y. E., Ahuja, S., Denford, J. S., Henfridsson, O., & Levallet, N. (2020). Digital Innovation and Entrepreneurship: The Challenges of an Ecosystem Perspective. *Academy of Management Proceedings, 2020*(1), 15203. https://doi.org/10.5465/AMBPP.2020.15203symposium

Corsini, L., Dammicco, V., & Moultrie, J. (2021). Frugal innovation in a crisis: The digital fabrication maker response to COVID-19. *R&D Management, 51*(2), 195–210. https://doi.org/10.1111/radm.12446

Fréry, F., Lecocq, X., & Warnier, V. (2015). *THE LEADING QUESTION Should.*

George, G., Howard-Grenville, J., Joshi, A., & Tihanyi, L. (2016). Understanding and Tackling Societal Grand Challenges Through Management Research. *Academy of Management Journal, 59*(6), 1880–95. https://doi.org/10.5465/amj.2016.4007

Hall, J., Matos, S., Sheehan, L., & Silvestre, B. (2012). Entrepreneurship and innovation at the base of the pyramid: A recipe for inclusive growth or social exclusion? *Journal of Management Studies, 49*(4), 785–812.

Harris, M., Bhatti, Y., Buckley, J., & Sharma, D. (2020). Fast and frugal innovations in response to the COVID-19 pandemic. *Nature Medicine,* 1–4. https://doi.org/10.1038/s41591-020-0889-1

Heeks, R., Foster, C., & Nugroho, Y. (2014). New models of inclusive innovation for development. *Innovation and Development, 4*(2), 175–185. https://doi.org/10.1080/2157930X.2014.928982

Howell, R., van Beers, C., & Doorn, N. (2018). Value capture and value creation: The role of information technology in business models for frugal innovations in Africa. *Technological Forecasting and Social Change, 131,* 227–39. https://doi.org/10.1016/j.techfore.2017.09.030

Knizkov, S., & Arlinghaus, J. C. (2020). Frugal Processes: An Empirical Investigation Into the Operations of Resource-Constrained Firms. *IEEE Transactions on Engineering Management,* 1–18. https://doi.org/10.1109/TEM.2020.3016776

Knizkov, S., & Arlinghaus, J. C. (2021). Frugal Processes: An Empirical Investigation Into the Operations of Resource-Constrained Firms. *IEEE Transactions on Engineering Management, 68*(3), 667–84. https://doi.org/10.1109/TEM.2020.3016776

McMurray, A. J., & Waal, G. A. de. (2019). *Frugal Innovation: A Global Research Companion.* Routledge.

Nambisan, S., Lyytinen, K., Majchrzak, A., & Song, M. (2017). *Digital innovation management: Reinventing innovation management research in a digital world.* https://doi.org/10.25300/MISQ/2017/41:1.03

Nambisan, S., Wright, M., & Feldman, M. (2019). The digital transformation of innovation and entrepreneurship: Progress, challenges and key themes. *Research Policy, 48*(8), 1–1.

Prahalad, C. K., & Mashelkar, R. A. (2010, July 1). Innovation's Holy Grail. *Harvard Business Review, July–August 2010.* https://hbr.org/2010/07/innovations-holy-grail

Qureshi, I., Pan, S. L., & Zheng, Y. (2021). Digital social innovation: An overview and research framework. *Information Systems Journal 31*(5), 647–71. Wiley Online Library.

Radjou, N., Prabhu, J., Ahuja, S., & Roberts, K. (2012). *Jugaad Innovation: Think Frugal, Be Flexible, Generate Breakthrough Growth | Wiley.* Wiley.Com. https://www.wiley.com/

Santos, L. L., Borini, F. M., & Oliveira Júnior, M. de M. (2020). In search of the frugal innovation strategy. *Review of International Business and Strategy, 30*(2), 245–63. https://doi.org/10.1108/RIBS-10-2019-0142

Sarkar, S., & Mateus, S. (2022). Value creation using minimal resources – A meta-synthesis of frugal innovation. *Technological Forecasting and Social Change, 179,* 121612. https://doi.org/10.1016/j.techfore.2022.121612

Van Hove, L., & Dubus, A. (2019). M-PESA and Financial Inclusion in Kenya: Of Paying Comes Saving? *Sustainability, 11*(3), 568. https://doi.org/10.3390/su11030568

Weyrauch, T., & Herstatt, C. (2016). What is frugal innovation? Three defining criteria. *Journal of Frugal Innovation, 2*(1), 1. https://doi.org/10.1186/s40669-016-0005-y

Winterhalter, S., Zeschky, M. B., Neumann, L., & Gassmann, O. (2017). Business Models for Frugal Innovation in Emerging Markets: The Case of the Medical Device and Laboratory Equipment Industry. *Technovation, 66–67,* 3–13. https://doi.org/10.1016/j.technovation.2017.07.002

Yoo, Y., Henfridsson, O., & Lyytinen, K. (2010). Research Commentary—The New Organizing Logic of Digital Innovation: An Agenda for Information Systems Research. *Information Systems Research, 21*(4), 724–735. https://doi.org/10.1287/isre.1100.0322

APPENDIX

Methodology

Since the phenomenon of frugal digital innovation is relatively novel, most studies in extant literature focus on case studies to develop a deeper understanding of how frugal digital innovation takes place. In general, case studies are appropriate when researchers seek to describe phenomena, explore processes, and investigate why and how phenomena interrelate (Yin, 2017). We adopt an illustrative case study approach (Eisenhardt & Graebner, 2007; Miles, Huberman, and Saldana, 2018). A case research approach allows for the gathering of rich, qualitative data, supporting complex and comprehensive analyses (Yin, 2017). Furthermore, following the case approach also allows for the examination of a complex phenomenon while permitting 'retention of holistic and meaningful characteristics of real-life events' as well as the 'retention of contextual conditions' (Yin, 2017). Illustrative case studies can be used to explain phenomena and are appropriate if: 1) it is a revelatory case, i.e., it is a situation previously inaccessible to scientific investigation; 2) it represents a critical case for testing a well-formulated theory; or 3) it is an extreme or unique case (Eisenhardt & Graebner, 2007; Yin, 2017). For an emergent phenomenon such as frugal digital innovation taking place in digital platform ecosystems, the careful study of a single case can permit researchers to explore new theoretical relationships and uncover new insights for further research (Eisenhardt & Graebner, 2007).

The data presented here are part of a larger study, in which over 20 Indian and Canadian digital platform firms and participants of their ecosystems were interviewed. Executives, managers, and technical employees of each firm were interviewed. The researchers conducted over 70 in-depth, in-person interviews as well as web-based and phone-based interviews and surveys during the period between 2017 to 2021. In this chapter, we present a subset of these interviews for one of the digital platforms. The platform we showcase in this chapter was selected as an illustrative case that highlights constraints in an emerging country context, digital platform solutions, ecosystem processes, and frugal digital innovation. The quotes we present are snapshots from interviews conducted with various representatives of these firms as well as with participants within the ecosystem. The quotes were selected based on their clarity and brevity.

The researchers began by writing case histories of the process of frugal digital innovation for each firm. To ensure completeness and accuracy, a second researcher reviewed the data and formed an independent perspective that we integrated into each case. We had no a priori hypotheses. We used individual case histories for within-case analysis. Our goal was to establish broad constructs that could be tied to other constructs or theoretical elements in the extant literature. We considered antecedent conditions, constraints, voids, and social and environmental challenges. We then looked for conditions that led to the emergence of the platform and how the ecosystem was developed. To enhance the validity of our findings, a case study database was created. All interviews were audiotaped and transcribed. All transcripts were independently analyzed by the researchers and inter-rater agreement was ensured. We began by interviewing the founder of the platform firm. Then we interviewed key technical and managerial representatives of the firm. To corroborate this internal perspective of the platform firm with external perspectives, we interviewed other members or participants of the ecosystem of these firms.

For triangulation purposes (Yin, 2017), we used multiple sources of evidence. We referred to and analyzed internal company documents relating to technical and business architecture, HR, training, strategy, etc. as well as internal and external websites, social media, and marketing materials. We used DEDOOSE software (www.dedoose.com) to assist with data analysis and employed principles of 'analytical generalizability' (Yin, 2017) to assist with theorizing.

6. Analyzing social interactions and conflicting goals: Australian government ecosystem context

Sultana Lubna Alam and Asif Qumer Gill

INTRODUCTION

Technological developments such as social networks, online forums, and petition sites have renewed attention on the participatory role of citizens in government service delivery (e.g., Helander et al., 2020; Klievink et al., 2016; Linders, 2012; Mergel, 2013; Reddick & Norris, 2013). This participatory role is enabled through the increasing use of social media as a digital platform for public value co-creation (Meijer & Boon, 2021). Social media is defined as 'a group of internet-based applications that build on the ideological and technological foundations of web 2.0 and that allow the creation and exchange of user generated content' (Kaplan & Haenlein, 2010, p. 65). Digital technologies change the ways service users can co-create value at the point of co-production (Lusch & Nambisan, 2015). For example, the increased popularity of social media platforms (SMPs) promises to enhance interaction, collaboration and networking enabled by virtual interactions online (Silva et al., 2019; Yildiz et al., 2020) in non-transactional settings such as in the delivery and consumption of government services (Helander et al., 2020; Musso et al., 2020). In the current networked environment, citizens increasingly expect that public agencies cooperate with them, harmonize information requests and interact with citizens/businesses in a uniform way (Klievink et al., 2016). This, however, demands extensive transformations, truly changing the way public agencies exchange information.

In light of fiscal pressures and austerity regimes by governments around the world there is renewed interest in co-production of public services (Kleinhans et al., 2022). From an instrumental point of view, technology enables new practices of co-production and information exchange, lowering costs of large-scale and dispersed action, thus making co-production more social and playful. Governments around the world are increasingly using the social media platforms (e.g., Facebook, LinkedIn, Twitter) for active interactions with the community (Abdelsalam et al., 2013; Gill & Bunker, 2012; Yildiz et al., 2020). These interactions may involve sourcing and providing government services and related information to the community (Paulin, 2020). Online discussions provide an additional channel for providing formal information to citizens, for social and emotional support, and provide access to citizens' experiences to gauge additional signals. Forums represent an additional function to the existing forms of service provision in the sense that citizens can provide each other with information that agencies cannot (Alam, 2020). Government includes several public agencies, whereas community refers to both individuals and non-government organizations. Thus, this is a kind of an ecosystem that comprises of several stakeholders that interact with each other using social media platforms for achieving their goals (Helander et al., 2020). These platforms can enable information communication and collaboration between the government and community to support effective and timely decision-making, planning, public value co-creation, feedback and improvement (Kleinhans et al., 2022; Klievink et al., 2016; Meijer & Boon, 2021). These goals could be viewed from both government and community perspectives (Gill et al., 2015).

Facebook is one of the leading social media platforms used by public agencies in Australia in this fashion, correlating with a high degree of use by Australian citizens. Sensis reported in June 2018 that almost eight in 10 Australians (79 percent) use social media use social media, and 94 percent use Facebook (Sensis, 2018). Facebook enabled interactions seem to offer several benefits such as government agencies that may directly and actively connect, inform, coordinate and collaborate with different stakeholders in a community at a relatively fast pace and low cost (Alam & Walker, 2011; Musso et al., 2020; Silva et al., 2019; Yildiz et al., 2020). Social media used by government fits into the broader trend of the 'digitization efforts of [public] services as a new wave of the e-Government era' (Mergel, 2013, p. 328). However, despite governments' increasing move toward e-interactions with their citizens, existing research suggests that 'the dialogic affordances of social media remain under-utilized by even … democratic governments'. Social media sites are largely used to complement governments' other online and offline communication platforms and do not supplant e-government services (Mergel, 2013, p. 328). Researchers have found 'that practitioners are using [social networking sites] for one-way transmission of information', [that is], as 'information dumps' (p. 134), rather than to truly engage citizens (Abdelsalam et al., 2013; S. Alam & Gill, 2020; S. L. Alam & Diamah, 2012; S. L. Alam & Walker, 2011; Mergel, 2013). Consequently, a gap exists between the existing theoretical knowledge and practical application of government-based social networking sites, with '[m]any federal departments and agencies […] still in the middle of navigating the uncertainties of using social media as an extension of the use of their online presence' (Mergel, 2013, p. 328).

While such interactivity via social platforms like Facebook seems useful, however, this also presents several challenges. One such challenge is around the tension between the government and community due to their conflicting goals and expectations. Thus, there is a need for understanding and addressing conflicts between government and community goals for effective interactions and mutual benefits. There is a knowledge gap due to the limited analysis and research on the conflicting goal and impact of social media platforms, when they are used by the Australian Government and the community for interactions. Further, the overlapping perspectives of looking at digital platforms from functional, structural and organizational perspective, creates various scenarios for potential conflict (Klievink et al., 2016). For example, drawing on the conceptualization of a platform as a socio-technical concept, Klievink et al., (2016), argue that both the information technology (IT) infrastructure (e.g., interfaces and services) and governance mechanisms (e.g., multiple user groups of the infrastructure, terms, conditions, decision-making structures, and stakeholder objectives) should be addressed when studying public–private platforms as a means for transformation as both offer specific types of challenges and present different types of instruments. This chapter aims to address this knowledge gap for enhancing understanding of conflicting goals around interactions between government and community. The findings from the chapter can be used by agencies to identity and address conflicting goals when redesigning their social platforms (e.g., Facebook pages) and related interactions with the community for optimal outcomes.

This chapter is organized as follows. Firstly, it provides the analysis of the Australian Government Facebook case and reports two types of views and underpinning conflicts or tensions: interaction mode view and activity view. Secondly, it proposes the interaction architecture approach to address or minimize the conflicting government and community interaction goals. Finally, it provides key insights and learnings before concluding.

AUSTRALIAN GOVERNMENT FACEBOOK CASE

This chapter presents two different views for understanding and identifying the possible conflicting goals. These views are organized into Facebook interaction mode view and interaction activity view.

Interaction Mode View

Four modes or levels of interactions have been identified through the analysis of the use of Australian Facebook pages. These modes are classified as:

one-way broadcast mode, two-way interaction mode, dialogue mode and co-creation mode (Figure 6.1).

One-way broadcast mode

This mode is mainly used to achieve the goal of monitoring and informing the community, with no consideration of the community's own goal. This is also considered a low maturity (level 1) of interaction. Thus, here there is a possibility of misalignment of the government goal with the community goal. For instance, the community may not want the government to monitor them or push undesirable information for modifying their behavior.

Two-way interaction mode

This mode is mainly used to achieve the goal of responding to the community requests, perhaps with little to no consideration of community's own goal. Thus, here there is also a possibility of misalignment of the government goal with the community goal. For instance, the community may not want the government to take a more pro-active approach to interaction, rather a reactive request and response model.

Dialogue mode

This mode is mainly used to achieve the goal of achieving real participation with the community. There is a sense or consideration of the community's goal. Thus, here there is another possibility of a misalignment of goals between the government and the community. For instance, a conflict on a policy or activity between government and community may not result in a mutual agreement or outcome. Thus, there are chances of conflict or misalignment between government and community goals.

Co-creation mode

This mode of interaction is at the highest maturity level and enables the government and community to collaborate on concerns of mutual interest and co-create policies or services that address the mutual goals. This is contrary to the extreme broadcast or push mode where the community is mainly informed, rather, they are actively involved such as in the co-creation mode.

The interaction modes confirmed that, when defining engagement scope, it is important to identify both the type of use desired, and the level of engagement expected to maximize the value of a Page. Key to the interaction mode is an understanding that engagement is not a single process or set of activities. It is an ongoing process of conversation, involving building trust and relationships, to achieve a series of outcomes or goals over time.

Further, it is important to note here that each interaction mode has its own goal, use and tension points. For instance, if the government only uses the

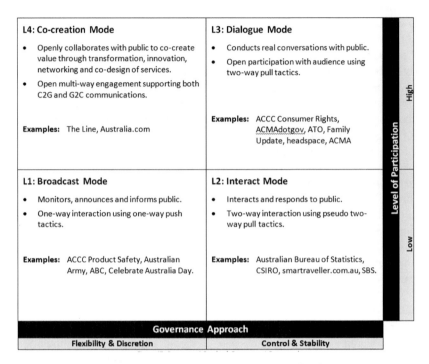

L4: Co-creation Mode	L3: Dialogue Mode
• Openly collaborates with public to co-create value through transformation, innovation, networking and co-design of services. • Open multi-way engagement supporting both C2G and G2C communications. **Examples:** The Line, Australia.com	• Conducts real conversations with public. • Open participation with audience using two-way pull tactics. **Examples:** ACCC Consumer Rights, ACMAdotgov, ATO, Family Update, headspace, ACMA
L1: Broadcast Mode	L2: Interact Mode
• Monitors, announces and informs public. • One-way interaction using one-way push tactics. **Examples:** ACCC Product Safety, Australian Army, ABC, Celebrate Australia Day.	• Interacts and responds to public. • Two-way interaction using pseudo two-way pull tactics. **Examples:** Australian Bureau of Statistics, CSIRO, smartraveller.com.au, SBS.

Level of Participation — High / Low

Governance Approach

Flexibility & Discretion	Control & Stability

Figure 6.1   Interaction modes across agency Facebook pages

broadcast mode to achieve their goal of monitoring and informing the community. It could be in conflict with the community goal where they expect to engage back with the government, or they need more or clearer information, whereas the government may want to share limited information through only certain channels and methods. This indicates a potential tension point due to the conflicting goals of the government and community. To address some part of this tension, an alternative mode of two-way communication can be used for enabling the community to engage with the government. However, this mode may introduce an additional expectation of the community from the government to respond instantly or engage in dialogue, which might not have been the original intention of the government. Thus, this introduces another conflicting goal and tension point. This could be addressed through the use of another available option of dialogue mode. However, dialogue mode may not be enough and may introduce issues such as limited engagement or strict moderation, where the community wants to have deep engagement with the government, not only to talk about the matters of interest but to also focus on how to address them and co-create solutions. Here, they can use another

Table 6.1   *Interaction activity types across agency Facebook pages*

Operational:(75 Pages)	Organizations involved in the implementation of public policy (includes Smaller Operational (under 1000 staff) and Larger Operational (over 1000 staff) (e.g.: Australia in the Caribbean, Royal Australian Navy, Screen Australia, Bureau of Meteorology, Screen Australia)
Policy: (8 Pages)	Organizations involved in the development of public policy (e.g.: Headspace, Australia's Chief Scientist, business.gov.au, Safe Work Australia, AusIndustry)
Regulatory: (18 Pages)	Organizations involved in regulation and inspection (i.e.: Australian Maritime Safety Authority, Great Barrier Reef Marine Park, ASADA)
Specialist: (46 Pages)	Organizations providing specialist support to government (e.g.: The Line, Australian Parliament – House of Representatives, DonateLife, Questacon)

available co-creation mode to address this tension. However, co-creation could be limited to certain matters where the government may only want to decide what, how and when to share certain information and co-creation tasks in an open public space. For instance, sensitive and classified information, strategies and tasks relevant to national security may not be feasible to discuss in a public space. In summary, these modes complement each other and have their own goals, uses and tensions. These modes can be mixed and matched for certain purposes.

Notably, the interaction modes also suggest four maturity stages: Broadcast (L1), Interaction (L2), Dialogue (L3), and Co-creation (L4). Each successive stage requires a higher level of openness and transparency from an agency to function effectively, coupled with a reduction in their operational barriers to active engagement, which fundamentally is the origin of the conflicting goals and expectations.

Interaction Activity View

Four categories of activities or services were identified: Operational, Policy, Regulatory and Specialist (Table 6.1). These categories support benchmarking of the core activities of agencies. Firstly, the majority of Australian Government Facebook Pages, per APSC classification of interaction activities, are managed by Operational Agencies (e.g.: Australia in the Caribbean, Royal Australian Navy, Screen Australia, and Bureau of Meteorology).

Secondly, it has been found (Table 6.2) that Policy type Pages achieved a far higher interaction rate than any other type, suggesting that these agencies were more interested and committed to soliciting user feedback.[1] Specialist Pages had the largest audiences on average, and made greater use of video, which reflects the particularly high sharing and commenting rates. Operational Pages used the most photos, which stimulated the highest level of likes, but lower sharing and commenting rates than video posts.

Further based on Table 6.2, the following trends were identified across the Agency Facebook Pages which have implications for designing interaction activities:

- Posting trends by Page: Operational and Regulatory Page posts per month increased considerably (almost doubled) over the study period, whereas Specialist Page post rate growth was more restrained (20 percent increase). This could be because Specialist agencies were already consistently using their Pages in their operations, whereas Operational and Regulatory agencies are building their internal mandates and progressively increasing the extent of topics they engage with on their Pages. Interestingly, Policy agency Page (e.g., headspace, ABARES, AusIndustry) posts per Page per month decreased over the three-year analysis period. This suggests that while Policy agencies generate the highest level of interaction by fan, they either are not seeking to engage the public in policy development, or do not yet see their Pages as an effective tool for this type of engagement activity.
- Posting trends by type of post by APSC agency type: Operational and Specialist Pages made the most use of photo posts, whereas Policy made the most use of link posts, followed by Specialist. Regulatory Pages published more photo posts than link posts. The difference becomes even more obvious when grouping visual (photo and video) and textual (link and status) posts. Operational Pages made significantly more use of visual imagery than any other category:
    - Photo post by Page: Pages with higher levels of photo posting were more successful at attracting both fans and interactions; there was a significant correlation between greater photo posting and higher engagement levels.
    - Video post by Page: Operational, Regulatory and Specialist agencies are all growing their use of video posts whereas Policy agencies reduced their video use in 2015.
    - Status posts by Page: Status posts – originally the only way to post to Facebook – have become the least used post type by all agency categories and is in rapid decline across Policy and Specialist agencies.

Operational

These Pages showed a clear focus on more operational-style informational content, such as the presentation of photos, information related to specific years and defense-related content. International and local news were also significant, and these pages included more technical self-references to Facebook

Table 6.2   *Average interaction rate per activity type*

Type	Median[2]	Average interactions (Interaction Types)				Post types (Information Sharing)			
	Fans	Likes	Shares	Comments	Interacts /fan	Photo	Link	Video	Status
Operational (74)	15 738	131 675	24 315	7157	0.05	56%	34%	7%	3%
Policy (8)	6583	36 279	17 481	1672	0.33	31%	59%	4%	6%
Regulatory (18)	14 100	44,450	17,196	4441	0.11	47%	34%	7%	12%
Specialist (46)	18 010	105 020	32 842	15 660	0.08	43%	41%	9%	8%

and posts, as well as to program and support/help information than the other categories. Operational Pages posted more photos (56 percent) than other categories but were less likely to link to information (34 percent), were moderate users of video (7 percent) but the least likely to make status posts (3 percent).

Policy

Policy pages exhibited a significant focus on business, with areas such as workplace safety and mental health (headspace) being distant second-level topics. Other topics were evenly spread, however some of the big policy topics by department, such as health, education, social services, science, or environment, received little mention on these pages, suggesting that policy conversations were not significantly involving the public through this channel. Policy Pages posted far fewer photos (31 percent) and videos (4 percent) than other categories but were most likely to link to information (59 percent). They were light users of status posts (3 percent).

Regulatory

These Pages clearly focused on regulatory matters, particularly related to product recalls, food and safety information. Less significant topics included business, borders, the Great Barrier Reef, the Murray Basin, standards, health and water, all topics expected from regulatory Pages. Consumers, people, rights, and industry were less commonly mentioned, and were clearly not targeted topics for these Pages. Regulatory Pages made the most use of status posts (12 percent) and were low users of links (34 percent), but moderately used both photos (47 percent) and videos (7 percent). Of all the categories these Pages appeared most focused across the core goals of their owning agencies.

Specialist

The Specialist category includes a collection of highly disparate agencies, and this was evident through the terms used in posts on their Pages. Behind a focus on national and news, innovation was a particularly strong term used in posts. Past this were a more eclectic range of terms, from the world and people, to science, advice and exhibitions and the only clear themes were around innovation and travel advice. Specialist Pages made the most use of video (8 percent) and were moderate users of other post types – photos (43 percent), links (41 percent) and status (8 percent).

Relationship Between Interaction Modes and Interaction Activity

It is evident that Australian public agencies are not consistently engaging with the public at higher interaction levels using Facebook. This provides a significant scope for ongoing evolution in engagement by government using the service. Our analysis of agencies found that 59 percent had a single dominant communications mode, fitting into one of the four quadrants of the interaction mode framework (Figure 6.1), while the other 41 percent had a co-dominant communications mode, spanning either L1/L2, L2/L3 or L3/L4. Mapped across the full framework, agency Facebook pages reflected the following breakdown (see Figure 6.2):

- For all classifications excluding Regulatory, more than half of agency Pages were performing at the L1 or L1/L2 levels, including 54 percent of Operational, 57 percent of Policy and 50 percent of Specialist agencies.
- Except for Policy agencies, three-quarters of agency Pages were performing at L1 or L2 levels (including L1/L2 and L2/l3), being 75 percent of Operational, 82 percent of Regulatory and 96 percent of Specialist agency Pages.
- Fifty-five percent of Regulatory and 46 percent of Specialist agencies performed at L2 or L2/L3 levels, representing their ongoing need to interact with citizens to, at minimum, address regulatory issues and customer service enquiries. In contrast only 21 percent of Operational and 14 percent of Policy agencies performed at this level.
- Far fewer Pages performed at L3 or higher levels, with Policy agencies having the highest share at 29 percent, followed by Operational on 25 percent, Regulatory on 18 percent and Specialist on 4 percent. This suggest that Policy agencies were more likely to perform consultative-style engagement using their Facebook Page than other agency types, with Specialist agencies the least likely to consult the community actively.
- L4 agency Pages were particularly rare as mentioned earlier, with only two Pages achieving this level, one Operational (Australia.com) and one

Specialist (The Line). Both are examples of exemplary engagement by the government using Facebook and have been the subjects of multiple case studies. These two Pages have several similarities that may reflect their level. Both have clearly defined goals and operate with a specific mandate to influence behavior. Australia.com is focused on encouraging international travelers to visit Australia and The Line influences young Australians towards respectful relationships.

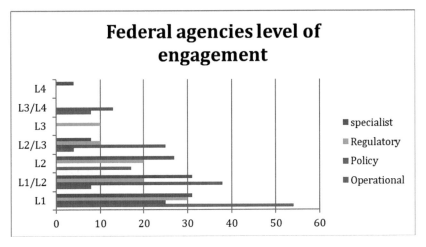

Figure 6.2   Federal agency Facebook pages by interaction mode and interaction activity

Agencies were being driven by the growth of social media and public awareness to increase their citizen engagement via social media services like Facebook. However, this engagement was still primarily outbound-centric, with most agencies focused on their own posting and citizens relegated to a reactionary or responsive commentary role. Citizen-led content – content developed and shared by citizens on pages independently of agency posts – was, across the board, limited and generally accorded little attention by agencies. This suggests that, while agencies understand the need to use Facebook for citizen engagement, they remain structurally, culturally, and strategically oriented towards traditional, one-way communication modes.

In a nutshell, both interaction and activity views are important for identifying and addressing the conflicting goals of government and community. The interaction mode view helped us to understand and identify the potential conflicts and tensions between the government and community goals. The activity view used helped to further investigate the activities that may be carried out during different interaction modes. Such analysis and understanding will help agencies to re-design their interactions and underpinning activities to address the mutual goals of government and community.

Interaction Architecture Approach to Social Media

Rather than having ad-hoc interaction modes and activities for a particular type of social media platform such as the Facebook, it is recommended to apply a systematic approach and design an interaction architecture (IA) for social interactions. IA needs to be aligned to the mutual government and community goals. This chapter proposes such approach based on social architecture framework (Alam & Gill, 2020; Gill et al., 2015) to design such IA.

IA can be designed to realize the mutual goals. These goals need to be embedded in the social media strategy, which can be used to guide the design of IA. IA can then be implemented using a specific social media platform such as Facebook. The following are the key iterative and incremental steps for designing the IA (based on Gill 2015).

1. Analyze key government and community stakeholders and design stakeholder map;
2. Design key stakeholder personas and map their expectations to formalize the mutual goals.
3. Embed goals in the social media strategy.
4. Priorities and select stakeholders' goals of mutual interest.
5. Identify and select relevant interaction modes to address the stakeholders' mutual goals (as discussed above).
6. Identify and select relevant interaction activities for each interaction modes to address the stakeholders' mutual goals (as discussed above).
7. Re-design social media such as the Facebook pages to support interaction modes and underpinning activities (number 5 and 6).
8. Implement Facebook pages (number 7).
9. Transition to Facebook governance.
10. Evolve interaction modes, activities and supporting Facebook pages.

LESSONS LEARNED

Public service provision on Facebook pages has resulted in interesting social interactions and behavior shifts that have created new relationships between traditional domains in following ways:

- Government ecosystem: Relationship between the government and its stakeholders has shifted in comparison to a traditional governance model

– from rigid controlled environment towards more flexible, loosely coupled relationships. The government-centric approach has shifted to a citizen-centric approach. As citizens engage in co-delivery, co-design, and co-evaluation of public services, the focus has shifted to citizens playing a participatory role in the government services they receive and, thereby co-producing benefits for both parties. Social media platforms, such as Feedback, provide access to citizens' experiences and responses within an online community. Government social media platforms can create opportunities for collating information or exchanging ideas through online live sessions. Citizens can participate on their own, for example, by responding to questions posed by other citizens, or have a deliberative conversation with a group of networked citizens on a topic of mutual interest. The relationship between government and citizens thus cab be short term, irregular, and flexible.

- Digital value and tension: The value from using digital platform-based (Alsufyani & Gill, 2022) citizen interactions are manifold. For example, knowledge is shared between government and citizens (i.e., G2C and C2G), between government and business (i.e., G2B, B2G) as well as between citizens (i.e., C2C). These knowledge contributions are characterized as small-scale contributions in the form of Q&A, information sharing, feedback, and potential for knowledge co-creation and spans over time. Government can use the digital platforms to address societal problems, but they can also use these platforms to source outside-in transformation ideas (Klievink et al., 2016). Further, businesses can also leverage these platforms to have access to government and community interactions and their data with a view to create value for themselves and also give back to the government and community. That is, knowledge is curated through small-scale contributions of government, citizens and businesses who add to the common area of concern or discussion over time – returning to the analogy of 'many hands make light work'. Here the focus of the chapter is government and community. Thus, the value propositions need to be optimized through understanding and addressing the tension and conflicts between government and community goals for effective interactions and mutual benefits. Finally, it is important to note here that each interaction mode has its own goal and use. Here, clear communication is needed to set expectations between the government and community when using a specific interaction mode. Interaction modes complement each other; thus, a mix and match approach may be appropriate when choosing a certain mode for interactions.

How to Choose an Interaction Mode Aligned with Interaction Activity

As with any public engagement activity, social interactions on social media offers an array of choices and complex governance risks. When selecting a form of interaction mode, government needs 'to reassess the need, opportunities and forms of interactions' (Meijer, 2012, p. 1170) in relation to their agencies' strategic goals (interaction activity). Based on the focus of Facebook Pages studied in this chapter (i.e., operational, regulatory, policy and specialist), public agencies can choose digital co-production strategies that suit each agency's focus and goals for engagement in the Facebook Page. For example, regulatory and policy focused agencies can promote open dialogue through engaging in real dialogue, feedback and encourage co-creation of ideas and solutions for solving significant complex issues. Specialist and operational government institutions can enrich cultural information through collating information from citizens seeking feedback and content. Embassies in external countries can reach target audiences with essential information through sharing, commenting and tagging of posts. Operational agencies can also engage in synchronous communications through live information and Q&A sessions. Again, all agencies can monitor non-official information provided by citizens and reduce the risks of misinformation through busting myths.

While the four modes outlined can be perceived as a progression of maturity levels for agencies and audiences (from one-way broadcast to co-creation), they all remain valid approaches for government Facebook Pages. As public agencies progress to each higher intensity interaction mode in their Facebook Page engagement, the public is more empowered to participate and take greater ownership of the subject of the engagement process. This can lead to greater public value and improved outcomes, including lifting positive perceptions of the agency within their engagement, and broadly improves long-term engagement with the government. On the other hand, higher intensity co-interaction also face increased technical and managerial complexity and greater challenges and risks. Also, it is worth mentioning that there is an increasing interest in digital technologies among the government and community (Bashir & Gill, 2017; Chohan & Hu, 2022). Facebook is only one of the digital interaction channels, agencies may also evaluate other digital channels such as conversational chatbots and Internet of Things (IoT) for interactions with a view to enhance community engagement. For instance, conversational chatbots can be used in the dialogue mode. IoT-enabled smart sensors and devices, such as smart watches, can be used for sourcing, providing and actioning information in an efficient manner.

Developing any effective engagement strategy starts with a solid understanding of an agency's strategy and mission, available digital channels, the theme and the audience that is to be engaged. Agencies must also ask what type of engagement matches their unique goals, capabilities, digital technologies and resources. An agency's functional focus and capabilities can lead to different engagement requirements and needs. It is a matter of combining the right mix of skills and resourcing, creative and talented communicators within an appropriate internal environment for government to maximize the effectiveness of its Facebook use along other available channels.

CONCLUSION

Public agencies are increasingly adopting social media platforms as communication channels, if not as a citizen engagement channel. The continued growth in social media adoption, such as Facebook, by agencies suggests that the platform is increasingly significant in their communication strategies. Most agencies remain focused on broadcast and basic audience interactions – using Facebook Pages to disseminate information and respond to direct citizen questions or complaints. This controlled and managed approach may suit risk-averse agencies, but ignores many potential benefits that Facebook offers for deep sustained engagement and consultation with citizens and stakeholders. This also gives rise to conflicting goals between government and citizens.

Using tools outlined in this chapter, such as the interaction view and activity view, will help agencies to identify and normalize the most appropriate models of engagement to use when engaging via their social media pages with citizens, stakeholders and communities.

KEY TAKEAWAYS

- Use of social media by public agencies has notably increased in maturity over time. Social media provides a platform for not only information sharing and communication between the government and community, but it also enables value co-creation via active engagement over the matters of mutual benefits. In this study, we found that public agencies have firmly adopted Facebook as a communication channel, if not consistently as a citizen engagement channel, and the continued growth in fans and posting by agencies suggests that the platform is increasingly significant in their communication strategies.
- There still exists a long tail of government Facebook Pages that appear to be under-managed and are achieving far less audience engagement success. Government Facebook Pages with fewer fans consistently evidenced significantly lower posting rates, less use of visual content and more bureaucratic and agency-centric language in their posts.

- Using tools such as the interaction view, activity view and IA approach, will help agencies to identify the tensions and conflicts within each mode of engagement and assist agencies to achieve their goals and the objectives of the government of the day, while ensuring that the outcomes meet the explicit and implicit needs of the community. Hence, it is important to have a clear communication about the expectations when selecting and using certain modes of interactions.

ACKNOWLEDGEMENTS

This research received funding from Facebook Inc. We would like to acknowledge Mia Garlick (Regional Director, Policy for Australia, New Zealand & the Pacific) for her contribution and the two research assistants who carried out the data collection and coding.

NOTES

1. 'Interaction rate' used here refers to fan interactions, NOT post interactions. Policy Page fans were more engaged, but posts received far less interactions due to fewer fan numbers on average.
3. The number of agencies has been estimated based on the named responsible agency for each page. This may not represent internal management practices or budget lines for Pages, which may be collectively managed by central teams in departments or individual agencies, decentralised and managed by individual teams within agencies or wholly or partially outsourced to a third-party.
4. Australia.gov.au – Social Media use (Facebook) (australia.gov.au/news-and -social-media/social-media/facebook).
5. APSC State of the Service Report 2014-15 (apsc.gov.au/about-the-apsc/ parliamentary/state-of-the-service/state-of-the-service-report-2014-15).

REFERENCES

Abdelsalam, H. M., Reddick, C. G., Gamal, S., & Al-shaar, A. (2013). Social media in Egyptian government websites: Presence, usage, and effectiveness. *Government Information Quarterly, 30*(4), 406–416. https://doi.org/10.1016/j.giq.2013.05.020

Alam, S., & Gill, A. Q. (2020). A social engagement framework for the government ecosystem: Insights from australian government facebook pages. *ICIS 2020 : Making Digital Inclusive: Blending the Local and the Global : International Conference on Information Systems.* Information Systems. Conference (2020 : Online from India). https://dro.deakin.edu.au/view/DU:30150061

Alam, S. L. (2020). Many hands make light work: Towards a framework of digital co-production to co-creation on social platforms. *Information Technology & People, 34*(3), 1087–1118. https://doi.org/10.1108/ITP-05-2019-0231

Alam, S. L., & Diamah, A. (2012). *Understanding user participation in Australian Government Tourism Facebook Page.* 11.

Alam, S. L., & Walker, D. (2011). The Public Facebook: A case of Australian Government Facebook Pages and Participation: Australasian Conference on Information Systems (ACIS) 2011. *Proceedings of the Australiasian Conference on Information Systems ACIS 2011: 'Identifying the Information Systems Discipline'* 1–13.

Alsufyani, N., & Gill, A. Q. (2022). Digitalisation performance assessment: A systematic review. *Technology in Society, 68*, 101894. https://doi.org/10.1016/j.techsoc.2022.101894

Bashir, M. R., & Gill, A. Q. (2017). IoT enabled smart buildings: A systematic review. *2017 Intelligent Systems Conference (IntelliSys)*, 151–59. https://doi.org/10.1109/IntelliSys.2017.8324283

Chohan, S. R., & Hu, G. (2022). Strengthening digital inclusion through e-government: Cohesive ICT training programs to intensify digital competency. *Information Technology for Development, 28*(1), 16–38. https://doi.org/10.1080/02681102.2020.1841713

Gill, A., Alam, L., & Eustace, J. (2015). Social Architecture: An Emergency Management Case Study. *Australas. J. Inf. Syst.* https://doi.org/10.3127/AJIS.V19I0.979

Gill, A., & Bunker, D. (2012). Crowd Sourcing Challenges Assessment Index for Disaster Management. *AMCIS.*

Helander, N., Sillanpää, V., Felicetti, A., Jussila, J., Paunu, A., Bal, A. S., & Ammirato, S. (2020). Co-creating digital government service: An activity theory perspective. *Proceedings of the 53rd Hawaii International Conference on System Sciences*, 10.

Kaplan, A. M., & Haenlein, M. (2010). Users of the world, unite! The challenges and opportunities of Social Media. *Business Horizons, 53*(1), 59–68. https://doi.org/10.1016/j.bushor.2009.09.003

Kleinhans, R., Falco, E., & Babelon, I. (2022). Conditions for networked co-production through digital participatory platforms in urban planning. *European Planning Studies, 30*(4), 769–88. https://doi.org/10.1080/09654313.2021.1998387

Klievink, B., Bharosa, N., & Tan, Y.-H. (2016). The collaborative realization of public values and business goals: Governance and infrastructure of public–private information platforms. *Government Information Quarterly, 33*(1), 67–79. https://doi.org/10.1016/j.giq.2015.12.002

Linders, D. (2012). From e-government to we-government: Defining a typology for citizen coproduction in the age of social media. *Government Information Quarterly, 29*(4), 446–54. https://doi.org/10.1016/j.giq.2012.06.003

Lusch, R., & Nambisan, S. (2015). Service Innovation: A Service-Dominant Logic Perspective. *MIS Q.* https://doi.org/10.25300/MISQ/2015/39.1.07

Meijer, A., & Boon, W. (2021). Digital platforms for the co-creation of public value. *Policy and Politics, 49*(2), 231–48. https://doi.org/10.1332/030557321X16115951032181

Mergel, I. (2013). A framework for interpreting social media interactions in the public sector. *Government Information Quarterly, 30*(4), 327–34. https://doi.org/10.1016/j.giq.2013.05.015

Musso, M., Pinna, R., Carrus, P., & Melis, G. (2020). Social Media Patient Engagement in Healthcare: An Italian Case Study. In Y. Baghdadi, A. Harfouche, & M. Musso (Eds.), *ICT for an Inclusive World: Industry 4.0–Towards the Smart Enterprise* (pp. 209–27). Springer International Publishing. https://doi.org/10.1007/978-3-030-34269-2_16

Paulin, A. A. (2020). *Open government concepts, methodologies, tools, and appli-cations*. IGI Global. http://services.igi-global.com/resolvedoi/resolve.aspx?doi=10 .4018/978-1-5225-9860-2

Reddick, C. G., & Norris, D. F. (2013). Social media adoption at the American grass roots: Web 2.0 or 1.5? *Government Information Quarterly, 30*(4), 498–507. https:// doi.org/10.1016/j.giq.2013.05.011

Sensis. (2018). *Sensis Social Media Report*. https://www.sensis.com.au/about/our -reports/sensis-social-media-report

Silva, P., Tavares, A. F., Silva, T., & Lameiras, M. (2019). The good, the bad and the ugly: Three faces of social media usage by local governments. *Government Information Quarterly, 36*(3), 469–479. https://doi.org/10.1016/j.giq.2019.05.006

Yildiz, M., Ocak, N., Yildirim, C., Cagiltay, K., & Babaoglu, C. (2020). *Usability in Local E-Government: Analysis of Turkish Metropolitan Municipality Facebook Pages* (pp. 966–84). https://doi.org/10.4018/978-1-5225-9860-2.ch045

APPENDIX

Methodology

To understand how the Australian Government uses Facebook, the researchers undertook an analysis of government Facebook Pages (Pages) in partnership with Facebook.

The Federal Government is responsible for the conduct of national portfo-lios such as defense and foreign affairs; trade, commerce, and currency; immi-gration; telecommunications and broadcasting; and social services. They are operated through headquarters in the Capital with service provision through Federal offices in major states in Australia.

The Australian Government has become a major user of Facebook over the last five years, with over 185 Pages currently listed as active in the Australia. gov.au website. 147 Facebook Pages, representing approximately 72 agencies across 17 portfolios,[3] were selected randomly from the Australia.gov.au social media directory[4] to be analyzed. Three years of posting and interaction data for these Pages (Jan 2013–Jan 2016) was provided by Facebook. This was analyzed using data analytics tools including CrowdTangle, FileMaker Pro, Excel and Nvivo.

Pages were initially classified based on the agency that operated and/ or funded them, using the Australian Public Service Commission's State of the Service report 2014-15.[5] The APSC divide agencies into five categories: Operational (Large), Operational (Small), Policy, Regulatory and Specialist. For ease of analysis the Operational (Large) and (Small) categories were com-bined into a single (Operational) category.

Content from 68 of the 147 pages in this study was analyzed. The sample set was chosen to be representative of each agency type (APSC State of Service classification) for sufficient spread. A genre analysis of 100 Facebook posts in

November 2015 and user comments for the selected Pages was carried out to examine levels of interaction and participation. It is important to distinguish between audience and agency engagement to understand the level of engagement evident in a specific initiative.

This approach produced a typology of communication practices into discrete categories (i.e., genres) for both agency and audience engagement. From this analysis a four-quadrant interaction mode was developed embodying the discrete characteristics of agency pages employing different dominant communication practices and engagement modes.

Finally, the 68 Facebook Pages were assessed and assigned to interaction modes quadrants based on their dominant communication approach, with pages displaying co-dominant practices assigned to sub-quadrants.

Genre Analysis Methodology

Acknowledging there are multiple ways to analyze communications, we adopted a genre analysis methodology to gauge dominant communicative practices within government Facebook Pages. Yates & Orlikowski (1992) coined the concept of 'genre of organizational communication' in their research on organizational communication. Yates & Orlikowski (1992, p. 301) define genre analysis as: 'typified communicative action invoked in response to a recurrent situation. The recurrent situation or socially defined need includes the history and the nature of established practices, social relations, and communication media within organization.' For the purposes of this research, the classification of communicative activities into genres was undertaken by understanding the purpose and type of each communication and engagement by both the agency and audience.

Practice 2. Practitioners viewpoint and reactions to 'unlocking digital value at the intersection of organizational digital transformation and digital business ecosystems'

Clay Pearson

Unlocking anything requires knowledge of the lock. One needs to know what are the correct tools (digital, biometric, encrypted?) and how to apply them? It also requires a desire to unlock and get to the other side. The academic chapter, 'Unlocking Digital Value at the Intersection of Organizational Digital Transformation and Digital Business Ecosystems' (Karenbogen, Oberlander, and Bovekamp) provides a tour of prior research and papers melding organizational technology transformations with the context, particularly with partnerships, in which that work happens. As somebody in the business, it strikes me that aspects of having the right tools (scale, expertise, prioritization/strategy) alongside organizational 'desire' make the best route to accessing the other side.

THE PUBLIC DIFFERENCE (AND SIMILARITIES)

Digital transformation on an organizational scale, particularly in the public sector, is hard. The referenced article pulls heavily from and describes academic research examples of the private sector. That is appreciated and necessary. The private sector with clear profit motivation to survive and thrive, can leverage that profit imperative and make choices on investment. The clear imperative gives a scorecard (Return on Investment (ROI)) on which various ideas and initiatives are regularly evaluated. The public sector does not have that clarity.

Public sector work does not start with the straightforward ROI evaluation. In the public sector, we have (recognizing those that exist in the business world too) politics of all sorts. Add a dose of inertia, and cumbersome decision-making to further slow and complicate. Plus, if large enough, many times the technology and transformation drive require procurements, evaluations, and decisions that can even get played out in newspaper headlines, public meetings, or election cycles. The public nature is a necessary and good thing for the public sector but that must be recognized when talking about business practices such as digital transformation.

The rules are different for government. When a local government I know wanted to transition from an antiquated software package to a new one, the standard technical evaluation was applied and recommendation made. When the incumbent vendor lost, they took their prerogative to lobby and go directly to policymakers before the final decision. Not too many corporate CIOs have similar concerns when making a recommendation to the CEO.

To round out the point, even the stated desired results have very different measuring sticks. As mentioned, a business has a clear financial ROI metric. The government results are measured in more vague efficiency, but also must be cognizant of who benefits and loses. Governments do not generally choose their customers. The ability to pay a premium can be a negative versus a desired customer with discretionary income. Administrative efficiency is but one of four pillars along with social equity, individual rights, and political responsiveness (Nalbandian).

All this is a context alert, not a rejection of the need to turn the key for digitalization and creating a helpful ecosystem. The administrator/manager job is to modernize, adapt, and bring new technologies. The point is that work here in city halls and county courthouses takes leadership willing to focus and be flexible with a good deal of uncertainties around.

THE CORRECT TOOLS AND CAPABILITIES

The chapter by Karenbogen, et. All provides an impressive literature review and melds streams to intersect Organizational Digital Transformation and Digital Business ecosystems. It strikes me that there are at least three factors for success in the public sector advancing in this regard: 1) Scale; 2) Expertise; and 3) Strategy with Prioritization.

Over 30 years, I have been fortunate to work alongside partners, interacted at professional forums, read/studied about, and collaborated with great dedicated professional colleagues across the world from everywhere to megalopolis like Tokyo to Ahmedabad to Auckland. I've had the opportunity to work intimately directly leading in three cities in different metropolitan areas of the United States. All that direct experience has been in suburban cities with populations between 60 000 and 130 000. So, while acknowledging the risk of bias towards the most familiar, I do think there's some sweet spots for scale to achieving success with technology to results.

I suggest that there is a 'Goldilocks' scale of operation. Somewhere between big enough that allows for the investment of resources for the technology and those to wield it and yet not so gigantic to be unwieldly for relatively gigantic organizations that must have a labyrinth of approvals, levels, and subdepartments to coordinate. That challenge may be more uniquely a United States dilemma with many independent small jurisdictions. Scale needs to be not too big and not too small for regular rapid Organizational Digital Transformation.

More important than absolute scale, but related, is the need for internal technical expertise to identify opportunities and carry out implementations. To bring digitization, it's logical that there has to be people, real human beings, who care, have the focus, and the knowledge to unlock the door to Organizational Digital Transformation. Dreams, aspirations, and ideas need a champion with knowledgeable expertise to move things forward. With scale, not too big and not too small a context, can be progress.

Those dreams and aspirations need focus and structure. The third factor would be having a clear strategy that sifts through competing possibilities to focus on desired end results. Cities with professional managers have the ability to provide continuity and direction. Cities without some consistency can be subject to more fluctuations in direction and implementation.

Regardless of governance structure, Information Technology, Geographic Information System, Digitization, and/or Smart Cities plans to develop the Digital Business Ecosystem development are essential.

COPRODUCTION ECOSYSTEMS

Finally, there's the opportunity developed in the Karenbogen paper that is the opportunity to supercharge transformation with partnerships, particularly coproduction. A timely recent article is by the Kettering Foundation's Valerie Lemmie, 'Relationship Between Public Engagement and Coproduction, (GFOA Government Finance Review, June 2022). Coproduction is a way to deeply integrate partners with expertise to developing integration. Taking community expertise through non-profits or private businesses into the process from beginning to end through coproduction can be a way to move the needle by collaboratively defining the problem before an RFP for a solution is even identified.

The coproduction system could also be thought of open-source government, akin to the early days of local government digitization with hackathons and 'Code for America' initiatives. In some ways, those cutting-edge initiatives are not embedded into local governments' work to meld entrepreneurship and start-ups into the City CIO collection of resources.

The Karenbogen paper provides an impressive literature review to synthesize experience and studies of the keys to unlock digitization. Local governments across the world at most any scale can use their expertise alongside prioritized strategies to achieve new levels of service and excellence to building their community.

GOING FORWARD

Looking ahead, the prospects are positive for more and more local governments leveraging digital value to improved and more efficient, perhaps even more equitable, services. While not on the 'bleeding edge' (thank goodness for slow adoption of cryptocurrency, for example) of technology, there is a growing cadre of professionals linking digital transformation to strategy and operations. While local governments in the USA may struggle with scale and divergent scopes of operation, there is a solid cadre of expertise that's taken hold to share examples and apply both hard and soft technologies. Aided in some cases with coproduction of vendors and community partners, the drones we see in the next few years could be from your local city providing a service just as easily as they are delivering an Amazon package.

7. The new in the old: managing inertia and resulting tensions in digital value creation

Thomas Haskamp, Christian Dremel, Carolin Marx, Ulla Rinkes and Falk Uebernickel

INTRODUCTION

Generating value from digital technology has become a core management task in today's competitive environment (Porter and Heppelmann, 2014, 2015). However, 70 percent of these activities – summarized under the term digital transformation – do not reach their objectives (Forth et al., 2020). This leads to massive cost explosions of transformation projects, disappointed project team members, and frustrated executives. A core reason for this pitfall is inertia, defined as 'the degree of stickiness of the organization being transformed' (Besson and Rowe, 2012, 105). Therefore, inertial forces present a crucial challenge for theory and practice (Vial 2019; Forth et al., 2020).

In practice, inertia is experienced on multiple levels. On the individual level, managers report about resistant behavior of employees who either reject or doubt digital transformation activities (Forth et al., 2020). On the organizational level, inertia is experienced in slow processes and rigid organizational structures that undermine the execution of digital transformation activities (Schmid, 2019). While executive teams are familiar with the phenomenon from numerous personal experiences such as delayed or failed projects and employees' resistance, inertia is hardly explicitly discussed.

From a research perspective, two different ways of thinking about inertia can be identified. The first stream of research understands inertia as an entity's strong persistence to stay in the status-quo (Rumelt, 1995; Polites and Karahanna, 2012; Orlikowski, 2000). From this understanding, a view of inertia as a form of resistance to change has emerged in literature around organizational change (Tushman and O'Reilly, 1996). The underlying idea is to think about change as a dual concept in which there is either stability or change (Stieglitz, Knudsen, and Becker, 2016). Inertia is then responsible for the former, keeping things how they are. This results in thinking about inertia as persistence, rigidity, and perseverance. While these concepts may become a challenge when it comes to changing the status quo, they are at the same time also responsible for driving organizational efficiency (Besson and Rowe, 2012). Beyond, persistence and perseverance are also core characteristics of successful entrepreneurs who stick to their ideas despite the challenges ahead. Thus, inertia may have a strong normative connotation depending on the context.

The second stream of research follows the idea of inertia being embedded in an ontological process perspective, in which things are continuously changing (Rescher, 2000). In terms of this view, processes are crucial to thinking. This implies to 'considering phenomena dynamically – in terms of movement, activity, events, change and temporal evolution' (Langley, 2007, 271). This line of thought refers to inertia as different rates of speed between separate entities moving in a temporal space (Hannan and Freeman, 1984). Thus, the distance between the temporal unfolding of things is understood as inertia.

Both schools of thought have advanced the understanding of inertia on the organizational level. However, much of this work has been conducted in pre-digital times (Besson and Rowe, 2012), not considering digital technology's generative capacity and boundary spanning effects (Yoo et al., 2012; Nambisan et al., 2017; Hund et al., 2021). The growing dispersion of digital technologies over the past years challenges the status quo and makes inertia a timely and vividly discussed topic (Vial, 2019; Schmid, 2019; Haskamp, Dremel, et al., 2021).

To summarize, both practice and academia are challenged in understanding and coping with inertia as part of digital transformation activities, which builds the motivation for this chapter. Many executives believe that inertia is hard to tackle and a natural barrier to overcome as part of a change initiative. Considering digital transformation activities' immense failure rates, we think there are more profound ways of dealing with inertia by executive teams.

Thus, the book intends to create awareness of different inertia effects and resulting tensions in the digital transformation activities of pre-digital companies. We focus on pre-digital companies as they are especially challenged with the integration of digital technology. They already have an existing business model, products, and services, including running operations. This makes it particularly challenging for them to transform digitally. We propose a conceptual model based on data from more than 70 interviews with three large-scale multinational companies and their digital transformation initiatives. The framework shall serve to help practitioners to understand better where they might need to deal with inertia and its associated tensions.

We understand inertia as the reproduction of the status quo. This status quo is challenged by the ongoing exploration and exploitation of digital innovation leading to different tensions in several organizational domains. Thereby, inertia unfolds on the individual and organizational level and can also be understood as 'organizational stickiness' (Besson and Rowe, 2012). We talk about different inertia domains as organizational areas in which inertia effects and occurrences were visible within our cases. We use the term tensions to refer to the challenges that executive teams experience when dealing with inertia, while at the same time aiming to implement and integrate digital innovation within their company.

This chapter is structured as follows: Firstly, we present a conceptual framework, including its three organizational domains: 1) Vision and Strategy; 2) Governance and Processes; and 3) Mindset and Culture. For each field, we present tensions occurring in subdomains. Based on our findings and contextualized with academic literature, we explain each subdomain and appearing tensions by giving examples and introducing their root causes. We end the chapter by discussing some ideas on the management of inertia in digital transformation initiatives of organizations.

INERTIA TRIGGERED BY DIGITAL INNOVATION: A CONCEPTUAL FRAMEWORK

Organizational inertia, as well as other forms and dimensions of inertia (e.g., socio-technical inertia, cultural inertia, socio-cognitive inertia, structural inertia) present a well-studied topic in management and information systems research (Besson and Rowe, 2012; Tushman and O'Reilly, 1996; Haskamp, Dremel, et al., 2021). Tripsas's work focuses on inertia imposed by technology (Tripsas, 2009; Tripsas and Gavetti, 2000; Tripsas, 2016) and coined the term of technological inertia. She defines it as 'the propensity of incumbent firms with historical expertise in one generation of technology to continue development of that generation and not effectively develop and commercialize products based on a new generation of technology' (Tripsas, 2016, 1).

We follow this vein but want to highlight the role of digital innovation for understanding inertia. Thereby, we understand digital innovation in its all-encompassing form, including the impact of digital technology on products and services, but also its impact on the process of development and resulting changes in the organizing logic of the firm (Hund et al., 2021; Nambisan et al., 2017; Nambisan, Lyytinen, and Yoo, 2020). We want to highlight the malleability of digital technology, which allows the editability and recombinability of digital innovation (Yoo et al., 2012). This again triggers the redefinition of boundaries on different levels and leads to the convergence of products and services (Hund et al., 2021). For instance, the integration and launch of digital innovation blur boundaries between products and services. This redefines departmental, organizational and industry boundaries (Porter and Heppelmann,

2015). We argue that these effects of digital innovation pose new and different occurrences or effects of inertia within existing organizational domains.

Our conceptual framework reflects this line of thinking and provides an overview of how digital innovation triggers different forms of inertia occurrences across three organizational inertia domains.

The first inertia domain evolves around the impact of digital innovation on incumbent organizations' strategic vision and corporate strategy (Vial, 2019; Chanias, Myers, and Hess, 2019). Within this domain, digital innovations require pre-digital companies to think about the current customer structure (Chanias, Myers, and Hess, 2019), to revise their product and service offerings (Svahn, Mathiassen, and Lindgren, 2017; Dremel et al., 2017), to think about new ways of monetizing their business model (Svahn, Mathiassen, and Lindgren, 2017) and challenges an organizations identity (Tripsas, 2009; Wessel et al., 2020).

Secondly, engaging in the exploitation of digital innovation requires organizations to substantially reconfigure their organizational systems, including their IT infrastructure (Schmid, 2019), their governance structure (Wiesböck and Hess, 2020; Tiwana and Kim, 2015) and, also their organizational processes (Hinings, Gegenhuber, and Greenwood, 2018).

Thirdly, digital innovation requires organizations to embrace a new digital mindset and culture, involving new capabilities and different values. It further relies on a different mental model that executive teams and employees need to build (van der Meulen, Weill, and Woerner, 2020; Hund et al., 2021; Vial, 2019).

The outlined inertia domains are tied to existing research on digital innovation and transformation. They rely on the main impact areas of digital innovation and the triggered transformation (Drechsler et al., 2020; Vial, 2019). This seems reasonable given that inertia occurrences appear most in areas of organizations in which organizational change unfolds. Within each inertia domain, we find different inertia occurrences. These are triggered through the implementation of digital innovation (Yoo et al., 2012). In the following, we describe the various occurrences as effects of inertia that can be observed in the organization's daily work. These effects are then visible in resulting tensions that explain how inertia occurrences appear. The resulting tensions display the inertial forces of the organization on the one hand and the organizational implications of digital innovation on the other hand.

VISION AND STRATEGY

The inertia domain vision and strategy reflects the impact of digital innovation on strategic decisions and the vision of the organization. The literature on digital innovation and transformation touches upon these issues with the terms

Inertia Domain	Inertia Occurrences/Effects	Resulting Tensions Inert Force vs Digital Innovation Implication
Vision and Strategy		
Customer	Department Ownership and Fear of Loosing Customers	Retention of Existing Customer Base vs. Generation of New Customers
Products and Services	Integration Struggles and Cannibalization Effects	Lock-In Effects due to Product Design Decisions vs. Smart Products and Services
Monetization	Protection of Profitability and Doubts of Financial Viability	Meeting Existing Profitability Targets vs. Required Investments for Digital Capabilities
Identity	Identity Threat, Fragmentation and Ambiguity	Past Success Legitimizes Historical Identity vs. Identity Uncertainty around Digital Innovation
Organizational Systems		
IT Infrastructure	Complexity of IT-Architecture limits Integration Efforts	Lock-In Decisions of IT Systems vs. Technical Requirements to Realize Digital Innovation
Governance Structure	Conflicts between Entities, Functions and Roles	Established Routinized Distribution of Responsibility vs. Collaborative and Fast Decision-Making
Organizational Processes	Workarounds, Continuous Task Force Mode, Redundancies	Rigidity of Established Processes vs. Flexibility and Demands of Agile Software Development
Mindset and Culture		
Capabilities	Confusion and Adoption Struggles	Existing Capabilities and Skills vs. New Skills and Capabilities for Digital Innovation
Values	Low Experimentation and Risk-Taking Behavior	Institutionalized Pursuit of Perfection vs. Required Exploration Mindset
Mental Models	Active and Passive Resistance	Fear of Becoming Redundant vs. Required Cognitive Flexibility to Deal with Change

Figure 7.1   Inertia domains, occurrences and resulting tensions

of digital innovation strategy and organizational determinants (Hund et al., 2021) as well as digital disruptions, strategic responses or structural changes in the value creation paths of organizations (Vial, 2019).

Drawing on existing research and our empirical data, four different subdomains and resulting tensions in each subdomain are distinguishable (see Figure 7.1).

Customer

Digital innovations often lead to shifts in the customer landscape of an incumbent organization (Vial, 2019). Thus, the launch of new digital services or products by new emerging start-ups that can quickly turn into serious competitors requires a strategic response from pre-digital companies (Vial, 2019; Chanias, Myers, and Hess, 2019). Hence, customers quickly learn to appreciate how digital technology delivers a faster and more customer-centered product or service, threatening existing products or services provided by established companies.

Addressing this competitive threat, incumbents also engage in developing new digital services and products that need to be tested with customers and launched at a point in time (Sebastian et al., 2017). With regards to customers, this often leads to a constellation in which organizations run the operations and sales of their existing products and services on the one hand, while at the same time try to digitize them or to position new digital services and products in the market on the other. Throughout these activities, we identified two main inertia occurrences.

Firstly, the development of digital services requires data access from several different sources within the organization. While new digital products and services are often developed in dedicated units or areas, they often have to be inte-

Table 7.1   Inertia domain vision and strategy

Sub-Domain	Inertia Occurrences	Resulting Tension
Customer	Department ownership refers to how existing departments (e.g., sales) want to retain their access to existing customers.	Retention of existing customer base vs. generation of new customers.
	Fear of losing customers refers to how exposing existing customers to new digital innovations may harm the customer relationship.	
Product and Services	Integration struggles refer to architectural challenges appearing when digitally extending an analog product.	Lock-in effects due to prior product design decisions vs. design requirements of smart products and services.
	Cannibalization effects refer to the fear that new digital services or products will undermine sales of existing core products and services.	
Monetization	Protection of profitability refers to the argument that old products guarantee certain profits that the executive team wants to keep.	Meeting specific profitability targets vs. required investments for digital infrastructure and capabilities.
	Doubt of financial viability refers to doubts that new digital services will lead to substantial financial income.	
Identity	Identity threat, fragmentation, and ambiguity refer to competitive actions within the market that challenge the existing logic of the organization leading to ingroup-outgroup situations within the organization.	Past success legitimizes historical identity vs. identity uncertainty around digital innovation.

grated within the organization at some point, which led to a conflict. Expressly, the responsible departments referred to an old IT policy ensuring that 'their' (sales) data is also processed in 'their' (sales) systems. Consequently, departments struggle to overcome their boundaries, which is visible in hesitant behavior in digital innovation activities that require cross departmental and organizational collaboration.

Secondly, in the development of digital services, teams often want to interview and test their ideas with current customers. Thus, they planned to approach customers directly and further tried to ask sales teams if they could provide access to customers. Sales teams were somewhat hesitant to grant access to their customers. They were afraid to expose their customers to something that sales teams were not in control of. The digital teams then perceived this as challenging as they relied on customer feedback to test and further develop their ideas.

In general, we can identify a tension between retaining an existing customer base versus generating new customers. On the one hand, pre-digital companies often serve established market segments with rather mature and old customers. The organizational processes, structures, and incentives are well-aligned towards targeting those customers and ensuring their value. Thus, the performance of sales departments may be assessed on customer satisfaction scores, of which exposing customers to new digital services and products might result in negative scores. On the other hand, new digital products and services need to be tested and experimented with. Specifically, close customer collaboration across the entire organization, going beyond sales departments, is vital to spurring the development of new digital products and services.

Products and services

In response to competitive moves and changing customer demands, digital innovations fundamentally alter an organization's product and service portfolio by either adding and complementing it or replacing and cannibalizing existing products and services (Porter and Heppelmann, 2015). This requires them to engage in redesigning their products and services, involving different issues that emerge. Two main inertia occurrences were observed within the products and services domain.

Firstly, the integration of digital technology within the given architecture often poses significant integration struggles. Thus, the prevalent product infrastructure may result in technological limits while integrating digital technologies into existing products. Thus, in some cases equipping the physical component with sensors or retrofitting is not possible from a technology perspective or may result in immense integration costs that may contradict the potential gain in value (at least in the short- to mid-term). A prominent example is the vehicle architecture of cars that incumbent car manufacturers aim to digitize to respond to new competitors in the market (NIO, Rivian, Li Auto, or Tesla) (Hylving and Schultze, 2020). In this context, car manufacturers aim to implement digital services such as on-demand functions that may be configurable or transmittable over the air. Accessing the data from the car components means accessing each electronic control unit attached to the car's components (Hylving and Schultze, 2020). Current car architectures often have more than 100 control units attached to single mechantronical components manufactured by decentralized suppliers. Centralizing these units to simplify data access and processing speed culminates in enormous integration costs. Established car manufacturers are redesigning their 'in-car' technologies and architectures to get hold of this technology-driven problem. Regarding cannibalization effects, recently launched digital services often replace and threaten existing products and service delivery infrastructure.

Secondly, when it comes to positioning these products in the market, new digital smart products cannibalize non-digital products, and the responsible organizational members are affected. Staying with the car manufacturer example, the implementation of over-the-air services allowing customers to receive bug fix updates on their cars replaces visits to workshops of the car manufacturers, threatening their business model. Hence, pre-digital companies need to find ways to deal with the redefined roles of existing stakeholders by redesigning their service structure and business model or, for example, by participating in generated sales through the over-the-air services.

The underlying tension is found between lock-in effects due to past product design decisions versus the characteristics and implications of new smart and connected products. Accordingly, this tension is rooted in the product architecture logic that was sufficient before and relied on a well-diversified supply process. Although incumbent car manufacturers have understood this issue and invested in building new product architectures, they still need to find solutions for transitioning older car models relying on the decentralized infrastructure. Earlier product design decisions (in this case, the decentralized architecture of control units) reinforce themselves. This leads to lock-in effects through the product architecture legacy.

Monetization

The adoption of digital products and services impacts an organization's business model by creating new forms of value for the servitization of businesses (Porter and Heppelmann, 2015). This leads to new and different forms of how organizations realize financial value through their products – monetization. Specifically, digital products or services often generate income based on subscription payment models, impacting an organization's profitability scheme. This often stands in strong contrast to non-digital business models. Within the subdomain of monetization, we find two occurrences of inertia.

Firstly, profitability protection means a strong attachment to revenues of previous analog products that are quite profitable and threatened by digital products. Regarding profitability protection, we build on differences in monetization strategies of analog vs. digital products and services. Analog products have often been commercialized solely through a single point of sale. Now, digital features complement and extend this value chain beyond this single point leading to continuous earnings and a different cost structure (Porter and Heppelmann, 2015). Specifically, digital products often generate small financial income continuously through payment models such as subscription services, whereas physical products often require customers to pay once. This shift in the monetization logic of a product may also involve cannibalization issues. The new digital product may replace or threaten existing product cash cows. An example is the automotive industry, in which most of the revenue is created through the sale of the vehicle with rather high profit margins. Now, being confronted with selling digital mobility services, small amounts of income are created over time. Hence, executives are challenged with shareholders' expectations of revenues from analog business models. As a result, executives need to justify why revenue and cost structures are different.

Second, questions on financial viability refer to arguments and the implementation that critically challenge the sustainability of the new digital services and products. The establishment of digital services and products comes with significant investments into the related capabilities. These investments burden the current revenues and can also stress the balance sheet. At the same time, the risk and opportunity of success are highly unforeseeable.

Striving to meet specific profitability targets stands in conflict with providing the required investments for the necessary digital infrastructure and capabilities for executive teams. Investments in infrastructure are often hard to justify as their rationale is not easy to explain, and assets are exceptionally high. These structural tensions are enforced through further issues. Analogue business models are often easy-to-understand business models. That results in individuals being afraid of losing these. Other biases like loss aversion – the observation that losses loom larger than gains (Kahneman and Tversky, 1979) – come into play at the individual level. At the organization's level, organizational budgeting and controlling practices reinforce current profitability schemes relying on a long-existing and well-established customer base that you can perfectly predict. This becomes a challenge when a budget needs to be provided for long-term digital products.

Identity

A core characteristic of digital transformation processes in organizations is that digital technology may pose significant challenges to the existing organizational identity (Wessel et al., 2020). Through the emergence of new start-ups, incumbents experience a threat on two levels. Instantly implementing digital technology itself may threaten the organizational purpose. Additionally, new competitors and emerging start-ups that enter the market based on exploiting a new digital technology pose a threat to incumbents. Hence, the adaption of digital technologies impacts different levels of the organizational identity (Tripsas, 2009; Tripsas and Gavetti, 2000).

Another inertia occurrence addresses effects around identity threats from new emerging competitors that pre-digital companies need to deal with. This led to different forms of fragmentation within the organization and created an ambiguous space. With the launch of digital innovation activities within organizations, one car manufacturer experienced a vital form of identity fragmentation. With fragmentation, we refer to situations in which the implementation of digital technology leads to two opposing groups. On the one hand, tradition keepers challenge the feasibility of new digital features and services and argue for focusing on the organization's core strength instead of adapting to a new normality. On the other hand, tech-savvy pioneers stress the urgent need for embracing the new digital approach, often pushing new agile ways of working across organizational areas challenging existing ways of doing things that are tied to analog businesses. Additionally, digital technologies lead to boundary-spanning activities and behavior (Hund et al., 2021). Specifically, roles and boundaries between organizational structures blur while implementing agile product development practices. This again creates an ambiguous space in which employees struggle to formulate a coherent answer in terms of the organizational identity. While they aim to follow digital pioneers like Google, Amazon, or Apple, many pre-digital companies are bounded to the material conditions of their products or to their legacy, leading to liminal periods of innovation (Orlikowski and Scott, 2021).

In consequence, the parallel existence of the old non-digital products and services and the new digital value creation triggers questions around organizational purpose. On the individual level, this is often caused by the imminent transformation of identity that is not yet made sense of by individuals. However, this can become dangerous for organizations as the current interpretations of what the organization represents might undermine ongoing activities. Additionally, this observation is seen on the organizational level through strategic moves that the organization makes (e.g., through M&A activities) that no longer reflect the old identity, altering the prevalent organizational logic and identity.

Thus, a tension emerges between the old identity that is often legitimized based on a success story that builds the organization and a new form of identity uncertainty around the pursued digital innovation strategy. Organizational identity can serve as a filter for recognizing new digital innovations, highlighting the vital role of identity within the digital transformation of incumbent organizations. Prior work has shown that organizations adopting digital technologies experience identity shifts. They go through different stages in which a new identity emerges and is subsequently incorporated (Tripsas, 2009). The car manufacturer, in our case, often argued that new digital technologies would extend rather than replace the existing organizational identity.

Organizational Systems

The inertia domain deals with issues around the existing IT infrastructure, governance structure, and organizational processes (see Table 7.2).

IT infrastructure
While implementing digital innovation, incumbent organizations often need to touch upon their given IT infrastructure, on which solutions need to be built upon. Specifically, realizing digital innovation often builds on new micro-service-based architectures and the use of application programming interfaces (APIs) is essential in ensuring modularity and speed. While independent development is often pursued as an easier way for implementation, the

Table 7.2   Inertia domain organizational systems

Sub-Domain	Inertia Occurrences	Resulting Tension
IT Infrastructure	The complexity of IT architecture refers to how the existing landscape of IT systems may impose limits for the integration of new digital innovations requiring substantial integration efforts.	Lock-in decisions of IT systems vs. technical requirements to realize digital innovation.
Governance Structure	Conflicts between entities, functions, and roles refer to issues around established stakeholder constellations that need to be reorganized to realize digital innovation with new internal units emerging and trying to find their role.	Established routinized distribution of responsibility vs. collaborative and fast decision-making involving new stakeholders.
Organizational Processes	Workarounds refer to activities and actions of digital innovation teams in which they try to find a way of executing the required activities for digital innovation while trying to circumvent with existing rigid processes. Continuous task force mode refers to an organizational setup in which normal processes and organizational structures are ignored due to high external pressure and slowness of these processes.	The rigidity of established processes vs. flexibility and demands for agile software development.

integration of these new digital systems needs to be considered. Thus, executive teams need to ensure that existing enterprise resource planning systems or IT systems deployed for specific organizational functions are tied to the new digital architecture. Otherwise, when implementing digital innovation, the existing IT infrastructure becomes a source of rigidity (Schmid, 2019).

Inertia within IT infrastructures emerged due to the complexity of the given IT architecture. Often systems have been developed over time, and functions and features are continuously added, resulting in a large monolithic IT system in which interdependencies between applications have become hard to control. Thus, the high complexity leads to the fear of imposing changes to the IT system, of which unintended side-effects may lead to the malfunction of parts of these systems. Dealing with the existing IT infrastructure requires organizations to decide, whether they want to pursue a new greenfield approach in which new IT applications are developed from scratch and as stand-alone products, or if they wish to integrate new digital solutions within the existing architecture in a brownfield approach. Within the case contexts, organizations were required to integrate digital innovations into the current IT systems as they needed to access data from old IT systems. A company's IS resources (existing legacy IT infrastructure) are integral to its complex business processes and services. Its renewal or alteration changes many non-IS resources (Liang et al., 2017).

Furthermore, companies need to face invested costs. Financial resources are already spent on these infrastructures, and the organization will tend to stick to these built IS resources. For example, firms spending millions of dollars on an enterprise resource planning (ERP) system do not easily switch to another system (Liang et al., 2017).

Further, IT infrastructures have a 'hardness' to them, which is difficult to break through their intertwining with the organizational processes and the complementarities of its components for their functioning (Geels, 2004). As a consequence, 'it becomes nearly unthinkable for the technology to change in any substantial fashion' (Geels, 2004, p. 911). The past choices in the design and development of IT legacy infrastructures requires an intense reflection of those choices and imagination of how one would build the same IT capabilities with prevalent emerging technologies. An organization may purposefully decide for an 'in-between' state, or a more disruptive change of core IS systems. Despite this decision, modularity and adequate capsulation (e.g., through asynchronous message and event brokering) will be key to keeping hold of emerging technologies' ever-increasing opportunities.

Consequently, lock-in decisions made in the IT system and specific design options that come along with it stand in contrast with the technical requirements necessary to realize digital innovations and corresponding characteristics of speed and modularity.

Governance structure
With efforts to adjust the current organization for digital innovation, governance becomes a core topic in the redesign of a pre-digital company (Wiesböck and Hess, 2020). Hence, digital transformation's success depends upon transforming an organization as a whole, including its technical structures, work practices and capabilities, ways of decision-making, and in particular rigid established governance structures and mechanisms (Keen, 1981). Governance structures represent a structure (who is governed, what is governed, how is governed) for ensuring that business objectives are achieved through an organization's work. Specifically, they refer to structural decisions such as which kinds of functions, roles, and goals are pursued and by whom.

Within the course of digital transformation, many organizations establish dedicated organizational units and labs – often referred to as digital innovation units (Dremel et al., 2017; Haskamp, Mayer, et al., 2021). Tasked with the development of digital innovations, these innovation units and labs emerge, including trying to find their role within the organization. This leads to the reorientation of several stakeholders within and around the organization, making conflicts between entities, functions, and roles an emerging inertia occurrence within the transformation of an organization. On the entity level, new organizational entities that are either established or bought shackle the status quo. Prior existing entities and functions such as sales, IT, or production may see their traditional business in jeopardy and they may feel that they have lost control. This potentially results in a 'not-invented-here' phenomenon in which they may block access to their operations or in which they undermine the integration at a later stage. Therefore, new emerging entities pose conflicts between different organizational functions and their role in pushing digital technology. Similarly, organizations often adopt new agile frameworks in digital transformation (Fuchs and Hess, 2018), coming along with new organizational structures and roles. This undermines existing roles and structures, and at the same time different corporate players need to reposition themselves, searching for a new place in the organization. This often results in a complexity of stakeholder decisions that, in turn, slows down decision-making. A successful transformation will alter how work practices are controlled and governed while changing the roles and responsibilities in an organization – independent of the future use of digital technologies.

Beyond this, the automation and radical innovation of work practices through generative digital technologies put an organization in jeopardy of aligning its technical constituents and related governance structures and mechanisms. So, digital transformation initiatives need to consider governance from two sides: prevalent governance in the organizations which are being changed and governance of the initiative itself. While the first should target the unfreezing rigid and established structures, the latter should replicate the 'new normal' in the initiative itself. Relational governance or its manifestation of informal control may provide a supportive environment for strategically innovating and transforming the organization (Weeks and Feeny, 2008).

Thus, the established routinized distribution of responsibility and work within governance structures may conflict with the need for collaborative and fast decision-making involving new stakeholders.

Organizational processes

Within changing the organization and creating a future-ready company (Weill and Woerner, 2018; Vial, 2019), pre-digital companies often already have clearly defined processes for product development, management, and manufacturing. These processes acted as a source of stability and efficiency in the past, but in implementing digital innovation and creating digital value, they become a source of rigidity (Besson and Rowe, 2012).

Processes and organizational routines as a source of inertia are a well-researched form of structural inertia (Hannan and Freeman, 1984; Schwarz, 2012). Yet, organizations aiming to implement digital innovations and transform their processes and structures are a core impediment for pre-digital companies (Vial, 2019; Drechsler et al., 2020). Thus, organizations try to master digital transformation targets by improving and renewing their overall work processes and respective business models. Often organizations lose sight of this goal by focusing on the mere implementation of new digital technologies or the replacement of established IS infrastructures. An organization remains in routine rigidity by failing to change organizational processes that use those resources (Besson and Rowe, 2012).

Inertia emerges when digital innovation teams are challenged and circumvent internal processes. We see an intense process conflict between other organizational logics, such as the agile development of digital innovations and waterfall project management for physical goods (Lappi et al., 2018). Furthermore, a low speed of transformation efforts and bureaucratic processes appears to be characteristic of implementing digital innovation. As such, employees may 'choose to use technology to retain their existing way of doing things the reinforcement and preservation of the structural status quo, with no discernible changes in work practices or the technological artifact; (Orlikowski, 2000, p. 421). It ultimately requires the countering of 'intruding' changes to both technical infrastructures and organizational design and work practices (e.g., setting up dedicated units that aim to explore and develop digital innovations) or to the readjustment of internal processes (e.g., reinvention of work practices through agile methods) (Drechsler et al., 2020). Routinized rigid rules may also provide security for employees to do things right and persevere with established power structures. Yet, the previously referred to transformation will lead to an alteration of the organization that needs to be taken care of through transparent communication measures (e.g., rationale for transformation, benefits for the individuals and the organization, as well the guided transformation to the 'new normal' through change management). Digital innovation teams react by using workarounds. They try to find a way of executing the required activities for digital innovation while circumventing and dealing with existing rigid processes. For example, the car manufacturer relied on 'backarounds', an organizational practice in which teams changed software artifacts silently in the background. However, the official process does not account for this affordance. Further, incumbent organizations often try to deal with their slow processes by moving into a continuous task force mode, referring to an organizational setup in which normal operations are circumvented due to high external pressure and slowness of these processes. Lastly, process redundancies not being synergized are a typical inertia occurrence. These examples provide evidence for the tension between the rigidity of established processes that stands in contrast to the required flexibility and the demands of agile software development used for digital innovations.

Mindset and Culture

With increasing technological possibilities and environmental complexity, firms experience higher levels of uncertainty and ambiguity (Vial, 2019). This also affects employees' organizational culture and mindset (van der Meulen, Weill, and Woerner, 2020). For example, prior research has shown that uncertainty amplifies inertia through regret aversion and indecisiveness and that ambiguity concerning existing habits is a powerful source of inertia (Sautua, 2017). Hence, being aware of how people deal with the uncertain nature of change and potential ambiguous interpretations of the future is a crucial managerial task in the context of transformation initiatives. Possible signs indicating an inability to deal with ambiguity should be alarming, as they can accelerate inertial forces.

The inertia domain mindset and culture express the personal and cultural impact of digital innovation. These elements are discussed in current work (Hund et al., 2021; Vial, 2019) that highlights, for example, the need for an iterative and agile mindset and incorporation of digital values into the organizational philosophy and culture (van der Meulen, Weill, and Woerner, 2020; Tabrizi et al., 2019). Throughout our data analysis, we found three inertia domains that emerged (see Table 7.3).

Table 7.3   Inertia domain mindset and culture

Sub-Domain	Inertia Occurrences	Resulting Tension
Capabilities	Confusion refers to the lack of sensemaking of employees in which new work practices, activities, and outcomes are not yet understood, leading to the response of confusion.	Existing capabilities and skills vs. new skills and capabilities for digital innovation.
	Adoption struggles refer to how new practices are not yet enacted, which results in situations in which employees are acting on old practices in a new setting.	
Values	Low experimentation and risk-taking behavior refer to inactivity due to the fear of punishment and doing things in the wrong way, which is often rooted in the organization's enforced pursuit of perfectionism.	Institutionalized pursuit of perfection. vs. required exploration mindset.
Mental Models	Active resistance refers to disagreement and expressed misunderstandings with the new course of action that is actively challenged.	Fear of becoming redundant vs. required cognitive flexibility to deal with change.
	Passive resistance refers to undermining or ignoring activities of employees in which a coalition is built against the intended change.	

Capabilities

Lifelong learning and the ability to acquire knowledge on the individual and organizational level represent a key resource for achieving and maintaining a competitive advantage in digital transformation (Caloghirou, Kastelli, and Tsakanikas, 2004). As a power and resource, knowledge and corresponding capabilities are significant assets for individuals and organizations. Almost every transformation or change initiative requires building or reconfiguring knowledge-based capabilities based on generating, capturing, sharing, and applying knowledge (Yang and Chen, 2007). Conversely, this also means that the inability to create and transmit the required novel knowledge on an individual level and structures that impede knowledge creation and transfer on the organizational level can evoke inertial forces. The significant role of skills and knowledge when leveraging new technologies, implementing agile methods, or transforming corporate culture as instantiated puzzle pieces show how digital transformation may manifest in practice (Fuchs and Hess, 2018).

The lack of capabilities unfolds in two inertia occurrences within the cases. Firstly, confusion refers to the lack of sensemaking of employees, in which new work practices, activities, and outcomes are not yet understood. Secondly, adoption struggles to refer to how new approaches are not yet enacted, resulting in situations in which employees act on old practices in a new setting.

This might be caused by a systematic lack of knowledge about the new approach, its reasons for necessity, and missing potential benefits for the organization and the individual. The research underlines that the necessary changes in products, services, and business processes to digitally transform an organization and the maintenance of ongoing operations will require new skills and knowledge capabilities (Vial, 2019). In our cases, we have observed people who are reluctant to learn about newly introduced functionalities and those, who rush into action before being adequately equipped with the necessary knowledge. Both can severely endanger the success of the transformation initiative and impose a risk of frustration and rejection. On an individual level, such observations can be caused by a lack of appropriate training due to the unavailability of training possibilities or unwillingness to get involved as employees have mentally left the organization.

Further, the lack of ability to anchor and apply the trained knowledge into daily practice and the unsuccessful transfer of learning are key barriers. The latter is also fostered when there is skepticism about the transformation initiative present and people question the effectiveness of investing time and effort to extend their knowledge base. The former is often rooted in organizational factors. Insufficient investments in training on new methods, technologies, or working approaches can hinder knowledge creation and transfer regarding the subject of change, which impacts skill and capability building. Similarly, a lack of change agents, who advocate the transformation initiative and help to share knowledge on the necessity and causes of change, increases the risk of skepticism and resistance. Top management support and visibility in embracing the new change is essential for addressing upcoming opposition. Hence, establishing a learning culture and incentivizing life-long learning can be crucial counteracting elements in this context.

Thus, a tension between the existing capabilities and the newly required ones emerges, which individuals and organizations need to address along with their transformation.

Values

Digital transformation also implies adopting different values, driving customer centricity, speed, and action to cope with new competitors, and embracing a digital mindset (van der Meulen, Weill, and Woerner, 2020). This again affects the lives of organizational members, including their values. The nature of work and performance expectations may change, usually requiring more effort. Relationships may be lost or have to be re-build. There exist multiple aspects of organizational transformation that can easily be experienced as distressing. This promotes anxiety which alerts threat perceptions and evokes psychologically defensive responses (Allcorn and Diamond, 1997). Fear, loss, and anger are frequently accompanying emotions. Perfectionism, characterized as striving for flawlessness, setting excessively high standards for performance, and evaluating one's behavior overly critically (Flett and Hewitt, 2002), is a common and potentially accelerating factor for interpreting organizational change as a threat. Hence, perfectionistic behavior, which is frequently accompanied by fear of failure and reinforcement of risk and experimentation aversion, is an occurrence of inertial forces threatening the success of transformation initiatives managers should watch out for. Otherwise, fear and uncertainty can damage morale and prevent the successful implementation of the desired transformations at multiple levels of the organization.

While perfection is often associated with overachievement, much of the literature shows a relationship between perfectionism and underachievement (Harari et al., 2018). In characterizing the sub domain, we identified the resulting reinforcement of risk and experimentation, hostile behavior, and negative emotions like fear of failure and anticipated regret as crucial. On the individual level, not embracing change but being skeptical and hesitant about becoming involved can be caused by the fear of becoming redundant, of not fulfilling and performing below expectations, or the fear of simply failing while trying. Those emotions are accelerated by a perfectionistic organizational culture, in which failure is used frequently as a label, and individuals fear the consequences of reporting errors. Also, a low level of individual autonomy and stakeholders suppressing their opinions might reinforce cautious behavior and skepticism towards change and eventually signal inertia. Organizational factors might also accelerate the ripple effects of perfectionism by hindering individuals from getting involved in change because they anticipate and try to avoid failure.

For instance, we see anecdotal evidence in our cases that strong hierarchical structures combined with the lack of incentivizing experimentation can endanger transformation initiatives because individuals fear professional drawbacks when taking risks. When interpreted as a loss of status, a change of title, role or reporting line can be counterproductive and might even spill over to other employees involved. Incentivizing experimentation and framing failures as gains in experiences instead of losses might counteract these effects. Similarly, embracing an organizational failure culture can weaken the inertial forces accelerated by perfectionism and fear of failure.

Thus, many pre-digital companies face tensions between an institutionalized pursuit of perfection and the required digital and explorative mindset to realize digital innovation efforts within the company.

Mental models
Digital transformation presents a deep-structure change, affecting every employee and their mental model (Vial, 2019). Hence, organizations must be aware of the human element and its implications for digital transformation-related decisions. The success of transformation initiatives depends on individuals' willingness to work towards the transformation-related goals and mental models (Brisson-Banks, 2010). Leaders who ignore this element guarantee an uphill battle against inertia, if not a sure failure. The level of engagement in forming a response to transformation efforts depends on the socio-cognitive process used to make sense of new information. Emphasis should be given to anticipating and monitoring cognitive responses to a digital transformation initiative, as recognizing and changing mindsets is extremely difficult. Once established, there is a danger that actors may become overly dependent on their mental models, especially if the intention is to change existing individual mental models into an organizational shared mental model (Nag, Hambrick, and Chen, 2007), which can result in passive or active resistance to the initiative.

Given the relevance of socio-cognitive processes, active and passive resistance from employees and other stakeholders are crucial inertia signals to anticipate and watch out for. The cognitive responses are observable in behaviors that restrict transformation activities because they are not aligned with the mental model of the change agents and receivers. Hence, one relevant managerial task based on identifying cognitive responses as inertia signals is to deal with the heterogeneity of attitudes, respective mental models, and eventually response behaviors to transformation initiatives. On the individual level, resisting behavior can be amplified by many causes. A simple disagreement with the direction or execution of the transformation, for instance, and more subtle causes such as the fear of losing power or relevance with changing structures and general risk aversion in the face of ambiguity can accelerate resistance. In general, changing attitudes and formerly established mental models is highly challenging and requires active engagement in change management, training, and leadership. When additionally, there is a mismatch of speed or direction of mental model alignment, resisting behavior is probable. An essential aspect of cognitive responses and potential behavioral resistance to transformation is communication on the organizational level. We have observed in our cases that not offering sufficient information and training – especially when it comes to cultural shifts – bears the danger of accelerating resistance. A misalignment between change agents and receivers can result in a mismatch of mental models about the transformation and eventually in resisting behaviors. Besides interpersonal and communication-related factors, an organization's structure can also reinforce or incentivize sticking to established mental models.

These inertia occurrences of active and passive forms of resistance result from a tension between employees' fear of becoming redundant and the required cognitive flexibility to deal with organizational change.

MANAGEMENT OF INERTIA AND RESULTING TENSIONS

Figure 7.2 summarizes all inertia domains based on our cases of pre-digital companies and their digital innovation and transformation. The figure builds on the three main organizational domains. Firstly, the inner part of the circle contains the inertia domain vision and strategy. Secondly, the intermediate part contains the inertia domain of organizational systems. Lastly, the outer circle covers the inertia domain of mindset and culture. The framework's logic must be interpreted from the inside out, meaning that the first dimension needs to be addressed by the senior management. In contrast, the second and third dimensions should involve and affect more and more organizational members.

How to Manage Inertia?

The framework, including its different inertia domains and occurrences, raises the question of how executive teams should deal with inertia and whether it can be managed. The inertia occurrences within the cases and the framework are rooted in different forms of rigidities. Rigidities come from the material nature of the architecture of products and IT systems, organizational structure, processes, and systems. Further, they are also rooted in the social aspect of organizations, such as mindset and culture.

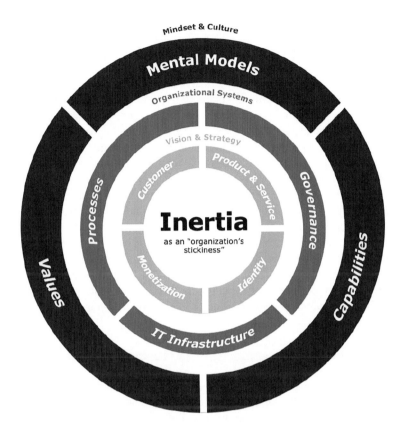

Figure 7.2   *Inertia domains including areas of occurrences*

Taking Back Control: In several cases, executive teams felt surprised and sometimes unable to cope with the challenges and tensions posed by inertia triggered by digital innovation activities. We argue that many of the challenges and uncertainties are – to some extent – addressable by reflecting on each domain of our framework when designing such initiatives. Thus, executive teams can incorporate and anticipate different forms of inertia in the design of such initiatives, which may not prevent inertia occurrences from appearing. Still, it allows executive teams to deal with upcoming tensions more professionally.

It's about the reaction: Further, the inertia occurrences were per se not an issue (they appear sometimes naturally), but rather how the organization decided to deal with them. Thus, finding the proper response to certain forms of inertia may be more critical, such as cutting pragmatic deals with actors when it comes to material conditions of inertia. For instance, some material forms of inertia can only be addressed through a certain transition period, whereas social conditions of inertia can be managed more shorthanded.

Inertia as a distraction: In the social context, inertia, e.g., in form of resistance to change, was often used as labels to distract from own failures by leadership members and teams. Explaining that employees resist change may be seen as a relatively easy way out for managers that do not want to engage with the underlying reasons and issues that employees deal with. This implies that executive teams should challenge reports about resistance to change. They should aim to understand the underlying reasons and motivations of those perceived as resistant.

Inertia as the status quo: Organizational systems, such as processes, governance structures, were often taken for granted as a status quo by many employees and executive teams. This, in a sense, assumes that organizational systems are defined and not malleable as a set natural environment of the organization. Teams and employees sometimes forget that all of these processes and structures result from human actions – and, therefore – can be changed with the required motivation to do so. Highlighting this and destroying this myth by reflecting and encouraging employees to broaden their horizons might be particularly useful.

CONCLUSION

Inertia, understood as an organization's stickiness (Besson and Rowe, 2012) is a decisive issue in the digital transformation of incumbent companies (Vial, 2019). While it cannot be solved quickly, the provided framework may help create awareness in the managerial community for this issue and bring it into management meetings so that potential upcoming transformation struggles can be sensed and addressed accordingly. This would significantly decrease the high failure rate among digital transformation initiatives (Forth et al., 2020).

This chapter is intended to contribute to this endeavor. We developed the inertia framework based on data from more than 70 interviews with three large incumbent companies and their digital transformation initiatives. The framework is not an instruction manual for circumventing inertia. For this, the phenomenon itself is too complex and, to some extent, also inherent and wanted for organizational transformation. Its value rather lies in the chance to be used for anticipating inertial forces when designing digital transformation initiatives. Having designed their digital transformation initiative and corresponding actions, the executive teams shall use the framework and go through each dimension to ensure that they have considered a potential upcoming force. Thus, they can prevent falling short of a conspiracy of optimism, a typical human fallacy of senior management teams having unrealistic expectations about what can be achieved on the ground. Using the dimensions, executive teams can reconcile their plans for digital transformation initiatives, set more realistic targets and achieve higher success rates of digital transformation initiatives.

Building on our research and findings around inertia, future research should explore a more integrated approach to the phenomenon of inertia, its positive and negative effects in organizational life, and how executive teams can deal with the diverse and multiple issues around inertia.

KEY TAKEAWAYS

- Inertia refers to keeping the existing way of doing things, which can be good when driving for efficiency but appears as a challenge when it comes to organizational transformation.
- Digital technologies and innovation challenge existing boundaries of roles, structures, and practices, triggering new occurrences of inertia and resulting tensions within three main organizational domains.
- Inertia and the resulting tensions do not need to be resolved, but executive teams need to set up ways and practices of dealing with them professionally. This involves proactive anticipation in planning digital transformation and innovation initiatives and a set of practices and methods as mitigation strategies for coping with tensions and forms of inertia when they emerge.

ACKNOWLEDGEMENTS

The authors are grateful to Nis-Jonas Harmsen for his support in the data analysis. Further, we would like to thank the participating organizations in our study, numerous interviewees, and their management representatives. Additionally, we want to thank the Hasso Plattner Foundation, specifically the Hasso Plattner Design Thinking Research Program between Hasso Plattner Institute and Stanford University, for the generous support that made this research possible.

REFERENCES

Allcorn, S, and Michael, A. D. (1997). *Managing People During Stressful Times: The Psychologically Defensive Workplace*. Greenwood Publishing Group.
Besson, P. and Frantz, R. (2012). Strategizing Information Systems-Enabled Organizational Transformation: A Transdisciplinary Review and New Directions. *The Journal of Strategic Information Systems 21*(2), 103–24.
Brisson-Banks, C. V. (2010). Managing Change and Transitions: A Comparison of Different Models and Their Commonalities. *Library Management 39*(May), 88.

Caloghirou, Y., Kastelli, I., and Tsakanikas, A. (2004). Internal Capabilities and External Knowledge Sources: Complements or Substitutes for Innovative Performance? *Technovation 24*(1), 29–39.

Chanias, S, Myers, M. D., and Hess, T. (2019). Digital Transformation Strategy Making in Pre-Digital Organizations: The Case of a Financial Services Provider. *The Journal of Strategic Information Systems 28*(1), 17–33.

Drechsler, K., Gregory, R. W., Wagner, H-T., and Tumbas, S. (2020). At the Crossroads between Digital Innovation and Digital Transformation. *Communications of the Association for Information Systems 47*(1), (23).

Dremel, C, Wulf, J., Herterich, M. M., Waizmann, J-C., and Brenner, W. (2017). How AUDI AG Established Big Data Analytics in Its Digital Transformation. *MIS Quarterly Executive 16*(2).

Flett, G. L., and Hewitt, P. L. (2002). Perfectionism and Maladjustment: An Overview of Theoretical, Definitional, and Treatment Issues. In *Perfectionism: Theory, Research, and Treatment , (Pp,* edited by Gordon L. Flett, 435:5–31. Washington, DC, US: American Psychological Association, xiv.

Forth, P, Reichert, T., de Laubier, R., and Chakraborty, S. (2020). Flipping the Odds of Digital Transformation Success. *BCG* (blog). October 29, 2020. https://www.bcg .com/de-de/publications/2020/increasing-odds-of-success-in-digital-transformation.

Fuchs, C, and Hess, T. (2018). Becoming Agile in the Digital Transformation: The Process of a LargeScale Agile Transformation. In *ICIS Proceedings 2018*.

Geels, F. W. (2004). From Sectoral Systems of Innovation to Socio-Technical Systems: Insights about Dynamics and Change from Sociology and Institutional Theory. *Research Policy 33*(6), 897–920.

Hannan, M. T., and Freeman, J. (1984). Structural Inertia and Organizational Change. *American Sociological Review 49*(2), 149.

Harari, D., Swider, B. W., Steed, L. B., and Breidenthal, A. P. (2018). Is Perfect Good? A Meta-Analysis of Perfectionism in the Workplace. *The Journal of Applied Psychology 103*(10), 1121–44.

Haskamp, T., Dremel, C., Marx, C., and Uebernickel, F. (2021). Understanding Inertia in Digital Transformation: A Literature Review and Multilevel Research Framework. In *ICIS Proceedings 2021*.

Haskamp, T, Mayer, S., Annalena, L., and Uebernickel, F. (2021). Performance Measurement in Digital Innovation Units - An Information Asymmetry Perspective. In *ECIS 2021 Proceedings*.

Hinings, B, Gegenhuber, T., and Greenwood, R. (2018). Digital Innovation and Transformation: An Institutional Perspective. *Information and Organization 28*(1), 52–61.

Hund, A, Wagner, H-T., Beimborn, D., and Weitzel, T. (2021). Digital Innovation: Review and Novel Perspective. *The Journal of Strategic Information Systems 30*(4), 101695.

Hylving, L., and Schultze, U. (2020). Accomplishing the Layered Modular Architecture in Digital Innovation: The Case of the Car's Driver Information Module. *The Journal of Strategic Information Systems 29*(3), 101621.

Kahneman, D., and Tversky, A. (1979). On the Interpretation of Intuitive Probability: A Reply to Jonathan Cohen. *Cognition 7*(4), 409–11.

Keen, P. G. W. (1981). Information Systems and Organizational Change. *Communications of the ACM 24*(1), 24–33.

Langley, A. (2007). Process Thinking in Strategic Organization. *Strategic Organization 5*(3), 271–82.

Lappi, T., Karvonen, T., Lwakatare, L. E., Aaltonen, K., and Kuvaja, P. (2018). Toward an Improved Understanding of Agile Project Governance: A Systematic Literature Review. *Project Management Journal 49*(6), 39–63.

Liang, H., Wang, N., Xue, Y., and Ge, S. (2017). Unraveling the Alignment Paradox: How Does Business—IT Alignment Shape Organizational Agility? *Information Systems Research 28*(4), 863–79.

Meulen, N van der., Weill, P., and Woerner S. L. (2020). Managing Organizational Explosions During Digital Business Transformations. *MIS Quarterly Executive 19*(3), 4.

Nag, R., Hambrick, D. C., and Chen M-J. (2007). What Is Strategic Management, Really? Inductive Derivation of a Consensus Definition of the Field. *Strategic Management Journal 28*(9), 935–55.

Nambisan, S., Lyytinen, K., Majchrzak, A., and Song, M. (2017). Digital Innovation Management: Reinventing Innovation Management Research in a Digital World. *Management Information Systems Quarterly 41*(1), 223–38.

Nambisan, S., Lyytinen, K., and Yoo, Y. (2020). Digital Innovation: Towards a Transdisciplinary Perspective. In *Handbook of Digital Innovation*. Edward Elgar Publishing.

Orlikowski, W. J. (2000). Using Technology and Constituting Structures: A Practice Lens for Studying Technology in Organizations. *Organization Science 11*(4), 404–28.

Orlikowski, W., and Scott, S. (2021). Liminal Innovation in Practice: Understanding the Reconfiguration of Digital Work in Crisis. *Information and Organization 31*(1), 100336.

Polites, G. L., and Karahanna, E. (2012). Shackled to the Status Quo: The Inhibiting Effects of Incumbent System Habit, Switching Costs, and Inertia on New System Acceptance. *Management Information Systems Quarterly 36*(1), 21–42.

Porter, M, and Heppelmann, J. (2014). How Smart, Connected Products Are Transforming Competition. *Harvard Business Review 92*(11), 64–88.

Porter, M., and Heppelmann, J. (2015). How Smart, Connected Products Are Transforming Companies. *Harvard Business Review 93*(10), 96–114.

Rescher, N. (2000). *Process Philosophy: A Survey of Basic Issues*. University of Pittsburgh Pre.

Rumelt, R. P. (1995). Inertia and Transformation. In *Resource-Based and Evolutionary Theories of the Firm: Towards a Synthesis*, 101–32. Springer, Boston, MA.

Sautua, S. I. (2017). Does Uncertainty Cause Inertia in Decision Making? An Experimental Study of the Role of Regret Aversion and Indecisiveness. *Journal of Economic Behavior & Organization 136*(April), 1–14.

Schmid, A. M. (2019). Beyond Resistance: Toward a Multilevel Perspective on Socio-Technical Inertia in Digital Transformation. In *Proceedings of the 27th European Conference on Information Systems*.

Schwarz, G. M. (2012). The Logic of Deliberate Structural Inertia. *Journal of Management 38*(2), 547–72.

Sebastian, I., Ross, J., Beath, C., Mocker, M., Moloney, K., and Fonstad, N. (2017). How Big Old Companies Navigate Digital Transformation. *MIS Quarterly Executive 42*, 150–54.

Stieglitz, N., Knudsen, T., Becker, M. C. (2016). Adaptation and Inertia in Dynamic Environments. *Strategic Management Journal 37*(9), 1854–64.

Svahn, F., Mathiassen, L., and Lindgren, R. (2017). Embracing Digital Innovation in Incumbent Firms: How Volvo Cars Managed Competing Concerns. *Management Information Systems Quarterly 41*(1), 239–53.

Tabrizi, B., Lam, E., Girard, K., and Irvin, V. (2019). Digital Transformation Is Not About Technology. *Harvard Business Review*, March 13, 2019.

Tiwana, A., and Kim, S. K. (2015). Discriminating IT Governance. *Information Systems Research 26*(4): 656–74.

Tripsas, M. (2009). Technology, Identity, and Inertia Through the Lens of 'The Digital Photography Company.' *Organization Science 20*(2): 441–60.

Tripsas, M. (2016). Technological Inertia. In *The Palgrave Encyclopedia of Strategic Management*, edited by Mie Augier and David J. Teece, 1–2. London: Palgrave Macmillan UK.

Tripsas, M., and Gavetti, G. (2000). Capabilities, Cognition, and Inertia: Evidence from Digital Imaging. *Strategic Management Journal 21*(10–11), 1147–61.

Tushman, M. L., and O'Reilly, C. A. (1996). Ambidextrous Organizations: Managing Evolutionary and Revolutionary Change. *California Management Review 38*(4), 8–29.

Vial, G. (2019). Understanding Digital Transformation: A Review and a Research Agenda. *The Journal of Strategic Information Systems 28*(2), 118–44.

Weeks, M. R., and Feeny, D. (2008). Outsourcing: From Cost Management to Innovation and Business Value. *California Management Review 50*(4), 127–46.

Weill, P., and Woerner, S. L. (2018). Is Your Company Ready for a Digital Future? *MIT Sloan Management Review; Cambridge 59*(2), 21–25.

Wessel, L., Baiyere, A., Ologeanu-Taddei, R., Cha, J., and Jensen, T. (2020). Unpacking the Difference between Digital Transformation and IT-Enabled Organizational Transformation. *Journal of Association of Information Systems 22*(1), 102–29

Wiesböck, F., and Hess, T. (2020). Digital Innovations. *Electronic Markets 30*(1), 75–86.

Yang, C., and Chen, L-C. (2007). Can Organizational Knowledge Capabilities Affect Knowledge Sharing Behavior? *Journal of Information Science and Engineering 33*(1), 95–109.

Yoo, Y., Boland, R. J., Lyytinen, K., and Majchrzak, A. (2012). Organizing for Innovation in the Digitized World. *Organization Science 23*(5), 1398–1408.

8. Digital value and organizational change: it's time to rethink organization for value-in-configuration

Gongtai Wang

INTRODUCTION

Firms are heading toward a new world of hybrid things. Not only everyday physical products but also livestock, plants, and even human bodies are embedded with sensors and chips for collecting, storing, processing, and exchanging digital data. A firm's digital technology (digital offerings, resources, and production tools) becomes a participant in a grand digital landscape constituted by all the present and future hybrid things and depends on them for functioning. The hybrid things may be designed by different firms without considering the firm's digital technology at all. Meanwhile, the firm may not have control over those hybrid things in use. As a result, the value of the firm's digital technology cannot be solely defined by its static technological characteristics or the firm's organizational and industrial boundaries. In turn, the corresponding organizational change for actualizing the digital value should not be restricted by the traditional idea that assumes a firm-centric and unidirectional value creation process.

In this chapter, we argue that, given such a background, research and practice need a new theoretical lens that can account for a 'relationist capacity' (DeLanda, 2016) nature of digital value. Correspondingly, organizational change for realizing digital value is beyond episodic events of the adoption or use of digital technology (Markus, 2004). Instead, it should pay attention to how digital value emerges and evolves as a firm's digital technology is constantly connected with and disconnected from the emergent digital landscape of evolving hybrid things.

In the rest of this chapter, we first review the organizational change literature to identify widely held views on organizational change and how they view value as a static property. Next, we review the conceptual transition of views on value, which brings the relational nature of value to the fore. It should be noted that both reviews do not intend to be exhaustive. Instead, they focus on major views shared by publications in quality journals and leading scholars. This selective focus is motivated by a scholarly goal to provoke an interest in exploring alternative perspectives for understanding digital value and organizational change (per the practice of Pettigrew et al., 2001) rather than concluding the conversation. Following this idea, we then discuss the unique characteristics of digital technology in a world of hybrid things and rethink their implications for understanding digital value and, in turn, organizational change. To facilitate the rethink, we advance a new theoretical lens resorting to Assemblage Theory (DeLanda, 2016) and discuss its implications for studies on organizational change for realizing digital value.

ORGANIZATIONAL CHANGE: TRADITIONAL VIEWS

Previous studies have commonly suggested five dimensions for understanding organizational change: environments, triggers, actors, actions, and results. First, *environments* refer to the conditions in which organizational change occurs (Baldridge & Burnham, 1975; Bielinska-Kwapisz, 2014; Jacobs et al., 2013). Environments include internal and external conditions. The former includes economic, societal, political, and industrial conditions, whereas the latter includes structural, cultural, and political conditions. Second, *triggers* refer to events that cause organizational change (Bielinska-Kwapisz, 2014). There are two types of triggers – social triggers, such as changes in cultural or psychological stability (Wiechers et al., 2016), and material triggers, such as changes in business routines and technological tools (Markus, 2004; Staudenmayer et al., 2002). Third, *actors* refer to stakeholders involved in organizational change (Battilana & Casciaro, 2012). An actor can be either an individual involved in changes of an organization (Thomas & Hardy, 2011; van den Heuvel et al., 2014) or an organizational actor that implements changes as a reaction to industry-level changes . Fourth, *actions* refer to how actors respond to organizational change. We identify two types of actions: resistance and adaptation . Resistance occurs as actors refuse to participate in organizational change, often due to negative perceptions or lack of resources to make the change. Adaptation occurs as actors recognize the necessity of organizational change and contribute to its implementation. Fifth, *results* refer to the outcome of organizational change. It is necessary to attend to the nuanced difference in studies' use of the term 'successful organizational change'. Some refer to it as the successful implementation of the planned change, while others refer to it as the business success resulting from the implemented change (Al-Haddad & Kotnour, 2015). Attention to the difference is necessary because successful implementation of planned changes may result in negative results, for example, productivity losses (Srivastava & Agrawal, 2020).

These five dimensions together suggest an open system view, which approaches an organization as an entity that takes inputs from its environment, transforms the inputs into goods/services, creates outputs for external users, and learns from feedback to improve its products/services and the transformation process (Luhman & Cunliffe, 2013). In other words, an organization is a value creation machine that converts value in one form – resources – to value in another form – products. Correspondingly, organizational change is viewed as an event of kinematic and dynamic optimization of the machine.

This view on organizational change has two issues. First, this view obscures the fact that an organization is a site where actors come and go. Although studies can artificially bracket organizational change in the spatiotemporal scope of an episodic event (Michel, 2014), an organization's inner sociotechnical constituents often have a long and ongoing history of making, maintaining, and breaking relations with the outer sociotechnical environment, which is highly fluid and dynamic (Baygi et al., 2021). Second, this view oversimplifies value as a static property. However, as reviewed below, the value justification of a good/service may depend on its relations with other artifacts and human actors. Such value justification becomes increasingly common on the rise of the recombinational use and design practice of digital technology (Henfridsson et al., 2018). Attention to the relational aspect of value and its justification is necessary for better understanding value creation in the digital age (Barrett et al., 2015).

VALUE: THE CONCEPTUAL TRANSITION

Value has been a central concept in management studies. The diverse theoretical perspectives and empirical contexts of previous studies have resulted in competing explanations of what value is and how it is created. In the explanations, Vargo and colleagues (Vargo & Lusch, 2012; Vargo et al., 2010) have identified a conceptual transition from value-in-exchange via value-in-use to value-in-context.

First, *value-in-exchange* refers to the value of a good as the amount of another good for which it can be traded. For example, if a barrel of crude oil can be obtained in exchange for 1.5 grams of gold, then we may say that value of a barrel of crude oil is equal to 1.5 grams of gold. This view focuses on tangible offerings – goods. Value is viewed as a static property embedded in a good, which is created as a form that transforms value from one form (resource) to another (product). The value creation process is organized based on a delivery logic and has a range bracketed by resource obtainment and offering delivery. The main role of a firm is producing goods. Users are excluded from the value creation process and only play a role in purchasing the good after the firm delivers it to the market. Users judge the value of the good based on its features at the moment of exchange. As more and better features imply more value, the organization's primary goal is to increase operational efficiency to create more quality features faster.

Second, *value-in-use* refers to the benefit from using an offering. For example, the actual value of an iPhone depends on how a user uses it. It has more value if the user makes full use of its functionality. Unlike value-in-exchange, this view goes beyond tangible offerings to include intangible offerings – services. This inclusion of services shifts the focus from an offering to how the users use it. In other words, value is no longer a property embedded in an offering but a capability to solve a problem. The range of value creation, therefore, is extended beyond resource obtainment and offering delivery to the stage of offering consumption. Correspondingly, value creation is organized with a cocreation logic that the firm does not create value within its internal production process and then deliver the value to the market for users to accept. Instead, the firm and users create value together: the firm acts as a resource provider whose internal production process is to create resources for users to create value at a particular moment of use. In this regard, the whole value creation process is constituted by two collaborative parts – the firm's *value creation through production* and the users' *value creation through consumption*. The output of the former is the input of the latter. Therefore, the eventual value cannot be entirely determined by the firm's output but depends on how users use the offering to solve a problem. Given such a cocreation logic, the communication between cocreators becomes a critical concern of the organization as the firm must effectively invite and motivate users to participate and complete the value cocreation process.

Third, *value-in-context* refers to the benefit from using an offering in relation to other objects and actors in a particular use context. For example, the value attained from watching a movie at a cinema is decided not only by the script, characters, acting, visual and sound effects, the audience's genre preference and intention and behaviors of movie watching but also by the quality of the projector and audio equipment, the comfortableness of the seat, and if other audience members follow movie manners. This view regards value as a satisfying experience of using an offering that depends not only on the offering's features (e.g., value-in-exchange) and use behavior (e.g., value-in-use) but also on other human and non-human surroundings that shape the experience. In this regard, value creation must go beyond the value of a single offering and the directly targeted users. The firm should systematically create a contextual stage to frame interactions between users, its offering, and human and non-human surroundings for the best possible consumption experience (Pine & Gilmore, 2011). As the objects and actors may be diverse, the focus of organization should be on coordinating the creation of potentially involved resources and the participation of potentially involved actors.

Such a conceptual transition of views on value has important implications for organizational change as it suggests that value is not a static property but emerges from the processual complexity and contextual relations of the creation and use of an offering. To acknowledge the full significance of this transition, a study should attend to the trend that as the business environment becomes more dynamic and complex, the responsibility and control of value creation become increasingly shared by a firm and its users, and, in turn, value emergence becomes increasingly contingent (see Henfridsson et al., 2018). However, the extant studies – even those that adopt the latest views on value – seem to still adhere to an idea that value creation is a *firm-centric* and *unidirectional* process (see Figure 8.1). Specifically, although the three views on value argue for different timing and locus of value emergence, value creation is depicted as always starting with a firm's internal production process. Although the value-in-context view has shed light on how an offering can become more valuable to a user as it is related to other human and non-human surroundings, the eventual value is viewed as offered by the firm to the user. As discussed in the next section, this firm-centric and unidirectional idea does not fit with the new phenomena of value creation in the digital age.

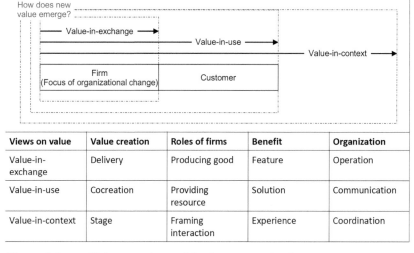

Views on value	Value creation	Roles of firms	Benefit	Organization
Value-in-exchange	Delivery	Producing good	Feature	Operation
Value-in-use	Cocreation	Providing resource	Solution	Communication
Value-in-context	Stage	Framing interaction	Experience	Coordination

Figure 8.1   *Value creation and business organization*

THE VALUE OF DIGITAL TECHNOLOGY IN A WORLD OF HYBRID THINGS

In this section, we first establish the connection between the evolution of digital technology, value, and organizational change through a historical reflection on how digital technology has been changing value logic and in turn organizations during the past decades. Together with the afore-mentioned conceptual transition of value, we then explain why the emerging world of hybrid things requires a new understanding of value.

Digital Technology, Value, Organizational Changes

In the 1940s, the invention of the Electronic Numerical Integrator and Computer (ENIAC) opened the epoch of the digital computer and fundamentally changed how business problems were solved. Since then, advances in data processing capabilities have been continuously ratcheting up operational speed and accuracy, enabling firms to realize more profit. Incentivized by this value of digital technology, firms engaged in unceasing organizational change that focuses on substituting automated processes for manual processes, which continues today.

Twenty years later, the launch of the Advanced Research Projects Agency Network (ARPANET) inaugurated the era of the Internet and essentially changed how digital computers were used. The connection of digital computers across functional and geographical boundaries allowed firms to manage massive production and reach broader markets for more profit. Fueled by this value of digital technology, we saw the accelerating emergence of megacorporations and multinational corporations as firms integrated previously scattered internal and external stakeholders within and across industries.

After another two decades, the development of wireless networks and portable computers ushered in the age of mobile computing and profoundly changed the usage of the Internet. The ubiquitous access to computing resources beyond a building's walls allowed firms to increase profit by identifying and acting on emergent business opportunities and threats in the field in real-time. Agility became a central tenet for contemporary businesses to capture this value of digital technology. Based on this tenet, firms created new organizational forms for direct and real-time information exchange between the powerhouse of decision making and the locale of decision execution or relocation of the locus of control.

Such a historical reflection shows that new digital technology comes with new value, and firms change their organization to realize the value. In this regard, both organizational change research and practice should attend to emerging digital technology for a better understanding of the technology's implications for value creation and in turn how organizations should be changed accordingly to seize the opportunity.

The Value of Digital Technology

Studies on the value of digital technology reflect the conceptual transition of value. Early studies reflect the value-in-exchange view. They often understand digital technology as a good – a self-contained product packed with a bunch of functional features predecided by their producing firms. Yoo (2010) referred to such an idea of digital technology as a 'beige box' (p. 216). In turn, the value of digital technology is represented by the unit price of each self-contained product. The price is often correlated with the number and quality of functional features packed in the product, although users might never use some features.

Later, as the value-in-use view emerges, we see the rise of the so-called 'X-as-a-service' movement (e.g., database as a service, software as a service, platform as a service) and the 'pay-as-you-go' business models in the digital technology industry. The development of digital networks allows functional features to be transferred to where they are used in real-time. As a result, the geographical divide between the creation and storage of the functional features and their use becomes increasingly irrelevant. Unlike the beige-box digital technology in which features are decided and packaged by their producing firms, users can subscribe and unsubscribe features based on their actual needs at a particular time of use. In contrast to the expense at the point of buying a beige-box digital technology, which must be spread even to the never-used features, a functional feature in an X-as-a-service business model becomes valueless as soon as users decide to stop using it and discontinue the subscription. In other words, the value of the functional feature is mostly determined by use.

In recent years, there has been increasing research interest in the adoption and use of digital technology in everyday life (Bodker et al., 2014; Prasopoulou, 2017; Yoo, 2010). As digital technology moves beyond work contexts to various daily contexts, the contextual diversity and complexity start to have a more significant impact on the value of the digital technology created in use. For example, embedding social networking functions in traditional products such as bicycles and running shoes extends the experience of using digital technology beyond its spatiotemporal locus. Connecting to other users drastically shapes how a user interacts with and experiences a digital technology. The networking, competition, and collaboration between users add a new layer of meaning to the digital technology above its technical functionality (Yoo, 2010). Such meaning-based value of digital technology is largely situated, depending on the actual use context, which legitimates value-in-context as an important view for studying value in the digital age (Mikusz, 2017; Turetken et al., 2019).

However, this development of studies on the value of digital technology in particular – like the conceptual transition of value in general – is also dominated by the idea that value creation is firm-centric and unidirectional. A firm is assumed to be in the driver's seat of the value creation process, from the input of resources to the output of offerings. When the digital technology of interest is a gearwheel of the corporate machine, the value of the digital technology is measured as the surplus between the firm's investment in the digital technology and its economic outcomes (Kohli & Grover, 2008). When the digital technology of interest is an offering, its value is measured at the market value or the utility and experience users extract in using the digital technology provided by a firm. Either way, the 'gearwheel' digital technology (digital infrastructures that support the operation of a firm, e.g., business intelligence systems) is barely concerned with the 'offering' digital technology (products/ services) a firm provides to users. Although this firm-centric view has offered significant guidance to firms for improving their organizations and value creation, it is of limited use when considering value creation and organizational change in a world of hybrid things.

A World of Hybrid Things: The Rise of Bidirectional Value Creation Processes

Hybrid things refer to living and non-living things embedded with digital technology. A significant characteristic of a world of hybrid things is that everything is connected. In such a context, gearwheel or offering digital technologies are not created on a blank slate but in a landscape with history, as earlier digital technologies pave the ground for later digital technologies. For example, Amazon's recommendation algorithm (gearwheel digital technology) relies partially on the data from consumer devices using Alexa (offering digital technology), and Alexa devices (offering digital technology) may use data from other Alexa devices (offering digital technology).

Such reliance on connections between digital technology means that creating a more valuable digital technology is different from creating a better stand-alone technology packaged with more and new functions. It is different from cooking the most delicious cake that barely considers other snacks and beverages consumed with it. Doubtlessly, it still holds that an excellent digital technology itself is indispensable for market success. However, unlike a cake that may function well alone, it is increasingly rare to find a digital technology that can fully function by itself. Instead, it is more likely that a digital technology becomes less valuable, if not valueless, as soon as it loses connection to other digital technology, and that this value drop is often bidirectional. For example, in one direction, if Amazon's server breaks down, Alexa devices become less valuable as they lose most of the intelligent functions. In the other direction, if Alexa devices stop submitting data to Amazon's server, the server becomes less valuable as it cannot provide intelligence for optimizing Amazon's operation.

In a similar vein, it is more likely that a digital technology will become more valuable as it makes new connections to other digital technologies (Henfridsson et al., 2018; Yoo et al., 2010). This value increase can also be bidirectional, which may or may not be initiated and driven by the firm. For example, Amazon's functional updates on the server may grant Alexa devices more intelligent functions. Conversely, Alexa users' creative interactions with the devices may create new behavioral data, giving rise to new patterns in Amazon's business intelligence system for better operation and new services.

Such a *bidirectional* value creation process where the firm may not necessarily be the initiator of the process necessitates a new theoretical lens to understand value creation in the time of hybrid things. We believe Assemblage Theory (DeLanda, 2016) applies to this end. In the next section, we first introduce the theory and explain why it is a suitable theoretical foundation and then develop a *value-in-configuration* lens for understanding digital value and its creation.

A PROVOCATIVE VIEW ON DIGITAL VALUE

In this section, we advance a provocative view on value for understanding the uniqueness of value creation in a world of hybrid things. We build the view on DeLanda's (2016) assemblage theory.

Assemblage Theory for Understanding Digital Technology

The essential argument of the theory is that everything can be viewed as an assemblage constituted by components that themselves are also assemblages. The relationships between the components are contingent. Any component can be unplugged from an assemblage and replugged into the same assemblage or other assemblages. All assemblages are on the same ontological plane, which means an assemblage can directly interact with the larger assemblage it constitutes and smaller assemblages that constitute it. Here the 'larger' and 'smaller' are 'relative scales' (DeLanda, 2016, p. 16) only defined by the whole-component relation. This whole-component relation follows a double determination logic. In the bottom-up direction, a whole assemblage is created through a historical trajectory where its components keep interacting. The whole assemblage attains emergent properties and capacities that are irreducible to the properties and capacities of the components. In the top-down direction, as soon as a whole assemblage emerges, its emergent capabilities exert enabling and constraining forces on its components and their interactions.

Such a conceptualization of how things exist and work shows good conceptual compatibility with the essential characteristics of digital phenomena – reprogrammability, data homogenization, and self-reference (Yoo et al., 2010). First, *reprogrammability* means that a digital device is a combination of software and physical parts, and its total capability can be changed by changing the software codes. For example, a Tesla car can become a game console if users download games to its tablet. This characteristic reflects the ontological idea of Assemblage Theory that a whole assemblage can maintain its identity and obtain new capabilities through substituting new components for old components (DeLanda, 2016). Second, *data homogenization* means that digital contents have the same format, allowing heterogeneous contents to be stored, transmitted, processed, and displayed by the same digital device and the same content to be used across heterogeneous digital devices. For example, a smartphone can receive diverse types of files from laptops and smartwatches and share files with those devices. This characteristic reflects the ontological idea of Assemblage Theory that an assemblage arises from interactions between heterogeneous components, and a component can be detached from one assemblage and reattached to another assemblage (DeLanda, 2016). Third, *self-reference* means that the creation, change, diffusion, and use of one digital technology requires the use of another digital technology. For example, the emergence of the Internet requires price decrease and performance increase of computers. This characteristic reflects the ontological idea of Assemblage Theory that an assemblage and its components interact on the same ontological plane, and the capacities of the whole and those of its components mutually determine each other (DeLanda, 2016).

This comparison between the characteristics of digital phenomena and Assemblage Theory, although brief, shows that the theory has the potential to offer a useful theoretical foundation for theorizing digital phenomena in a way that will not lose track of its essential characteristics. In fact, high-quality Information Systems studies have already used it to theorize the emergence and evolution of an infrastructure entity (Hanseth & Modol, 2021) and the combinatorial nature of digital innovation (Henfridsson et al., 2018). These studies showcased the theory's power in interpreting how digital phenomena are created from fluid and complex interactions between living and non-living things.

Digital Value Redefined: Value-in-Configuration

What new insights into digital value can we gain with the aid of Assemblage Theory? The above brief on the theory's essential idea highlights a particular concept that can help rethink the nature of digital value – capacity. DeLanda (2016) distinguishes 'capacity' from 'property'. A property is a variable or a parameter that describes the state of an assemblage, for example, the sharpness of a knife. A capacity is what an assemblage can do, for example, the ability to cut tofu. He further distinguishes between substantialist and relationist views on properties and capacities. From a substantialist view, the property and capacity of an entity exist in their own right and are a simple sum of their components' properties and capacities. From a relationist view, the property and capacity of an entity are causal results of the interactions of its components, and the entity can exhibit novel properties and capacities that all its components do not have. Further, an entity's capacity (to affect) is merely potential and only becomes actual in relation to the presence of another entity who has a corresponding capacity (to be affected). For example, the to-cut capacity of a knife can only be actualized to cut tofu when the tofu is present and has the to-be-cut capacity. If you keep tofu in a freezer for several weeks, the to-cut capacity of a knife cannot be actualized, although the potential remains (for other things that have a to-be-cut capacity). These ideas have important implications for rethinking the nature of value.

As reviewed before, there have been three views on value: value-in-exchange, value-in-use, and value-in-context. Conventionally, the differences between these three value conceptualizations are interpreted in a practical sense in terms of the scope and timing of value creation (see Figure 8.1). Resorting to Assemblage Theory's distinctions between property and capacity and between substantialist and relationist views, we may reinterpret their differences in an ontological sense. Specifically, first, as the value-in-exchange of an offering is a sum of the value of resources used for producing it and remains the same across exchange contexts (Vargo et al., 2010), value-in-exchange is essentially a substantialist property of a good. Second, as value-in-use refers to value as the ability of an offering to solve a set of problems across use contexts (Vargo et al., 2010), value-in-use mostly reflects the idea of a substantialist capacity. Third, as value-in-context maintains that value is created as users extract benefits from an offering, shaped by the relations to surrounding actors and artifacts (Vargo et al., 2010), value-in-context is primarily a relationist property.

However, it is not easy to fit digital value (especially in the context of hybrid things) in either of the above three categories. The above discussion on hybrid things suggests that it is increasingly common for a digital technology to become incapable of anything as soon as it loses connection to other digital technologies and, in turn, becomes valueless. As the value is defined by what a digital technology can do and the capability relies on the capability of other digital technologies with which it is connected, digital value is a capacity and fits with a relationist view. The value creation does not seek to create and manage all the artifacts and actors relevant to the value of a digital technology (unlike value-in-context) because it is increasingly difficult as the digital technologies on the other end of the connection are often not in the custody of the firm. Instead, the value creation features a *configuration* process that 'creates value by configuring a digital technology in certain ways so that it can be connected well with a targeted set of digital technologies to form an assemblage where the intended capacity of the digital technology can be actualized'. For example, users may not be able to tap into a smartphone's professional video production capacity if the phone does not have a speedy connection to transfer large files to professional video-editing computers. The capacity can only be actualized by configuring the smartphone with an efficient data transfer protocol and hardware interfaces (e.g., USB-C) that most professional video-editing computers have already used.

It should be noted that, given the increasing malleability of digital technology, the configuration may take place on the user side as users make changes to a focal digital technology for other digital technology or make changes to other digital technology for the focal technology. Besides, as the digital technology on the user side is connected to the digital technology on the firm side, it is also reasonable to expect that the configuration on the user side may change the value not only of a firm's offering but also its internal digital technology. For example, users' configuration of the privacy settings of their mobile devices may enable or prevent a social media firm from offering new digital functions to the users or using their business intelligence system for operational decision-making support.

We refer to digital value that features such ontological and processual characteristics as *value-in-configuration*. Figure 8.2 illustrates how value-in-configuration is positioned differently along the property-capacity and substantialist-relationist dimensions.

	Property	Capacity
Substantialist	Value-in-exchange	Value-in-use
Relationist	Value-in-context	Value-in-configuration

Figure 8.2   Digital value as value-in-configuration

DISCUSSION: RETHINKING ORGANIZATIONAL CHANGE FOR DIGITAL VALUE

As reviewed above, organizational change research mostly focuses on episodic events where individual or organizational actors respond to sociotechnical interruptions from their organizational or industrial environment, such as the implementation of a new technology. The main reason for responding to interruptions is because they disturb the existing value creation process or transform the fundamental logic of value creation. Either way, organizational change is arguably driven by the motivation for better value creation.

Traditionally, organizational change for better value creation has focused on the efficiency and effectiveness of operation, communication, and coordination. These three focuses are still important for today's business as operation determines the speed and quality of the creation and provision of an offering, communication shapes users' perception and interaction with the offering, and coordination increases the potential for users to extract additional value beyond the offering. However, the idea that a firm is always the initiator of a value creation process does not fit well with the evolving practice. It beclouds the fact that the process may not be in the firm's custody. Given the history of digital technology in the past 80 decades, a firm's offering most likely comes into existence after the current digital landscape. As a result, the firm is more of a participator in the landscape who barely has full control of the value of its digital technology because the value depends on the other external digital technology with which it will be connected.

Attending to the unique characteristics of digital technology in the time of hybrid things, we have developed an alternative theoretical lens – *value-in-configuration* – for understanding the value of digital technology in this context. As we have learned from reviewing the value and organizational change studies, how value is viewed shapes how an organization is structured and managed. However, we have a limited understanding of what the new focus of organization for value-in-configuration should be and how an organization should be changed for the new focus. In what follows, we discuss two possible research directions that may help us understand organization for value-in-configuration.

Research Direction 1: Technochange Management

Technochange refers to 'technology-driven organizational change' (Markus, 2004). Technochange management research seeks to complement traditional IT project management research that focuses on ensuring the quality of an IT solution development process and its outcome. It also seeks to complement traditional organizational change management research that focuses on the people aspects of an organization. Technochange management emphasizes that implementing an IT solution requires complementary organizational change and vice versa. Although technochange management research brings together the mutual enabling and constraining effects of IT solution change and organizational change, its primary scope is still within a firm.

Our value-in-configuration lens, however, suggests that configuration can happen on both the firm side and the user side. The connection between a firm's gearwheel digital technology, its offering digital technology, and other firms' digital technology makes it increasingly difficult for the firm to have complete control over the value of its digital technology, whether it is within or outside the firm. Therefore, technochange management research may attain new insights by paying attention to the cross-boundary effect of configuration, specifically, by studying the following research questions: 1) how does user-side configuration shape within-firm organization logic; 2) how does firm-side configuration lead to changes in its organization logic for engaging and managing users; and 3) how does user-side configuration enable or constrain a firm's intended organizational change?

Research Direction 2: The Alignment of Organizational Structure and Product Architecture

Research has found that the misalignment of organizational structure and product architecture negatively affects the quality of product development (Gokpinar et al., 2010). Therefore, it is necessary to increase the alignment between the two, especially when designing highly complex products. However, the complexity of a product under design increases if it depends on connections with other products beyond the firm's custody because its quality is not the same as its value. It is reasonable to argue that the development of a digital technology cannot only consider the product under design, and, in turn, the organization cannot only be structured according to the product architecture. Instead, firms must evolve their product architecture and organizational structure for emerging opportunities and constraints as other potentially relevant digital technologies emerge and change. In this regard, the alignment of product architecture and organizational structure should be ongoing; however, this alignment is under-researched. To better understand the dynamics of the ongoing alignment process, we need to understand, for example, 1) how does an organizational structure or a product architecture shape project members' sense of the use environment of their digital product; and 2) how do organizational structure and product architecture coevolve with the external sociotechnical environment?

CONCLUSION

Evolving digital technology evolves the logic of value creation. Organizational change is conducted for better value creation. Therefore, organizational change should attend to emerging digital technology. However, although emerging digital technology in the time of hybrid things exhibits unique characteristics indicating changes in the nature of value, most organizational change research still adheres to the traditional viewpoint that value is a static property of an offering. To this end, we have developed an alternative theoretical lens – *value-in-configuration* – that views digital value as a relationist capacity of digital technology. It suggests that value emerges when the to-affect capacity of a digital technology is connected with the to-be-affected capacity of another digital technology. Therefore, value creation is a configuration process that changes and matches the capacity of one digital technology for actualizing the capacity of another. We hope our theoretical lens inspires future research to explore new insights into organizational change for better creation and realization of digital value.

We also hope the ideas introduced in this chapter offer new angles for firms to rethink their business organization. For a long time, firms have assumed they should be at the center of a value creation process. Although they sometimes invite users to the research and development of a product/service, they have full control over value creation in terms of who are invited and how user opinions should be reflected in the design, redesign, and upgrade of the product/service. Such value creation is innately unidirectional as firms transform resources into products/services and deliver them to users. However, in a world of hybrid things where everything connects to everything, the value of digital offerings, resources, and production tools depends on each other. The input of new data on the user side may affect the digital resources and production tools right away, and vice versa. For this reason, firms should not draw an arbitrary boundary to cut digital technology within their organization off the huge amount of digital technology on the user side. Firms should engage in effortful, careful, and continuous configuration of their digital technology to make it better connect with related digital technologies to form an assemblage where the intended capacity of their digital technology can be actualized.

KEY TAKEAWAYS

- Firms are heading into a world of hybrid things characterized by unprecedented fusion and connection between digital technology and living and non-living things.

- Evolving digital technology evolves the logic of value creation, which in turn requires corresponding organizational change.
- In a world of hybrid things, digital value should be viewed as a relationist capacity of digital technology.
- In a world of hybrid things, value creation may not be firm-centric and is usually bidirectional.
- In a world of hybrid things, digital value is created through configuring a digital technology in certain ways so that it can be connected well with a targeted set of digital technologies to form an assemblage where the intended capacity of the digital technology can be actualized.

REFERENCES

Al-Haddad, S., & Kotnour, T. (2015). Integrating the organizational change literature: a model for successful change. *Journal of Organizational Change Management*, *28*(2), 234–62.

Baldridge, J. V., & Burnham, R. A. (1975). Organizational Innovation - Individual, Organizational, and Environmental Impacts. *Administrative Science Quarterly*, *20*(2), 165–76. https://doi.org/Doi 10.2307/2391692

Barrett, M., Davidson, E., Prabhu, J., & Vargo, S. L. (2015). Service Innovation in the Digital Age: Key Contributions and Future Directions. *MIS Quarterly*, *39*(1), 135–54. 8

Battilana, J., & Casciaro, T. (2012). Change Agents, Networks, and Institutions: A Contingency Theory of Organizational Change. *Academy of Management Journal*, *55*(2), 381–98. https://doi.org/10.5465/amj.2009.0891

Baygi, R. M., Introna, L. D., & Hultin, L. (2021). Everything Flows: Studying Continuous Socio-Technological Transformation in a Fluid and Dynamic Digital World. *MIS Quarterly*, *45*(1), 423–52.

Bielinska-Kwapisz, A. (2014). Triggers of Organizational Change: Duration, Previous Changes, and Environment. *Journal of Change Management*, *14*(3), 405–24. https://doi.org/10.1080/14697017.2014.885461

Bodker, M., Gimpel, G., & Hedman, J. (2014). Time-out/Time-in: The Dynamics of Everyday Experiential Computing Devices. *Information Systems Journal*, *24*(2), 143–66.

Campbell, K. M. (1996). Information technology and organizational change in the British census, 1801–1911. *Information Systems Research*, *7*(1), 22–36. https://doi.org/DOI 10.1287/isre.7.1.22

DeLanda, M. (2016). *Assemblage Theory*. Edinburgh University Press.

Gokpinar, B., Hopp, W. J., & Iravani, S. M. R. (2010). The Impact of Misalignment of Organizational Structure and Product Architecture on Quality in Complex Product Development. *Management Science*, *56*(3), 468–84.

Grimm, C. M., & Smith, K. G. (1991). Management and Organizational-Change - a Note on the Railroad Industry. *Strategic Management Journal*, *12*(7), 557–62. https://doi.org/DOI 10.1002/smj.4250120708

Hanseth, O., & Modol, J. R. (2021). The Dynamics of Architecture-Governance Configurations: An Assemblage Theory Approach. *Journal of the Association for Information Systems*, *22*(1), 130–55.

Henfridsson, O., Nandhakumar, J., Scarbrough, H., & Panourgias, N. (2018). Recombination in the Open-Ended Value Landscape of Digital Innovation. *Information and Organization*, *28*(2), 89–100. https://doi.org/10.1016/j.infoandorg.2018.03.001

Jacobs, G., van Witteloostuijn, A., & Christe-Zeyse, J. (2013). A theoretical framework of organizational change. *Journal of Organizational Change Management*, *26*(5), 772–92. https://doi.org/10.1108/Jocm-09-2012-0137

Kohli, R., & Grover, V. (2008). Business value of IT: An essay on expanding research directions to keep up with the times. *Journal of the Association for Information Systems*, *9*(1), 23–39.

Luhman, J. T., & Cunliffe, A. L. (2013). *Key Concepts in Organization Theory*. Sage.

Markus, M. L. (2004). Technochange management: using IT to drive organizational change. *Journal of Information Technology*, *19*(1), 4–20. https://doi.org/10.1057/palgrave.jit.2000002

Michel, A. (2014). The Mutual Constitution of Persons and Organizations: An Ontological Perspective on Organizational Change. *Organization Science*, *25*(4), 1082–1110. https://doi.org/10.1287/orsc.2013.0887

Mikusz, M. (2017). Value-In-Context with Service Innovation in the Digital Age: A Service-Dominant Logic Perspective. *Proceedings of the 50th Annual Hawaii International Conference on System Sciences*, 1267–76.

Oborn, E., Barrett, M., Orlikowski, W., & Kim, A. (2019). Trajectory Dynamics in Innovation: Developing and Transforming a Mobile Money Service Across Time and Place. *Organization Science*, *30*(5), 1097–1123. https://doi.org/10.1287/orsc.2018.1281

Orlikowski, W. J. (1996). Improvising Organizational Transformation Over Time: A Situated Change Perspective. *Information Systems Research*, *7*(1), 63–92. https://doi.org/10.1287/isre.7.1.63

Pettigrew, A. M., Woodman, R. W., & Cameron, K. S. (2001). Studying organizational change and development: Challenges for future research. *Academy of Management Journal*, *44*(4), 697–713. https://doi.org/Doi 10.2307/3069411

Pine, B. J., & Gilmore, J. H. (2011). *The Experience Economy*. Harvard Business Review Press. https://books.google.com.au/books?id=edtOyzyKgXUC

Prasopoulou, E. (2017). A Half-Moon on My Skin: A Memoir on Life with an Activity Tracker. *European Journal of Information Systems*, *26*(3), 287–97.

Srivastava, S., & Agrawal, S. (2020). Resistance to change and turnover intention: a moderated mediation model of burnout and perceived organizational support. *Journal of Organizational Change Management*, *33*(7), 1431–47.

Staudenmayer, N., Tyre, M., & Perlow, L. (2002). Time to change: Temporal shifts as enablers of organizational change. *Organization Science*, *13*(5), 583–97. https://doi.org/DOI 10.1287/orsc.13.5.583.7813

Thomas, R., & Hardy, C. (2011). Reframing resistance to organizational change. *Scandinavian Journal of Management*, *27*(3), 322–31.

Tsoukas, H., & Chia, R. (2002). On Organizational Becoming: Rethinking Organizational Change. *Organization Science*, *13*(5), 567–82. https://doi.org/10.1287/orsc.13.5.567.7810

Turetken, O., Grefen, P., Gilsing, R., & Adali, O. E. (2019). Service-Dominant Business Model Design for Digital Innovation in Smart Mobility. *Business & Information Systems Engineering*, *61*(1), 9–29. https://doi.org/10.1007/s12599-018-0565-x

van den Heuvel, M., Demerouti, E., & Bakker, A. B. (2014). How psychological resources facilitate adaptation to organizational change. *European Journal of Work and Organizational Psychology*, *23*(6), 847–58.

Vargo, S. L., & Lusch, R. F. (2012). The Nature and Understanding of Value: A Service-Dominant Logic Perspective. In S. L. Vargo & R. F. Lusch (eds), *Special Issue – Toward a Better Understanding of the Role of Value in Markets and Marketing* (Vol. 9, pp. 1-12). Emerald Group Publishing Limited. https://doi.org/10.1108/S1548-6435(2012)0000009005

Vargo, S. L., Lusch, R. F., Archpru Akaka, M., & He, Y. (2010). Service-Dominant Logic: A Review and Assessment. In N. K. Malhotra (ed), *Review of marketing research* (Vol. 6, pp. 125-167). Emerald Group Publishing Limited. https://doi.org/10.1108/S1548-6435(2009)0000006010

Wiechers, H., Lub, X., & Have, S. t. (2016). Triggers of Transition: Psychological Recontracting in Organizational Change. *Academy of Management Proceedings*, *2016*(1), 14741. https://doi.org/10.5465/ambpp.2016.14741abstract

Yoo, Y. (2010). Computing in Everyday Life: A Call for Research on Experiential Computing. *MIS Quarterly*, *34*(2), 213–31.

Yoo, Y., Henfridsson, O., & Lyytinen, K. (2010). The New Organizing Logic of Digital Innovation: An Agenda for Information Systems Research. *Information Systems Research*, *21*(4), 724–35. https://doi.org/10.1287/isre.1100.0322

9. Digital maturity models

Christina Wagner, Verena Kessler Verzar, Rainer Bernnat and Daniel J. Veit

INTRODUCTION

'Being 'digital' is paramount for companies to stay competitive in today's business world.' (Thordsen et al., 2020, p. 358)

Digital technologies drive change in organizations and affect all levels of the firm. The degree to which an organization is successful in their digital transformation, however, differs vastly across organizations (Rossmann, 2018). To understand why these differences exist and how an organization's path towards digital transformation may succeed, digital maturity models have become popular over the past few decades.

These digital maturity models for the most part have been developed by practitioners, i.e., consultancies – and are highly valued and applied by them and their clients (Thordsen et al., 2020). In previous years, industry and academia seem to have developed maturity models in a vacuum. The path forward, however, is to collaborate and co-create to develop more robust models (Mettler & Ballester, 2021). As a consequence, academia and practice need to collaborate to create more robust and relevant models (Becker et al., 2009; Lasrado et al., 2016; Mettler & Ballester, 2021; Thordsen et al., 2020).

The goal of this chapter is to provide an overview of the meaning of digital maturity models, their origins, and to lay out exemplary instantiations to be employed by practitioners. To achieve this, we conduct a review of academic literature in Information Systems (IS) and related disciplines, as well on relevant practitioner publications. With that, we aggregate studies dispersed over academic and practitioner literature. As our outcome, we present and structure them in a way that aids both academics and practitioners. The former to build upon those foundations for research. The latter for choosing an informed approach to apply adequate models in specific situations of digital transformation that organizations might find themselves in.

The next sections will be structured as follows. We start with an overview of the definitions and emergence of digital maturity models. This is followed by laying out in detail one of the foundations of digital maturity models: The capability maturity model (CPM) and digital maturity models developed for the public sector. Next, we present and describe selected digital maturity models. Finally, we will provide guidelines for how to develop, choose, and implement digital maturity models in practice.

DEFINING MATURITY MODELS

To have a common understanding of digital maturity models, we will now provide an overview of the emergence and definition of extant digital maturity models.

Maturity Models

The concept behind maturity models originates from early stage models, such as Maslow's hierarchy of human needs (Maslow, 1954) or the theory of economic growth (Kuznets, 1965). Maturity models can be defined as 'conceptual multistage models that describe typical patterns in the development of organizational capabilities' (Poeppelbuss et al., 2011, p. 506). Organizational capabilities can refer to different types of organizational resources: the maturity of processes, the maturity of objects or technologies, or the maturity of people's capabilities (Mettler, 2011). Maturity models describe different degrees of maturity as stages that build on one another (Poeppelbuss et al., 2011).

The purposes of maturity models can be described along three dimensions (De Bruin et al., 2005; Poeppelbuss et al., 2011):

- *Descriptive*: Snapshot of an organization's performance at a certain point, assessing the situation.
- *Comparative*: Based on this snapshot, benchmarking and comparison against other organizations.
- *Prescriptive*: Guidelines and roadmaps for step-by-step progression and improvement to move up maturity stages.

Even though maturity models enjoy great popularity and impact, in practice they are criticized by academics for lack of methodological rigor (Mettler & Ballester, 2021; Pereira & Serrano, 2020). One source of that lack in rigor is the high diversity and ambiguity in conceptualization and theoretical foundation on which the development of maturity models is based. Another source is that maturity models can be aimed at a wide variety of areas of application: from assessing organizational development and growth, to benchmarking process and outcome improvements (Mettler & Ballester, 2021). Further, maturity models can widely differ in their generalizability – ranging from maturity models that are only applicable to certain industries or processes, to widely applicable more generalized maturity models (Thordsen et al., 2020). Recent academic research has aimed at assessing established maturity models and deriving guidelines and criteria for developing maturity models, which will be discussed in the next sections (Mettler & Ballester, 2021).

In IS research, maturity models typically consider a specific type of IS as the maturity entity (such as a business intelligence system, a knowledge management system, or business process management). Another perspective that IS research takes on maturity models is the perspective of the IS development as the maturity entity. Finally, some studies consider the role of individuals and groups (such as CIO leadership or employees' acceptance of organizational changes) as the entity of analysis (Poeppelbuss et al., 2011).

Digital Maturity

To pin down the status quo of an organization's degree of digitalization and its path towards digital transformation, the term digital maturity has become popular (Thordsen et al., 2020). Kane and colleagues describe digital maturity as the continuous process of adaptation to an increasingly digital environment, including strategy, workforce, culture, technology, and structure, in order to stay competitive and meet the expectations of all stakeholders (Kane et al., 2017). Rossman aids our understanding of digital maturity by conceptualizing it in terms of an organization forming a set of capabilities to manage its digital transformation. They classify these capabilities into eight dimensions: strategy, leadership, business model, operating model, people, culture, governance, and technology (Rossmann, 2018). Thereby, digital maturity goes far beyond simply implementing new technology (Kane et al., 2017). To summarize, digital maturity is about achievements with regard to digital transformation (Thordsen et al., 2020).

Digital Maturity Models

While maturity models in IS research have existed for a long time and considered, as laid out above, a wide spectrum in which IS can play a role in an organization's maturity, digital maturity models have only gained increased and broader attention in the past few years. Beginning with the early 2010s, in order to assess and provide an aid to achieving their clients' digital maturity, a variety of consulting firms started building models to measure digital maturity (e.g., Catlin et al., 2015; PwC, 2011; Westerman et al., 2012). With this focus on determining digital maturity, digital maturity models form a subset of maturity models that relate to pinning down the status quo of an organization's path towards digital transformation. In contrary to the specification of the entity of maturity as a specific IS (Poeppelbuss et al., 2011), the entity of the digital maturity model is the maturity of the organization's digital transformation as a whole. Since then, most digital maturity models were developed and published by practitioners, whereas a few have been published in academic outlets (Thordsen et al., 2020).

ORIGINS OF DIGITAL MATURITY MODELS

The foundation of many digital maturity models are IT maturity models, where IT maturity refers to matching IT services with business requirements (Thordsen & Bick, 2020). In the following, we will describe their most prominent representative, the CMM, maturity models that stem from it, as well as digital maturity models from an area where they emerged first: the public sector.

Basis for Digital Maturity Models: The Capability Maturity Model

Research on maturity models did not gain significant attention until the emergence of the first CMM, which has been developed by the Software Engineering Institute at Carnegie Mellon University. The purpose of the CMM was to find an approach towards the continuous improvement of organizational software processes (Humphrey, 1987; Paulk et al., 1993). Ever since its release in 1987, the CMM and its five-level structure have served as a basis for other maturity models across a variety of disciplines (Humphrey, 1987; Poeppelbuss et al., 2011).

Each maturity level in the CMM is characterized through a range of process features, that will be outlined in the following. In addition, a graphical representation of the distinct maturity stages is given in Figure 9.1.

The *initial* level is the least mature stage. Here, only a sparse number of processes are clearly defined, and the organization does not have management practices that allow for effective development and maintenance of software. Instead, processes are driven by poor planning practices and reactive decision-making. The overall process capability as well as performance indicators, such as schedule or product quality, are unpredictable in this maturity stage (Humphrey, 1987; Paulk et al., 1993).

The second level is the *repeatable* stage. At this level of maturity an organization has defined policies and procedures for project management in place. These guidelines help to repeat the successful practices of past projects. In addition, an organization is able to monitor fundamental software management controls, for example cost and schedule. Process capability can thus be characterized as stable and disciplined (Humphrey, 1987; Paulk et al., 1993).

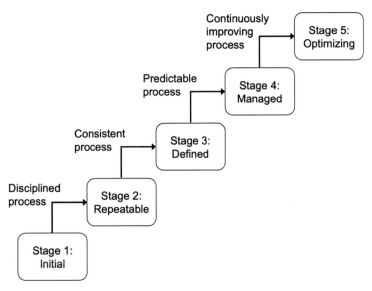

Source: Humphrey, 1987; Paulk et al., 1993.

Figure 9.1   The five stages of the Capability Maturity Model

In the third or *defined* level, all software engineering and management activities are consistently applied and well documented. Organizations at this stage have their own standard software processes for software development and maintenance, which also takes unique project needs into account (Humphrey, 1987; Paulk et al., 1993).

The fourth or *managed* maturity level is characterized by the organization-wide collection and analysis of detailed process data. Prevailing processes and indicators are thus well understood and quantitative goals are set. The overall process capability can be described as predictable (Humphrey, 1987; Paulk et al., 1993).

The fifth and most mature stage is the *optimizing* level. Here the organization as a whole is continuously working towards sustainable process improvement. Weaknesses of a process are analyzed to prevent their future reoccurrence. In addition, new technologies and approaches are implemented to enhance process performance (Humphrey, 1987; Paulk et al., 1993).

The CMM was originally intended to improve the effectiveness of software development projects. However, it soon gained popularity in other domains as well, such as engineering firms, who applied the CMM for project management purposes. Research suggests that successful CMM implementation can significantly increase performance in terms of time and cost optimization. In addition, the CMM was shown to be a tool for quality improvement by means of defects reduction (Titov et al., 2016).

Extensions of the Capability Maturity Model

Based on the original CMM, the Software Engineering Institute at Carnegie Mellon University introduced several more models, which exhibit the same stages of maturity applied to different backgrounds. One of these is the People CMM, which adopts the maturity stages from the CMM and applies them to a human resources context, offering organizations a framework for successful workforce management and development (Curtis et al., 2001). Other related concepts are the Systems Engineering CMM (Bate et al., 1995), and the Systems Security Engineering CMM (Hefner, 1997).

The Capability Maturity Model Integration (CMMI), whose first version launched in 2000, expanded the context of the initial model even more. Systems engineering, software engineering as well as process and product development were merged into a single model. Hence, the CMMI offers organizations a full range of comprehensive guidelines for the development of products and services, taking quality measures such as stakeholder satisfaction into account (CMMI Product Team, 2010; Paulk, 2009). As the CMMI and its maturity guidelines are widely applied in practice, the framework is continuously improved and developed further. Their most recent publication from 2019 features version 2.0 of the CMMI, which integrates a set of customized views from different business environments, allowing an organization to tailor the model according to their individual performance improvement demands (CMMI Institute, 2019).

Digital Maturity Models in the Public Sector

The success of the CMM and its subsequent models triggered related research in the IS field. Before digital maturity models emerged for the private sector, they became popular in the public sector. In the early 2000s, several concepts aiming at explaining the maturity of electronic government (E-government) were developed into various versions of approaches which comprised of four to six maturity stages (e.g., Baum and Di Maio, 2000; Layne and Lee, 2001; Ronaghan, 2002; Wescott, 2001). Along with the CMM family, these models have served as another foundation for many private sector maturity concepts. One exemplary model is the E-government framework by Hiller and Bélanger (2001), in which the authors proposed five distinct stages of digital government maturity. These stages along with their attributes will be outlined in the following as well as in Figure 9.2.

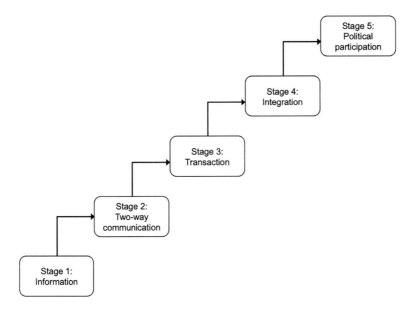

Source: Hiller & Bélanger, 2001.

Figure 9.2   *Stages of the e-government maturity framework*

The first stage describes the most basic form of digital government. At this level, public institutions only provide one-way communication, such as *information* regarding election dates and regulations on a website. At the second stage, simple *two-way communication* between government and citizens is possible, for example through e-mail exchange or the option to request information via online forms. When E-government resources are not limited to just commu- nication, but when *transactions*, such as paying taxes online and applying for financial aid are also possible, this would be the third stage of maturity. In the fourth stage, all government services are *integrated*, most commonly though a single portal that citizens can utilize to access all services they need regardless of which departments or agencies offer them. The fifth and most mature stage of E-government is characterized by *participation in political matters* being offered. This can be accomplished through internet voting services for instance, or the possibility to file comments online (Hiller & Bélanger, 2001).

A more recent maturity model in the public sector was published in a report of the IBM Center for The Business of Government (Desouza, 2021). This article presents six areas, based on research and practice, in which authorities must succeed in order to pave the way for effective adoption of Artificial Intelligence (AI) in public settings. The first aspect is *Big Data*, meaning agencies need to implement machine learning algorithms to make use of large data streams. Second, *authorities must adopt AI systems* that enable the effective transformation, analysis, and processing of data. Third, agencies must ensure that their workforce has the *capability to analyze the data correctly* and draw conclusions from it. Fourth, agencies need to *create an environment* where new ideas and approaches as well as experimenting are promoted. Fifth, *effective and responsible leadership* must be in place to ensure responsible data usage. And finally, AI initiatives need be part of the *overall strategy* and must be taken into account when making decisions at a strategic level. The model then suggests five distinct levels of maturity in the above mentioned areas, which are namely the ad-hoc level, experimentation, planning and deployment, scaling and learning, and the highest level which is enterprise-wide transformation (Desouza, 2021).

SELECTED DIGITAL MATURITY MODELS

Thordsen and colleagues aid in assessing the quality of different digital maturity models along various criteria such as their precision of definitions, generalizability, theoretical basis, or the implications they derive (Thordsen et al., 2020). Based on their structured overview, we will present three digital maturity models with high quality ratings.[1] In addition, two more recent extensions of digital maturity models will be introduced.

Model 1: Digital Maturity Matrix

The first model is from the MIT Sloan School of Management. Instead of a progressive stepwise approach, Westerman and colleagues (2012) propose a matrix structure for the classification of digital maturity along two dimensions based on an organization's standing in the ecosystem. *Digital intensity* on one side is the amount of investment in technology-driven projects that are intended to transform the way the organization operates. *Transformation management intensity* on the other side describes the amount of investment in leadership capabilities which are required for digital transformation. Based on this, there are four categories of organizations, which will be described hereafter. In addition, a visual overview is given in Figure 9.3.

Companies with low digital intensity as well as a low level of transformation management intensity can be described as *Digital Beginners*. Organizations in this category may be experienced with standard applications, such as ERP software, but they have no or very limited advanced digital capabilities in place. *Digital Fashionistas* have implemented more mature digital solutions,

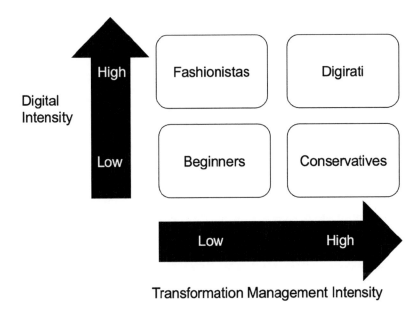

Source: Westerman et al., 2012.

Figure 9.3   *Four types of digital maturity*

but their transformative impact is limited. Organizations here have the motivation to initiate digital transformation but lack the experience and knowledge to actually benefit from their efforts. Companies in the category of *Digital Conservatives* are aware of the need for successful governance and leadership, but they are hesitant to adopt new technologies. They rather stick with digital applications that are well-established and familiar. The most mature class of organizations are the *Digirati*. Companies in this category exhibit a high digital intensity, along with a high transformation management intensity. They manage to adopt technological trends through diligent governance and to continuously improve their competitive advantage through them (Westerman et al., 2012). The practical value of this model is twofold. First, it can assist managers in benchmarking their organization's standing regarding digital transformation in comparison to others. Second, it can help in deriving fields of activity to improve the company's digital maturity.

Model 2: Digital Maturity Model 4.0

The next maturity model was published by Forrester Research in a report for E-business and channel strategy professionals (Gill & VanBoskirk, 2016). The

202 Digitalization and sustainability

authors developed a questionnaire, which assists organizations in determining their degree of digital maturity so that they can derive a strategy to increase their maturity based on the results. The assessment is based the following four dimensions:

1. *Culture*: An organization's mindset towards digital technologies.
2. *Technology*: An organization's adoption and usage of technologies.
3. *Organization*: A company's alignment regarding strategy, governance, and execution.
4. *Insights*: The degree to which an organization utilizes business data for benchmarking success.

The developed questionnaire consists of 28 statements from the above-mentioned dimensions. The organization is then asked to rate their agreement regarding each statement on a scale between zero (completely disagree) and three (completely agree). These rating are summed up in the end and gives the organization their final score, which determines their degree of digital maturity. Figure 9.4 gives an overview of all maturity stages and their respective scores (Gill & VanBoskirk, 2016). Companies at the lowest level of maturity are called *Skeptics*. They only

Maturity segment	Score range
Differentiators	72 – 88
Collaborators	53 – 71
Adopters	34 – 52
Skeptics	0 – 33

Source: Gill & VanBoskirk, 2016.

Figure 9.4   Segments of the Digital Maturity Model 4.0

possess limited experience with digital innovations and no clear strategy for implementing technologies. Further they hardly ever make use of online sales channels and digital marketing. Organizations on the *Adopters* level are more practiced in dealing with technologies. They are ready to invest into digital infrastructure, but their focus is mainly on automating operational procedures, so that they are not exploiting the full potential of digital means. *Collaborators* on the other side additionally make use of online marketing channels and collaborate to enable the implementation of innovations. The fourth and most advanced stage in terms of digital maturity is the group of *Differentiators*. Companies at this level exhibit strong revenue growth and a competitive advantage, for instance through the successful implementation of advanced marketing and online sales infrastructures (Gill & VanBoskirk, 2016).

Model 3: Maturity Model of Digital Transformation

The maturity model of digital transformation was designed after conducting a literature review, and expert and focus group interviews (Berghaus & Back, 2016; Berghaus, 2016). It has nine dimensions of organizational areas of activity with distinct criteria of maturity for each of them.

The first activity field is *customer experience*. The authors found that digitalization makes it more important than ever to understand customer needs and wishes and to adjust the corporate offer based on that assessment. One maturity criterion is thus analytics as it enables meaningful insights into customer data. Cross-channel experience is another aspect, which can be defined as a firm's ability to tailor their digital offers to customer needs.

Product innovation is the second area of activity. The first maturity criterion here is a company's willingness to integrate digital innovations into their product and service portfolio. Furthermore, an organization's general ability to develop and integrate innovative ideas is crucial in this field of activity. A third maturity attribute is digital customer involvement, for example through integration of lead users into the development of new ideas.

Another field of activity refers to the *strategic planning of digital innovations*. It is important that innovation in general plays a fundamental role in the overall corporate strategy, which is the first maturity criterion. Further, there should also be a strategic focus on digital means, which the authors label as 'Digital Commitment'.

Digitalization also affects *intraorganizational structures*. In this dimension, firms should ensure that digital competencies are widely spread across all departments and areas of the company, not just limited to a separate IT-division. A second criterion is entrepreneurial agility, which enables the firm to quickly and flexibly respond to the dynamics coming along with digital transformation. These dynamics also emphasize the need for a network of partners, which the organization can come back to in case of short-term bottleneck situations or the need for specialized services.

Three maturity criteria have been identified regarding *process digitization*. Firstly, firms should digitalize and integrate communication with external partners, such as suppliers and customers, which the authors refer to as *Touchpoint*

Management. Similarly, it is necessary for a mature organization to be able to control communication and make decisions based on data. The third attribute in this field of activity is automation of routine operational processes to make business more efficient.

Digital technologies influence the ability to *transform the collaboration in organizations*. For instance, knowledge management solutions can be used to connect staff from different divisions and enhance reciprocal learning. Another application area is cooperation among employees, where digital technologies can be utilized to share information and communicate. A third criterion is time and location-independent working, which is made possible by digital solutions.

Another field of activity refers to *IS operation and development*. One criterion in this dimension is the application of agile methods, which enables organizations to quickly implement innovative solutions and flexibly adapt them when needed. In order to integrate new technologies more easily into existing systems, it is necessary for firms to have an integrated and scalable IT-architecture. Moreover, there is the need for human IT expertise within the company to ensure a high-quality selection and implementation of technologies.

Corporate culture is also an important component of digital transformation. The first aspect in this regard is digital affinity, which means that employees do not only require the knowledge to operate new systems, but also the motivation to integrate them into their routines. Further, organizations must be willing to take risks and critically evaluate errors to improve in the future.

One last area of activity is *effective transformation management*, which includes successful governance with clearly defined responsibilities. Secondly, top level managers need to actively support digital transformation by, for example, offering financial resources. A final aspect is performance measurement and monitoring to ensure successful implementation.

The before-mentioned fields of activity, criteria and specific characteristics were then clustered into five stages of digital transformation maturity. Due to the complexity and size of the original model, we decided to present only a selection of exemplary items and fields of activity for each maturity stage in Table 9.1. Please refer to Berghaus (2016) for a complete and detailed overview.

Model 4: A Human-Centeredness Maturity Model

With the current shift from a product-centric to a service-centric and an experience-centric approach of companies to deliver value to their customers – designing with and through the user – the necessity for companies to change their mindset regarding the role of the human in their value creation processes

Table 9.1   *Five stages of maturity with exemplary fields of activity and specific items (based on Berghaus (2016))*

Maturity Stage	Activity Field	Short Description of Item
1	Strategy	Digital transformation is seen as continual strategic change project.
	Collaboration	Employees work from home or on the move.
	Customer Experience	Customer interaction through both traditional and digital channels.
2	Collaboration	Tools with videoconferencing and screen sharing are in use.
	Process Digitization	Check core processes for improvements on a regular basis.
	Corporate Culture	Errors are evaluated in order to improve.
3	Product Innovation	Employees contribute ideas for digital products on a regular basis.
	Transformation Management	Roles, responsibilities and decision-making processes are defined.
	Organization	Ability to react quickly to changes.
4	Information Technology	New products are tested and modified using prototypes.
	Transformation Management	Digital transformation goals are reviewed periodically.
	Product Innovation	Customers are included in the development of new products.
5	Transformation Management	Digital transformation goals are defined in a measurable way.
	Customer Experience	Customer and interaction data are collected across different channels.
	Process Digitization	Expertise in big data is used to develop new products.

emerges (Guerrero et al., 2022). The human-centeredness maturity model indicates the 'evolutionary path towards maturity for companies to become truly human-centered' (Guerrero et al., 2022, p. 1). In the following, the five stages of human-centeredness maturity that a company can be situated at on this 'evolution' are described shortly (Guerrero et al., 2022).

1. *Infancy*: Customers are viewed as merely consumers of services, strictly separated from the provider, not involved in the design and development of services.

2. *Developing*: Increased focus on customer needs in service design, though still inconsistent customer engagement.
3. *Transforming*: Co-creation as a necessity, customer engagement in service design and development as a priority, shift of understanding from designing services to designing experiences..
4. *Assimilating*: Co-creation and co-design as part of a company's strategy, customers as the biggest source of value contribution, concrete strategy towards improved service experiences.
5. *Truly human-centered*: Customers as the biggest source of value contribution, all firm decisions based around the customer, company mindset of seeing customers as humans.

Within each stage, an organization is evaluated regarding the extent to which they develop capabilities in five areas (Guerrero et al., 2022):

1. *Co-creation*: The extent to which customers are actively involved in designing services.
2. *Customer experience*: Assessment of company from customer perspective in terms of satisfaction, empathy, well-being, and trust.
3. *Service personalization*: Assessment of company's ability to offer customized services regarding different aspects of their customer's lives.
4. *Strategy and leadership*: Assessment of the company's ability to deploy a human-centered mindset and culture across all organizational levels.
5. *Technology*: Related to company's understanding about data collection.

GUIDELINES FOR DESIGNING MATURITY MODELS

Researchers have sought to guide the designing of maturity models through guidelines and frameworks (Becker et al., 2009; Mettler & Ballester, 2021). These guidelines take a generalized view and can be applied to different types of maturity models – including digital maturity models.

Based on the guidelines for designing maturity models by Becker and colleagues (Becker et al., 2009) and a review of publications on maturity models, Mettler and Ballester critically assess the degree to which those guidelines are applied and implemented, and derive further recommendations on designing maturity models (Mettler & Ballester, 2021). Each step of Becker and colleagues' maturity model design process and the respective extensions for improvement by Mettler and Ballester are laid out below.

Table 9.2 *Guidelines for developing (digital) maturity models (based on Mettler and Ballester (2021))*

Guideline	Description by Becker et al. (2009)	Extension by Mettler and Ballester (2021)
1. Problem definition	Defining the application domain of the maturity model as well as conditions for its application and benefits.	Provide clear definitions of 'maturity', differentiate between subject of investigation and evolution of the subject, define optimization problem faced.
2. Comparison with existing maturity models	Motivate need for development of a new maturity model through comparison with existing models (novelty, improvement, …).	Clearly state to what extent the new model is an improvement of existing models as well as how the new model differentiates in terms of theoretical assumptions, operationalization, practical goals, and envisioned application domain from other models.
3. Identification of problem relevance	Demonstrate theoretical and practical relevance of problem solution proposed by the projected maturity model.	Thoroughly assess the necessity for developing a new maturity model; define need in practice; explain why specific design of maturity model is appropriate for this problem; more complex is not always better.
4. Multi-methodological procedure	Employ methods that are well-founded and finely attuned for developing maturity models	Triangulate findings from empirical and logic-based methods; mix judgmental and theory-based evidence.
5. Iterative procedure	Maturity models must be developed iteratively, i.e., step by step.	Lay out the extent to which the design process followed an iterative procedure: how many iterations, initial and end goal
6. Evaluation	All principles and premises for the development of a maturity model, as well as usefulness, quality and effectiveness of the artifact, must be evaluated iteratively.	Thoroughly define criteria and setting for evaluation of maturity model; mention reliability and validity of findings; evaluate real impact in practice.
7. Scientific documentation	Document the design process of the maturity model in detail, consider each step of the process: parties involved, applied methods, results.	Pay more attention to documentation of design process – next to explaining the form and functioning of the model; explicitly state potential limiting factors of model application; use graphical representations.
8. Targeted presentation of results	Target presentation of maturity model with regard to conditions of its application and needs of its users.	Concretize how to apply new maturity models in practice; clearly outline how to interpret results and how to deal with ambiguous situations.

IMPLEMENTING DIGITAL MATURITY MODELS

The effective implementation of digital maturity models in an organization may pave the way to successful digital transformation. Gurbaxani and Dunkle (2019) identify dimensions, which need to be addressed in an organization to achieve the best possible outcome of digital transformation efforts. These dimensions include a clearly defined strategy and vision, a corporate culture that promotes innovation as well as technological skills and assets. Another factor is strategic alignment, which involves collaboration between different stakeholders or ecosystem members within the company (Gurbaxani & Dunkle, 2019). Such stakeholders include management as well as employees throughout all departments of the firm including IT, marketing, product development, strategy and human resources (Berghaus, 2016).

The collaboration between these ecosystem members may, however, lead to certain challenges. First, there may be differences in technological affinity and commitment between individual employees, which results in disparate levels of motivation to support digital transformation efforts. A second challenge could be a lack of collaboration between departments. Since digital transformation affects the organization as a whole, it needs to be ensured that transformative activities are not limited to the IT department (Berghaus, 2016). Instead, business departments and IT should collaborate closely, for instance through increasing business capabilities among IT employees (Bassellier & Benbasat, 2004) or by advancing IT skills of executive staff (Berghaus, 2016; Turel & Bart, 2014). Third, there may be information asymmetries or differences in motivation and goals between the management and the workforce. For example, top-level managers might see the strategic need to implement digital maturity throughout the organization more clearly than employees on lower levels of the organization, who could thus be less motivated to support the transformation process. Therefore, special attention needs to be paid to employees' attitudes towards digital transformation so that they actively support necessary change processes (Meske & Junglas, 2021).

For a successful implementation of digital maturity models in practice the beforementioned tensions need to be overcome by the ecosystem members and effective collaboration on all levels of the organization must be ensured. When a company however fails to resolve these challenges or is doing it poorly, it may face serious consequences. First, organizations may not be able to ensure their digital readiness, meaning they are unable to satisfy customer needs and react to changing circumstances as quickly as needed. Second, companies may not be able to engage in innovating digital products, which results in a lowered competitiveness and ultimately lower revenues (Berghaus & Back, 2017; Osmundsen et al., 2018).

One practical example of successful digital transformation is the LEGO Group, the Danish company famous for construction kits and children's toys. In 2004, LEGO was close to bankruptcy. As a result, the company needed to resolve issues concerning their organizational structure and supply chain To do this, they expanded into the virtual world by offering video games as well as online virtual-interaction games, which helped them to achieve growth rates again. The growth on the other side drastically strained the information systems supporting the business. Order management and fulfillment were especially affected, leading to an inability to meet customer demands. In order to address these problems, LEGO created a modularized and standardized architecture for their information systems, making it possible to expand faster and dynamically add capacity and functionality. They implemented an integrated enterprise system that included new applications for human capital management, operations support, product life cycle management, and data management. In summary, LEGO demonstrated a successful digital transformation approach. First, by recognizing the need for change and adjusting their business model accordingly. And second, by adopting technology into all levels of the organization through effective collaboration (Pearlson & Saunders, 2013; Sebastian et al., 2017).

PRACTITIONER INSIGHTS

This section is based on decades of practical experience of our third author Prof. Dr. Rainer Bernnat.

Applying a digital maturity model as a diagnostic tool provides transparency on digital capabilities and enables a valuable comparison of these capabilities with peers, industry average, or best-in-class digital leaders. However, transparency of a company's ability to create value through digitization only defines a starting point and requires the adaptation of the strategic agenda and an operational implementation plan to meet the desired state. Successful companies institutionalize the implementation of key projects to support the digital transformation based on the outcome of digital maturity models, as part of an overarching program organization, or as part of a 'digital factory' where cross-cutting activities are centralized and managed. Equally important is regular controlling of the impact of the implementation plan on the model outcome, e.g., by repeating the assessment on a regular basis. Although there is an ongoing requirement of increased scientific foundation and comparability of different digital maturity models, their implementation provides valuable strategic insights for senior leadership towards leveraging digital technologies to bolster competitiveness through disruption or simply to ensure current market positioning.

The digital transformation journey of private sector companies and public institutions typically rely on six pillars (customer relationship, operations, business support, new products and business models, data and technology, culture and people) from internal to customer facing capabilities. This requires a holistic approach towards successful implementation across the entire value chain and business enablers. To attract, keep, and interact with customers, digital channels, tools and instruments play an important role. Digitally transformed customer relationships impact brand awareness, products and services, conversion of sales via existing and new channels, and fulfillment of individual customer experience. Operations and business support also undergo a fundamental transformation through digital capabilities, from engineering, supply chain management, logistics and service towards optimized customer service and other support functions, such as procurement, finance, and HR. The value chain transformation is being complemented by the creation of new products, services, and business models potentially outside the core business, driven through digital innovation and value generation with digital products. To transform the core value chain, capabilities in developing technology need to be implemented that, for example, support the integration of data analytics as a core function, or that establish digital development methodologies to speed up traditional implementation processes. Finally, organizational adjustments are required to support the digital vision, primarily from a cultural point of view that enable innovation and collaboration, to hire and to retain digital talents, and to sponsor digital transformation from the top leadership across the entire organization.

Archetypes of Digital Maturity Stages of Organizations

Before discussing the selective challenges of practical implementation of digital maturity models, some archetypes will be outlined to get a better understanding of differentiated challenges for public and private sector institutions during a digital transformation journey.

The first archetype consists of *legacy institutions* that are typically characterized by a traditionally grown organization, process architecture, governance, and culture. This archetype can be found for example among healthcare payor organizations or within the manufacturing industry. Healthcare payor organizations sometimes have a pedigree that goes back many decades, at times also centuries. In that context, the German 'Knappschaft Bahn See' payor organization has its roots in the year 1260 which illustrates tradition and culture as an integral part of the 'organizational DNA'.

The next archetype are *early adopters* who have leveraged digital capabilities at a very early stage. Leading players in banking and finance, retail or pharmaceutical industry are examples of this archetype. All these players have gradually integrated technology across their value chains. Typically, this has been performed through the increased centralization of digital initiatives as the initial stage, until – subsequently – each part of the organization has acquired sufficient capabilities to leverage technology as part of their daily activities. ING's agile transformation is a good example of a banking institution that complements digital capabilities with the appropriate flexibility and ability of the entire organization.

Lastly, *digital natives* are institutions that have been established within the digital age. Their individual business models, operations, and customer relationship management directly rely on applying technology as the core differentiator vis-à-vis competition. The international startup ecosystems, but also many established cloud-based service providers (e.g., for artificial intelligence, data analytics or cybersecurity) can be found among this archetype. One example is the rise of the US-based software company Palantir that specializes in big data analytics.

Digital leaders can be found in all archetypes and industries – primarily in those who base their success mostly on disruption within the value chain. The heterogeneity of digital maturity within different industry sectors illustrates the need for systematically baselining status and desired state through applying maturity models.

Contemporary Dynamics in Applying Digital Maturity Models

The last two years have been impacted strongly by the global pandemic. This situation has practically served as an accelerator for increased digitization, particularly in sectors that were lagging behind. Governments in many countries were operating in an environment that was not positioned at the forefront of leveraging digital innovation to optimize end-user interaction, operations, or collaboration. However, the pandemic required governments to quickly adapt to the new way of working, basically to ensure delivery and operations. As a result, this new way of working has leapfrogged traditional resistance towards a desperately required change.

As digital maturity models typically embrace a holistic perspective of status and desired state of a digital transformation within an institution, apparently there is a requirement to identify relevant expertise of comparable situations among competitors within the considered industry or beyond, and the need to provide an objective and unbiased view on status and 'to-be' state. Moreover, it is difficult to define the desired state within the customer interaction of an organization that is characterized by legacy processes, as it might result in major disruption of the current way of working. Therefore, in most cases a need to include an outside-in perspective through external advice, or, alternatively, through inhouse consulting, is a well-established way to ensure objectivity in applying digital maturity models and to provide qualitative benchmarking/best practice capabilities.

As outlined in the sections before, digital maturity models typically have a comprehensive scope, addressing the entire value chain and additional enablers, such as data and technology, and organization and culture. In many cases, this scope is too broad and would require an increased focus on the specific challenges along the digital transformation journey of an individual institution. In banking for example, the definition of digital products and the optimization of the customer relationships based on digital channels are already part of most banks' strategic agenda, whereas the internal organization would strongly benefit from increased agility. In these cases, standard digital maturity models would require adaptations and focus to accommodate for these specific challenges.

CONCLUSION

In this chapter, we presented the ancestors of maturity concepts in the private context, being the CMM and its related models, along with maturity models in the public sector. Based on this foundation, selected prominent digital maturity models developed by practitioners and in academic literature were introduced. We outlined guidelines for how to deploy digital maturity models and addressed tensions regarding their implementation.

KEY TAKEAWAYS

- Digital maturity models are a class of maturity models which aim at assessing and guiding an organization's path towards digital transformation.
- Most digital maturity models present a kind of evolutionary, stepwise process that an organization may take towards digitalization.
- The assessment of an organization's digital maturity is based on a variety of factors such as organizational culture and effective transformation and change management. The selection of factors that are included in each specific model represent the most significant difference between the maturity models.
- It can be viewed critically that some models were developed without following or documenting a rigorous design process, but they may still be useful for practitioners.
- The effective implementation of digital maturity models requires collaboration between different ecosystem members. This collaboration involves tensions, which need to be resolved successfully. A failure in overcoming these tensions can result in serious losses for the organization.

- Digital maturity models are useful tools for organizations as they provide strategic insights towards leveraging digital technologies. However, their practical implementation is not without challenges.

NOTE

1. Thordsen et al. (2020) define high quality models as those with a high degree of validity, which is measured by the five requirements: observation, generalizability, theory-based interpretation, exploration, and implication.

REFERENCES

Bassellier, G., & Benbasat, I. (2004). Business Competence of Information Technology Professionals: Conceptual Development and Influence on IT-Business Partnerships. *MIS Quarterly*, *28*(4), 673–94. https://doi.org/10.2307/25148659

Bate, R., Kuhn, D., Wells, C., Armitage, J., & Clark, G. (1995). *A Systems Engineering Capability Maturity Model, Version 1.1*. Carnegie-Mellon University, Software Engineering Institute.

Baum, C. H., & Di Maio, A. (2000). *Gartner's Four Phases of E-Government Model*. Gartner.

Becker, J., Knackstedt, R., & Pöppelbuß, J. (2009). Developing Maturity Models for IT Management. *Business & Information Systems Engineering*, *1*(3), 213–22.

Berghaus & Back. (2016). Gestaltungsbereiche der Digitalen Transformation von Unternehmen: Entwicklung eines Reifegradmodells. *Die Unternehmung*, *70*(2), 98–123. https://doi.org/10.5771/0042-059X-2016-2-98

Berghaus, S. (2016). Stages in Digital Business Transformation: Results of an Empirical Maturity Study. *Proceedings of the 10th Mediterranean Conference on Information Systems*, 1–17.

Berghaus, S., & Back, A. (2017). Disentangling the Fuzzy Front End of Digital Transformation: Activities and Approaches. *Proceedings of the 38th International Conference on Information Systems*, 1–17.

Catlin, T., Scanlan, J., & Willmott, P. (2015). Raising your Digital Quotient. *McKinsey Quarterly*, 1–14.

CMMI Institute. (2019). *CMMI V2.0: Model at-a-Glance* (pp. 1–36).

CMMI Product Team. (2010). *CMMI® for Development, Version 1.3*. Carnegie-Mellon University, Software Engineering Institute.

Curtis, B., Hefley, W. E., & Miller, S. A. (2001). *People Capability Maturity Model (P-CMM)*. Carnegie-Mellon University, Software Engineering Institute.

De Bruin, T., Rosemann, M., Freeze, R., & Kaulkarni, U. (2005). Understanding the Main Phases of Developing a Maturity Assessment Model. *Proceedings of the 16th Australasian Conference on Information Systems*, 8–19.

Desouza, K. C. (2021). *Artificial Intelligence in the Public Sector:* IBM Center for The Business of Government.

Gill, M., & VanBoskirk, S. (2016). The Digital Maturity Model 4.0. *Forrester Research*, 1–16.

Guerrero, R., Lattemann, C., Michalke, S., & Siemon, D. (2022). A Human-Centeredness Maturity Model for the Design of Services in the Digital Age. *Proceedings of the 17th International Conference on Wirtschaftsinformatik*, 1–16.

Gurbaxani, V., & Dunkle, D. (2019). Gearing Up For Successful Digital Transformation. *MIS Quarterly Executive, 18*(3), 209–20.

Hefner, R. (1997). Lessons Learned with the Systems Security Engineering Capability Maturity Model. *Proceedings of the International Conference on Software Engineering*, 566–67.

Hiller, J., & Bélanger, F. (2001). *Privacy Strategies for Electronic Government.* The PricewaterhouseCoopers Endowment for The Business of Government. http://www.businessofgovernment.org/sites/default/files/PrivacyStrategies.pdf

Humphrey, W. S. (1987). *Characterizing the Software Process: A Maturity Framework.* Carnegie-Mellon University, Software Engineering Institute.

Kane, G. C., Palmer, D., Phillips, A. N., Kiron, D., & Buckley, N. (2017). *Achieving Digital Maturity* (pp. 1–29). MIT Sloan Management Review.

Kuznets, S. (1965). *Economic Growth and Structure.* Heinemann Educational Books.

Lasrado, L., Vatrapu, R., & Andersen, K. N. (2016). A Set Theoretical Approach to Maturity Models: Guidelines and Demonstration. *Proceedings of the 37th International Conference on Information Systems*, 1–20. https://aisel.aisnet.org/icis2016/Methodological/Presentations/12

Layne, K., & Lee, J. (2001). Developing Fully Functional E-Government: A Four Stage Model. *Government Information Quarterly, 18*(2), 122–36. https://doi.org/10.1016/S0740-624X(01)00066-1

Maslow, A. H. (1954). *Motivation and Personality.* Harper and Row.

Meske, C., & Junglas, I. (2021). Investigating the Elicitation of Employees' Support Towards Digital Workplace Transformation. *Behaviour & Information Technology, 40*(11), 1120–36.

Mettler, T. (2011). Maturity Assessment Models: A Design Science Research Approach. *International Journal of Society Systems Science, 3*(1/2), 81–98. https://doi.org/10.1504/IJSSS.2011.038934

Mettler, T., & Ballester, O. (2021). Maturity Models in Information Systems: A Review and Extension of Existing Guidelines. *Proceedings of the 42nd International Conference on Information Systems*, 1–16. https://aisel.aisnet.org/icis2021/is_design/is_design/3

Osmundsen, K., Iden, J., & Bygstad, B. (2018). Digital Transformation: Drivers, Success Factors, and Implications. *Prooceedings of the the 12th Mediterranean Conference on Information Systems (MCIS)*, 1–17.

Owais, S. T., Khanna, S., & Mani, R. S. (2017). Building Multi-Channel e-Service Delivery Platform: Opportunities and Challenges. *Proceedings of the Special Collection on EGovernment Innovations in India*, 58–63. https://doi.org/10.1145/3055219.3055233

Paulk, M. C. (2009). A History of the Capability Maturity Model for Software. *Software Quality Professional, 12*(1).

Paulk, M. C., Curtis, B., Chrissis, M. B., & Weber, C. V. (1993). *Capability Maturity Model for Software, Version 1.1:* Defense Technical Information Center. https://doi.org/10.21236/ADA263403

Pearlson, K. E., & Saunders, C. S. (2013). *Strategic Management of Information Systems.* Wiley.

Pereira, R., & Serrano, J. (2020). A Review of Methods Used on IT Maturity Models Development: A Systematic Literature Review and a Critical Analysis. *Journal of Information Technology, 35*(2), 161–78. https://doi.org/10.1177/0268396219886874

Poeppelbuss, J., Niehaves, B., Simons, A., & Becker, J. (2011). Maturity Models in Information Systems Research: Literature Search and Analysis. *Communications of the Association for Information Systems*, *29*(1). https://doi.org/10.17705/1CAIS .02927

PwC. (2011). *Measuring Industry Digitization: Leaders and Laggards in the Digital Economy*. https://www.strategyand.pwc.com/gx/en/insights/2011-2014/measuring -industry-digitization-leaders-laggards.html

Ronaghan, S. (2002). *Benchmarking E-government: A Global Perspective*. United Nations Division for Public Economicsand Public Administration and American Society for Public Administration.

Rossmann, A. (2018, December 13). Digital Maturity: Conceptualization and Measurement Model. *Proceedings of the 39th International Conference on Information Systems*. https://aisel.aisnet.org/icis2018/governance/Presentations/8

Sebastian, I. M., Ross, J. W., Beath, C., Mocker, M., Moloney, K. G., & Fonstad, N. O. (2017). How Big Old Companies Navigate Digital Transformation. *MIS Quarterly Executive*, 197–213. https://doi.org/10.4324/9780429286797-6

Thordsen, T., & Bick, M. (2020). Towards a Holistic Digital Maturity Model. *Proceedings of the 41st International Conference on Information Systems*, 1–9. https://aisel.aisnet.org/icis2020/governance_is/governance_is/5

Thordsen, T., Murawski, M., & Bick, M. (2020). How to Measure Digitalization? A Critical Evaluation of Digital Maturity Models. In M. Hattingh, M. Matthee, H. Smuts, I. Pappas, Y. K. Dwivedi, & M. Mäntymäki (eds), *Responsible Design, Implementation and Use of Information and Communication Technology* (pp. 358–69). Springer International Publishing. https://doi.org/10.1007/978-3-030 -44999-5_30

Titov, S., Bubnov, G., Guseva, M., Lyalin, A., & Brikoshina, I. (2016). Capability Maturity Models inEengineering Companies: Case Study Analysis. *ITM Web of Conferences*, *6*(03002), 1–4. https://doi.org/10.1051/itmconf/20160603002

Turel, O., & Bart, C. (2014). Board-level IT Governance and Organizational Performance. *European Journal of Information Systems*, *23*(2), 223–39. https://doi .org/10.1057/ejis.2012.61

Wescott, C. (2001). E-government in the Asia-Pacific Region. *Asian Journal of Political Science*, *9*(2), 1–24.

Westerman, G., Tannou, M., Bonnet, D., Ferraris, P., & McAfee, A. (2012). The Digital Advantage: How Digital Leaders Outperform their Peers in Every Industry. *MIT Sloan Management and Capgemini Consulting*, *2*, 2–23.

Practice 3. A practitioner's view on the organizational perspective

Dorine Andrews

Organizations miss the mark in realizing digital value because they fail to fully integrate their digital technologies and organization operations to keep customer-defined value at the forefront. As Wang et al conclude, customers find digital value through their evolving experience with products and service based on how they perceive it. Too often organizations think they know best, falling back onto defining value without customer engagement. In my experience, I found the intensity of the problem increases when the customer looks to the services provided with the physical product that makes the difference between satisfaction and dissatisfaction.

Most recently, a company I'll call MNO sells digitally enabled products that include custom digital documents and virtual videos and conferencing events. MNO's sales team promises customers that MNO products will deliver benefits (e.g., exposure to new audiences, opportunities to engage, and industry knowledge). However, customers are disappointed in the services required from the delivery organization to develop and deliver the products that meet customer expectations (e.g., targeted audiences, influencers opportunities, or needed industry knowledge). The crux of the problem is threefold:

- MNO initiates the product creation process internally, defining product value without understanding what it takes to create and deliver that value. To accommodate customers, the sales group promises special features and benefits that are difficult to develop and deliver.
- The MNO staff tasked to develop and deliver are only engaged after a product is sold. They are faced with unrealistic requests that, if not met, fail to meet customer expectations.
- The two groups worked in organizational silos, did not collaborate or share data and were in conflict due to conflicting performance reward systems. The MNO sales team was rewarded for selling the product, not delivering it and customer satisfaction was the responsibility of the development and delivery group. All dissatisfaction was attributed to its failure to meet customer expectations.

The nugget of insight for organization change practitioners is to help companies create 'customer configured' value instead of 'organization unit configured value'. Failing to consider the impact of a promised product on the operations side of the organization results in the company shooting itself in the foot, so to speak when, as a whole, it fails to meet what the customer considers of most value. As Wang theorizes, it is the misalignment in organization structure and product architecture that create customer dissatisfaction. As practitioners, it is our job to help organizations keep the focus on:

- Understanding customers' relationships with their environment, what is important value to them, and how the company can leverage those socio-technical relationships.
- Creating organization structure, cross-organization process design, and management practices that unite, not silo operational units. [1]

A focus on customer 'configured' value is only a piece of the digital transformation puzzle. Like young children, organizations must be nurtured and supported to evolve. Digital transformation requires an evolutionary growth process. They are organic and dynamic entities with their own personalities (cultures) with many complex moving parts. If you're a practitioner working in the digital transformation arena, multi-faceted organization assessments are a first step in creating concrete actionable change plans that can be successfully implemented.

To use a simple analogy, modernizing a house starts with an assessment of what needs to be done to achieve the homeowner's objectives for the change. The same applies to digital transformation. It requires: (1) understanding what needs to be fixed, added to or replaced; (2) creating a digital transformation vision – a picture of how the organization will operate when the change is completed; and (3) identifying the gaps between the two. Only within that framework is it possible to architect the transformation – to set the boundaries of customers, products/services, and organization entities to be transformed given finite resources and environmental conditions. Key questions include 'How much can we do at once?", "In what sequence?" and "What expertise and leadership do we need to pull it off?

No one digital transformation model is perfect and we know from Wanger's et al research, change will continue to be needed as technology evolves; hence, continual process improvement must be part of the transformation vision. As a practitioner, I'm not a purist. I steal from multiple models to create questions that structure my assessment work. For example, the *Digital Maturity Matrix Model* stimulates questions like these:

1. What types of IT system(s) is the organization using today and what makes them insufficient?

2. Has the organization gone beyond standard applications, but with limited business impact? What happened to cause this?
3. What is the organization's leadership history with technology investment? Hesitant to invest or one of adopting technological trends? What in the culture caused this?
4. Has leadership recognized digital technology as an asset and embedded it in business strategy through governance? If not, how has digital transformation been accomplished historically?

To assess groups, teams and individual readiness for transformation the *Digital Maturity Model 4.0* stimulates questions such as:

1. Who is skeptical, embracing or 'one the line' toward digital technologies?
2. Who has adopted automation to pilot what is possible? How was it recognized by leadership? Are they punished for trying and failing?
3. Who is eager to use digital technology to collaborate outside organization boundaries as well as across siloed departmental entities? How have they done this?

By leveraging the dimensions of the *Maturity Model of Digital Transformation* and *Human Centeredness Models*, questions to stimulate visionary thinking come to mind:

1. What do customers contribute to product/service innovation? Is it sufficient? Is it systemic?
2. What customer data can predict behavior, needs, and trends? Is it sufficient? Is it systemic?
3. How are business processes and product/services improvements made?
4. How can budgets reflect commitment to building digital transformation expertise?
5. What intra-organizational structures and processes create collaboration barriers or reduce agility?
6. How is IT involved in business strategic, operational, and tactical planning? Are they partners, leaders or considered just an assumed utility?
7. How are people valued, developed, evaluated, and rewarded for embracing digital technology?

The reality is simple. Digital Transformation creates tension within organizations. It is a disruptive, painful and wrenching process to move from what is comfortable to an environment full of insecurity, uncertainties, and conflicts of interest – the very disruptive nature of transformation activity. It takes very hard work, committed leadership, time, and resources, to undertake an organizational change journey. People may intellectually acknowledge that the transformation makes logical sense, but until people can embrace it emotionally and adapt their behavior, transformation is unlikely to be realized. New traditions, values, reward systems and evidence of success must incentivize change across an organization's many complex moving parts.

To prove the point, the success rate has proven elusive. Since the 1980s and the introduction of cross functional ERP systems, the mantra '70% of digital transformation activities do not reach their objectives while leading to massive cost explosions' is a familiar one. Adding external customers and supply chain partners to the internal mix of organization players only increases complexity.

Haskamp's et al 'sticky' web of inertia fields is an excellent framework for identifying all the components that must be addressed in creating actionable change plans. The Vision and Strategy Inertia field address business purpose and profitability (break even for non-profits). Governance and Process address all aspects of business operations. Mindset and Culture, the often ignored or forgotten, address what it takes to stimulate adaption and creativity in people. The key to success for practitioners is to engage the multi-level groups whose work will become interdependent and simultaneous. Dictating change from the top down is viewed as patronizing. Information Technology (IT) driven transformation is often ill conceived, because 35 years of experiences tells us that techies do not understand the organic nature of organization dynamics. As stated earlier, departmentalized operations are territorial silos reinforced physically and culturally where people perceive the drive for change as attacks on their autonomy and power.

My recommendation is to build *change ownership of those directly impacted by the anticipated transformation to break through inertia.* I use the analogy of owning vs. renting a home. When you own your home, you invest in its maintenance to grow its value. If you rent, maintenance is someone else's problem. The same applies to organization health. You build *change ownership* through the intentional orchestration of four core sets of activities integrating all inertia fields to build *awareness, which leads to involvement, that matures into partnerships, and culminates in joint decision making.* For example:

1. Raise awareness through multi-level and intergroup meetings and media to communicate issues affecting business health that must be addressed for its survival. Use data AND stories (e.g., 'Voices of our customers') to put on a personal perspective everyone can relate to.
2. Create involvement by conducting focus group discussions and listening sessions for individuals and groups (external and internal) directly impacted. Publish results and share them so everyone sees they have been heard and share many common problems, needs and desires.
3. Create executive cross organization partners by having them develop and commit to a transformation vision and strategy that incorporates key find-

ings results from focus groups and listening sessions. When executives behave as a team, those below them have a behavior model to replicate.

4. Triage the groups and individuals that will be impacted by the transformation – (1) laggards will never be convinced that transformation is necessary (yes, there will be some); (2) early adopters who will enthusiastically embrace it all; and (3) respected skeptics who, if properly engaged, will become strong advocates, influencers, and motivators for transformation.

5. Use facilitated structured workshops to enable joint decision-making techniques with inter-group teams consisting of business and technology early adopters and respected skeptics members. Their job is to redesign and develop new supporting business systems –policies, practices, processes, relationships that harness digital technologies. Clear roles and rules for discussion, decision-making and issue management will provide everyone the opportunity to contribute and influence final decisions. These teams become change owners.

6. Expand ownership by adding intergroup and cross organization teams to test/pilot designs with digital technologies and business systems, measuring results, and recommending refinements for roll-out.

7. Reconvene change owners to plan the more expansive roll-out and identify human and financial resources required to execute the roll-out.

8. Acquire organization leaders' commitment to financing, people, transition support systems, facilities, et al.

9. Execute roll-out plans monitoring to provide adjustments as needed.

10. Institutionalize cross-organization teamwork to ensure continual process improvement, learning, performance improvement, and issue management.

This iterative approach ensures that the right decisions are made by the right people, at the right time, and at the right level in the organization. Using the Inertia Field model ensures all critical components required for change success are addressed. Although there may be some 'low hanging fruit', there are no quick fixes. A new digital technology may inspire transformation initiatives, but technology providers don't own them. That's the job of the business. Technology providers are partners with the business, members of change owner teams. Digital transformation is a messy business and organizations should undertake it with everyone's eyes wide-open.

NOTE

1.   A story about the struggle over customer vs. product 'configured' value is told in the recent article from the *New York Times* (1 May 2022), 'How Technocrats Triumphed at Apple' by Tripp Mickle: https://www.nytimes.com/2022/05/01/technology/jony-ive-apple-design.html.

10. Achieving structural ambidexterity through bimodal IT: a conceptual model and research agenda

Kristina Kusanke

INTRODUCTION

Companies find themselves in a situation where the need for a focus on digital transformation is unquestioned but, at the same time, ensuring stable and reliable operations remains of unabated importance (Haffke et al., 2017a; Leonhardt et al., 2017). As a consequence, companies' information technology (IT) functions are facing challenges arising from changed expectations towards and perceptions of their role within an organization. One the one hand, IT functions are expected to 'keep the lights on', while on the other hand they are also expected to drive the digital change (Haffke et al., 2017b). In most cases, traditionally structured unimodal IT setups, constrained by their legacy information systems, are not suited to accompany these contradicting needs (Haffke et al., 2017b). Instead, companies have sought *bimodal* forms of organization that provide both, explorative and exploitative, capabilities and thus allow them to reach – what previous researchers also called – structural ambidexterity e.g., (Haffke et al., 2017a; Fortmann et al., 2019).

Bimodal IT has been coined by Gartner market research as 'the practice of managing two separate, coherent modes of IT delivery, one focused on stability and the other on agility' (Colella et al., 2014). The concept is widely applied in practice by companies such as Ford, DHL, and Deutsche Bahn (Boulton, 2015; Fortmann et al., 2019). Bimodal IT can take different organizational forms (Haffke et al., 2017a). While some companies regard bimodal IT as a way to run different (e.g., plan-driven versus agile) projects within the same IT unit, others regard the structural division of IT units as key to meeting the strategic and operational expectations towards IT in digitally transforming companies (Haffke et al., 2017a). More recently, practitioners have also discussed the concept more controversially. Bimodality has been criticized for creating organizational silos and slowing down transformation to a fully agile state (Haffke et al., 2017b; Horlach et al., 2016). In addition, the common characterization of the traditional mode as being the slower one fuels employees' unwillingness to participate in bimodal IT and creates a cultural division between mode 1 and mode 2, ultimately impeding the alignment between business and IT (Ellerman, 2017). For some, bimodality 'sets the path for IT's long-term transformation' (Marko, 2015) while others declare it as a 'recipe for disaster' (Bloomberg, 2015).

Although the discourse around bimodal IT has primarily been led by practice, the academic literature on bimodal IT has grown considerably within the last five years. Since Horlach et al.'s 2016 study (Horlach et al., 2016), who identified only one academic paper on this phenomenon, research has made progress in the fields of how to organize bimodal IT, e.g., (Haffke et al., 2017a; Horlach et al., 2016), its influencing factors e.g., (Tai et al., 2019; Zhen et al., 2021) and governance mechanisms e.g., (Jöhnk et al., 2019). Other researchers focused on showing the strategic and business performance related benefits of this phenomenon (Fischer et al., 2020). From this growing stream of literature, and in the light of the continued controversies in the practitioner discourse, emerges a need to structure the knowledge domain. Although previous authors have reviewed various topics related to bimodal IT, including digital transformation and IT, e.g., (Albino & Souza, 2019; Gerster, 2017), strategies for successful IT projects (Holgeid et al., 2018), and ambidexterity research (Lee et al., 2015; Saxena, 2020), we lack a dedicated review of the current state of research regarding bimodal IT to discuss our understanding of this contemporary IT phenomenon in the light of the critique among practitioners. The goal of this chapter is, therefore, to: (1) provide an overview of the current academic knowledge; (2) collect and synthesize findings in an overall conceptual model; and (3) identify potential paths for future research on bimodal IT and structural ambidexterity.

To this end, this chapter first explains the practical and theoretical foundations of the three related concepts of bimodal IT, structural ambidexterity, and IT ambidexterity. We then explain our systematic literature review (SLR) approach, in which we retrieved 42 articles based on defined criteria. We analyzed this body of literature for bimodal IT forms, antecedents, facilitators, potential barriers, and outcomes of bimodal IT. Our key contribution is a conceptual model that integrates the cumulative knowledge of the literature on bimodal IT and structural/IT ambidexterity. We discuss our model findings in the light of the controversies in the practitioner discourse and close with an agenda with four directions for further research on the phenomenon of bimodal IT.

BACKGROUND

How organizational aspects effectively contribute to the firm's performance has been a focal point in Information Systems (IS) research and practice ever since (Bossert et al., 2014), and especially in the recent debate on digital transformation (Fitzgerald et al., 2013).

A relatively new model of organizational structure, driven by practitioners and adopted in academia, is the concept of bimodal IT (Horlach et al., 2016). Synonyms such as 'dual IT' or 'two-speed IT' have also been used (Cuomo, 2015). Due to its wider recognition, we use the term bimodal IT throughout this chapter. The approach of bimodality was introduced by the market research and advisory firm Gartner as '(...) the practice of managing two separate but coherent styles of work: one focused on predictability; the other on exploration' (Colella et al., 2014). These two modes differ not only in their project management approach, but are also embedded in different cultures, based on and steered with different strategic and operational management styles, and aiming at fulfilling unique objectives (Haffke et al., 2017b). The traditional mode, mode 1, is used for mission and business critical information systems and the operation of a company's core processes (Horlach et al., 2016). This exploitative side is responsible for minimizing operational risk, using sequential project management methods, e.g., waterfall methodologies (Haffke et al., 2017b). Within this unit management promotes a risk averse culture accentuating safety and accuracy (Haffke et al., 2017b). In contrast, the agile mode, mode 2, focuses on customer experience and business outcomes driven by rapidly changing market needs (Zhen et al., 2021). Such explorative activities are usually employed for projects with less certain outcomes, targeting at short release cycles and choosing iterative project management styles, such as Scrum (Haffke et al., 2017b). The mode 2 culture is driven by the principles of agility and speed (Haffke et al., 2017b).

In past research, the concept of bimodal IT has been viewed as a device through which organizations aim to reach IT ambidexterity (Haffke et al., 2017b). IS research views IT ambidexterity as *the ability to simultaneously explore new IT opportunities and exploit existing IT resources and practices* (Haffke et al., 2017b; Zhen et al., 2021). IT exploration, referring to activities associated with terms such as experimentation and innovation, and IT exploitation, referring to activities associated with terms such as efficiency and execution, are indispensable for organizations (March, 1991). However, experimentation and exploration also compete for resources (March, 1991). To foster exploration and enhance a company's capability for innovation, organizations can set up agile IT teams that may be structurally separated from the traditional IT (Saxena, 2020). In IS research the term structural ambidexterity, rather than the term bimodal IT, has been used to describe *the pursuit of IT exploration and IT exploitation through an organizational separation* (Saxena, 2020). Thus, bimodal IT is a term coined by practitioners that is used for different IT organizational forms through which organizations aim for structural ambidexterity. These endeavors are undertaken to ultimately support an organization's overall IT ambidexterity (Colella et al., 2014; Jöhnk et al., 2019).

METHODOLOGY

Literature reviews play an important role in IS research and are seen as powerful information sources for practitioners and researchers alike (Bandara et al., 2015; vom Brocke et al., 2015). The literature review method can be used to build on existing knowledge and to identify areas or gaps where further research is needed (Slack, 2004; Webster & Watson, 2002). The goal of this descriptive literature review is to accumulate existing knowledge, to synthesize the findings in a conceptual model, and to derive possible directions for future research (Paré et al., 2015).

The literature search was conducted between May and July 2021 using the databases AIS Electronic Library (AISeL) and EBSCOhost with the following search string: 'Bimodal IT' OR 'Dual IT' OR 'Two Speed IT' OR 'Multimodal IT' OR 'IT Ambidexterity' OR 'Structural Ambidexterity'. In addition, we performed a cross-check with Google Scholar (search term 'Bimodal IT') to find other potential relevant studies outside the outlets indexed by the mentioned databases. Following the recommendations of Rowley and Slack (2004) and Webster and Watson (2002), we focused on articles published in scholarly journals and proceedings of conferences. The initial set of search results was reduced by excluding duplicates and papers in other languages than English. To assess the potential relevance of each paper, we screened the articles based on their titles and abstracts. If the fit to the research purpose was not clear from this screening, we performed a full text analysis. During this quality assessment, each paper was evaluated based on ex-ante defined inclusion and exclusion criteria, see Table 10.1.

Once the database search was completed, a forward and backward search was performed in order to find papers that previous search attempts did not yield (Webster & Watson, 2002). Saturation could be assumed as no additional paper of potential relevance was found (Engesmo & Panteli, 2020). Finally, the search and selection process, as described above, led to the finding of 20 eligible papers for the search term 'bimodal IT', nine papers for the search term 'structural ambidexterity' and 12 papers for the search term 'IT ambidexterity' (see Table 10.2).

Our cross-check with Google Scholar resulted in one additional paper that was found relevant in terms of our inclusion and exclusion criteria (Table 1)

Table 10.1   Inclusion and exclusion criteria

Inclusion criteria	Exclusion criteria
• Study is a peer-reviewed journal or conference paper	• Study is a duplicate
	• Study is not written in English
• Study focuses on bimodal IT, structural ambidexterity or IT ambidexterity	• Study is research-in-progress w/o first results
	• Study focuses on ambidexterity in general
• Study researches the phenomenon of interest in the light of Information Systems	• Study focuses on dynamic, temporal or contextual ambidexterity
	• Study focuses on Digital Innovation Units (DIU's)

Table 10.2   Search strings and results of the literature search process

Source	Search String	Hits	Included
AISeL	'Bimodal IT' OR 'Dual IT' OR 'Two Speed IT' OR 'Multimodal IT'	111	20
EBSCO	'Bimodal IT' OR 'Dual IT' OR 'Two Speed IT' OR 'Multimodal IT'	115	
AISeL	'Structural Ambidexterity'	31	9
EBSCO	'Structural Ambidexterity'	45	
AISeL	'IT Ambidexterity'	89	12
EBSCO	'IT Ambidexterity'	20	

and thus included in the analysis (Nah & Xiao, 2018). As vom Brocke et al. (2015) note, 'there is no reason to exclude a relevant publication from a literature review if the researcher came across it by means other than the keyword search'.

Papers included in the search were published between 2014 and 2021 with an increasing number over the years and with a peak of 12 papers in 2020. In total, 26 studies were published in conference proceedings and 16 in refereed journals. Each paper included in the final set of eligible papers was thoroughly read, analyzed and synthesized through written memos (Bandara et al., 2015). We started analyzing the literature selection based on the pre-codification scheme dimensions proposed by Bandara et al. (2015). This served as a base but evolved over time through recoding and restructuring the coding dimensions to make them heterogenous across but homogenous among each other. During the coding and analysis phase, which was conducted by the authors independently and included several iterations, we eventually assigned all papers to the final codification scheme presented in chapter 4.

Table 10.3   Research themes and retrieved references

Research themes	Description	References
Forms.	Organizational structures and alignment in which bimodal IT is embodied.	(Haffke et al., 2017a), (Haffke et al., 2017b), (Nah & Xiao, 2018), (Horlach et al., 2016), (Engesmo & Panteli, 2020; Heckmann & Maedche, 2018), (Tumbas & Brocke, 2017), (Horlach et al., 2020).
Antecedents.	Motivations underlying a bimodal separation of the IT function.	(Haffke et al., 2017a), (Haffke et al., 2017b), (Horlach et al., 2016)
Facilitators and barriers.	Intervening factors that drive or hinder the implementation and operation of bimodal IT.	(Haffke et al., 2017a), (Haffke et al., 2017b), (Tai et al., 2019)- (Jöhnk et al., 2019), (Chi et al., 2017; Horlach et al., 2020), (Kalgovas et al., 2014).
Outcomes.	Desired and observed outcomes of bimodal IT.	(Haffke et al., 2017a), (Leonhardt et al., 2017), (Nah & Xiao, 2018), (Zhen et al., 2021), (Fischer et al., 2020), (Muehlburger, Rückel, et al., 2019), (Zhen et al., 2021), (Ortiz de Guinea & Raymond, 2019), (Abbas et al., 2020), (Syed et al., 2019), (Gregory et al., 2015; Syed et al., 2020), (Ortiz de Guinea & Raymond, 2020).

FINDINGS

The literature analysis brought up four main research themes related to bimodal IT: forms, antecedents, facilitators and barriers, and outcomes of bimodal IT. The research themes are described in Table 10.3.

In the following, we describe the themes derived from the literature and end by presenting a conceptual model that brings together the findings.

Forms of Bimodal IT

The first research theme seeks to find a deeper understanding of the operation of bimodal IT, specifically the organizational forms and their needed alignment with business and within IT units. *Organizational forms* are found with different characteristics.

The most cited classification is the archetype model of Haffke et al. (2017a) who propose four archetypes differentiated by the *level of separation*: project-by-project (A), sub-divisional (B), divisionally separated (C), and reintegrated bimodal IT (D). The chosen form depends on the company's internal and external environment and is not ultimate (Haffke et al., 2017a). Haffke et al. (2017a) use the analogy of an urban metro map to demonstrate that switching between archetypes is common and a consequence of experiences and learnings made during a company's IT transformation journey. This transformational path was taken by Deutsche Bahn Vertriebs GmbH, a subsidiary of Deutsche Bahn Group, starting around the year 2000. At that time the company was facing the challenge of responding to changing customer requirements on digital sales channels which required them to establish a flexible and agile working environment and routine. Thus, they built a small and agile IT function, with its own rules and culture, outside the traditional, existing IT unit. This setup of a divisionally separated bimodal IT (Archetype C) allowed for exploration without jeopardizing stable and secure operations for existing traditional channels and backend systems. This setup was seen as a transitory phase which ultimately led to a reintegrated bimodal IT setup (Archetype D) merging the online and traditional IT unit in one digital division (Fortmann et al., 2019).

A different classification is presented by Horlach et al. (2016) who distinguish between five types of bimodal IT. They characterize forms of bimodal IT as: (1) traditional IT with bimodal development processes, (2-3) project-based while outsourcing one of the both modes and/or partnering with third-party providers, (4) bimodal IT, and (5) agile IT (Horlach et al., 2016). While the designs and focus of the classifications substantially differ, both author groups agree on the fact that the individual environment and situation drives the chosen form of bimodal IT (Haffke et al., 2017a, 2017b; Horlach et al., 2016).

While the aforementioned studies present concepts and types of bimodality along the level of separation, Jöhnk et al. (2017) follow the question of how to realize bimodal IT, more specifically on how to implement the agile mode (mode 2). Jöhnk et al. introduce a taxonomy of design options, which gives practical guidelines along seven dimensions, such as staffing, technical integration, and location (Urbach, 2017).

The *duration of separation* between modes 1 and 2, which can be transitory or ultimate, depends on a companies' structure and resource situation.

A bimodal IT structure itself might be considered as desired final stage (Nah & Xiao, 2018), intermediate state to a fully agile organizational set-up (Gerster, Dremel, & Kelker, 2018; Gerster et al., 2020) or an even more fine-grained, multi-speed structure (Nah & Xiao, 2018). However, there is a broad consensus that in most cases bimodal IT is rather employed as a transitory state within an overarching transformation process rather than an organizational target state (Haffke et al., 2017a; Horlach et al., 2016). Haffke et al. (2017a) found that in most cases companies arriving at archetype D (reintegrated bimodal IT) eventually aim for a unimodal agile design.

Another decision to be made when defining bimodal forms of IT is the *reporting line*, which refers to the functional and hierarchical superior bimodal IT organization. Setting up the right management structure can help avoid barriers faced when balancing the conflicting and often competing activities of exploration and exploitation (Engesmo & Panteli, 2020; Tumbas & Brocke, 2017). Engesmo and Panteli (2020) found that, within their four studied scenarios of structures and leadership for the IT function, it is most often the Chief Digital Officer (CDO), rather than the Chief Information Officer (CIO), who takes the leadership to enable bimodal IT. Tumbas et al. (2017) present three types of CDO's and identify the 'Digital Accelerator CDO Approach', with the key capability of digital innovation and primary objective of experimentation and implementation, as best suited to adopt bimodal IT.

The importance of *alignment* has been emphasized between modes 1 and 2 IT as well as between business and IT (Horlach et al., 2016; Leonhardt et al., 2017). The triangular structure of business units, mode 1 IT, and mode 2 IT, brings forth three new forms of alignment: (1) bimodal business IT alignment; (2) bimodal IT alignment; and (3) business digital IT alignment (Horlach et al., 2016) and respective alignment mechanisms (Horlach et al., 2016, 2020). Alignment is seen as an important management task (Haffke et al., 2017a) that also creates the need for additional skill development among IT staff (Horlach et al., 2016, 2020).

Antecedents

The second theme, *antecedents*, sheds light on the motivations underlying a bimodal separation of the IT function. Using explorative and exploitative capabilities at the same time is foremost seen as a strategic construct and 'inevitable' step towards digital business transformation by achieving the most advantageous balance of agility and high reliability (Haffke et al., 2017b).

Specifically, studies have shown that bimodality shall settle incompatible goals of stability and experimentation and deliver effective support for digitization (Haffke et al., 2017a). Haffke et al. (2017b) also studied the antecedents of bimodal IT and found that the main reasons for companies to realize bimodal IT is to achieve ambidexterity and agility. In a similar vein, Horlach et al. (2016) highlighted the need for flexibility in companies' IT as an underlying motivation to implement bimodal IT design. In a second publication on this, Haffke et al. (2017a) added companies' insufficient level of explorative capabilities and need for structural alignment to the list of antecedent factors.

Facilitators and Barriers

The third identified research theme, *facilitators* and *barriers*, investigates the intervening factors that might drive or hinder the implementation and operation of bimodal IT.

With regards to business environment, Syed et al. (2020) suggest that a high level of dynamism and complexity within a firm's business environment can have a positive impact on IT ambidexterity. Moreover, the study of Ortiz de Guinea and Raymond (2019) adds that bimodal IT might be less suitable for small- and medium-sized enterprises (SMEs) due to their limited size and resources. They suggest that these types of companies benefit more from a sequential employment of exploration and exploitation rather than a simultaneous approach (Ortiz de Guinea & Raymond, 2020). Horlach et al. (2020) point out that companies with a B2C focus, due to their customer centricity and higher risk of market volatility, tend to favor enterprise-wide approaches towards agility instead of unit-based approaches as in bimodal IT design.

From a managerial perspective, Horlach et al. (2016) highlight the facilitative role of leadership roles on the IT-IT and business-IT alignment in bimodal IT. Tai et al. (2019) researched the importance of leaderships' understanding of business situations, while Syed et al. (2019) show that both studied decision-making styles, directive decision-making and participative decision-making, enable IT ambidexterity and thus bimodal IT. In a similar vein, Badr (2018), Park et al. (2020) and Haffke et al. (2017a) studied internal and external practices that facilitate bimodal IT and enhance structural ambidexterity, such as communication and collaboration between the modes and towards the business. Furthermore, Tai et al. (2019) add flexible technology assets, such as sharable IT hardware/software as facilitators for bimodal IT.

Haffke et al. (2017a) also highlight appropriate and formalized governance mechanisms as critical success factors to achieve and operate in a bimodal form. With a focus of dealing with challenges during initializing and operating bimodal IT, Jöhnk et al. (2019) define two categories of governance mechanisms, namely impeding governance mechanisms and coping governance mechanisms. More recently, Zhen et al. (2021) studied the positive influence of process-based and relational governance on IT exploration and exploitation. From a different standpoint and focus Chi et al. (2017) investigated which governance strategy to choose depending on the level of IT ambidexterity stating that companies with low IT ambidexterity choose a balancing governance strategy rather than a complementing governance strategy.

Only two papers were identified during the literature search process that deal with potential *barriers* of bimodal IT (Jöhnk et al., 2019; Kalgovas et al., 2014). Jöhnk et al. (2019) assign the observed challenges to either being of transformational nature, arising while implementing bimodal IT, or operational nature, experienced while operating bimodal IT. During the implementation phase, challenges are attributed to the required organizational shift with regards to structures, processes and culture while operational challenges are, among other areas, experienced due to resource allocation or technical barriers (Jöhnk et al., 2019). Kalgovas et al. (2014) add that barriers might also arise from a cost driven focus of the IT function resulting when responsibility and accountability is with the Chief Financial Officer (CFO). Emerging from their work on challenges and governance mechanisms, Jöhnk et al. (2019) identify five paradoxical tensions within bimodal IT (flexibility vs. predictability, business/IT vs. IT/IT, simplicity vs. complexity, comparability vs. differentiation, integration vs. autonomy).

Outcomes

With regards to the outcomes of bimodal IT, research shows that bimodality supports companies with their transformation endeavors (Muehlburger, Rückel, et al., 2019). Studies suggest that ambidextrous IT capabilities, achieved through establishing a bimodal IT organization, support addressing concurrent demands experienced in overall digital transformation activities (Gregory et al., 2015; Haffke et al., 2017a). Studies underscore the benefit of bimodal IT structures while initializing (Muehlburger, Rückel, et al., 2019), implementing (Muehlburger, Rückel, et al., 2019), managing (Schiffer, 2021) and building the right mindset to transformation endeavors (Nah & Xiao, 2018). It is to be noted that El-Tabany et al. (2020) found that the impact of bimodal IT, within digital transformation endeavors, might be considered of less importance in emerging markets. This can, among other reasons, be ascribed to budget and talent recruiting constraints. Furthermore, a study among IT managers conducted by Fischer et al. (2020) mention bimodal IT as one of the coping mechanisms to rapid change. Holotiuk and Beimborn (2017) analyzed industry reports on digital business strategy and indicated that bimodal IT is listed as one of the critical success factors. Bimodality has also been studied as a success factor for agility. Simultaneous exploitation and exploration positively relate to and enhance organizational agility (Zhen et al., 2021, 2021) as well as utilize the beneficial aspects from IT agility (Leonhardt et al., 2017). In a performance related manner, studies show that IT ambidexterity can enhance service innovation performance (Ortiz de Guinea

& Raymond, 2019, 2020), new product development performance (Syed et al., 2019, 2020), IT success (Abbas et al., 2020) and IS alignment (Tai et al., 2019).

Figure 10.1 synthesizes the presented findings in a conceptual model of bimodal IT forms, antecedents, facilitators and barriers, and outcomes.

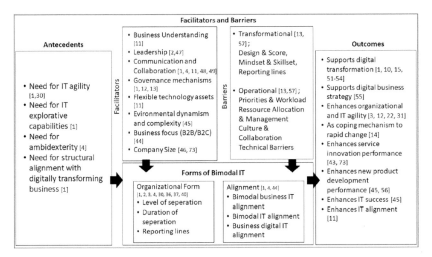

Figure 10.1   Conceptual model of current research on bimodal IT

DISCUSSION

With the goal of synthesizing existing knowledge and providing directions for further research on bimodal IT, we conducted a systematic literature review. We synthesized the aggregate findings from 42 eligible papers in a conceptual model of forms of bimodal IT, antecedents, facilitators and barriers, and outcomes (Figure 10.1). In the following, we first discuss two observations that emerged from our analysis, before we reflect our research findings against two points of critique in the practitioner discourse on bimodal IT.

First of all, our analysis of existing research has shown that the number of publications on bimodal IT, and its related concepts structural and IT ambidexterity, has increased (from one peer-reviewed paper in 2014 to 12 peer-reviewed papers in 2020). This suggests that the phenomenon of bimodal IT is of relevance and growing research interest, which can positively influence the discourse among IS practitioners.

Second, based on the findings of the presented literature review, controversies around bimodal IT might be ascribed to a diverging understanding of the concept itself. Although bimodal IT has been studied as a success factor to strategic and performance related outcomes, such as mastering digital transformation programs (Muehlburger, Rueckel, et al., 2019), the concept provokes discussions and receives critique among practitioners and academics (Ellerman, 2017). This brings up uncertainties and might hinder or slow down the realization of benefits resulting from bimodal IT. Therefore, we will elaborate on the critique by linking it to the findings of the literature analysis.

The mentioned drawbacks of bimodal IT can be ascribed to two main aspects. The most often mentioned point of critique is the strict separation of the two modes with all its attributed consequences, such as cultural conflicts and misalignment (Boulton, 2016; Haffke et al., 2017b). The presented review shows that, although the base for bimodality is indeed a separation into two modes, it is not intentionally creating irreversible structures and competing organizational silos with no interaction and interference for possible tensions. For example, according to Remfert and Stockhinger (2018), resolving inter- and intra-organizational problems arising in bimodality settings are seen as an important leadership task. In addition, within a bimodal setup the level and duration of separation shall be constantly reevaluated and adjusted based on requirements and learnings made (Haffke et al., 2017a). Haffke et al. (2017a) have used the analogy of an urban metro map to visualize that companies might progress through various states of bimodal IT.

As a second point of critique, there is the assumption that all companies will ultimately try to reach a fully agile or multimodal state (Gerster et al., 2020). First, the literature review shows that there is a consensus that for some companies, bimodality itself might be the desired architectural end state while for others it is a transitory state. Depending on the firms' circumstances and preferences, each organizational setup, including the aforementioned bimodal archetypes has potential advantages and disadvantages. According to Haffke et al. (2017a) decisions regarding the chosen organizational form can be evaluated in the light of level of tolerance towards internal disruption, preference on level of cultural divide, focus of resource management and reluctance to deal with alignment challenges. Although the presented studies suggest that some of the companies ultimately desire to progress to a state beyond bimodality, potentially leading to a fully agile state (Haffke et al., 2017b), the interim state can serve as valuable time for generating learnings with regards to governance, modus operandi, and alignment processes (Haffke et al., 2017a). Thus, it can be seen as a learning journey, supporting organizational restructuring during IT transformation, or more metaphorically spoken, serving as a bridge that connects the old to the whatsoever 'new world'. In addition, it should not be neglected that a fully agile, or similar form, might not be suitable, or desired, for all companies due to their market environment or resource structure (O'Donnell, 2008).

In summary, the reviewed literature suggests that the multi-faceted nature of bimodal IT empowers companies to optimize processes and resource allocation for tasks and challenges with different requirements (Marko, 2015; Saxena, 2020). We conject that bimodal IT will likely be a phenomenon of interest for research and practice for many years to come.

RESEARCH AGENDA

While our findings (summarized in Figure 10.1) show that the antecedents and outcomes as well as facilitators and barriers of bimodal IT have been researched, we also see opportunities for future research. We discussed the potential white spots emerging from the synthesis of the literature and identified from these a small set of research opportunities and new perspectives that we consider to have theoretical and practical relevance. Specifically, we propose avenues for further research regarding the human, cultural, and technological factors as well as the general applicability of bimodal IT.

Human Factors in Bimodal IT

Structure-related questions of bimodal IT are mostly studied at organization level (Engesmo & Panteli, 2020; Haffke et al., 2017a; Horlach et al., 2016). Past research on bimodal IT has somewhat ignored the individual level of IT professionals. This is surprising since it is conceivable that different modes require different skillsets and mindsets (Haffke et al., 2017b). The psychology and social science literature stresses the importance of the interplay of personality and job characteristics, such as the impact of person-job fit on job satisfaction (Ehrhart, 2006; Peng & Mao, 2015). Therefore, we propose that future research should seek to identify the different personality (character) traits of individuals needed to successfully operate in bimodal architecture. In a similar vein, although Horlach et al. (2016) briefly mention the importance of training with regards to bimodal IT, and Remfert et al. (2018) emphasize the willingness to change, there has been a lack of research on how to support this transformation process on an individual level. Therefore, we propose to investigate how companies can support employees in adapting and enhancing their skillset needed to work in bimodal IT. These research questions are expected to have high relevance for IT human resource management in practice.

Technological Factors in Bimodal IT

Our literature review did not identify many publications with a focus on more technical questions of bimodal IT. We believe that enterprise architecture (EA) thinking can enrich bimodal IT research since EA is a strategic capability and response capability of organizations to emerging change drivers (Gill, 2015; Lumor et al., 2021). EA, which provides a long-term view of technologies, systems and business processes in the organization (Ross et al., 2006), is a central topic in the agile literature e.g., (Gill, 2015; Lumor et al., 2021) and studies have identified architecture as one of the areas impacted when organizations adopt agile practices (Gerster, Dremel, & Prashant, 2018). For example, Gill (2015) points at the risk to overlook the need for holistic enterprise architecture when agile practices are introduced (Gill, 2015). Drawing on a systematic review of 43 articles, a study of Lumor et al. (2021) provides an overview of architectural properties of EA products and process practices that organizations can employ to build and sustain organizational agility. We believe there is a potential to transfer and validate these findings in a bimodal context.

Cultural Factors in Bimodal IT

The characteristics of modes 1 and 2 show that they are based on and operate within different sets of values when they employ different project management methods (Haffke et al., 2017b). While research investigated the importance of and fit with organizational culture when scaling agile methods (i.e., present in mode 2) (Hsing-Er Lin & McDonough, 2011; Kalenda et al., 2018) there is a lack of research that considers the environment in which both modes are existent and the consequences on a common (organizational) culture. The importance of cultural capabilities is also reflected in the recently published Individual and Organizational Ambidexterity Maturity Model (IOAMM) by Huber et al. (2021), which measures individual and organizational capabilities, including cultural capabilities, along five maturity stages. We see a need for drilling deeper into which organizational culture and values are needed for bimodal environments to thrive.

Applicability to Industries and Company Types

Our literature review showed that bimodality might be more suitable for some companies than for others (Abbas et al., 2020). Some facilitators (see Figure 10.1) have been studied separately, but only a compromised analysis can foster the understanding of the relation between company type and benefits received from bimodal IT. For example, Horlach et al. (2020) found that B2C companies favor targeting a fully agile approach. Also, benefits received from structurally separated IT departments differ depending on the market situation, for example, within emerging markets (El-Telbany et al., 2020) and company size (Ortiz de Guinea & Raymond, 2019, 2020). In a similar vein, although not specifically investigated for structural ambidexterity, previous studies question the superiority of ambidexterity for SMEs (Mathias, 2014; Wenke et al., 2021). As a consequence, to fully harness the potential of bimodal IT, further research needs to be done in evaluating which types of companies and industry sectors are most (or least) suited for employing bimodality as an organizational design principle in IT.

LIMITATIONS

Limitations of our work arise from the review method and the search strategy itself. Only defined keywords in mentioned databases were searched and the selection of the final set of papers was based on defined inclusion and exclusion criteria (see Table 10.1). Furthermore, we excluded literature that studies potential parts of bimodal IT, e.g., literature on digital innovation units (DIU's). In addition, readers may see further research avenues beyond the four directions outlined in our research agenda.

CONCLUSION

This chapter expands knowledge about the concept of bimodal IT by bringing together and discussing the status quo of academic work and the critique the phenomenon is facing in practice. Our review delineated the related concepts of structural ambidexterity and IT ambidexterity, but included these in the search process to ensure broad coverage. Through our review, we identified four major research themes, namely forms of bimodal IT, antecedents, facilitators and barriers, and outcomes, which are synthesized in a conceptual model. The presented literature review helped us identify four suggested paths for future research with regards to: (1) human factors in bimodal IT; (2) technological factors in bimodal IT; (3) cultural factors in bimodal IT; and (4) applicability to industries and company types.

KEY TAKEAWAYS

- Bimodality of the information technology (IT) function is one answer to the changed expectations towards and perceptions of IT's role within an organization.
- Bimodal IT is a term coined by practitioners that is used for different IT organizational forms through which organizations aim for structural ambidexterity.
- Structural ambidexterity aims at leveraging ambidextrous capabilities, allowing to engage in explorative and exploitative activities at the same time.

REFERENCES

Abbas, T., Blome, C., & Papadopoulos, T. (2020). Resolving paradoxes in IT success through IT ambidexterity: The moderating role of uncertain environments. *Information & Management*. https://doi.org/10.1016/j.im.2020.103345

Albino, R., & Souza, C. A. (2019). Information and Technology's role and digital transformation challenges: A systematic literature review. *CONF-IRM*.

Badr, N. G. (2018). Enabling Bimodal IT: Practices for Improving Organizational Ambidexterity for Successful Innovation Integration. *AMCIS 2018 Proceedings*. https://aisel.aisnet.org/amcis2018/OrgTrasfm/Presentations/1

Bandara, W., Furtmueller, E., Gorbacheva, E., Miskon, S., & Beekhuyzen, J. (2015). *Achieving Rigor in Literature Reviews: Insights from QualitativeSDuaptpaoArnt alysis and Tool*. 52.

Bloomberg, J. (2015). *Bimodal IT: Gartner's Recipe For Disaster*. Forbes. https://www.forbes.com/sites/jasonbloomberg/2015/09/26/bimodal-it-gartners-recipe-for-disaster/

Bossert, O., Ip, C., & Laartz, J. (2014, December). *A two-speed IT architecture for the digital enterprise | McKinsey*. https://www.mckinsey.com/business-functions/mckinsey-digital/our-insights/a-two-speed-it-architecture-for-the-digital-enterprise

Boulton, C. (2015, December). Why Ford's CIO is shifting gears to bimodal IT. *CIO*. https://www.cio.com/article/242896/why-fords-cio-is-shifting-gears-to-bimodal-it.html

Boulton, C. (2016). *Why bimodal IT kills your culture and adds complexity*. CIO. https://www.cio.com/article/240840/why-bimodal-it-kills-your-culture-and-adds-complexity.html

Chi, M., Zhao, J., George, J. F., Li, Y., & Zhai, S. (2017). The influence of inter-firm IT governance strategies on relational performance: The moderation effect of information technology ambidexterity. *International Journal of Information Management*, *37*(2), 43–53. https://doi.org/10.1016/j.ijinfomgt.2016.11.007

Colella, H., Mesaglio, M., Rowsell-Jones, A., & Nunno, T. (2014, November). *Three Steps to Successfully Implementing Bimodal-Aware IT Governance*. Gartner. https://www.gartner.com/en/documents/2901217

Cuomo, J. (2015). *The Era of the Now: Embracing Two Speed Integration by IBM*. https://www.redbooks.ibm.com/abstracts/www.redbooks.ibm.com/abstracts/redp5191.html

Ehrhart, K. H. (2006). Job Characteristic Beliefs and Personality as Antecedents of Subjective Person–Job Fit. *Journal of Business and Psychology*, *21*(2), 193–226. https://doi.org/10.1007/s10869-006-9025-6

Ellerman, H. (2017). *Radikale Kehrtwende: BMW-CIO hält Bimodal IT für einen Irrweg*. https://www.cio.de/a/bmw-cio-haelt-bimodal-it-fuer-einen-irrweg,3562374

El-Telbany, O., Abdelghaffar, H., & Amin, H. (2020). Exploring the Digital Transformation Gap: Evidence from Organizations in Emerging Economies. *PACIS 2020 Proceedings*. https://aisel.aisnet.org/pacis2020/79

Engesmo, J., & Panteli, N. (2020). *Digital Transformation and Its Impact On It Structure And Leadership*. 15.

Fischer, T., Jaeger, K., & Riedl, R. (2020). *Coping with Rapid Changes in IT: An Update*. 6, Article 2. https://doi.org/10.17705/1atrr.00045

Fitzgerald, M., Kruschwitz, N., Bonnet, D., & Welch, M. (2013). *Embracing Digital Technology*. 16.

Fortmann, L., Benlian, A., & Haffke, I. (2019). *Navigating Through Digital Transformation Using Bimodal IT: How Changing IT Organizations Facilitates the Digital Transformation Journey at Deutsche Bahn Vertrieb GmbH*. Digitalization Cases. https://www.springerprofessional.de/en/navigating-through-digital-transformation -using-bimodal-it-how-c/16140772

Gerster, D. (2017). Digital Transformation and IT: Current State of Research. *PACIS*.

Gerster, D., Dremel, C., Brenner, W., & Kelker, P. (2020). How Enterprises Adopt Agile Forms of Organizational Design: A Multiple-Case Study. *ACM SIGMIS Database: The DATABASE for Advances in Information Systems*, *51*, 84–103. https://doi.org/10.1145/3380799.3380807

Gerster, D., Dremel, C., & Kelker, P. (2018). Scaling Agility: How enterprises adopt agile forms of organizational design. *Thirty Ninth International Conference on Information Systems, San Francisco 2018*, 10.

Gerster, D., Dremel, C., & Prashant, K. (2018). *"Agile Meets Non-Agile": Implications of Adopting Agile Practices at Enterprises*.

Gill, A. Q. (2015). *Adaptive enterprise architecture drivenagiledevelopment*. https:// opus.lib.uts.edu.au/handle/10453/43283

Gregory, R. W., Keil, M., Muntermann, J., & Mähring, M. (2015). Paradoxes and the Nature of Ambidexterity in IT Transformation Programs. *Information Systems Research*, *26*(1), 57–80. https://doi.org/10.1287/isre.2014.0554

Haffke, I., Kalgovas, B. J., & Benlian, A. (2017a). Options for Transforming the IT Function Using Bimodal IT. *MIS Q. Executive*.

Haffke, I., Kalgovas, B. J., & Benlian, A. (2017b). The Transformative Role of Bimodal IT in an Era of Digital Business. *HICSS*. https://doi.org/10.24251/HICSS.2017.660

Heckmann, C. S., & Maedche, A. (2018). IT ambidexterity for business processes: The importance of balance. *Business Process Management Journal*, *24*(4), 862–81. https://doi.org/10.1108/BPMJ-04-2016-0078

Holgeid, K. K., Krogstie, J., Stray, V., & Thompson, M. (2018). Strategizing for Successful IT Projects in the Digital Era. *Undefined*. https://www.semanticscholar .org/paper/Strategizing-for-Successful-IT-Projects-in-the-Era-Holgeid-Krogstie/ 0d90849e9ab892ec481ebc0b730a7f94b17b1cbd

Holotiuk, F., & Beimborn, D. (2017). Critical Success Factors of Digital Business Strategy. *Wirtschaftsinformatik 2017 Proceedings*. https://aisel.aisnet.org/wi2017/ track09/paper/5

Horlach, B., Drews, P., Drechsler, A., Schirmer, I., & Böhmann, T. (2020). *Reconceptualising Business-IT Alignment For Enabling Organisational Agility*.

Horlach, B., Drews, P., & Schirmer, I. (2016). Bimodal IT: Business-IT alignment in the age of digital transformation. *Multikonferenz Wirtschaftsinformatik (MKWI)*. https://www.semanticscholar.org/paper/Bimodal-IT%3A-Business-IT-alignment-in -the-age-of-Horlach-Drews/57847e7461bd8497db94dbba435e0f82c298a43e

Hsing-Er Lin, & McDonough, E. F. (2011). Investigating the Role of Leadership and Organizational Culture in Fostering Innovation Ambidexterity. *IEEE Transactions on Engineering Management*, *58*(3), 497–509. https://doi.org/10.1109/TEM.2010 .2092781

Huber, R. X. R., Renner, J., & Stahl, B. (2021). Combining Individual and Organizational Capabilities: An Integrated Maturity Model for Ambidexterity. *Hawaii International Conference on System Sciences 2021 (HICSS-54)*. https://aisel.aisnet.org/hicss-54/ os/design/2

Jöhnk, J., Oesterle, S., Winkler, T. J., Nørbjerg, J., & Urbach, N. (2019). Juggling the Paradoxes: Governance Mechanisms in Bimodal IT Organizations. *ECIS 2019*

Proceedings. 27th European Conference on Information Systems: Information Systems for a Sharing Society, ECIS 2019. https://research.cbs.dk/en/publications/ juggling-the-paradoxes-governance-mechanisms-in-bimodal-it-organi

Kalenda, M., Hyna, P., & Rossi, B. (2018). Scaling agile in large organizations: Practices, challenges, and success factors. *Journal of Software: Evolution and Process*, *30*(10), e1954. https://doi.org/10.1002/smr.1954

Kalgovas, B., Toorn, C. V., & Conboy, K. (2014). *Transcending the Barriers to Ambidexterity: An Exploratory Study of Australian Cios*.

Lee, O.-K. (Daniel), Sambamurthy, V., Lim, K. H., & Wei, K. K. (2015). How Does IT Ambidexterity Impact Organizational Agility? *Information Systems Research*, *26*(2), 398–417.

Leonhardt, D., Haffke, I., Kranz, J., & Benlian, A. (2017). Reinventing the IT function: The Role of IT Agility and IT Ambidexterity in Supporting Digital Business Transformation. *ECIS*.

Lumor, T., Hirvonen, A., & Pulkkinen, M. (2021). The Role of Enterprise Architecture in Building and Sustaining Information Technology – Enabled Organizational Agility. *Hawaii International Conference on System Sciences 2021 (HICSS-54)*. https://aisel.aisnet.org/hicss-54/os/it_governance/9

March, J. G. (1991). Exploration and Exploitation in Organizational Learning. *Organization Science*, *2*(1), 71–87.

Marko, K. (2015). *Bimodal IT Doesn't Mean Bipolar Organizations: The Path to IT Transformation*. Forbes. https://www.forbes.com/sites/kurtmarko/2015/07/07/ bimodal-vs-bipolar-it/

Mathias, Ph. D., Blake. (2014). *Exploration, Exploitation, Ambidexterity, and Firm Performance: A Meta-Analysis* (pp. 289–314). https://doi.org/10.1108/S1479 -067X20140000014009

Muehlburger, M., Rückel, D., & Koch, S. (2019). A Framework of Factors Enabling Digital Transformation. *AMCIS*.

Muehlburger, M., Rueckel, D., & Koch, S. (2019). A Framework of Factors Enabling Digital Transformation. *AMCIS 2019 Proceedings*. https://aisel.aisnet.org/ amcis2019/org_transformation_is/org_transformation_is/18

Nah, F. F.-H., & Xiao, B. S. (eds). (2018). *HCI in Business, Government, and Organizations: 5th International Conference, HCIBGO 2018, Held as Part of HCI International 2018, Las Vegas, NV, USA, July 15-20, 2018, Proceedings* (Vol. 10923). Springer International Publishing. https://doi.org/10.1007/978-3-319-91716 -0

O'Donnell, M. (2008). *EuroSPI O'Donnell Richardson Agile Methods in a Very Small Company*. https://www.slideshare.net/MichaelODonnell14/eurospi-odonnell -richardson-agile-methods-in-a-very-small-company

Ortiz de Guinea, A., & Raymond, L. (2019, January 8). Improving SMEs' Service Innovation Performance in the Face of Uncertainty Through IT Ambidexterity: A Configurational Approach. *Proceedings of the 52nd Hawaii International Conference on System Sciences | 2019*. http://hdl.handle.net/10125/59988

Ortiz de Guinea, A., & Raymond, L. (2020). Enabling innovation in the face of uncertainty through IT ambidexterity: A fuzzy set qualitative comparative analysis of industrial service SMEs. *International Journal of Information Management*, *50*, 244–260. https://doi.org/10.1016/j.ijinfomgt.2019.05.007

Paré, G., Trudel, M.-C., Jaana, M., & Kitsiou, S. (2015). Synthesizing information systems knowledge: A typology of literature reviews. *Information & Management*, *52*(2), 183–199. https://doi.org/10.1016/j.im.2014.08.008

Park, Y., Pavlou, P. A., & Saraf, N. (2020). Configurations for Achieving Organizational Ambidexterity with Digitization. *Information Systems Research*, *31*(4), 1376–97. https://doi.org/10.1287/isre.2020.0950

Peng, Y., & Mao, C. (2015). The Impact of Person–Job Fit on Job Satisfaction: The Mediator Role of Self Efficacy. *Social Indicators Research*, *121*(3), 805–13. https://doi.org/10.1007/s11205-014-0659-x

Ross, J. W., Weill, P., & Robertson, D. (2006). *Enterprise Architecture As Strategy: Creating a Foundation for Business Execution.* Harvard Business Review Press.

Saxena, A. (2020). The Field of Ambidexterity Research: Perspective from Information Systems Domain. *ACIS 2020 Proceedings*. https://aisel.aisnet.org/acis2020/51

Schiffer, S. (2021). Structural Ambidexterity as an Approach for an Incumbents Digital Transformation. *AMCIS 2021 Proceedings*. https://aisel.aisnet.org/amcis2021/org_transform/org_transform/6

Slack, F. (2004). *Conducting a Literature Review.* https://www.academia.edu/32140958/Conducting_a_Literature_Review

Syed, T. A., Blome, C., & Papadopoulos, T. (2019). *Driving NPD Performance in High-Tech SMEs Through IT Ambidexterity: Unveiling The Influence Of Leadership Decision-Making Styles.* 17.

Syed, T. A., Blome, C., & Papadopoulos, T. (2020). Impact of IT Ambidexterity on New Product Development Speed: Theory and Empirical Evidence. *Decision Sciences*, *51*(3), 655–90. https://doi.org/10.1111/deci.12399

Tai, J. C. F., Wang, E. T. G., & Yeh, H. Y. (2019). A study of IS assets, IS ambidexterity, and IS alignment: The dynamic managerial capability perspective. *Information and Management*, *56*(1), 55–69. https://doi.org/10.1016/j.im.2018.07.001

Tumbas, S., & Brocke, J. vom. (2017). Three types of chief digital officers and the reasons organizations adopt the role. *MIS Quarterly Executive*, *16*, 121–34.

Urbach, N. (2017). *How To Implement Agile It Setups: A Taxonomy Of Design Options.* https://core.ac.uk/reader/301372370

vom Brocke, J., Simons, A., Riemer, K., Niehaves, B., Plattfaut, R., & Cleven, A. (2015). Standing on the Shoulders of Giants: Challenges and Recommendations of Literature Search in Information Systems Research. *Communications of the Association for Information Systems*, *37*. https://doi.org/10.17705/1CAIS.03709

Webster, J., & Watson, R. (2002). Analyzing the Past to Prepare for the Future: Writing a Literature Review. *MIS Quarterly*, *26*. https://doi.org/10.2307/4132319

Wenke, K., Zapkau, F. B., & Schwens, C. (2021). Too small to do it all? A meta-analysis on the relative relationships of exploration, exploitation, and ambidexterity with SME performance. *Journal of Business Research*, *132*, 653–65. https://doi.org/10.1016/j.jbusres.2020.10.018

Zhen, J., Xie, Z., & Dong, K. (2021). Impact of IT governance mechanisms on organizational agility and the role of top management support and IT ambidexterity. *International Journal of Accounting Information Systems*, *40*.

11. Building digital platform leadership through affordances and generativity

Andreas Hein, David Soto Setzke, Sebastian Hermes, Jörg Weking, Philipp Kernstock, and Helmut Krcmar

INTRODUCTION

Digital platforms shifted the locus of value creation from inside the firm to an ecosystem of complementors (G. Parker et al., 2016). An example is Apple's App Store, where most applications originate from an ecosystem of third-party developers. The platform owner provides boundary resources such as software development kits (SDKs) to increase the digital affordances of the platform, where affordances represent opportunities for complementors to co-create value-adding complements (Ghazawneh & Henfridsson, 2013; Nambisan et al., 2019). Those value-adding complements result from the actualization of affordances and can produce unprompted changes by autonomous actors, which defines the generativity of a digital platform ecosystem (Zittrain, 2005). For example, Apple's provision of ARKit provides developers with new affordances or ways to develop applications. In turn, developers can use the generativity of the ecosystem by sharing their knowledge with peers to develop novel applications in the field of augmented reality.

This interplay of providing digital affordances and the subsequent actualization of those affordances with an ecosystem of autonomous complementors illustrates that the success of digital platform ecosystems depends on both the internal innovation capabilities of the platform owner and the capabilities of external complementors in a digital platform ecosystem. Hence, by combining research on the internal facilitation (Baldwin & Woodard, 2009; Tiwana et al., 2010) and the external actualization of affordances, which define generativity (Henfridsson & Bygstad, 2013; Yoo et al., 2010), it is possible to understand why some platforms strive and others fail.

Research on the internal perspective of digital platforms (Baldwin & Woodard, 2009; Tiwana et al., 2010) elaborates on how the platform owner can increase digital affordances of the technical platform (Nambisan et al., 2019). The measures to increase affordances include design criteria such as the malleability of the digital platform (Tilson et al., 2010; Tiwana et al., 2010) or the innovation capabilities of the platform owner represented by patents (Pavitt, 1985). Research on the external perspective evaluates an ecosystem of autonomous actors (Adner & Kapoor, 2016; Jacobides et al., 2018) and incorporates external measures such as the degree of knowledge sharing in an ecosystem (Dokko et al., 2014) or the autonomy of complementors (Ye & Kankanhalli, 2018) that influence the generativity of a digital platform.

To synthesize both perspectives, scholars introduced new concepts such as the distributed tuning of boundary resources through the interaction of the platform owner and actors in the ecosystem (Eaton et al., 2015). These and other results (Henfridsson et al., 2018; Karhu et al., 2018) hint toward the complex and interdependent relationship between the provision of digital affordances through boundary resource development and their actualization by external complementors, which leads to generativity. However, on a holistic perspective, it is still unclear how the interplay of affordances and generativity influence the success of digital platforms (de Reuver et al., 2018). The importance of the provision of affordances, such as ARKit, to gain a competitive advantage is unclear. Alternatively, it is essential to know whether digital platforms depend more strongly on the capabilities of peers, like in the case of knowledge sharing, to utilize the generativity of the ecosystem. In addition, it is necessary to know whether platforms that depend on the provision of affordances are more successful than those that depend on the generativity of their ecosystem. To identify patterns of interaction between the internal and external innovation perspective, we pose the research question: *How do affordances and generativity influence the success of digital platforms?*

Owing to the complexity and interdependencies between affordances provided by the platform owner and generativity created by the ecosystem, we adhere to a fuzzy-set qualitative comparative analysis (fsQCA) (Fiss, 2007; Ragin, 2008) in the context of 47 digital platforms. The platforms are in different stages of a venture life cycle such as conceptualization, monetization, and growth stages (Fisher et al., 2016). To obtain more detailed results, we added platform cases that failed to establish a new venture and cases where the platform achieved platform leadership (Gawer & Cusumano, 2002). On the basis of these stages, we use the concepts of affordances and generativity to derive patterns of successful digital platforms that increase our understanding of how leading platforms use the provision of affordances and the generativity of autonomous complementors to strive. The patterns of the interplay between internal and external innovation capabilities can further guide research toward a more nuanced understanding of platform leadership (Gawer, 2014) and inform practitioners on the design criteria of digital platforms.

As part of an ongoing research effort, we preliminarily identify four configurations of affordances and generativity that foster digital platform leadership.
However, this is only the first iteration to derive more robust and compelling
results on interaction patterns between internal and external innovation capabilities in digital platform ecosystems. For future research work, we plan to
conduct further interviews to refine and recalibrate the causal conditions of
internal innovation as affordances and those of external innovation as generativity. In addition, we plan to extend the results toward the patterns of failing
platform ecosystems.

BACKGROUND

This chapter is based on the literature on digital platforms (Constantinides
et al., 2018; de Reuver et al., 2018) and includes the internal construct of
technological platforms (Baldwin & Woodard, 2009; Tiwana et al., 2010) or
digital infrastructures (Henfridsson & Bygstad, 2013; Tilson et al., 2010), and
the external construct of ecosystems (Adner & Kapoor, 2016; Jacobides et al.,
2018). From an internal perspective, the platform owner provides boundary
resources to increase digital affordances, as shown by the example of Apple
providing ARKit. From an external perspective, autonomous complementors
in the ecosystem actualize the affordances by using the generativity of the ecosystem to develop value-adding complements. An example is combining capabilities of complementors to develop novel augmented reality applications.

The Provision of Affordances in Digital Platforms

Digital platforms are central to an ecosystem and orchestrate supply and
demand between different actors (G. Parker et al., 2016; G. G. Parker et
al., 2016). From a technical perspective, actors in the ecosystem access
a digital infrastructure through boundary resources such as application programming interfaces (APIs) to create and cultivate digital goods or services
(Constantinides et al., 2018; Ghazawneh & Henfridsson, 2013). An example is
the application platform iOS, where third-party developers use APIs and SDKs
to develop applications. Then, the digital platform distributes the applications
to an ecosystem of users. In the remainder of this chapter, we refer to the
construct of a digital platform as 'a set of digital resources—including services
and content—that enable value-creating interactions between external producers and consumers' (Constantinides et al., 2018; G. G. Parker et al., 2016).

Digital platforms, like any other form of technology venture, pass through
various stages of development (Evans, 2009; Fisher et al., 2016). First, the conceptualization stage describes how new ventures act under uncertainty regarding the plausibility of their underlying technology and the targeted market

segment. Second, the commercialization stage demonstrates how the new ventures decrease technological and market-based uncertainties and establish a plausible business model (Kazanjian, 1988). Third, the growth stage indicates how the new venture exploits its technology to harvest short-term financial returns (Rajgopal et al., 2003). On the basis of the target market, ventures can either try to ignite the platform into a mass-market, as shown by the example of Facebook, or establish a niche as demonstrated by Dribbble. Consequently, the aggressive ignition of a digital platform requires more capital than the slow growth in a niche market (Evans, 2009). Last, there can be the stage of platform leadership that emphasizes how the platform establishes a central and dominant position in the market (Gawer & Cusumano, 2002).

A crucial characteristic of digital platforms is the provision of digital affordances (Nambisan et al., 2019; Tan et al., 2016), which defines 'what an individual or organization with a particular purpose can do with a technology' (Majchrzak & Markus, 2013). The digital platform needs to be inherently malleable to provide new affordances; specifically, it can be reconfigured to adapt user needs and to prompt new technological advances (Yoo et al., 2010). In addition, digital platforms are built on a modular architecture that ensures composability by integrating new modules without compromising the entire system (Baldwin & Clark, 2000; Tiwana et al., 2010). An example is Apple's introduction of the ARKit that complements the iOS platform and is now a breeding ground for third-party developers. This measure illustrates that the degree of malleability or ease with which a platform or modules can be reconfigured can create new affordances for the entire ecosystem (Tiwana et al., 2010). This observation also implies that the platform owner depends on the internal innovation capabilities to introduce new functionality that an ecosystem of complementors can use as new affordances. Studies that try to operationalize the internal innovation capability of a firm use metrics such as patents or the number of new products developed (Balkin et al., 2000; Romijn & Albaladejo, 2002).

Furthermore, the platform owner provides boundary resources that enable an ecosystem of complementors to actualize affordances on the digital platform (Eaton et al., 2015; Ghazawneh & Henfridsson, 2013). Boundary resources can be APIs that define the openness of digital platforms, SDKs that provide boilerplate code to decrease the cognitive distance between platforms and their ecosystems, and documentation that define work processes on how to use boundary resources (Hein et al., 2019; Karhu et al., 2018). In addition, boundary resources represent the joint effort of the platform owner and complementors to increase the generativity of a digital platform ecosystem. An example is the process of distributed tuning that describes the dynamics between the platform owner and the ecosystem actors on altering boundary resources (Eaton et al., 2015).

Establishing Generativity by Integrating Complementors

The creation of economic value shifted during the last decades from production within single firms to collaboration with individual customers to the co-creation of value in complex ecosystems. From a theoretical perspective, the integration of external actors into the value creation process of a firm goes back to the concept of lead-user innovation (Von Hippel, 1986) and was seized by other researchers as open innovation (Chesbrough, 2012) and value co-creation (Prahalad & Ramaswamy, 2004; Vargo & Lusch, 2016; Vargo et al., 2008). In addition, the literature on digital platform ecosystems is inherently built on the integration of customers and other partners to leverage external innovation capabilities (G. Parker et al., 2016). More recently, scholars in the field of strategy research emphasized the importance of ecosystems as a construct of scientific inquiry (Adner & Kapoor, 2016; Jacobides et al., 2018). We follow Jacobides et al. (2018) who define ecosystems as 'a set of actors with varying degrees of multilateral, nongenetic, complementarities that are not fully hierarchically controlled'.

A crucial characteristic of a digital platform ecosystem is its generativity (Henfridsson & Bygstad, 2013; Yoo et al., 2010), which defines 'a technology's overall capacity to produce unprompted change driven by large, varied, and uncoordinated audiences' (Zittrain, 2005). While the digital platform provides affordances in the form of digital infrastructure, the large variety of ecosystem actors fuels the generativity with individual innovation capabilities (Nambisan et al., 2019). An example is the application development industry, where more external complementors on the platform lead to a wider variety and number of complements on the platform (Boudreau, 2012). Thus, the decision-making and work-method autonomy of complementors directly influence the number of innovative complements on the digital platform (Ye & Kankanhalli, 2018). In addition, the degree of knowledge-sharing in the ecosystem is another factor that increases the creative generativity in the ecosystem (Dokko et al., 2014).

Furthermore, the degree of openness determines the boundaries of an ecosystem and, thus, the generative potential of the digital platform (Nambisan et al., 2019). Gawer (2014) classifies platforms as internal, supply chain, and industry platforms on the basis of the autonomy of agents and the degree of competition in the ecosystem. Internal platforms limit the ecosystem to internal employees with little competition, while technological platforms include an ecosystem of autonomous agents that can compete with one another. Restricting the degree of openness can further reduce competition and increase the control of the platform owner over the installed base of complements (Ghazawneh & Henfridsson, 2013). In turn, relinquishing control and increasing the degree of

Table 11.1   *Key concepts*

Concept	Operationalization	Perspective
Affordance	Malleability of platform and internal innovation capabilities of platform owner.	Platform internal.
Generativity	Knowledge-sharing and autonomy of complementors.	Ecosystem.
Boundary resources	Platform openness (APIs) and cognitive distance through provisioning SDKs.	Aligning internal and ecosystem perspective.

openness can limit the platform owner's influence on complementors but fuel the generativity of the broader ecosystem (Remneland-Wikhamn et al., 2011). Thus, the success of a digital platform can be operationalized through the different stages of platform development; digital affordances can be operationalized through the degree of malleability and internal innovation capabilities of the platform owner; generativity of the platform ecosystem can be operationalized through the degree of knowledge-sharing and the autonomy of complementors in the ecosystem. Finally, boundary resources align both perspectives and can be operationalized by APIs and the degree of platform openness and the cognitive distance through the provision of SDKs.

METHODOLOGY

This study builds on a fsQCA as a novel methodology for modeling complex and causal relations 'that are frequently better understood in terms of set-theoretic relations rather than correlation'. (Fiss, 2007; Ragin, 2008). The fsQCA has proven to be useful in conditions where the relationship between different causal conditions cannot be observed in isolation but can be classified as a 'conjunctural causation' (Durand & Vaara, 2009). FsQCA consists of three subsequent steps: calibration, which is the assignment of fuzzy-set membership scores to each case, identification of necessary conditions, and identification of sufficient configurations (Ragin, 2009). Necessary condition analysis reveals conditions that are present in every case and result in a specific outcome. Analyzing sufficient conditions reveals configurations of conditions that guarantee a specific outcome if present in a case (Ragin, 2008). Unlike necessary conditions a specific configuration does not need to be present to produce the outcome. Thus, there can be multiple configurations leading to the same outcome (Soto Setzke et al., 2021).

In the context of digital platforms, both affordances provided by the platform and the interactions of an ecosystem to actualize those affordances to create generativity are needed to make a digital platform strive. To determine configurations of core and peripheral conditions of an outcome, such as platform leadership, the fsQCA uses logical minimization of a truth table that represents causal conditions such as affordances and generativity. The design of APIs refers to technological openness, and the design of SDKs describes cognitive distance between platform owner and complementors (Ragin, 2008).

The fsQCA identifies differences and commonalities across a set of cases (digital platforms) to yield configurations that share the same outcome. Hence, we use a sampling strategy that incorporates digital platforms at different lifecycle stages ranging from failure, conceptualization, monetization, small growth in niche markets, ignition into mass markets, and platform leadership. On the basis of the recommendation of Ragin (2008), we selected 47 digital platforms, which we categorized as follows: six – failure stage, four – conceptualization stage, nine – monetization stage, 13 – small niche market growth stage, eight – mass-market growth stage, and seven – platform leadership stage cases. As an empirical basis, we conducted 51 semi-structured interviews with the platform owners to gather information on how they provide affordances, how the ecosystem contributes to the generativity, and on the design of boundary resources. We triangulated the data with market reports, patent data, and archival data gathered in a period from mid-2018 to the end of the first quarter of 2019.

We used the literature on digital platforms to guide the calibration process of the causal conditions regarding the set membership. We integrated the internal perspective of the platform owner and the provision of affordances and the external perspective of ecosystem actors that foster generativity by identifying antecedents of platform failure and leadership. During the calibration process, we followed prior research (Ragin, 2008) that defines 0 as full-non membership, 0.5 as maximum ambiguity, and 1 as full membership. In addition, we used qualitative data in the form of interview transcripts and quantitative data such as archival data from GitHub to calibrate hard to measure constructs, such as knowledge sharing in an ecosystem (Vasilescu et al., 2014). We followed the stepwise procedure of Basurto and Speer (2012) to calibrate the qualitative data starting with the operationalization of conditions, development of anchor points, conduction of content analysis, summarizing of the coded data, and determining the fuzzy-set scale. Because this contribution is part of an ongoing research endeavor, further iterations of interviews will provide new insights that help to recalibrate causal conditions to obtain more meaningful configurations.

Data Sources

Measuring the success of digital platforms can be a challenging task. For example, Uber is an undisputed platform leader in terms of market share even though in the year of 2018 its losses were greater than profits (Zaveri

& Bosa, 2019). However, niche markets may have a low degree of market penetration but sustainable profits. Hence, we decided to use digital platform lifecycle stages (OUT) as a proxy for platform success. We used market data from CrunchBase, empirical results from interviewees and market reports, and archival data to calibrate a platform's current lifecycle stage. The value of 0 means that the platform went bankrupt or failed, 0.2 refers to a newly emerging platform that tries to establish a concept, 0.4 refers to platforms that try to monetize their concepts, 0.6 refers to platforms growing into niche markets, 0.8 refers to platforms that rapidly ignite into mass markets, and 1 refers to platform leadership.

The first causal condition represents the platform owners' ability to file patents (PU) as a preliminary proxy of the ability to provide *digital affordances*. We coded companies that filed patents subject to their digital platform as 1 and companies without patents as 0. During the next iteration of interviews, we plan to inquire on more sophisticated metrics such as the degree of the malleability of the technical infrastructure to refine the first results of the fsQCA.

We measured the *generativity* of a digital platform on the basis of the complementors' autonomy (CA) and the degree of knowledge sharing (KS). For the complementor's autonomy, we adhered to decision-making autonomy (Ye & Kankanhalli, 2018). We differentiated between no autonomy, which refers to the internal provision of complements by the platform owner as 0 to a low degree of autonomy, which is represented by the tight coupling with few, strategic partnerships as 0.33, to a tight coupling with many contractually-bounded partners as 0.66, to high autonomy and loosely-coupled complementors as 1. In addition, on the basis of the active number of GitHub repositories, we determined the degree of knowledge-sharing (Vasilescu et al., 2014). We fuzzified the repositories on the basis of the direct method and the three anchor points (Ragin, 2008) of 10 repositories, which indicate limited-knowledge sharing, 50 as the cross-over point, and more than 500 as a high degree of knowledge sharing. We selected the anchor points on the basis of the substantive knowledge of reviewing GitHub commits and issues discussed in the repositories.

Furthermore, we measured the use of *boundary resources* on the basis of the degree of cognitive distance (CD) between platform owner and complementor and the technological openness (TO) of APIs. The cognitive distance indicates the ease of providing new products or service on the platform by offering tools and information on how to interact. We coded a high degree of cognitive distance as 0, when the platform owner does not provide SDKs, code snippets, or documentation on how to interact with the platform; 0.33 if documentation, such as code snippets, or an internal developer website, is available; 0.66 if the platform owner provides SDKs that lack documentation; and 1 if the platform owner provides both documentation and SDKs. The degree of technological

Table 11.2   *Overview of employed configuration elements*

Configuration Element	Explanation	Theme
PU – Patent use.	Platform owner's ability to file patents.	Affordances.
CA – Complementor autonomy	Decision-making autonomy for complementor.	Generativity.
KS – Knowledge-sharing	Degree of knowledge sharing based on GitHub repositories.	
CD – cognitive distance	Tools and information on how to interact with platform (SDKs).	Boundary resources.
TO – technological openness	Degree of technological openness regarding integration of complements (APIs).	
OUT	Digital platform lifecycle stages.	Platform success.

openness describes whether the platform is closed or open. We adhered to similar metrics to measure the cognitive distance that codes digital platforms: 0 if they provide no APIs or other ways to integrate complements; 0.33 if the platform does not offer APIs but has a restricted process to integrate complements; 0.66 if APIs are available but there is no further documentation; 1 if both APIs and documentation are available.

Analysis

On the basis of the five causal conditions and the calibrated fuzzy sets, the fsQCA proceeds with a three-step approach (Fiss, 2007). First, we use the R package QCA to construct a truth table where each row includes zero to many cases that describe all logically possible combinations of causal conditions toward an outcome variable. Second, the fsQCA proceeds with a minimization of the truth table to derive cases that fulfill the minimum number of cases, and that adhere to a minimum consistency level required. We set the minimum number of cases to two and the consistency level to 0.80, which is above the suggested threshold of 0.75 (Ragin, 2008). Last, the truth table algorithm calculates the consistency scores of raw consistency and proportional reduction in inconsistency (PRI), both of which determine the reliability of configurations. While the raw consistency gives credit for inconsistencies resulting from 'near misses', the PRI accounts for cases that have simultaneous membership in both the complements and outcome. Similar to prior studies (Park et al., 2017), we set the cutoff for the raw consistency and PRI to 0.80. Table 11.3 shows the minimized truth table of succeeding digital platform configurations.

Table 11.3   *Minimized truth table of succeeding digital platform configurations*

PU	CA	KS	TO	CD	OUT	Number	Raw consistency[1]	PRI consistency[2]	Cases
0	1	1	1	0	1	2	1.00	1.00	37, 39
1	1	1	1	0	1	2	1.00	1.00	33, 43
1	1	1	1	1	1	8	.97	.97	22, 38, 41, 42, 44, 45, 46, 47
1	0	0	0	1	1	2	.96	.93	28, 34
1	0	0	0	0	1	2	.92	.86	35, 40

Notes: 1. Raw consistency assesses the degree of reliability with which a configuration yields a result and can be roughly compared to the meaning of significance in regression analysis [46]; 2. PRI consistency is an alternative consistency measure that 'eliminates the influence of cases that have simultaneous membership in both the outcome and its complement' [46];

FINDINGS

The results yielded by the intermediate solution of our analysis suggest that there are four configurations of sufficient conditions for the leading digital platforms (Table 11.4). We build on the notation introduced by Fiss [49], who uses large circles to denote core conditions and small circles to denote peripheral conditions. Black circles indicate the presence of a condition, while crossed-out circles indicate its absence. Empty cells indicate that the condition is not relevant for a particular configuration.

The core conditions indicate that each configuration utilizes different aspects of affordances, generativity, and boundary resources. *Innovation platforms* rely both on the internal provision of affordances and the generativity of the ecosystem, which can be illustrated by the core conditions of patent use and knowledge sharing. In addition, innovation platforms indicate technological openness through the provision of APIs that complementors can use to co-create value-adding complements. Examples are application stores, where the platform provides boundary resources that an ecosystem of autonomous complementors can use to create new applications. In turn, each complementor has access to a variety of applications to obtain new ideas, which increases the generativity of the ecosystem.

Technology platforms depend solely on the internal provision of affordances, as indicated by the core condition of patent use. In addition, technology platforms show the absence of complementor autonomy, knowledge-sharing, and technology openness. This occurs because technology platforms are closed and are only fueled by the internal innovation capabilities of the platform owner. The direct consequence is that the platform does not take advantage

Table 11.4   *Configurations of the leading digital platforms*

Theme	Configuration elements	Configurations for leading platforms			
		Innovation	Technology	Transaction	Integration
Affordances	Patent use	●	●		X
Generativity	Complementor autonomy	●	X	●	●
	Knowledge-sharing	●	X	●	X
Boundary resources	Technological openness	●	X	●	●
	Cognitive distance			X	●
Consistency[1]		.97	0.91	1.00	0.80
Raw coverage[2]		.35	.11	.17	.18
Unique coverage[3]		.30	.11	.04	.10
Overall solution consistency[4]		**.91**			
Overall solution coverage[5]		**.68**			

Notes: 1. Consistency refers to the percentage of observations that conform with the configuration. A consistency of 1.000 means that all observed cases of this configuration had the same outcome, which indicates a very high level of confidence in the solution [50]; 2. Raw coverage indicates the total percentage of the result explained by a configuration [50]; 3. The unique coverage reflects the unique share of the outcome that is explained by the configuration [50]; 4. Overall solution consistency represents the extent to which the cases in the dataset match the relationships in the solution [49]; 5. Analogous to the R^2 measure in regression, overall solution coverage is a measure of fitness for the entire set of configurations [50].

of the generativity of ecosystem partners, because the technology platform enables value-creating interactions only within the boundaries of the partners' company. Hence, partners do not mirror innovations back to the platform owner. The examples include technology platforms that aid ecosystem partners to co-create new applications using artificial intelligence.

Transaction platforms do not rely on the provision of new affordances. Rather, they rely on the generativity of a vibrant ecosystem, as shown by the core condition of knowledge sharing. The generativity is further fueled by the high autonomy of complementors and technological openness. In addition, the cognitive distance is high, as the main goal is the orchestration of generic services between the supply and demand and not the integration of innovative complements. The examples include digital platforms that focus on the convenient facilitation of generic goods and services such as marketplaces and transportation services.

Integration platforms do not utilize the provision of affordances and only partly take advantage of the generativity of their ecosystem. They are characterized by the high degree of complementor autonomy, technological openness, and the absence of patents and knowledge sharing. A key characteristic is the low cognitive distance, which demonstrates that integration platforms try to make the provision of new complements as easy as possible. This configuration illustrates that integration platforms are reactive and either allow complementors to use the data provided by the platform or to integrate their services on a meta platform. Both cases can be illustrated based on the case of mobility, where the platform can be the source of data due to open APIs and SDKs or the aggregator of mobility services acting as a meta platform.

DISCUSSION

The four configurations reveal how internal innovation capabilities or affordances and the external actualization of those affordances, which are represented as generativity, influence the success of digital platforms. First, innovation platforms rely on internal innovation capabilities by providing boundary resources that allow deep integration of complements into the digital platform (Ghazawneh & Henfridsson, 2013). The complements are supermodular, which means that every new complement increases the overall value of the platform (Jacobides et al., 2018), which makes the platform less vulnerable to multi-homing effects and fuels the generativity of the ecosystem. However, innovation platforms need internal resources to keep up with the latest innovations and development to stay competitive. In addition, they need a malleable and composable infrastructure (Tiwana et al., 2010) to continuously provide new affordances to the ecosystem.

Second, technology platforms depend solely on their internal resources to provide affordances to a closed set of ecosystem partners. The complements show a unique complementary, which means that companies need to use the platform to create new services (Jacobides et al., 2018). However, because the services are not mirrored back to the platform owner, the platform does not profit from the generativity of the ecosystem. While this allows for more control over the ecosystems, it creates the risk of competitive disadvantages. The generativity caused by new applications that do not apply to platform standards and that are created when organizations combine the applications and services according to their institutional logic can lead to increased value for the whole ecosystem (Hein et al., 2019).

Third, transaction platforms benefit from a first-mover advantage and strong indirect network effects (McIntyre & Srinivasan, 2017). Similar to innovation platforms, transaction platforms build a high degree of knowledge sharing and technological openness regarding the integration of APIs. However, the interviews also revealed that they are prone to multi-homing effects because they do not have internal innovation capabilities and rely on generic goods and services.

Fourth, integration platforms build on SDKs to reduce the cognitive dissonance and technological openness through APIs to enable autonomous actors to either integrate their services or to use the data provided. The integration fosters supermodularity because new services increase the value of the platform. However, the boundary resources strictly define what services can be integrated, which limits the generativity of the ecosystem.

The intersection analysis reveals that only innovation platforms and technology platforms intersect; all other configurations are disjointed (Park et al., 2017). A reason for this intersection is that patents can be filed in transaction platforms to improve the efficiency of transaction platforms. However, patents are not used to mirror new affordances to the ecosystem, which indicates that patents need to be analyzed more carefully to determine the provision of affordances. By interpreting conditions as patterns of equifinality (Fiss, 2011), the configurations reveal that transaction platforms can transition toward innovation platforms if they build internal innovation capabilities. However, technology platforms need to shift from the absence of technology openness, knowledge-sharing, and complementor autonomy toward fostering generativity by opening up the digital platforms (Ondrus et al., 2015). The potential for the success of digital platform ecosystems is based on the contributions of complementors. Complementor activities spur generativity across the ecosystem, bringing the products and services offered to scope and scale. Digital platforms that focus on single organizations, such as technology platforms, have difficulties replicating this effect (Hein et al., 2020). Further, leveraging the generativity of the ecosystem allows platforms to cope with exogenous shocks and become resilient to future disruptions by capturing new opportunities and engaging in transformative activities (Floetgen et al., 2021).

This creates tension for the platform owner, as granting access to the platform and opening it is required to establish platform leadership (Boudreau, 2010). Giving external actors more access also means losing absolute control over the ecosystem. At the same time, the platform owner and complementors might interact in the form of coopetition, for example, when knowledge is shared between the parties. The configurations reveal the different patterns on how successful platforms utilize affordances and the generativity of an ecosystem. Research on digital platforms can use the four configurations to specify the term digital platform more carefully, hence, accounting for the different patterns of providing affordances and utilizing the ecosystem generativity through boundary resources. While this research shows that affordances and generativity influence platform leadership, it is still scarcely researched how the different configurations leverage contributions of complementors and how boundary resources should be designed and provided to enable engagement of complementors (Engert et al., 2022). Future research could also investigate when and how the provision of affordances and the leveraging of generativity has negative effects on the platform ecosystem. Practitioners can use the results to learn how different platform configurations use internal and external innovation capabilities to be successful.

CONCLUSION

Digital platforms integrate and orchestrate an ecosystem of autonomous actors to co-create value instead of relying solely on internal innovation capabilities. To achieve this, the platform owner provides digital affordances through boundary resources that an ecosystem of complementors can use to create value-adding services. The platform combines internal innovation capabilities by providing digital affordances and utilizes external innovation capabilities between complementors that refer to the generativity of the ecosystem. To disentangle both internal and external innovation capabilities, we conducted a fsQCA analysis based on a set of 47 platforms. We measured the provided affordances, the ecosystems generativity and the boundary resources integrating internal and external perspective. The results reveal four configurations of leading platforms that combine affordances of the platform and generativity in an ecosystem: technology, innovation, transaction, and integration platforms.

KEY TAKEAWAYS

- Affordances concern what an individual or an organization can do with a technology.
- Generativity concerns the digital platform ecosystem's capacity to produce unprompted change driven by a large, varied, and uncoordinated number of complementors.
- Boundary resources such as APIs and SDKs allow actors to access a digital platform.
- The four digital platform configurations (technology, innovation, transaction, and integration) reveal how affordances and generativity influence the success of digital platforms.

REFERENCES

Adner, R., & Kapoor, R. (2016). Innovation ecosystems and the pace of substitution: Re-examining technology S-curves. *Strategic Management Journal, 37*(4), 625–48.

Baldwin, C. Y., & Clark, K. B. (2000). *Design rules: The power of modularity* (Vol. 1). MIT Press.

Baldwin, C. Y., & Woodard, C. J. (2009). The architecture of platforms: a unified view. In A. Gawer (ed), *Platforms, markets and innovation* (Vol. 1). Edward Elgar Publishing Limited.

Balkin, D. B., Markman, G. D., & Gomez-Mejia, L. R. (2000). Is CEO pay in high-technology firms related to innovation? *Academy of Management Journal*, *43*(6), 1118–29.

Basurto, X., & Speer, J. (2012). Structuring the calibration of qualitative data as sets for qualitative comparative analysis (QCA). *Field Methods*, *24*(2), 155–74.

Boudreau, K. (2010). Open Platform Strategies and Innovation: Granting Access vs. Devolving Control. *Management Science*, *56*(10), 1849–72. http://www.jstor.org/stable/40864743

Boudreau, K. J. (2012). Let a Thousand Flowers Bloom? An Early Look at Large Numbers of Software App Developers and Patterns of Innovation. *Organization Science*, *23*(5), 1409–27.

Chesbrough, H. (2012). Open innovation: Where we've been and where we're going. *Research-Technology Management*, *55*(4), 20–27.

Constantinides, P., Henfridsson, O., & Parker, G. G. (2018). Introduction—Platforms and infrastructures in the digital age. *Information Systems Research*, *29*(2), 3–6.

de Reuver, M., Sørensen, C., & Basole, R. C. (2018). The digital platform: a research agenda. *Journal of Information Technology*, *33*(2), 124–35.

Dokko, G., Kane, A. A., & Tortoriello, M. (2014). One of us or one of my friends: How social identity and tie strength shape the creative generativity of boundary-spanning ties. *Organization Studies*, *35*(5), 703–26.

Durand, R., & Vaara, E. (2009). Causation, counterfactuals, and competitive advantage. *Strategic Management Journal*, *30*(12), 1245–64.

Eaton, B., Elaluf-Calderwood, S., Sorensen, C., & Yoo, Y. (2015). Distributed tuning of boundary resources: the case of Apple's iOS service system. *MIS Quarterly*, *39*(1), 217–43.

Engert, M., Evers, J., Hein, A., & Krcmar, H. (2022). The Engagement of Complementors and the Role of Platform Boundary Resources in e-Commerce Platform Ecosystems. *Information Systems Frontiers*. https://doi.org/10.1007/s10796-021-10236-3

Evans, D. S. (2009). How catalysts ignite: the economics of platform-based start-ups. In A. Gawer (Ed.), *Platforms, markets and innovation* (pp. 99–128). Edward Elgar Publishing.

Fisher, G., Kotha, S., & Lahiri, A. (2016). Changing with the times: An integrated view of identity, legitimacy, and new venture life cycles. *Academy of Management Review*, *41*(3), 383–409.

Fiss, P. C. (2007). A set-theoretic approach to organizational configurations. *Academy of Management Review*, *32*(4), 1180–98.

Fiss, P. C. (2011). Building better causal theories: A fuzzy set approach to typologies in organization research. *Academy of Management Journal*, *54*(2), 393–420.

Floetgen, R. J., Strauss, J., Weking, J., Hein, A., Urmetzer, F., Böhm, M., & Krcmar, H. (2021). Introducing platform ecosystem resilience: leveraging mobility platforms and their ecosystems for the new normal during COVID-19. *European Journal of Information Systems*, *30*(3), 304–21.

Gawer, A. (2014). Bridging differing perspectives on technological platforms: Toward an integrative framework. *Research Policy*, *43*(7), 1239–49.

Gawer, A., & Cusumano, M. A. (2002). *Platform leadership: How Intel, Microsoft, and Cisco drive industry innovation* (Vol. 5). Harvard Business School Press Boston, MA.

Ghazawneh, A., & Henfridsson, O. (2013). Balancing platform control and external contribution in third-party development: the boundary resources model. *Information Systems Journal*, *23*(2), 173–92.

Hein, A., Schreieck, M., Riasanow, T., Setzke, D. S., Wiesche, M., Böhm, M., & Krcmar, H. (2020). Digital platform ecosystems. *Electronic Markets*, *30*(1), 87–98. https://doi.org/10.1007/s12525-019-00377-4

Hein, A., Weking, J., Schreieck, M., Wiesche, M., Böhm, M., & Krcmar, H. (2019). Value co-creation practices in business-to-business platform ecosystems. *Electronic Markets*, *In print*, 1-16.

Henfridsson, O., & Bygstad, B. (2013). The generative mechanisms of digital infrastructure evolution. *MIS Quarterly*, *37*(3), 907–31.

Henfridsson, O., Nandhakumar, J., Scarbrough, H., & Panourgias, N. (2018). Recombination in the open-ended value landscape of digital innovation. *Information and Organization*, *28*(2), 89–100.

Jacobides, M. G., Cennamo, C., & Gawer, A. (2018). Towards a theory of ecosystems. *Strategic Management Journal*, *39*(8), 2255–76.

Karhu, K., Gustafsson, R., & Lyytinen, K. (2018). Exploiting and defending open digital platforms with boundary resources: Android's five platform forks. *Information Systems Research*, *29*(2), 479–97.

Kazanjian, R. K. (1988). Relation of dominant problems to stages of growth in technology-based new ventures. *Academy of Management Journal*, *31*(2), 257–79.

Majchrzak, A., & Markus, M. L. (2013). Technology affordances and constraints in management information systems (MIS). In E. Kessler (ed), *Encyclopedia of Management Theory* (Vol. 1, pp. 832). SAGE Publications.

McIntyre, D. P., & Srinivasan, A. (2017). Networks, platforms, and strategy: Emerging views and next steps. *Strategic Management Journal*, *38*(1), 141–60.

Nambisan, S., Wright, M., & Feldman, M. (2019). The digital transformation of innovation and entrepreneurship: Progress, challenges and key themes. *Research Policy*, *In print*, 1-9.

Ondrus, J., Gannamaneni, A., & Lyytinen, K. (2015). The impact of openness on the market potential of multi-sided platforms: a case study of mobile payment platforms. *Journal of Information Technology*, *30*(3), 260–75.

Park, Y., El Sawy, O. A., & Fiss, P. (2017). The role of business intelligence and communication technologies in organizational agility: a configurational approach. *Journal of the Association for Information Systems*, *18*(9), 649–86.

Parker, G., Van Alstyne, M., & Jiang, X. (2016). Platform ecosystems: how developers invert the firm. *MIS Quarterly*, *41*(1), 255-266.

Parker, G. G., Van Alstyne, M. W., & Choudary, S. P. (2016). *Platform revolution: how networked markets are transforming the economy and how to make them work for you* (Vol. 1). WW Norton & Company.

Pavitt, K. (1985). Patent statistics as indicators of innovative activities: possibilities and problems. *Scientometrics*, *7*(1-2), 77–99.

Prahalad, C. K., & Ramaswamy, V. (2004). Co-Creation Experiences: The Next Practice in Value Creation. *Journal of Interactive Marketing*, *18*(3), 5–14.

Ragin, C. C. (2008). *Redesigning social inquiry: fuzzy sets and beyond* (Vol. 6). Univ. of Chicago Press.

Ragin, C. C. (2009). Qualitative comparative analysis using fuzzy sets (fsQCA). *Configurational comparative methods: Qualitative comparative analysis (QCA) and related techniques*, *51*, 87–121.

Rajgopal, S., Venkatachalam, M., & Kotha, S. (2003). The value relevance of network advantages: the case of e–commerce firms. *Journal of Accounting Research*, *41*(1), 135–62.

Remneland-Wikhamn, B., Ljungberg, J., Bergquist, M., & Kuschel, J. (2011). Open innovation, generativity and the supplier as peer: the case of Iphone and Android. *International Journal of Innovation Management*, *15*(1), 205–30.

Romijn, H., & Albaladejo, M. (2002). Determinants of innovation capability in small electronics and software firms in southeast England. *Research Policy*, *31*(7), 1053–67.

Soto Setzke, D., Riasanow, T., Böhm, M., & Krcmar, H. (2021). Pathways to digital service innovation: The role of digital transformation strategies in established organizations. *Information Systems Frontiers*, 1-21.

Tan, T. C. F., Tan, B., & Pan, S. L. (2016). Developing a leading digital multi-sided platform: examining IT affordances and competitive actions in alibaba.com. *Communication of the AIS*, *38*, 739–60.

Tilson, D., Lyytinen, K., & Sørensen, C. (2010). Research commentary—Digital infrastructures: The missing IS research agenda. *Information Systems Research*, *21*(4), 748–59.

Tiwana, A., Konsynski, B., & Bush, A. A. (2010). Research commentary—platform evolution: coevolution of platform architecture, governance, and environmental dynamics. *Information Systems Research*, *21*(4), 675–87.

Vargo, S. L., & Lusch, R. F. (2016). Institutions and axioms: an extension and update of service-dominant logic. *Journal of the Academy of marketing Science*, *44*(1), 5–23. https://doi.org/10.1007/s11747-015-0456-3

Vargo, S. L., Maglio, P. P., & Akaka, M. A. (2008). On Value and Value Co-Creation: A Service Systems and Service Logic Perspective. *European Management Journal*, *26*(3), 145–52.

Vasilescu, B., Serebrenik, A., Devanbu, P., & Filkov, V. (2014). How social Q&A sites are changing knowledge sharing in open source software communities. Proceedings of the 17th ACM conference on Computer supported cooperative work & social computing, Baltimore, MD.

Von Hippel, E. (1986). Lead users: a source of novel product concepts. *Management Science*, *32*(7), 791–805.

Ye, H., & Kankanhalli, A. (2018). User Service Innovation on Mobile Phone Platforms: Investigating Impacts of Lead Userness, Toolkit Support, and Design Autonomy. *MIS Quarterly*, *42*(1).

Yoo, Y., Henfridsson, O., & Lyytinen, K. (2010). Research commentary—the new organizing logic of digital innovation: an agenda for information systems research. *Information Systems Research*, *21*(4), 724–35.

Zaveri, P., & Bosa, D. (2019). *Uber's growth slowed dramatically in 2018*. CNBC. Retrieved 01.04.2019 from https://www.cnbc.com/2019/02/15/uber-2018-financial-results.html

Zittrain, J. L. (2005). The generative internet. *Harvard Law Review*, *119*, 1975–2039.

12. The evolution of IT leadership

Thomas Hess and Christian Sciuk

INTRODUCTION

Information technologies (IT) have been making steady progress since the 1960s. This has resulted in several opportunities for organizations to leverage these technologies, ranging from initial applications to increase efficiency in accounting and simplify supply chains to services such as online banking (Chun & Mooney, 2009). Thus, from modest beginnings in the back offices of large corporations, IT has evolved into a subject of significant strategic interest in most boardrooms (Ross & Feeny, 1999). However, the use of IT does not happen automatically but requires a targeted management approach. An important consideration is how to govern the systematic utilization of IT. This question – often referred to as IT leadership – has been discussed in the literature for many years, given the rising relevance of IT for the business has increased the strategic importance of IT leaders (Drechsler, 2020). Nonetheless, it is not yet apparent that the topic of IT leadership has been finally resolved, especially since it is subject to dynamic developments. In particular, technological and competitive factors – both internal and external to the organization – force organizations to constantly rethink and re-strategize the use of their IT resources (Chen et al., 2010).

For a long time, the focus of IT leadership has been primarily on supporting and optimizing operations by providing IT infrastructure and systems (Haffke et al., 2016). However, in an increasingly digital business environment, technologies lead to changes throughout the entire organization and can create novel digital business offerings (Hess et al., 2016). In addition, there are constantly novel technical solutions in established fields of application, such as the analysis of large data sets. Finally, the advancement of digital technologies is by no means complete. Instead, technologies penetrate more and more areas of life, which is also relevant for organizations – just consider the digitalization of the car. This gives rise to various challenges, such as volatile customer demands or altered competitive dynamics (Bharadwaj et al., 2013). As a result, there is a paradigm shift in the perception of the IT function, moving away from its traditional role as a service provider. Instead, IT functions are taking the lead in discovering and experimenting with digital innovations that satisfy emerging digital customer needs and thus give the business a competitive edge (Haffke et al., 2017).

Accordingly, the challenges of the digital age also impact IT leadership, as organizations frequently adapt their structure and hire new senior executives for digital transformation (Tumbas et al., 2017), leading to a separation of the distinct IT leadership roles (Ghawe & Brohman, 2018). Yet, with the exception of Haffke et al. (2016), previous research on the evolution of IT leadership has mainly examined changes in the role of the Chief Information Officer (CIO) from a variety of perspectives (e.g., Chun & Mooney, 2009). Thus, the following chapter aims to holistically trace the development of IT leadership to the present day, taking recent developments in the wake of digital transformation into account and examining the forces that have historically shaped the various concepts. Special attention is paid to how value is captured by the corresponding IT leaders in the different evolutionary phases. The theoretical basis for this is provided by the notion of ambidexterity (Duncan, 1976), which suggests that IT functions must balance competing priorities by ensuring robust and cost-effective applications on the one hand and developing innovative solutions on the other (Kusanke & Winkler, 2022). The chapter also aims to highlight issues that arise as the concepts of IT leadership evolve, both against the backdrop of technical development and the practicability of the existing approaches.

The next sections are organized as follows. First, we outline the conceptual background of our chapter by introducing the concepts of IT leadership and ambidexterity. The following three sections focus on one evolutionary stage of IT leadership and elaborate on the corresponding developments in this phase. We then synthesize the observations by presenting an aggregate picture of the evolution of IT leadership. We also discuss possible developments in IT leadership in this section. We conclude our chapter with a summary.

BACKGROUND

IT leadership is the management of IT in organizations. Thus, the term pertains to the executives in an organization who are accountable for the IT infrastructure and applications that enable and drive the overarching business strategy and goals (Haffke et al., 2016). The topic of IT leadership is not new but has been discussed for more than 50 years in the literature on information systems and related areas in business administration. Recently, the subject gained traction as academia debates how to shape IT leadership in digital transformation.

In the literature, different conceptualizations of digital transformation exist. In this chapter, we adopt the definition of Vial (2019, p. 118), who understands digital transformation as a 'process that aims to improve an entity by triggering significant changes to its properties through combinations of information, computing, communication, and connectivity technologies'. While some authors refer to digital transformation only when the value proposition is redefined by digital means, forcing the creation of a new organizational identity (Wessel et al., 2021), Vial's (2019) definition implies a broad understanding that addresses significant changes induced by digital technologies throughout the organization. For instance, advances in digital technologies and the rapid adoption of digital products have increased the demand for digital sales and communication channels and led to digitized products and services replacing or complementing physical offerings (Haffke et al., 2017). However, although these examples already hint at the altered requirements for the IT function in the digital transformation (Bharadwaj et al., 2013), the focus of IT leadership is still on the management of (digital) technologies. This must be distinguished from the digital competence of managers, which is often referred to as digital leadership (Eberl & Drews, 2021).

The use of IT in an organization is concerned with both the reliable operation and ongoing development of the IT landscape, whereby the latter can result either from the opportunities offered by new technical solutions or from changes in business requirements (Wiesböck & Hess, 2020). Theoretically, this is described as ambidexterity, referring to an organization's ability, including its IT, to combine capacities from conflicting dimensions (Cao et al., 2009) and thus be efficient and innovative at the same time (Kusanke & Winkler, 2022). Accordingly, the interaction between the development of new competencies (exploration) and the utilization of existing structures (exploitation) is an important challenge in management (Duncan, 1976). More precisely, exploration describes how an organization develops a new competency base through search, experimentation, and risk-taking. Exploitation refers to the process by which organizations create improvements within the existing competency base through refinement and focused attention (March, 1991).

In the context of IT management, ambidexterity is regarded as the capability of an IT function to simultaneously discover new IT resources and practices (IT exploration) as well as utilize existing IT resources and practices (IT exploitation) (Gregory et al., 2015). Accordingly, IT exploration relates to demand-side leadership, i.e., the ability to lead the organization to discover new IT-enabled business opportunities that drive organizational innovation and business growth. On the other hand, IT exploitation can be viewed as supply-side leadership, i.e., the capability to leverage existing IT resources and competencies to improve the efficiency of business operations. While demand-side leadership is more externally focused on partnering with the business to innovate, supply-side leadership tends to be internally oriented toward delivering cost-effective IT support (Chen et al., 2010).

In this context, it is important to note that a new IT-based solution for an organization arises from the interplay of technical possibilities and business requirements. This relationship is expressed in the concept of digital innovations, which captures the notion that digital innovations are composed of two digital artifacts: a novel digital technology and a new business concept (Yoo et al., 2010). Both dimensions can be actuators for innovation processes and, therefore, must be integrated and harmonized. As such, digital technologies can be combined in creative ways to form digital innovations, which again enable organizations to derive digital business concepts. Innovative digital business concepts can be the foundation for developing follow-up solutions, eventually resulting in a recursive, iterative, and dynamic digital innovation cycle. This idea is depicted in the 'technology-push-pull model' (Wiesböck & Hess, 2020).

IT leadership has its beginnings in the private sector. However, the concept is not only pertinent for firms but is also of growing relevance to the public sector. Especially the digital transformation – similar to the massive impact on companies – poses challenges to the public sector on various levels that need to be addressed. For example, increased demands of citizens and budgetary pressures are critical drivers of digital transformation (Eggers & Bellman, 2015). Thus, IT leaders who are concerned with the exploration and exploitation of IT can also increasingly be found in government organizations. Emerging topics include the digitalization of internal processes and the design of innovative e-government solutions. In particular, the digitalization of the services offered to citizens is at the forefront. Therefore, citizens should, to some extent, be involved in the solution development process, which is why concepts such as open innovation, crowdsourcing, or ideation are also relevant in government institutions (Dawson & Denford, 2015). Besides, the public sector relies on new technologies and applications such as big data, artificial intelligence, and blockchain to achieve efficiency gains (Stern et al., 2018). For instance, government organizations apply artificial intelligence as part of holistic development concepts – such as smart cities – for intelligent traffic control that increases citizen satisfaction and reduces emissions.

Concepts for structuring the genesis of IT leadership already exist in the literature (Chun & Mooney, 2009; Haffke et al., 2016; Ross & Feeny, 1999). While the models of Ross and Feeny (1999) and Chun and Mooney (2009) investigate the development up to the position of the CIO, the work of Haffke et al. (2016) also takes the role of the Chief Digital Officer (CDO) into account. Thus, we draw on the latter model in this chapter. However, for the sake of simplicity and to focus on the most important trends, we only distinguish three evolutionary stages of IT leadership.

IT LEADERSHIP IN A FUNCTIONAL ROLE

The concept of IT leadership has its origins in the early 1960s when the introduction of mainframe computers into corporate back offices constituted the earliest application of computing in business (Ross & Feeny, 1999). Organizations recognized the potential of IT to reduce time, cost, and human error in performing and automating repetitive business tasks. Besides, they started to appreciate the value of data for business decision-making, which led to the development of electronic data processing capabilities (Gibson & Nolan, 1974). Initially, organizations viewed IT and, in particular, electronic data processing as an accounting tool (e.g., for simplifying general ledger entries). However, they soon became enthusiastic about the range of tasks the systems could support, which is why IT had penetrated most functional areas relatively quickly. For instance, in production planning and control, IT was utilized to support organizing activities along the value chain.

At that time, IT (hardware and software) was regarded as a resource that should primarily be provided efficiently and in accordance with the functional requirements of the organization. To this end, organizations have increasingly appointed so-called Directors of IT. Typically, Directors of IT were operational managers, focused on acquiring, implementing, and maintaining the technical infrastructure rather than exploring the opportunities presented by new technologies (Chun & Mooney, 2009). Instead, the direction and pace of the development of new applications were mainly determined by the dominant suppliers such as IBM. The Directors' of IT tasks were to implement new systems on time and on budget and to operate existing systems with high reliability and to agreed service levels, thus ensuring user satisfaction. As organizations embarked on large IT projects that resulted in a rapid expansion of IT staff, Directors of IT were also confronted with internal organization and human resource management issues (Rockart, 1980). But while the challenges increased over time, the role of the Director of IT remained essentially that of an operational manager in a specialized domain (Ross & Feeny, 1999). Cost objectives were still the focal point of their attention as they needed to manage the costs of ongoing operations and sprawling IT projects. Besides, IT was seen as a cost-cutting tool, which meant that decisions to invest in new information systems were based primarily on the expected return on investment.

Accordingly, Directors of IT were positioned in middle management and typically reported to the Chief Financial Officer, thus reflecting the perception that IT was first and foremost a cost factor that needed to be kept under control (Applegate & Elam, 1992). Most Directors of IT had a technical background both in terms of career (often previous positions in an IT company and thus on the provider side) and academic (frequently degrees in computer science or engineering). In addition to pure technical expertise, Directors of IT increasingly needed management and communication skills to manage large projects and instill the necessary performance orientation in the IT area (Ives & Olson, 1981). In line with the increasing importance of IT, virtually every large organization had a Director of IT and thus adopted this concept. Corresponding positions have also increasingly been created in the public sector to increase efficiency and effectiveness through IT by enabling authorities to store, process, and manage public data (Moon et al., 2014).

THE CIO CONCEPT

Since the 1980s, dramatic technological improvements have resulted in IT becoming a strategic business resource. The shift caused numerous changes in the way IT is used, e.g., as emerging telecommunications technologies led to an increasing perception of IT as a tool that enables a new level of integration and collaboration among business functions and across organizational boundaries (Rockart & Short, 1989). This can be exemplified by the emergence of enterprise resource planning systems, which offer seamless integration of all transaction processing. By this time, many business executives have already recognized the strategic importance of IT for the competitiveness of organizations. It was no longer sufficient to keep IT costs under control and ensure efficient and secure operations. Instead, the IT function needed to support the requirements of the business by designing an IT organization that could meet immediate business needs while simultaneously sustaining ongoing operations (Chun & Mooney, 2009). Accordingly, the IT function in many organizations evolved from having a supporting role to acting as a crucial strategic partner for the business units and thus being a driver of competitive advantage. Therefore, strong business alignment and a shared vision between business and technology became critical (Haffke et al., 2016).

These developments raised questions about how organizations should manage and assess the value of IT, i.e., how they can convert IT from a cost factor to be minimized into a strategic asset (Ross & Feeny, 1999). In response, the concept of a CIO emerged, which is based on two central ideas. First, organizations needed a manager who – besides providing the technical systems – also deals with the (strategic) use of information, which has become a critical resource for organizations and requires active management. In this sense, the term 'information' is deliberately used rather than 'IT' to emphasize the more business-oriented role. Second, this position only had the necessary power and visibility if it was located in the top management, thus assuming senior executive accountability of the organization's information resources (Peppard et al., 2011). The inclusion in the C-suite was intended to express this. In this regard, the purpose of the position was to initiate discussions at the executive level about how information and technology can be used to achieve a competitive advantage. Compared to the Director of IT, the CIO was seen as a business manager (albeit with significant technical focus) capable of implementing value-creating information systems and acting as a strategic partner to the business (Chun & Mooney, 2009).

Many organizations adopted the CIO position. Especially in industries where information and its processing are particularly relevant (such as in insurance and financial service companies), the CIO has quickly risen to become a central figure and was consequently represented on the organization's board. Accordingly, among the first people to have a CIO title were Alfred Zipf (Bank of America) and Max Hopper (American Airlines) in the early 1980s (IBM, 2011). By contrast, it took several years for the public sector to embrace the CIO concept. For example, Australia was a pioneer at the government level, being one of the first nations to install a CIO only in 2005 (Bushell, 2006).

According to the basic idea underlying the creation of the position, CIOs often displayed the ambition to deal with innovative IT-based concepts in the organization. However, despite the opportunities offered by the C-level title, many CIOs encountered problems in their efforts to prove their merit as they were responsible for a function that consumed considerable resources but provided little direct evidence of value (Peppard et al., 2011). Cost-oriented goals and achieving service levels remained a frequent focus, presenting significant obstacles for CIOs trying to meet strategic expectations and optimize value from IT (Haffke et al., 2016). Accordingly, most CIOs continued to report to the CFO and were not anchored at the first level. Besides, CIOs still typically had a technical background and held degrees in computer science or cross-functional studies such as information systems. Their professional careers were also often characterized by previous positions in the IT sector or with IT companies, thus exhibiting little orientation towards the business side. In practice, the typical CIO was concerned with providing technology (in strong alignment with the business) and occasionally with innovating business processes.

SPLITTING IT LEADERSHIP INTO TWO ROLES

With the commercial launch of the public Internet in the early 1990s, which led to concepts such as e-commerce and e-business, IT has become a competitive weapon as it directly influenced the organizations' offerings. For instance, organizations extended their existing business models by adding an electronic customer interface and recognized the opportunity to offer value-adding services to their customers via the Internet, which required a market-oriented perspective on IT and thus exploring technical possibilities (Ross & Feeny, 1999). Examples include online services of financial service providers and retail companies or digital interfaces of airlines. The development has been reinforced by the advent of digital technologies, such as the Internet of Things, platforms, and clouds, which have 'fundamentally altered consumers' expectations and behaviors, pressured traditional firms, and disrupted numerous markets' (Verhoef et al., 2021, p. 889). They can lead to the digitalization of an organization's offerings, replacing or complementing physical offerings. Moreover, digital technologies massively impact sales and communication channels by providing new opportunities to interact and engage with customers across dozens of media channels and a rapidly growing number of touchpoints in the customer journey (Lemon & Verhoef, 2016). As a result, digital technologies can trigger strategic business moves through data-driven insights, leading to the adoption of digital business models that enable new ways of creating value (Bharadwaj et al., 2013). Companies such as Airbnb, Uber, and Netflix have transformed entire industries by positioning themselves with digital business models and quickly capturing market share from established players with traditional business models (Haffke et al., 2016). Considering these trends, it is evident that IT has become a strategic differentiator in recent decades, influencing corporate strategy to an unprecedented extent and requiring organizations to explore opportunities offered by technologies better or faster than competitors. Thus, to ensure competitiveness in the digital age, established organizations must develop IT-related capabilities that enable them to leverage the potential of digital technologies (Bharadwaj et al., 2013).

Alongside the changing requirements on the market side, the provision and adjacent governance of IT, i.e., hardware, networks, and applications, has become significantly more complex. The underlying reasons are manifold. First and foremost, digitalization inevitably leads to more and highly integrated IT in organizations, complicating its management. Accordingly, the ubiquity of digital technologies increased the difficulty of providing reliable systems that cover an ever-growing number of users, devices, business processes, and organizational functions (Haffke et al., 2017). Second, to meet this demand, outsourcing is gaining significance (Chun & Mooney, 2009). While initially, entire IT landscapes were outsourced, over time, smaller systems in demarcated areas were also affected, further complicating the management of the landscapes. Finally, highly integrated systems and the increasing significance of IT for the business render security, operational reliability, and efficiency more critical. In a nutshell, to compete in the digital economy and have a stable foundation for launching new digital products and services, organizations must build an operational backbone that ensures 'the efficiency, scalability, reliability, quality and predictability of core operations' (Sebastian et al., 2017, p. 202).

For several years, organizations have expected their CIOs to expand their role from pure technologists to business strategists, aiming to explore emerging technology opportunities for the business. This implies that they should spend less time managing IT services and emphasize delivering business value, i.e., addressing the demand-side of IT (Peppard et al., 2011). However, as outlined above, the provision of IT, i.e., the supply-side, has increased in complexity. Therefore, it is often not feasible for CIOs to take on additional tasks on top of their core responsibilities (Singh & Hess, 2017) and IT departments struggle to keep up with the increasing demands of the organization. In addition, many CIOs still do not have a business background, either in education or in previous career experiences. Yet, digital technologies follow different logics (Tumbas et al., 2018) and require distinct mindsets and skills (Fitzgerald et al., 2013). Besides, digital innovations typically unfold as a combination of emerging technologies and novel business solutions (Wiesböck & Hess, 2020). As a result, many organizations turn away from the CIO concept in the original sense, i.e., with the ambition of exploring IT-enabled innovations. Instead, they appoint someone who focuses on the complex supply-side in a way that facilitates agility and adaptiveness. Besides, tasks often include encouraging process change (Chun & Mooney, 2009). This manager is either still referred to as the CIO or occasionally as the Chief Technology Officer (CTO).

In response to the challenges of digital transformation and the amplified requirements on the demand-side of IT, organizations are increasingly hiring digital leaders, namely CDOs (Tumbas et al., 2017). The role of the CDO can be centralized at the corporate level or decentralized at the subsidiary level (especially in large organizations with very heterogeneous business areas). In most cases, however, the CDO acts centrally at the highest level of an organization, i.e., in top management or as the head of a digitalization function, such as a digital innovation unit (Hess et al., 2022; Singh et al., 2020). Regardless of the positioning, CDOs are entrusted with various aspects of digital transformation and share responsibility for developing and implementing a transformation strategy. However, the specific tasks are not clearly defined and in practice, CDOs can have different focuses: 'Everyone defines the CDO role and its scope differently' (Haffke et al., 2016, p. 8). The role of CDOs depends on various factors, such as the organization's digital maturity, the digital mindset of the employees, the size of the organization, and the reporting structure of the CDO. Specifically, three different CDO role types are outlined (Singh & Hess, 2017):

- As *Entrepreneurs*, CDOs explore innovations brought about by digital technologies, develop a digital transformation strategy and implement it in their organization. In this role, CDOs sometimes change entire business models.

- As *Digital Evangelists*, CDOs aim to ignite enthusiasm for digital technologies. This usually requires a cultural change, which can be driven, for example, by communicating progress in digital activities.
- As *Coordinators*, CDOs dismantle existing silo mentalities and steer the controlled change toward cross-functional collaborative organizations. Since digital transformation is not an isolated process but affects many areas, CDOs of this type contribute to the interconnectedness of the entire organization.

The CDO phenomenon found its origin in 2005, with the firm MTV Networks being the first company to hire a CDO. Since then, the CDO function has rapidly gained popularity and is one of the fastest-growing top management positions globally (Singh & Hess, 2017). CDOs are installed across many sectors. For example, Columbia University hired a CDO back in 2012 with the aspiration to develop a plan to expand the university's online education programs (Columbia University, 2012). A recent study shows that in 2018, about 120 companies in the S&P 1500 index had a CDO, with the trend pointing upwards (Kunisch et al., 2020). However, this figure also illustrates that the appointment of a CDO can be an adequate response to the challenges of digital transformation, but CDOs are not installed in all organizations. Firk et al. (2021) argue that the decision to centralize responsibilities for digital transformation in the position of a CDO depends significantly on two factors:

- The *transformation urgency* signals how important the transition to digital business models is for organizations. Information- and knowledge-based business models, such as those of media or service companies, are particularly vulnerable to being replaced by digital substitutes. Such organizations can benefit from CDOs accelerating the digital transformation by designing new (digital) business models and building the necessary digital capabilities.
- The *coordination needs* of digital transformation also influence the benefit of a CDO in a top management team. These are particularly pronounced in highly diversified organizations, which are susceptible to the emergence of business silos that pursue digital initiatives in a decoupled manner. CDOs can aggregate such decentralized digital activities and realize synergies in developing and applying digital technologies across functions.

If organizations install a CDO, they must pay particular attention to a functioning relationship between the CDO and the CIO and actively promote it. Digital transformation can only succeed if the CIO's expert IT knowledge and the CDO's strategic digital business knowledge work together. However, CDOs' and CIOs' different backgrounds and expertise harbor the potential for conflict, as they can quickly lead to different perspectives and thus obstruct digitalization programs. Since the role of the CDO is still emerging, collaboration with the CIO is only beginning to be clarified. Initial research shows that four factors are crucial for the interaction between CDO and CIO (Horlacher, 2016):

- *A shared understanding* of the goals of digital transformation.
- *Specialization* and clearly delineated role definitions.
- *Trust* in each other's expertise.
- *Coordination* concerning the concrete collaboration.

In addition, due to the cross-functional orientation of the CDO, the cooperation of the CDO with other top managers or even the entire board is also highly pertinent. However, there is yet little scientific evidence on this. In particular, the interaction with the CEO is worth-investigating as CDO positions are frequently created with a direct reporting to the CEO (Singh & Hess, 2017), which is something that many CIOs have failed to attain (Haffke et al., 2016).

EVOLUTION OF IT LEADERSHIP

From the three phases described in the previous sections, an aggregated picture of the evolution of IT leadership can be derived (Figure 12.1). In the first of the three stages, IT leadership is in the hands of the Director of IT, i.e., an operational manager (located in middle management) responsible for delivering IT on time while staying within budget and ensuring reliable operations. At that time, IT was mainly seen as a cost factor, requiring Directors of IT to convince the top management of the value of further spending on IT by demonstrating the return on investment. However, as IT became more widespread, it was no longer sufficient for organizations to focus solely on costs but also take the strategic opportunities offered by IT and information into account. As a response, organizations deployed CIOs, who acted as a partner of the business by aligning investments in IT with strategic business priorities. The primary objective in this phase was to develop a complex IT organization meeting the business needs while supporting ongoing operations. Unlike Directors of IT, CIOs often held a top management position, highlighting the importance of IT and information to the organization. While CIOs were initially involved in exploring technologies and opportunities for new business models based on the Internet, i.e., the demand-side of IT, this is often no longer feasible due to the massive increase in complexity of the IT landscape and changing market requirements in the course of digital transformation. Accordingly, many organizations split IT leadership into two top management positions in the third phase. On the supply-side, the CIO or CTO manages the more sophisticated IT infrastructure and is often entrusted with modifying processes. On the demand-side, organizations are increasingly appointing CDOs who, among other things, experiment with digital innovations and evaluate the potential of digital technologies for the organizations' business models.

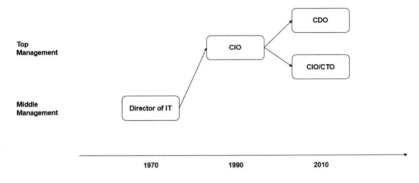

Figure 12.1   Evolution of IT leadership

Looking at the evolution of IT leadership in the three phases, it is apparent that a key difference between the various IT leaders lies in the way they capture value through IT in their organizations (Figure 12.2). The Director of IT was primarily responsible for the cost-efficient provision of IT, i.e., the exploitation of technical possibilities. At the same time, the opportunities offered by technologies were explored almost exclusively by the dominant suppliers during this period. Likewise, the CIO focused on ensuring flawless and reliable operations by optimizing the IT infrastructure, thus realizing exploitation. However, the aspiration for this position was partly the exploration of strategic applications of IT and information, e.g., in the course of new opportunities created by the launch of the commercial Internet. As IT and, in particular, digital technologies become increasingly important and digital innovations often form the core of entire (digital) business models, many organizations created a dedicated position with the CDO to explore the opportunities offered by technologies. The ongoing refinement of the IT infrastructure, i.e., exploitation, is typically not part of the CDO's job profile. Due to the increased complexity of the IT landscape, this has become even more the focus of the CIO/CTO. Accordingly, the exploration of digital innovations is only peripherally performed by these managers and to a lesser extent than initially envisaged for the CIO role.

It is noteworthy that only exploration, i.e., demand-side leadership, directly impacts IT's contribution to strategic growth. On the other hand, exploitation, i.e., supply-side leadership, does not enable strategic growth as it focuses on refinement and not on creating unique organizational capabilities. Nevertheless, supply-side leadership is a necessary foundation for demand-side leadership, as reliable and efficient operations are required to explore innovative solutions (Chen et al., 2010).

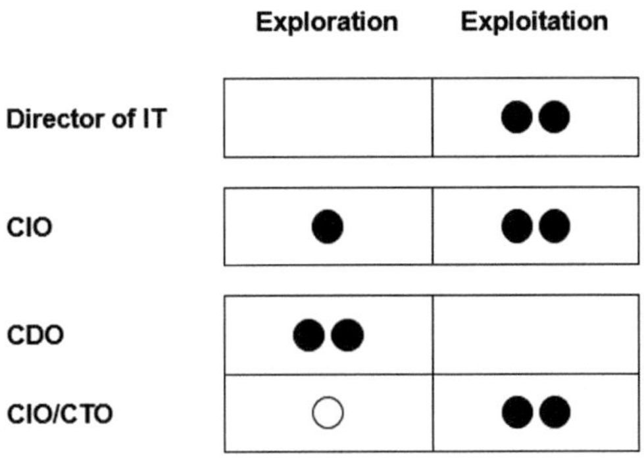

Figure 12.2   Value capturing of the different IT leaders

Concerning the further trajectory of IT leadership, it is indeterminate whether the separation concept of the CDO and CIO/CTO is the final solution. In particular, it corresponds to the current competencies of the executives in question but also the short cycles of new (digital) technologies and the constantly increasing complexity of the IT infrastructure. However, the separation of demand-side and supply-side IT leadership can also present challenges, as many interdependencies exist. One example is integrating a new solution, e.g., digital customer interfaces, into an IT landscape. While the definition of corresponding interfaces to the existing systems is feasible, the handling of redundant databases and the maintenance of the system are more complex. This involves both parties permanently and thus requires a high degree of coordination.

The concept of bimodal IT vividly illustrates this issue. Bimodal IT refers to dividing an IT function into two modes – similar to the division of tasks between CDO and CIO/CTO – to effectively balance both explorative and exploitative duties, i.e., the management of secure systems on the one hand and agile applications facing customers on the other (Horlach et al., 2016). The two modes differ structurally and usually follow dissimilar governance principles as they strive to achieve unique objectives. The basic idea of such an organizational form is to create a 'speedboat' for digital transformation projects alongside the traditional IT development. Traditional IT (Mode 1) is geared towards optimizing the business-critical systems and core processes based on

clearly defined requirements, thus following a stability and reliability paradigm. This mode facilitates a risk-averse culture by accentuating safety and
accuracy. The speedboat (Mode 2), on the other hand, focuses on 'disruptive'
IT solutions and is accordingly characterized by customer- or business-driven
digital transformation projects. The main focus in this mode is on innovation
and differentiation. Such explorative activities are often endeavors with less
certain outcomes, aiming for short release cycles and commonly using agile
(iterative) project management methods such as Scrum. The culture is driven
by the principles of agility and speed (Haffke et al., 2017).

While studies show that bimodal IT can be a way to transform the IT function and prepare it for the digital age by enabling ambidexterity (Kusanke &
Winkler, 2022), there are also critical voices concerning the concept. First,
a two-tier system can increase complexity. When organizations need to act fast
and agile, it is counterproductive to maintain two IT groups, each vying for
resources and recognition. Second, bimodal IT is based on a technology-centric
rather than a customer-centric mindset, which counters the idea of creating
cross-functional roles and achieving an overarching omnichannel mode as
organizational silos are maintained. Finally, employees working in traditional
IT will likely feel left behind in the long run as the market side is more
esteemed (McCarthy & Leaver, 2016). Based on these considerations, bimodal
IT can be regarded as a temporary intermediate stage in a more extensive
transformation process. In the long term, organizations should reassemble the
IT function into a single mode of operation rather than relying on structural
mechanisms to implement ambidexterity (Haffke et al., 2017). In this regard,
a potential approach is the concept of dynamic ambidexterity, which proposes
a dual strategy of exploration and exploitation to be sustained through the constant rebalancing of resources and capabilities (Dixon et al., 2017). However,
the appropriate IT leadership has yet to be clarified for this concept.

Therefore, it will be exciting to monitor how IT leadership and, in particular,
the division of roles will develop in the future. One crucial aspect is how the
competence of managers and employees to explore new technical possibilities
is evolving. On the one hand, digital literacy is now a basic requirement for
every member of the top management team since digital transformation affects
all areas of the organization (Haffke et al., 2016). In addition, it can be noted
that many projects for generating digital innovations emerge bottom-up out
of the respective departments and also involve the employees in the process
(Chanias et al., 2019). It is conceivable that the exploration of ideas for digital
innovations will no longer require support units or a distinct management position but will instead take place directly in the organization's various departments. In organizations that are 'born-digital', this already occurs to some
extent. Hence, organizations that have undergone a digital transformation and

can be described as digital-defined organizations (Hess, 2022) could also rely on such an approach in the long term.

Another feasible scenario is that the complexity of IT landscapes is reduced in the long term, thus relieving the CIO/CTO. Efforts in this direction, which were piloted under the heading of service-oriented architectures (Widjaja & Buxmann, 2009), have just sporadically been successful. By contrast, outsourcing IT systems via a cloud approach could be more promising. Nevertheless, established organizations still have very intricate structures that have grown over time, so the complexity of the IT landscape is likely to be curtailed only in the long term. In addition, the requirements for IT security will continue to increase due to issues such as cybercrime. Overall, the demands on the IT function are therefore not expected to decline. Yet, it is worth mentioning that there are also CIOs who have a business rather than a technical background and take on an important role in the demand-side of IT leadership by widening their responsibilities (Weill & Woerner, 2013). Here, it is apparent that this is especially feasible when CIOs operate in more stabilized and standardized IT infrastructures and can thus emphasize exploring technologies for process and product innovations (Chun & Mooney, 2009). However, it is crucial that CIOs first ensure efficient and reliable operations, i.e., serve the requirements of supply-side leadership, before demand-side leadership responsibilities can be embraced (Chen et al., 2010).

Finally, sustainability issues are increasingly important in today's world, which makes it intriguing to monitor the role that IT plays in this regard. On the one hand, IT directly impacts organizations' carbon footprint, for example, through the disposal of technology waste or increased electricity consumption. On the other hand, IT is also part of the solution by enabling significant efficiency gains. Here, organizations need to evaluate how technologies and data can be leveraged to use or reuse materials more effectively, eliminate friction in supply chains, invest in circular economies, or minimize waste (Osburg & Lohrmann, 2017). Besides, IT can support the transformation of workflows and thus sustainability goals, if only because the switch from paper-based to digital processes saves resources such as water and paper. However, sustainability is not just a question of internal processes but an imperative that customers increasingly demand. Therefore, organizations must also monitor the impact on their business models and integrate sustainability objectives. While some organizations have hired Chief Sustainability Officers (Fu et al., 2020) to answer these questions, sustainability is also anchored in the area of responsibility of IT leaders. Here, the tension between the goals of profitability and sustainability must be resolved. Analogous to the previous considerations, a separation of exploration (CDO) and exploitation (CIO/CTO) of the technical possibilities in terms of sustainability appears to be reasonable at this point in time. Nevertheless, the division of IT responsibilities regarding sustainability issues will also have to be reassessed in the future.

CONCLUSION

This chapter traces the evolution of IT leadership through its major phases. It elaborates on the triggers for change due to technological advancements as well as the success of the different concepts. Besides, current issues of IT leadership are discussed and an outlook on potential future directions is given. The theoretical basis was the notion of ambidexterity and thus different ways of capturing value in organizations. In terms of IT leadership, this implies that new technical possibilities and changing business requirements demand the constant advancement of an organization's IT landscape (exploration). At the same time, the IT infrastructure must be operated efficiently and securely (exploitation). In the beginnings of IT leadership, it is apparent that the focus was primarily on exploiting IT. In contrast, in the era of the Internet and, in particular, digital transformation, the exploration of technical possibilities has become increasingly important. Yet, the provision of IT has also become more complex due to growing requirements on the market side.

Initially, the tasks of IT leadership were typically assumed by one manager (i.e., the Director of IT or the CIO). Yet, the rising demands from digital transformation often separate IT leadership into demand-side (i.e., CDO) and supply-side (i.e., CIO/CTO) roles. Thus, it is crucial to assess whether the changed requirements can be distributed among existing top managers or whether a new position should be created to support the organization in managing the digital transformation. In this regard, appropriate governance mechanisms are essential, as the demand-side and supply-side of IT leadership are highly interdependent. When tasks are split between the CDO and CIO/CTO, organizations need to ensure that there is flourishing collaboration and tight coordination, which has the potential to align IT and business functions more closely. However, it is important to note that the separation concept of CDO and CIO/CTO is by no means robust as it is subject to dynamic developments, especially concerning organizations' ongoing digital transformations and increased digital maturity. Therefore, it is conceivable that further shifts in IT leadership will occur, for example, as the digital empowerment of the entire organization – including its employees – progresses and issues such as sustainability render more important.

KEY TAKEAWAYS

* Academics and practitioners alike have observed the continuous appreciation of the value of IT since its first emergence in organizations in the

1960s. Yet, the utilization of IT does not happen automatically but requires systematic management, i.e., IT leadership.

- Drawing on ambidexterity, IT leadership is concerned with discovering new IT-enabled business opportunities that drive organizational innovation (exploration) and leveraging existing IT resources and capabilities to improve efficiency (exploitation).
- The historical development of IT leadership demonstrates that IT leaders were primarily concerned with the exploitation of IT in the early phases. Accordingly, cost minimization and effectiveness were focal objectives. Over the years, however, the importance of IT for the business has become increasingly apparent.
- In digital transformation, the requirements on both the demand-side and supply-side of IT leadership have intensified, leading to a separation of IT leadership into demand-side (i.e., CDO) and supply-side (i.e., CIO/CTO) responsibilities in many organizations.
- However, the currently prevailing concept of separating IT leadership into the roles of CDO and CIO/CTO is by no means robust. Thus, it is worth monitoring how tasks are distributed in the long term, especially when digital technologies penetrate organizations even deeper.

REFERENCES

Applegate, L. M., & Elam, J. J. (1992). New information systems leaders: A changing role in a changing world. *MIS Quarterly*, *16*(4), 469–90.

Bharadwaj, A., El Sawy, O. A., Pavlou, P. A., & Venkatraman, N. (2013). Digital business strategy: Toward a next generation of insights. *MIS Quarterly*, *37*(2), 471–82.

Bushell, S. (2006). *Government CIO role still developing, but Australia ahead of pack.* Retrieved 12.05.2022 from https://www.cio.com/?id=401118652&eid=601

Cao, Q., Gedajlovic, E., & Zhang, H. (2009). Unpacking organizational ambidexterity: Dimensions, contingencies, and synergistic effects. *Organization Science*, *20*(4), 781–796.

Chanias, S., Myers, M. D., & Hess, T. (2019). Digital transformation strategy making in pre-digital organizations: The case of a financial services provider. *The Journal of Strategic Information Systems*, *28*(1), 17–33.

Chen, D. Q., Preston, D. S., & Xia, W. (2010). Antecedents and effects of CIO supply-side and demand-side leadership: A staged maturity model. *Journal of Management Information Systems*, *27*(1), 231–72.

Chun, M., & Mooney, J. (2009). CIO roles and responsibilities: Twenty-five years of evolution and change. *Information & Management*, *46*(6), 323–34.

Columbia University. (2012). *Sreenivasan named university's first Chief Digital Officer.* Retrieved 19.05.2022 from https://magazine.columbia.edu/article/sreenivasan-named-universitys-first-chief-digital-officer

Dawson, G. S., & Denford, J. S. (2015). *A playbook for CIO-enabled innovation in the federal government.* IBM. Retrieved 17.05.2022 from https://www.businessof government.org/sites/default/files/A%20Playbook%20for%20CIO-Enabled %20Innovation%20in%20the%20Federal%20Government.pdf

Dixon, J. A., Brohman, K., & Chan, Y. E. (2017). Dynamic ambidexterity: Exploiting exploration for business success in the digital age. International Conference on Information Systems, Seoul, South Korea.

Drechsler, K. (2020). Information systems executives: A review and research agenda. European Conference on Information Systems, Marrakesh, Morocco.

Duncan, R. B. (1976). The ambidextrous organization: Designing dual structures for innovation. *The management of organization*, *1*(1), 167–88.

Eberl, J. K., & Drews, P. (2021). Digital leadership - Mountain or molehill? A literature review. International Conference on Wirtschaftsinformatik, Duisburg-Essen, Germany.

Eggers, W. D., & Bellman, J. (2015). *The journey to government's digital transformation*. Deloitte. Retrieved 19.05.2022 from https://www2.deloitte.com/de/de/pages/public-sector/articles/journey-to-governments-digital-transformation.html

Firk, S., Hanelt, A., Oehmichen, J., & Wolff, M. (2021). Chief Digital Officers: An analysis of the presence of a centralized digital transformation role. *Journal of Management Studies*, *58*(7), 1800–31.

Fitzgerald, M., Kruschwitz, N., Bonnet, D., & Welch, M. (2013). Embracing digital technology: A new strategic imperative. *MIT Sloan Management Review*, *55*(2), 1–16.

Fu, R., Tang, Y., & Chen, G. (2020). Chief Sustainability Officers and corporate social (ir)responsibility. *Strategic Management Journal*, *41*(4), 656–80.

Ghawe, A., & Brohman, K. (2018). Conceptual foundations of information systems leadership. Americas Conference on Information Systems, New Orleans, USA.

Gibson, C. F., & Nolan, R. (1974). Managing the four stages of EDP growth. *Harvard Business Review*, *52*(1), 76–88.

Gregory, R. W., Keil, M., Muntermann, J., & Mähring, M. (2015). Paradoxes and the nature of ambidexterity in IT transformation programs. *Information Systems Research*, *26*(1), 57–80.

Haffke, I., Kalgovas, B., & Benlian, A. (2017). Options for transforming the IT function using bimodal IT. *MIS Quarterly Executive*, *16*(2), 101–20.

Haffke, I., Kalgovas, B. J., & Benlian, A. (2016). The role of the CIO and the CDO in an organization's digital transformation. International Conference on Information Systems, Dublin, Ireland.

Hess, T. (2022). *Managing the digital transformation: A guide to successful organizational change* (1st edn.). Springer.

Hess, T., Barthel, P., Lohoff, L., & Sciuk, C. (2022). Governance for the digital transformation. In S. Roth & H. Corsten (Eds.), *Handbuch Digitalisierung* (pp. 20–40). Vahlen.

Hess, T., Matt, C., Benlian, A., & Wiesböck, F. (2016). Options for formulating a digital transformation strategy. *MIS Quarterly Executive*, *15*(2), 123–39.

Horlach, B., Drews, P., & Schirmer, I. (2016). Bimodal IT: Business-IT alignment in the age of digital transformation. Multikonferenz Wirtschaftsinformatik (MKWI), Ilmenau, Germany.

Horlacher, A. (2016). Co-creating value - The dyadic CDO-CIO relationship during the digital transformation. European Conference on Information Systems, Istanbul, Turkey.

IBM. (2011). *The emergence of the CIO*. Retrieved 18.05.2022 from https://www.ibm.com/ibm/history/ibm100/us/en/icons/emergenceofcio/

Ives, B., & Olson, M. H. (1981). Manager or technician? The nature of the information systems manager's job. *MIS Quarterly*, *5*(4), 49–63.

Kunisch, S., Menz, M., & Langan, R. (2020). Chief Digital Officers: An exploratory analysis of their emergence, nature, and determinants. *Long Range Planning*, *101999*, 1–17.

Kusanke, K., & Winkler, T. J. (2022). Structural ambidexterity through bimodal IT - A literature review and research agenda. International Conference on Wirtschaftsinformatik, Nuremberg, Germany.

Lemon, K. N., & Verhoef, P. C. (2016). Understanding customer experience throughout the customer journey. *Journal of Marketing*, *80*(6), 69–96.

March, J. G. (1991). Exploration and exploitation in organizational learning. *Organization Science*, *2*(1), 71–87.

McCarthy, J. C., & Leaver, S. (2016). *The false promise of bimodal IT*. Forrester. Retrieved 19.04.2022 from https://go.forrester.com/wp-content/uploads/Forrester -False-Promise-of-Bimodal-IT.pdf

Moon, M. J., Lee, J., & Roh, C.-Y. (2014). The evolution of internal IT applications and e-government studies in public administration: Research themes and methods. *Administration & Society*, *46*(1), 3–36.

Osburg, T., & Lohrmann, C. (2017). *Sustainability in a digital world*. Springer.

Peppard, J., Edwards, C., & Lambert, R. (2011). Clarifying the ambiguous role of the CIO. *MIS Quarterly Executive*, *10*(1), 31–44.

Rockart, J. F. (1980). The changing role of the information systems executive: A critical success factors perspective. *Sloan Management Review*, *85*, 3–13.

Rockart, J. F., & Short, J. E. (1989). IT in the 1990s: Managing organizational interdependence. *MIT Sloan Management Review*, *30*(2), 7–17.

Ross, J. W., & Feeny, D. F. (1999). The evolving role of the CIO. Center for Information Systems Research, Working Paper 308, Sloan School of Management, Massachusetts Institute of Technology.

Sebastian, I., Ross, J., Beath, C., Mocker, M., Moloney, K., & Fonstad, N. (2017). How big old companies navigate digital transformation. *MIS Quarterly Executive*, *16*(3), 197–213.

Singh, A., & Hess, T. (2017). How Chief Digital Officers promote the digital transformation of their companies. *MIS Quarterly Executive*, *16*(1), 1–17.

Singh, A., Klarner, P., & Hess, T. (2020). How do Chief Digital Officers pursue digital transformation activities? The role of organization design parameters. *Long Range Planning*, *53*(3), 1–14.

Stern, S., Daub, M., Klier, J., Wiesinger, A., & Domeyer, A. (2018). *Government 4.0: The public sector in the digital age*. McKinsey. Retrieved 18.05.2022 from https:// www.mckinsey.de/~/media/mckinsey/locations/europe%20and%20middle%20east/ deutschland/publikationen/2018%20compendium/government%2040%20the %20public%20sector%20in%20the%20digital%20age/kompendium_04_ps.pdf

Tumbas, S., Berente, N., & Brocke, J. v. (2018). Digital innovation and institutional entrepreneurship: Chief Digital Officer perspectives of their emerging role. *Journal of Information Technology*, *33*(3), 188–202.

Tumbas, S., Berente, N., & vom Brocke, J. (2017). Three types of Chief Digital Officers and the reasons organizations adopt the role. *MIS Quarterly Executive*, *16*(2), 121–34.

Verhoef, P., Broekhuizen, T., Bart, Y., Bhattacharya, A., Dong, J. Q., Fabian, N., & Haenlein, M. (2021). Digital transformation: A multidisciplinary reflection and research agenda. *Journal of Business Research*, *122*, 889–901.

Vial, G. (2019). Understanding digital transformation: A review and a research agenda. *The Journal of Strategic Information Systems*, *28*(2), 118–44.

Weill, P., & Woerner, S. L. (2013). The future of the CIO in a digital economy. *MIS Quarterly Executive, 12*(2), 65–75.

Wessel, L., Baiyere, A., Ologeanu-Taddei, R., Cha, J., & Blegind-Jensen, T. (2021). Unpacking the difference between digital transformation and IT-enabled organizational transformation. *Journal of the Association for Information Systems, 22*(1), 102–29.

Widjaja, T., & Buxmann, P. (2009). Service-oriented architectures: Modeling the selection of services and platforms. European Conference on Information Systems, Verona, Italy.

Wiesböck, F., & Hess, T. (2020). Digital innovations - Embedding in organizations. *Electronic Markets, 30*(1), 75–86.

Yoo, Y., Henfridsson, O., & Lyytinen, K. (2010). Research commentary - The new organizing logic of digital innovation: An agenda for information systems research. *Information Systems Research, 21*(4), 724–35.

Practice 4. CIO perspective

Jagdish Dalal

EVOLUTION OF THE DIGITIZATION OF BUSINESS

With the advent of higher levels of computing capabilities, businesses are focusing on digitizing their business and creating new models of business. Professors Andreas Hein, David Soto Setzke, Sebastian Hermes, Jörg Weking, Philipp Kernstock and Helmut Krcmar have said in Chapter 11 that: 'The increasing importance of digital platforms is undisputed.' It has also created a different organizational structure than in the past. The author of Chapter 10 has identified it as bimodal IT. Professsor Kusanski and Winkler wrote in Chapter 10: 'Thus, bimodal IT is a term coined by practitioners that is used for different IT organizational forms through which organizations aim for structural ambidexterity. These endeavors are undertaken to ultimately support an organization's overall IT ambidexterity.'

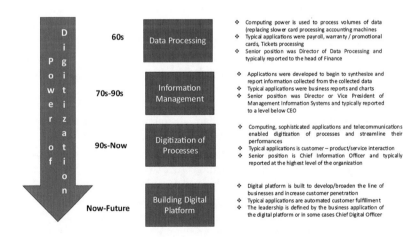

Figure 12. 3   Evolution of computing

As a practicing professional in the IT field for the last 50 years, I have been a participant in this evolution of digitization. The leadership for the function has evolved with the evolution in computing and telecommunication technology. This is reflected in functionality and the titles that have evolved over a period of time. It is further evolving today. Professors Hess and Scuik have detailed this evolution of IT management positions in section 3 of Chapter 12. They also have noted that 'For a long time, the focus of IT leadership has been primarily on supporting and optimizing operations by providing IT systems and IT infrastructure.'

Impact of Digitization on the Organization

Over the last 50 years, the organization overseeing the computing has changed for the most part, however many businesses see the role as overseeing the computing capabilities. This notion of managing computing resources goes back to the introduction of business computers back in the 1960s. Since computers were an expensive resource and were mainly used for routine large data processing, the leadership was held responsible for asset management as much as creating digitized value. Professors Hess and Sciuk also noted this: 'To this end, organizations have increasingly appointed a so-called Director of IT. Typically, the role of these managers was that of an operational manager, focused on IT delivery rather than exploring the opportunities presented by new technologies.' When I was asked to lead the function back in the late 1960s, my title was 'Director of Data Processing' and my qualification was the fact that I had a background in Engineering and Finance; and not programming. After 40 plus years of managing the function, I retired as Chief Information Officer and VP of E-business. The expectation from my last position was to manage information and initiate digitization activities. This was a recognition of my business background supported by the long term management of the technology.

However, the recent evolution of digitization and competitive advantages offered through digitization has led many to rethink the traditional 'computing' organization. There is a model that is used by businesses: Maintain the traditional computing management organization to provide infrastructure management and digitization of existing processes while establishing a separate organization that is dedicated to building a digital platform. The title of CIO – Chief Information Officer, remains with the first set of activities while assigning a new title of CDO – Chief Digital Officer is assigned to the new position of creating a digital platform and building that business. There have been examples of the current CIO with a strong business background taking over the role of the CDO. As the digitization driven-organization begins to mature, the CDO creates the opportunity to head up the digital business unit, or even the entire business when the digital business becomes a critical part of the success. While the CIO position remains somewhat stagnant. However, a CIO with business acumen and strategic thinking can achieve the BDO position and lead a business unit.

However, the differentiating line between the CIO and CDO position blurs when the building digital platform requires the exploitation of data analytics. This is observed in the use of customer data for revenue generation by websites like Amazon and Google.

Another impact of digitization – both for the existing business process automation as well as for creating the digital platform is potential exposure to security issues. The world has seen a dramatic increase in security violations – both incidental and criminal. It has created exposure for businesses that didn't exist before. As a result, many businesses are appointing a senior executive to oversee computing security. This position is often identified as CISO – Chief Information Security Officer. This position often reports to an independent executive such as the head of Audit or Finance.

In many organizations, this division of responsibilities around the digital ecosystem can create a level of conflict and confusion.

Reformation of the Ecosystem around the Evolving Model

Professors Kusanski and Winkler have identified this evolving model for the ecosystem and have recognized the evolution of a new model. They state:

'In most cases traditionally structured unimodal IT setups, constrained by their legacy information systems, are not suited to accompany these contradicting needs. Instead, companies have sought bimodal forms of organization that provide both, explorative and exploitative, capabilities and thus allow them to reaching—what previous researchers also called—structural ambidexterity.'

I am in agreement with the evolution of the bimodal IT setup, but I believe that there is another model that should be further explored. This bimodal IT definition doesn't account for the management of the Infrastructure Management as a key component of the IT ecosystem. Again, Professors Kusanski and Winkler do recognize this sharable resource and noted that: '...add flexible technology assets, such as sharable IT hardware/software as facilitators for bimodal IT'.

Managing infrastructure management is akin to managing a utility. The ecosystem around infrastructure management is dependent on the evolution of the technology, managing the security of information, and providing uninterrupted power. Since a typical facilities management organization is well equipped to do so, there may be a case made that the infrastructure management should no longer be managed by a CIO or a CDO. This will lead to a 'trimodal' IT model. This model then can support the infrastructure through an ecosystem-based on cloud-based computing and professional hosting services.

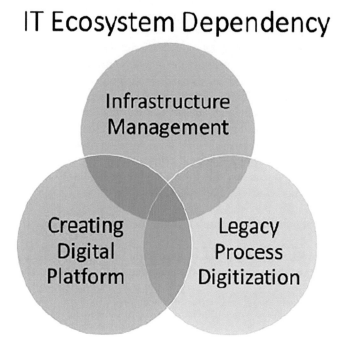

Figure 12.4   Ecosystem dependency

On the other hand, most businesses are still struggling to improve their legacy processes and systems. Digitization of these processes continues to be a challenge and needs investment and focus by an executive, such as a CIO. Since its ecosystem depends on the business process owners, a case can also be made that the business process owner owns the digitization program while a CIO becomes one of the providers of the services. In such an environment, outsourcing the legacy process digitization becomes a viable option, to be managed by either the business process owner or the CIO. Professors Hein et al. identify this as an opportunity of inviting outside entities to participate in the ecosystem. They wrote: 'The creation of economic value shifted during the last decades from production within single firms to collaboration with individual customers to the co-creation of value in complex ecosystems.' In some cases, these legacy processes will be replaced or retracted by the digital platform and thereby reduce the importance of digitization.

Creating a digital platform is a process that is quite different than the traditional IT application development where the emphasis is on strategy, product, market, and customer base. Most often the digital platform is created with a strategic intent in mind that may or may not utilize the legacy platform. The ecosystem for creating a digital platform may also require a different technology infrastructure, hence furthering the importance of the third dimension of the 'trimodal' IT.

Challenges in Transforming Ecosystems in the New Digitized World

It is easy to envision creating the new bimodal IT environment and developing the ecosystem in a 'greenfield' business environment. We have several examples of this that we have seen in recent times – Amazon and Netflix. However, the CIOs of established companies face the challenge of implementing the future digital platform in concert with the legacy environment. Established IT organizations generally lack the capabilities and support of the process owners. Thus, the legacy IT environment and legacy business process ownership provide resistance in the new ecosystem. One of the challenges that I faced leading the information technology function was the fact that almost 75-80 percent of the resources was dedicated to keeping the legacy environment operational supporting the ongoing business.

Professors Hein et al. have recognized this as: '...that the success of digital platform ecosystems depends on both the internal innovation capabilities of the platform owner and the capabilities of external complementors in a digital platform ecosystem'. The legacy IT environment also is restricted by its existing architecture, resistance to innovation and dearth of the necessary skills in digitization. Unless directly addressed through external partnering or increased investments in the platform building, it limits the digitization efforts. Professors Hein et al. have stated:

'In addition, technology platforms show the absence of complementor autonomy, knowledge-sharing, and technology openness. This occurs because technology platforms are closed and are only fueled by the internal innovation capabilities of the platform owner.'

CONCLUSION

Rapid digitization of platforms has altered the traditional models of technology management. Whether we recognize bimodal or trimodal of the function, the leadership roles are evolving. We may be headed towards several variations of the position.

- CITO – Chief Infrastructure Technology Officer, responsible for overseeing the disparate infrastructure supporting legacy and the new digital platforms as well as managing the security of the infrastructure.
- CIRO – Chief Information Resource Officer, responsible for managing the digital assets of the business created from both the legacy and the new digital platforms and managing the security of underlying information.
- CDPO – Chief Digital Platform Officer, responsible for creating and managing product/customer-centric digitized environment.

Professors Hess and Scuik acknowledge this shift as well and state: 'It is conceivable that the ongoing digital transformation and increased digital maturity of companies will lead to further shifts in IT leadership, for example, as digital empowerment of the entire company, including its employees, commences.'

The ecosystem for these models will require businesses to rethink their governance of the function, including inviting external resources to enable advancement so as to remain competitive in the changing world.

Index